Being Human

Being Human

Ethics, Environment, and
Our Place in the World

Anna L. Peterson

UNIVERSITY OF CALIFORNIA PRESS
Berkeley   Los Angeles   London

University of California Press
Berkeley and Los Angeles, California

University of California Press, Ltd.
London, England

Library of Congress Cataloging-in-Publication Data

Peterson, Anna Lisa, 1963–
    Being human : ethics, environment, and our
place in the world / Anna L. Peterson.

        p. cm.
    Includes bibliographical references and index.
    ISBN 0-520-22654-2 (hardcover : alk. paper)—
ISBN 0-520-22655-0 (pbk. : alk. paper)
    1. Ethics. 2. Environmental ethics. I. Title.

BJ1012.P454 2001
179'.1—dc21

                                00-055170

Printed in the United States of America

The paper used in this publication is both acid-free
and totally chlorine-free (TCF). It meets the mini-
mum requirements of ANSI/NISO Z39.48-1984 (R
1997) (Permanence of Paper). ∞

The fragment from the poem "Animal of Light,"
from Winter Garden © 1986 by Pablo Neruda, William O'Daly trans., is reprinted by permission of
Copper Canyon Press, P.O. Box 271, Port Town-
send, WA 98368.

A different version of chapter 3 was published as
"Environmental Ethics and the Social Construction
of Nature," Environmental Ethics 21, no. 4 (winter
1999): 339–57.

For my family,
by nature and by nurture,
and especially for Gabriel,
animal de luz

Soy en este sin fin sin soledad
un animal de luz acorralado
por sus errores y por su follaje

I am in this endless lack of solitude
an animal of light corralled
by his mistakes and by his foliage

Pablo Neruda, "Animal de Luz"

Contents

Acknowledgments

I owe thanks to many people who offered support, information, and constructive criticisms at various points during the writing of this book. I am especially indebted to Bron Taylor and Kay Read, who reviewed the entire manuscript and provided countless helpful suggestions and references. I am grateful more generally for their pioneering and insightful work in comparative ethics. Many thanks also go to Manuel Vásquez, who read the whole manuscript, some chapters more than once. A number of other colleagues kindly read various parts of the manuscript at different stages; special thanks to Kim Emery, Richard Haynes, Steve Horst, Maureen Schwarz, Elise Springer, and Jeremy Zwelling. I am also grateful to Mary Midgley, both for the inspiration and erudition of her work and for her encouraging comments on a chapter that she kindly read. Two reviewers for the journal *Environmental Ethics,* Tom Birch and Simon Glynn, along with Eugene Hargrove, editor of the journal, offered very helpful comments on an article that represents a revised form of an earlier version of chapter 3. Reading a different article, anonymous reviewers for the *Journal of Agricultural and Environmental Ethics* made useful suggestions regarding Christianity and nature. Baird Callicott provided valuable comments on an initial proposal for the University of California Press. At the Press, Doug Abrams Arava's early enthusiasm and suggestions helped get the project off the ground, Reed Malcolm's advice and encouragement made it happen, and the superb production editing by Bonita Hurd and Jacqueline Volin made it better.

I have been challenged and inspired by conversations with many friends, students, and colleagues at different stages of my thinking about this project. For generously sharing their own work or taking the time to discuss some of the issues that have arisen in this project, or both, I thank in particular Richard Haynes, Steve Horst, Heidi Regier Kreider, Joe Rouse, Maureen Schwarz, and Les Thiele. For their suggestions and insights, I am also grateful to students in my classes at the University of Florida and Wesleyan University, particularly David Matthew and Michelle Johnson-Weider. Thanks also to Jane Brockman and Sue Rosser for letting me participate in the seminar "Evolutionary Biology and Feminism" at the University of Florida in spring 1998 and for sharing their knowledge of both zoology and feminism. Thanks are due also to the other members of the seminar, especially Connie Shehan and Laura Sirot. Kathryn Burns deserves special mention for her long-ago suggestion that *el discreto encanto de los animalitos* might be a worthy intellectual pursuit.

I am immensely grateful to my family and friends for their tolerance and support, and especially to Judith Peterson for helping with child care at crucial moments and to Manuel Vásquez for helping with everything all the time. Special thanks are also due to Jane Appling, Kristen Bole, Gustavo del Chucho Bravo, Jane Fischberg, Diane Marting, and Jeb Sharp, who have offered encouragement, diversion, and reality checks as needed. Finally, I remember reading once that the average observant pet owner has more insight into animal behavior than the average animal researcher who works only in a laboratory. Without endorsing that claim in its entirety, I have learned a great deal from Balo, Chula, Inti, and the late, great, Fred. I have learned even more from my son, Gabriel, who continually reminds me both how complicated *Homo sapiens* is and how close we are to our fellow creatures.

CHAPTER ONE

Introduction

Nature is one of the most complicated terms in English or any language. It carries the weight of projected human fears and hopes, the marks of history and political conflict, the grounds for moral legitimation or condemnation. Running throughout these discussions, tying many of them together, is an ongoing debate about what it means to be human. As Raymond Williams writes, "What is often being argued . . . in the idea of nature is the idea of man."[1] The reverse is also true: what is often being argued in the idea of "man" is the idea of nature. Just as we cannot speak easily of nature without referring, implicitly or explicitly, to some idea of the human, so we rarely speak of humanness without an underlying conception of nature, either as that which encompasses or excludes humans or, perhaps more often, as that which humans exclude.

Not only are ideas of humanness and of nature wrapped up with each other, but they also shape ethical systems and practices. Questions such as what counts as human, what does not, and what is natural or unnatural do not simply feed philosophical debates but help determine moral and political priorities, patterns of behavior, and institutional structures. This book explores the connections among ideas about nature, ideas about humanness, and environmental ethics. These relations are culturally and historically variable, theoretically complicated, and politically vital. In exploring them, we face central issues regarding the shape of our communities, the destruction of our natural environment, and the character of moral discourse. Rethinking our different natures can illuminate both the need for and the possibilities of transformation.

BEING HUMAN

To say that ethics are intimately connected to ideas about what it means to be human suggests that understandings of what humans ought to be or do rest, almost always, on ideas about what human beings are: individualistic or social, rational or emotional, violent or peaceful, biologically or socially constructed, among countless other possibilities. (It is worth noting that many of these ideas about human nature are really about the particular kinds of humans who count, usually the same ones who have made the definitions.) Social contract theory, for example, makes sense only in the context of a conviction that people are rational, autonomous, and self-interested. In light of these assumptions, the economic and political arrangements associated with philosophical liberalism, as well as its moral claims (e.g., the emphasis on rights to freedom from interference), seem not only "good" but also "natural," even inevitable. In contrast, the Roman Catholic tradition assumes that humans are fundamentally social and mutually dependent. In this framework, social and economic institutions should not assume conflicts among competing individuals. Instead, they ought to empower people to live and work together in pursuit of shared goals.

Like economic and political arrangements, environmentally harmful practices and lifestyles rest on definite, though often implicit, assumptions about human nature. Most Western belief systems define humans as unique among the rest of life: humans are the only animal with x, some essential trait lacking in all other animals and setting people not only apart from but also above them. Western religions generally point to an eternal soul as the candidate for x, while secular philosophies often focus on rational thought and the capacity for conceptual language. While there are important differences between (and within) the dominant Western theological and secular approaches to human uniqueness, central to both have been the assumptions that some crucial quality radically separates humans from nonhuman animals and "nature" generally. In Christian terms, this has often made humans "in but not of" the created world (John 17:14–15), including the world of nature. This distinction has momentous implications for the meaning of a good life for humans, the shape and direction that human communities should take, the ways that humans should relate to nonhuman nature, and the ways they ought to use that nature.

Belief in a qualitative gap shapes even some radical critiques of Western Christian and modernist traditions. Contemporary social constructionist approaches, for example, posit a new form of "special creation" in theories that stress the social "invention" of virtually all dimensions of experience, including human and nonhuman nature. "Human nature," in this light, is not a fixed essence but blank paper, open to endless possibilities of cultural and environmental shaping. This approach, while intended to avoid the problematic assumption of a universal human nature, nonetheless still identifies a unique characteristic that divides humans from all other species. As Carl Esbjornson puts it, poststructuralist definitions of human nature substitute "absence" for the modernist concept of "essence."[2] In this light, our lack of innate traits becomes precisely our defining, distinctive feature. Human self-invention substitutes for the work of a transcendent God. This view of human nature, no less than that of Thomas Aquinas or of René Descartes, shapes the ethical claims its adherents make and their justifications of those claims.

I argue both that any idea of human nature has ethical implications and that all ethical systems rest upon certain ideas of human nature. This is not an exclusive relationship: assumptions about humanness are not the only factor in ethical claims and decisions, any more than ethical consequences exhaust ideas about what it means to be human. Anthropological claims can never be sufficient to understand, let alone to sustain or to change, ethical systems. However, they are necessary, and they have not received sufficient attention. I bring anthropological assumptions to the fore in the ways we understand social and environmental ethics because much of what makes moral claims and their social, economic, and political consequences seem reasonable, natural, or right is their coherence with a particular idea of the human. These ideas need to be examined, just like other elements of our moral thought and practice. In what follows, I explore certain specific visions of humanness and the ethical and environmental consequences of such ideas. In so doing I hope to uncover, on the one hand, the destructive consequences of certain ethical assumptions and, on the other hand, visions of human nature that might help us find less harmful ways of being human in the midst of nonhuman nature. I do not, however, seek a single correct view of human nature or a single way to be ethical. While I reject reductive forms of cultural determinism, such as the notion that humans are "blank paper," I also believe that no single version of what it means to be human could possibly be correct. Recent histories of "ethnic cleansing" and other forms of genocide remind us of the enormous political dangers of such a narrow vision.

Perhaps the best way to understand my approach to specific belief systems is in light of a larger interest in what might be termed ethical anthropology,[3] paralleling the established subfield of theological anthropology. Just as theological anthropology explores the relations between ideas about human nature and ideas about God, ethical anthropology examines the connections between ideas about human nature and ideas about values. This subject raises other far-reaching questions, including those about epistemology, or theories of knowledge, since understandings of human nature shape our ideas about how we know what we know and on what grounds we think it is true. Ethical anthropology also touches on questions about the nature of being itself.[4] We cannot approach such questions except in and through anthropological ones. In other words, we cannot begin to ask, much less know, about "being" in general except insofar as it relates to being human and, more specifically, to being human in concrete ways, both embodied as physical animals and embedded in particular social and ecological settings.[5] It is not that being human is all there is to being, generally. I argue, to the contrary, that being human cannot be understood except in relationship to other beings and forms of being. The point is that being human is the only way of being that we have. Thus, we had better understand what our humanness means to us if we hope to change the ways we live in the world.

RELIGION AND ENVIRONMENTAL ETHICS

Environmental ethics is usually understood as a type of practical or applied ethics, in contrast to ethics that elaborate formal and abstract moral systems. However, rather than an "application" of ethical frameworks or rules to "practical" problems, environmental ethics might more fruitfully be conceived of as a type of lived ethics.[6] This suggests an approach to ethics that attends to the moral assumptions, principles, and ideals that shape, implicitly or (perhaps less often) explicitly, the ways individuals and groups make decisions, set and pursue goals—in short, live their lives. To speak of lived ethics points to the mutual shaping of ideas and real life and suggests that moral systems should not simply be applied to concrete situations but rather applicable to and livable in them.

The primary models for lived ethics are religious. Like philosophical ethics, religious ethics reflect upon conceptions of good and evil, correct and incorrect behavior and the consequences thereof, goals for individuals and communities to seek, and obstacles to realizing those goals. Religious ethics are distinguished, however, by their grounding in the histories, texts, rituals, practices, and institutions of particular communities. Just as religious ethics are lived ethics, the ideas studied in religious ethics are embodied ideas. In this sense, religion confronts philosophy with real life. Religion also, however, confronts real life with philosophy. Religion remains the primary way that most people conceptualize the "big questions" of ethics and metaphysics. If all people are philosophers, as Gramsci contended, then their philosophy—their "conception of the world and life"—is most often constituted by religion.[7] In and through religious narratives and rituals, people set everyday duties, concerns, conflicts, and hopes in a larger context, giving them meaning and significance beyond their own times and places.

This vital role of religion persists, despite reports of inevitable secularization, in the "developed" West as well as in more "traditional" parts of the world. Religions—those "cultural processes whereby individuals and groups map, construct, and inhabit worlds of meaning"[8]— change, but they rarely disappear. For the majority of the world's people, religion continues to offer the most important, or at least the most accessible, tools for thinking about how their world works, how it ought to work, and what their place is in it.

All this suggests that environmental ethics has much to gain from a turn to religion, and in fact a number of recent books examine both destructive and constructive dimensions of religion's relationships to the ways people think of and deal with nature. Some of these volumes simply collect religious texts, such as prayers, doctrines, sermons, and meditations, that bear on humanity's relations with nonhuman nature. Others focus on specific traditions, often revealing the diversity of attitudes within a single tradition. Still others are comparative and analytic, exploring the positive environmental values present in various traditions or the present "greening" of religion as different traditions turn attention to ecological problems. Although many of these works are valuable, few investigate the internal dynamics that make religion such a potent force in forming and sustaining or challenging ethical ideas and practices. In this book, I begin filling in this gap in the course of examining how certain ethics, religious and otherwise, recast people's ideas about what it means to be human, the value of nonhuman nature, and the possibilities and requirements of social and ecological transformation.

Before turning to this task, it is worth looking at two of the most rigorous, influential, and representative of recent studies of religion and environmental ethics, both to highlight their contributions and to suggest some additional areas in need of exploration. Max Oelschlaeger's 1994 book, *Caring for Creation: An Ecumenical Approach to the Environmental Crisis,* represents what might be termed a liberal-communitarian approach to both environmental ethics and the public role of religion. Oelschlaeger contends that people need a context for ethics in general, and for environmental ethics in particular, and that religion can most effectively provide such a context, at least in the present-day United States. His argument, as he summarizes it, "is not that religion alone can resolve the environmental crisis but that it has an irreplaceable function in the larger process."[9] Religion's overwhelming importance, in his view, stems from its generality and its relative insulation from the instrumental values that dominate the political and economic spheres: "Religion is the only form of discourse widely available to Americans . . . that expresses social interests going beyond the private interests articulated through economic discourse and institutionalized in the market."[10]

Oelschlaeger builds on the work of Robert Bellah and colleagues to argue that religion has a unique and valuable role to play in civic life in the United States because religion is, for all practical purposes, the only sphere capable of challenging the "first language" of utilitarian individualism, an atomistic understanding of human selfhood and society that emphasizes the exploitation of resources (human and natural) to reach the goals of profit and productivity.[11] Just as Bellah found utilitarian individualism destructive to community and civil life in the United States, Oelschlaeger believes it has contributed to destructive treatment of the natural environment, and that religion represents the only feasible alternative to it in the present situation. (Of course religion, especially Christianity, has also contributed to ecological damage, as many environmentalists have pointed out. Perhaps precisely because of the past emphasis on religion's negative consequences, Oelschlaeger concentrates on its positive potential.)

Like Bellah, Oelschlaeger examines religion's public role and the sources of religion's efficacy that are external to religion itself, rather than the internal dynamics of religious ideas and communities. In other words, neither is a theologian or religious ethicist, although both are sympathetic observers of religion's pervasive and powerful role in American public life. Thus Oelschlaeger makes it clear that his goal is not to find and defend the "best" or "greenest" religion but to explore different potentials that exist across a spectrum of faith.[12] These potentials are manifested in local churches, the best or at least most likely forum for ordinary people to inform themselves about environmental (or other) issues in a collective context, to begin conversations about what constitutes a good society, and ultimately to take action.

Oelschlaeger's interest in local churches, and in religion generally, stems very explicitly from his desire to identify an effective way to mobilize Americans around environmental issues, rather than find the most philosophically sophisticated theory of environmental problems or their solutions. Thus he criticizes environmental philosophy for being too technical and narrowly addressed to academic specialists: "The ethical theory of the professional environmental ethics community is powerless to overcome the pervasive influence of utilitarian individualism, an ideology institutionalized in political and economic institutions. Further, ecophilosophical discourse offers its ethical insights and ecological panaceas in a language inaccessible to lay publics." Rejecting the sterility of academic philosophy, Oelschlaeger hopes for a consensus to emerge within mainstream religious bodies in the United States in favor of "caring for creation," grounded in common themes in creation stories and the related ethics of conservative, moderate, and liberal Jewish and Christian groups. This new ethic rests on a shared appreciation for God's creative power and works, although it can be based, Oelschlaeger claims, on a wide range of claims to ultimate knowledge. He is less interested in the theological reasons for believers' appreciation of nature than in the political results of such appreciation: "Solidarity is the issue."[13] This pragmatic concern drives his focus on Judeo-Christian religious narratives, which, Oelschlaeger believes, are shared by most Americans and thus have the greatest potential to generate a consensus on environmental issues.

This solidarity can be fostered most effectively, he asserts, through creation stories, which are crucial both in shaping religious attitudes toward nature and in providing a potential common ground for a multidenominational approach to the environmental crisis. According to Oelschlaeger, "Creation stories across the spectrum of belief coalesce, despite their differences, around a politically efficacious or at least potentially useful metaphor of caring for creation." The value of this metaphor stems from the power of creation stories themselves. "A creation story is primordial, carrying both obligations with it and injunctions for human behavior toward all aspects of the world." What a creation story does, from a sociological perspective, "is to legitimate the present by locating it in sacred time. Creation stories generally attempt to close the gap between existence and meaning by situating human beings in a cosmic continuum that stretches from the origin of time to some unknown future. Humans find themselves, their place in the cosmic scheme, by being placed within a creation story, by being located in a context that legitimates and gives direction (meaning, purpose, significance) to existence." Later on, he elaborates on this definition by noting that origin myths have culture-forming power: "They possess both legitimacy through the prestige of origin and potency through the evocation of sentiment (emotion)."[14] In these quotations, he hints at a possible internal reason for religion's unique force in public and private ethics other than, as he implies elsewhere, the mere fact that it is omnipresent. He suggests that religious narratives have some unique features, such as their location in sacred time, and notes the emotional resonance of origin myths, which make them especially strong shapers of attitudes and behaviors. He does not elaborate this notion fully, because, again, his purpose is to examine what religion does—its political potential—rather than what it is. While this approach can produce valuable insights, it is also limited insofar as the political dimension of religious belief cannot, I contend, ever be separated fully from its content and internal structure. Thus assertions about religion's efficacy should perhaps be read not as the final word but rather as a starting place in explorations of religion's political importance.

In building on Oelschlaeger's work, I underline the extent to which both the creation stories he values and the utilitarian individualism he attacks rest on anthropological assumptions. Even though his argument depends on a critique of utilitarian individualism, Oelschlaeger does not spend much time on conceptions of human nature in ideas about nature or in social ethics generally. He does touch on this issue a few times. Early in the book, for example, he writes, "Human beings, living out their lives within a social matrix that creates ecocrisis, are more usefully described as storytelling culture-dwellers than as rational agents seeking ultimate knowledge of timeless foundations." He suggests here a vision of human nature—"storytelling culture-dwellers"—that contradicts the dominant vision of self-interested rational agents. The alternative vision, he contends, is more congenial to the kind of environmental ethic we need in order to begin to resolve the current crisis. We need, in other words, a theory of human nature and collective life that can meaningfully describe social relations, which utilitarian individualism most certainly cannot provide. Oelschlaeger describes his vision of human nature most explicitly in the following quotation, worth providing in its entirety:

> Each of us lives primarily within a social context of sustaining relationships, which can be neither empirically described nor theoretically conceptualized as nothing more than the aggregated interests of autonomous individuals. Given the Enlightenment definition of the individual, the "good society" serves private and primarily economic interests. Any vision of the social matrix as constituted by internal relations among people, especially when these are noneconomic, is inconsistent with the prevailing ideology, since relations between two or more people (for example, mother and child) or between generations violates the premise that the individual is (metaphysically) absolute: an atom, in splendid isolation.

This is both an explicit critique of our culture's dominant vision of human nature and an implicit argument that an effective environmental ethic will require different anthropological foundations. Oelschlaeger does not develop this critique or elaborate on the potential alternatives, although he hints at the importance of anthropological assumptions in the formation and transformation of ethical ideas. He suggests, for example, that "environmentalism may converge around a rejection of Homo oeconomicus." Despite such occasional examinations of the anthropologies underlying environmental ethics and critiques of dominant approaches, Oelschlaeger generally avoids radical critiques of liberal assumptions about the central position and uniqueness of human life.[15] This stems, no doubt, not from ignorance of the problems of such assumptions but rather from his focus on finding practical solutions to an increasingly urgent crisis.

This search for solutions also leads Oelschlaeger to concentrate on creation stories as the most important element of a revised religious-environmental ethic and, perhaps, to neglect other elements of such an ethic that might be just as important. Specifically, he does not examine the importance of ideas about desired or expected ends, which might provide crucial impetus for changes in ethical attitudes and practices. Visions of the end of human life tie together religious narratives, revealing not only the end of the story but also the reason for its telling in the first place. The beginning of the story establishes a particular vision of creation, as Oelschlaeger emphasizes, but the hoped-for (or

feared) end of the story may often be more important to motivating
action.[16] This might explain why, for example, religions such as Buddhism, Jainism, and Hinduism, in which individuals' fates are tied to
treatment of nonhumans, appear to be more successful in motivating
habits that are compassionate or sustainable or both (such as vegetarianism) than are Western traditions. It might also explain why, historically, Christianity has been most effective in motivating individual and
social changes when those changes affect personal salvation or the coming of the reign of God.

Attention to desired ends or to salvation can underline the importance
of narratives in shaping, and not just reproducing, religious ethics. Religious myths of origin not only tell about how people came to be but
also bring together images of a good life, of proper relations among
humans and with other elements of creation, and of where we ought to
be going, and they weave them into a compelling and coherent story
line. Oelschlaeger's approach to creation stories hints at this larger significance but does not explore their relationship to larger narratives of
humans' place in the world. However, his failure to dwell on narrative
theory or the theory of salvation is not so much a flaw in his approach
as an indication that much more work remains to be done in explorations of the elements that might make a religiously grounded environmental ethic efficacious.

Because of his concern for efficacy, Oelschlaeger highlights the possibilities of a consensus based on very general concerns. While an emphasis on consensus might be politically helpful in many circumstances,
it can also weaken much of the promise of environmental ethics, which
lies in the very profundity of its challenges to the underlying assumptions
and methods of, and not just the content of, ethical and political discourse. As other scholars have noted, radical environmental ethics such
as Deep Ecology, biocentrism, and ecofeminism can alter the way ethics
is conceived. They suggest not just a new content for established ethical
frameworks, an extension of traditional methods to new objects of
moral concern, but rather a new understanding of what ethics might be,
what it requires, and where it could and should reach.

One problem, as Oelschlaeger rightly notes, is that many of the more
radical approaches have little following, outside a small group of environmental philosophers and activists. In this context, his focus on mainstream religious language and communities fruitfully points to the possibility of a more widely effective environmental ethic. Building on his
insights, I explore in this book the possibility of combining the

greater public power of religious ethics with some of the more radical critiques of environmental ethics. This approach might sharpen his mostly implicit critique of the underlying assumptions in contemporary U.S. culture about the nature of human beings and communities. My approach also points, not incidentally, to the profound difficulties of addressing such problems in the context of consumer capitalism and all that accompanies it. In this context, I delve more deeply into the nature of religious ethics, what makes them powerful, and how they might need to change in response to environmental crisis.

Oelschlaeger himself hints at how we might approach this task in his short discussion of non-Western, and especially Native American, religious traditions, which provide alternative visions of both creation and humanity's relation to the natural environment. Borrowing an insight from Vine Deloria, Oelschlaeger writes that indigenous creation stories point to problems with the notion of stewardship, which is central to many attempts to devise a Christian environmental ethic. The stewardship ethic still places human beings apart from nature, describing them as qualitatively different from and thus somehow responsible for the rest of creation. Many Native American traditions, in contrast, envision creation as an ongoing process in which humans are one part, intimately related to all the other beings and objects that comprise the natural world, rather than placed above them.[17] Due to his focus on mainstream U.S. culture, however, Oelschlaeger does not devote much time to Native or other non-Western traditions.

Another book about religion's potential for transforming environmental ethics does concentrate primarily on such alternative worldviews. J. Baird Callicott's *Earth's Insights: A Multicultural Survey of Ecological Ethics from the Mediterranean Basin to the Australian Outback* explores a wide range of non-Western philosophies as well as certain themes within Judaism and Christianity that have the potential to undergird new ethical approaches to nonhuman nature. Like Oelschlaeger, Callicott aims for a consensus of sorts. However, while Oelschlaeger seeks common ground among mainstream religious traditions in the United States, Callicott looks to the unifying potential of postmodern ecological and evolutionary science. Different religious traditions are continuous with this scientific worldview, Callicott argues, and thus can contribute, in different cultures and settings, to a new environmental ethic that is both scientifically adequate and culturally grounded.[18]

Oelschlaeger hopes for a philosophically rather vague, but politically efficacious, consensus about the importance of caring for creation.

Callicott, in contrast, envisions a single, coherent environmental ethic that unites diverse religious and cultural traditions, on the one hand, and postmodern science, on the other. A key feature of both the religious and scientific approaches he uses is holism. Both reject the mechanism of modernist science in favor of a holistic, relational model. Thus in postmodern scientific perspective, "from the macrocosmic family of galaxies to the microcosmic dance of quanta, including the middle-size terrestrial environment we inhabit, nature is systemically unified by a hierarchy of internal relations."[19] The notion of "internal relations" suggests a profound interdependence among parts and between part and whole, in which "a thing's essence is exhaustively determined by its relationships . . . it cannot be conceived apart from its relationships with other things."[20] The holism of some postmodern scientific views of nature as a vast organism contrasts with Newton's and Bacon's visions of nature as a great mechanism, as well as with most Western philosophical and theological traditions. This leads Callicott to look to other cultures to fill out the ethical implications of contemporary science.

The holism of postmodern science implies, for Callicott, that an adequate environmental ethic must be *ecocentric,* meaning it takes into account the direct impact of human actions on nonhuman natural entities and nature as a whole. "This approach," he hopes, "would make the effects of human actions on individual nonhuman natural entities and on nature as a whole directly accountable, regardless of their indirect effects on other people."[21] This model is closely related to Aldo Leopold's land ethic, which "enlarges the boundaries of the community to include soils, waters, plants, and animals, or collectively: the land."[22] Leopold's ethic serves as the standard by which Callicott evaluates the diverse traditions under scrutiny. Throughout his survey, Callicott searches for elements that agree with the single, scientifically accurate and philosophically coherent ethic he hopes to construct. His search for a unitary environmental ethic both holds promise and presents problems, to which I will return after describing his approach to the various religious and cultural traditions in which he finds seeds of this ethic.

He begins with the Mediterranean basin and the origins of Christianity in Jewish and Greco-Roman sources. Although he agrees, in the main, with Lynn White's contention that Christianity contains the roots of environmentally damaging attitudes in the Western world, Callicott also finds redemptive possibilities within Christianity (as, in fact, does White). Both exploitative and ecocentric approaches can be grounded in Christian theology, he believes. Of the several possible Christian attitudes to nature, the concept of stewardship has the most potential to motivate environmentally responsible behavior. A stewardship ethic accounts for inherent value, stemming from God, in the nonhuman natural world, and it also provides guidelines for correct human action in that world to safeguard the creation. This attribution of inherent value is, for Callicott, Christianity's chief contribution to, or parallel with, the ethic he wishes to construct.

After assessing the hopeful but ambivalent ecological potential of Christianity, Callicott turns to non-Western traditions, which have wrought less damage historically, he believes, and which generally contain much that is of value to an environmental ethic. He identifies the emphasis on the reciprocal dependencies that define both human life and nonhuman nature, as well as the relations between the two, as the chief contributions of Hinduism and South Asian Buddhism. Such dependencies challenge tendencies to individualism and egoism and thus might ground a more ecocentric approach to nature. Further, both Hinduism and Buddhism generally encourage nonviolence and a sense of kinship with other species. Less positively, but pragmatically, Callicott also notes that South Asian traditions manifest a "world-denying" attitude that encourages a low-consumption lifestyle.

Callicott is particularly enthusiastic about East Asian religions, especially Taoism and Confucianism, which he sees as congenial to both his land ethic and an even more radical deep-ecological perspective. Much of the Chinese traditions' promise for environmental ethics stems from their relational understandings of human nature. While Western thought assumes an ontological discontinuity between individuals, East Asian worldviews "begin with the assumption that one is constituted by one's relationships."[23] In other words, they regard individuals as internally related both to other persons and to nonhuman natural objects and beings. This approach undermines efforts to maintain a sharp distinction between the individual and others or between individuals and their social context. Callicott believes that this approach can be expanded, with little difficulty, to encompass the natural environment as well, thus providing the metaphysical foundations of an environmental ethic that accords with scientific knowledge, with the political exigencies of the present situation, and, not incidentally, with the land ethic.

Moving to the "far west," Callicott highlights "the sense of relationship, of kinship, between human and nonhuman life implied in an evolutionary understanding of origins" in traditional Polynesian worldviews. A similar emphasis on relationship underlies Lakota

understandings of nature, in which, as the classic text *Black Elk Speaks*
puts it, all species, human and other, are "children of one mother and
their father is one spirit."[24] This emphasis on relationship and common
origins accords with evolutionary science and thus with the exigencies
of an adequate environmental ethic. Differing slightly but still valuable
is the Ojibwa view of plants and animals as "persons" with their own
societies, which enter into exchange relations with human persons and
groups. This community-based ethic shares much in common with contemporary ecological views, Callicott contends, and thus, again, can
contribute to a new environmental ethic.

A different view of personhood is the most important contribution
to this ethic from African and Australian Aboriginal traditions, just as
from Chinese philosophies. In many African cultures, Callicott writes,
self-identity is bound up with family, clan, village, tribe, and, more recently, nation. In traditional African perspectives, "the individualistic
moral ontology of utilitarianism and its associated concepts of enlightened rational self-interest, and the aggregate welfare of social atoms,
each pursuing his or her idiosyncratic 'preference satisfaction,' would
seem foreign and incomprehensible."[25] In contrast to the damaging consequences of this Western view of human nature, the African view of
individuality as embedded in communal relationships, if added to a sense
of embeddedness in a broader community with nonhuman beings and
objects, might be transformed into a nonanthropocentric African environmentalism. Such an approach already exists in Australian Aboriginal
thought, Callicott contends. In Aboriginal culture, human life is embedded in the relations among humans, between humans and other species,
and between all those beings and their physical landscape. The importance of the relations of all species to particular geographic areas, emphasized in Aboriginal thought, echoes the attachment to place that is
central to the land ethic, as well as to many Native American traditions.

Callicott's enthusiastic appraisal of Aboriginal culture leads to an
elaboration of his own environmental ethic, again based on Leopold's
land ethic and on contemporary ecological and evolutionary sciences.
He seeks "to unite the environmental ethics of the world's many cultures
into a systemic whole." This ambitious effort is justified, he believes, by
the international acceptance of contemporary science: "The postmodern
evolutionary-ecological environmental ethic here outlined may therefore
make a claim to universality simply to the extent that its scientific foundations are universally endorsed—whether openly and enthusiastically
or sub rosa."[26]

Callicott's project differs decisively from Oelschlaeger's. The latter shies away from constructing a complex environmental ethic as well as from uniting the various denominational approaches he describes, except in the most general of terms. Callicott, in contrast, insists on a single environmental ethic, into which elements of other approaches to nature can be incorporated. This ethic is holistic and ecocentric, "concerned less with sorting out the mutual obligations among specimens than with preserving species. Individual specimens ought to be respected, but specimens can claim no legitimate right to life in an economy of nature in which one being purchases life only at the expense of the life of others." While many may reject this demand to subordinate individual interest for the good of the whole, Callicott argues that it becomes less problematic when people shift their understanding of selfhood to an ecological point of view, in which "oneself is a nexus of strands in the web of life . . . a node in a matrix of internal relations."[27]

More than Oelschlaeger and more than most other environmental philosophers, Callicott shows that we cannot make sense of or begin to resolve ecological crises without transforming our thinking about what it means to be human. Despite the philosophical strength of his approach, however, it may suffer from precisely the weakness that Oelschlaeger identifies as endemic to environmental philosophy. Callicott does not offer a particularly compelling argument for practical change, at least not to the many people who are not deeply moved by, or even informed about, contemporary scientific models and insights. While Oelschlaeger's ethic of caring for creation, insofar as it is descriptive and not constructive, suffers from overgenerality, it does draw on ideas that are closer to home for many people and thus more likely to affect their behavior.

Callicott appears aware of these tensions, for his final chapter describes ways in which believers are applying environmental ethics to local problems. He lauds efforts to bring a Christian stewardship ethic to bear on agricultural practices in the North American Midwest, Chipko activists' struggle to limit timber cutting in India, and Buddhist approaches to sustainable development and environmental exploitation in East Asia. The problem, however, is that these diverse movements lack clear links to the grand postmodern environmental ethic that Callicott has constructed. Each shares particular elements with that ethic, as he shows, but all remain separate, highly distinctive approaches to human relations with nature. Implicitly, Callicott's turn to the practical in this final chapter suggests that, despite the elegance of his overarching philosophical vision, perhaps local ethics are, most of the time, the ones that get put into practice.

This echoes Oelschlaeger's argument that, on a practical level, environmental movements and policies will fail unless they are grounded in religious or other traditional worldviews. Both Oelschlaeger and Callicott, in different ways, turn to religion in the hope of understanding how the environmental crisis got so bad, to put it bluntly, and how we might begin to fix it. Their books make crucial points about the importance of religion to people's worldviews and behavior; the role of religion in challenging dominant ideas and institutions in the United States; the value of non-Western understandings of nature not only in themselves but also as critical reference points for evaluating Western worldviews; and the importance of diverse, locally grounded environmental ethics that can also come together in policies and institutions. Together, the two books cover a great deal of ground, and they point to the need for further reflection and research on the religious dimensions of environmental ethics.

One goal for such research is to illuminate not just the fact that religion is important to environmental ethics but also the specific ways in which it is important. The starting point, and a goal for both Oelschlaeger and Callicott, is to demonstrate the influence of religion on attitudes and behavior toward nature. Once this point is made, as I believe it is, the next necessary task is to ask how religious value systems, along with other lived ethics, actually work in the lives of individuals and communities. One part of this answer comes from Callicott's emphasis on the ways that understandings of selfhood in different traditions shape ideas about and attitudes toward nature. However, the disjuncture between the efficacy of local traditions and the abstractness of his postmodern scientific ethic undermines the power of his vision. On a practical and local level, Callicott fully recognizes that cultural traditions are often what motivates ethical action. Due to the power of these local traditions, he believes, they must be included in the construction of an effective environmental ethic. However, because he wants a single ethic rather than many disparate ones, he isolates elements of ethics embedded in unique cultures and places—a view of human nature here, a commitment to stewardship there—and merges them into a single, hybrid philosophy. The problem is that when different elements of worldviews or ethics are separated from their ecological, historical, cultural, and narrative settings, they rarely hold together, philosophically or practically. Much of their power, in other words, comes precisely from their embeddedness in particular contexts, histories, and stories. To understand and utilize religion in ecological action, then, perhaps what we need is less a single environmental ethic than new insights into what makes such ethics work, when they do work. This requires attention to the internal elements, structure, and dynamics of religious ethics generally, as well as to understandings of nature in particular.

ETHICS AND NARRATIVES

One of the elements of religious ethics that makes them especially powerful is their narrative quality. Of course, religious ethics are not uniquely narrative. Many kinds of ethical claims—suppositions about what it means to be human, and the values that such suppositions sustain—come embedded in narratives, stories about humankind's (or a group's) origins, purpose, and destiny. This is especially true of lived ethics, for which, again, religion provides the primary examples. For most people, values, priorities, and visions of what they ought to be and do and how their communities ought to look do not take the shape of abstract, formally stated maxims. More often they emerge from or remain implicit within a general notion of how the world is, what people are like, where we came from, and where we are headed, synthesized in narrative form. Only in light of such narratives can we make sense of our ideas about right and wrong. As Jim Cheney writes, "To contextualize ethical deliberation is, in some sense, to provide a narrative or story, from which the solution to the ethical dilemma emerges as a fitting conclusion."[28]

Mark Johnson addresses this issue at length in *Moral Imagination,* where he claims that humans continually organize and reorganize their experiences using imaginative resources, among which narrative is central. Thus action and selfhood—what it means to be human—are intimately bound up with narrative structures. Such narratives, according to Johnson, are not just stories we tell to organize prior, completed experiences. Rather, "narrative characterizes the synthetic character of our very existence, and it is prefigured in our daily activities and projects. The stories we tell emerge from, and can then refigure, the narrative structure of our experience. Consequently, the way we understand, express, and communicate our experience is derived from and dependent on the prior narrative structures of our lives. And yet, because we are imaginative narrative creatures, we can also configure our lives in novel ways."[29]

Because narrative is so central to our understandings of ourselves, our experiences, and our future possibilities, writes Johnson, "a central task for any moral theory . . . must be to understand how we narratively construct our lives and how our deliberations are framed by those narratives."[30] Narratives structure not just our interpretations of our experience but also our ways of living those experiences. For ethics, this means that narratives not only describe events but also shape them, via moral claims woven into the story itself: a critique of some actions, praise for others, models of admirable personhood, a vision of how things ought to be and even how they might in fact come to be.

In *After Virtue,* Alasdair MacIntyre suggests precisely this understanding. Morality or virtue, MacIntyre contends, resides not in certain rules or consequences, but in a particular sort of self, one with integrity or constancy. In turn, the unity and coherence of this concept of self "resides in the unity of a narrative which links birth to life to death as narrative beginning to middle to end." The good of a person's life, then, is living out the unity of the narrative it embodies. Further, we do not simply live out a narrative someone else has written but participate in the writing ourselves. We are always both actors and authors. More precisely, we are coauthors, MacIntyre claims: we are part of the stories of others, as they are part of ours; "the narrative of any one life is part of an interlocking set of narratives." Thus MacIntyre suggests another crucial dimension of the self: humans are not just storytelling animals but social ones as well. This sociability is in fact central to MacIntyre's narrative view of the self, insofar as the stories of individuals' lives are always embedded in the stories of their communities.[31]

MacIntyre summarizes the intricate ways ethics, anthropologies, and narratives implicate each other thus: "I can only answer the question 'What am I to do?' if I can answer the prior question 'of what story or stories do I find myself a part?' "[32] Only in light of stories can people come to understand themselves, the multiple roles they play, and the origins and trajectories of their communities. This insight provides the foundation for an explicitly narrative approach to ethics, as advocated and explicated by some feminist theorists, among others. They contend that moral decisions emerge out of history, relationships, and setting, rather than abstract rules or reasoning, or at least that narrative provides a context within which rules and reasoning make sense and can be compelling.

In addition to ethics that are deliberately grounded in narratives, I believe that values have a narrative dimension even when they do not obviously rely on first-person testimonies, fiction, or other stories. This claim is inherent in Johnson's and MacIntyre's contention that humans understand their lives and themselves in terms of narratives. Because humans constantly create and recreate narratives, in the light of which we make sense of our personal and communal histories, even ethical systems that do not refer explicitly to narratives rely on a sense that we are participating in an ongoing story and that our lives and values make sense in light of this story. Thus contract theory, to return to an earlier example, rests not only on a notion of human nature but also on a particular narrative framing of human history and experience. The autonomous self of philosophical liberalism gains legitimacy from creation myths that posit a precontract epoch when humans were independent and self-sufficient and that express hope for a return to that original ideal in and through particular economic and political arrangements. Roman Catholicism, in contrast, holds a social, relational view of personhood that rests heavily on a particular interpretation of Biblical narratives and especially on a belief in humans' common origins as children of a benevolent creator-God and their shared task of helping to build the reign of God.

Such narrative frameworks shape not only ideas but also behavior and communities, often reinforcing the "naturalness" and correctness of certain ways of living (and, in turn, narratives themselves rest on existing worldviews and practices). Ethical narratives are usually constructed, maintained, or diffused by participants in shared social events, communities, or movements. The collective and ethical dimensions of narrative come together most commonly and perhaps most powerfully in religion. What distinguishes religious narratives, for my purposes, is that they incorporate in some way the sacred: forces, ideas, and events with meaning, location, or value—or all three—beyond (but not necessarily opposed to) the human. Like any narrative, religious narratives tell a story, but theirs is one in which secular history is linked in some way to sacred history, so that the latter gives a deeper meaning to events in the former. In academic terms, religion "universaliz[es] and spiritualiz[es] the local and particular."[33]

Religious narratives join the secular and the sacred in various ways. The link may be allegorical (if secular events are "like" sacred ones) or more direct (if divine forces or figures irrupt into secular events, human figures participate in events with transcendent significance, or both). In either case, the connection between the sacred and the secular imbues the latter with special meaning and significance. What happens here and now is more important, for religious believers, because of its connections to sacred history. Thus in El Salvador, the killings of progressive activists took on tremendous meaning and power because of the perceived parallel between their deaths and the Christian tradition of martyrdom. Political assassinations were not just manifestations of mundane conflicts but part of the ongoing story of the construction of the reign of God on earth. Sacred-secular narratives explained what was happening in the present, in light of what had gone before, and they provided guidelines for action, charging believers with particular tasks in order to make the story continue to unfold as it should.[34]

The often negative historical role of religion highlights the potential dangers of viewing human lives and history in terms of a "grand narrative." Such a perspective can conceal differences and conflicts, forcing all actors to conform to a unitary vision, imagined by the powerful, of what the story ought to be. In contrast, much contemporary theory highlights pluralism and change and encourages skepticism toward claims that all of humanity's (or a nation's) history fits neatly within a single, overarching story. Critical awareness, however, need not entail rejecting all sorts of narratives. Many religious narratives, especially those imagined and lived out by groups without power, are liberative in both personal and political terms.

While acknowledging that we cannot rely on any single metanarrative and that narratives alone are not all there is to ethics, I believe that narrative frameworks can still illuminate people's lives and values, if these narratives are understood as partial, contextual, and subject to change. Narrative-based ethics can counter the overly abstract, mechanistic approaches that have dominated Western philosophical traditions and can help us understand the complex ways that values, worldviews, and social movements are constructed, maintained, and transformed. Attention to religion is crucial here because religious ethics, much more than most secular ones, are lived ethics. Very few secular moral philosophies, with the notable exception of feminism, are practical in the same way that virtually every religious ethic is.

I am interested in narratives that are not only lived but also have the potential to challenge, rather than reinforce, dominant worldviews. This can happen in several ways. First, narrative can provide a sense of connection to others (past and present, human and nonhuman) that sometimes proves more powerful than abstract principles. Stories of origins and shared experiences of crucial historical events ground understandings of appropriate relationships to other people and other species. An example that may be familiar to environmental ethicists and activists is the Chipko (tree-hugging) movement that resists logging in India. As Baird Callicott describes, the movement relies on tales of past heroes and martyrs as well as traditional Hindu sacred stories. These narratives provide Chipko activists with "an identity between themselves and the trees they embrace."[35] Jim Cheney provides another example in his discussion of the ways that Pacific Northwest coast Native Americans understand salmon, the center of their mythic world as well as a primary food source. Stories about salmon provide guidelines not only for dealing with the fish themselves but also for living in a community that includes both human and nonhuman members.[36] This example also highlights the growing importance in environmental philosophy of *place,* understood as the result of "human culture's peculiar and fascinating interpenetration with all the vagaries of topography, climate, and evolving ecology that define landscapes."[37] Stories by indigenous groups often tie people to particular places, creating commitments that can inspire activism aimed at protecting both the land and the human communities that depend on it.

Such narratives, Cheney claims, provide a kind of truth that cannot be expressed in scientific terms but that helps make possible right relationships with the land and ensure both human and environmental health. The emphasis on correct relationships is also central to contemporary Christian reworkings of the concept of "stewardship" for environmental ethics. Stewardship, interpreted as a more responsible approach to nature than the traditional model of "dominion," depends on relationships—between God and humans, God and the rest of creation, and human and nonhuman creatures—that take shape in narratives of origins and ends.[38]

Again, as MacIntyre has suggested, an intimate connection exists between a narrative view and a social view of selfhood. Put otherwise, the narrative view of self is almost necessarily a social self. Few stories have only one character, and narrative visions of what it means to be human and to live well almost always unfold in the context of the lives and stories of other people. The relationships, in fact, often make both the story and the person. This is clear in many biblical narratives, where the real moral drama comes not in the events by themselves but in the way that events, such as the widowing of Ruth or the arrest of Jesus, serve as context and catalyst for particular relationships, good or bad. In the Bible, these relationships exist not only among persons but also between persons and God and even between persons and nonhuman entities, most notably the land of Israel. These multiple relationships help define a believing community as it is and as it should be.

By shaping relationships, religious narratives help create a collective identity, encouraging people to see themselves as part of a group with a past and future and ties to particular places in which these narratives take place. These collective stories help make sense of and resonate with individuals' histories. This is obvious in biblical stories about the history of Israel or early Christian communities, but it also emerges in other sorts of narratives. For example, leftist parties, guerrilla movements, and other oppositional or minority political groups have long found stories and histories to be invaluable resources in struggles to create and sustain group solidarity. In Central America during the 1970s and 1980s, progressive movements drew on tales of past martyrs and heroes ranging from Jesus to indigenous rebels during the colonial period to contemporary activists.[39] Such stories provide people with a connection to a group, a sense that the group does in fact exist, that it has origins and goals, and that its existence is essential to members' own identity.

I underline the importance of future visions in these narratives: the importance of their capacity to present a utopian horizon toward which present events and actions should move. Like narratives generally, utopian dreams can lead to flawed attitudes and actions, to unrealistic expectations and dangerous single-mindedness. These dangers, however, stem largely from the power of utopian visions to motivate ethical behavior. Rather than reject dreams of a better world entirely, as do some postmodernist ethicists, I hope for a restrained utopianism, one capable of motivating action without generating intolerance, of inspiring hope without leading to paralyzing disappointment. This version of utopianism may be described less as goal seeking than as "ideal-setting," in Joanna Macy's term. Goals change over time and are "never completely realizable," but they present a horizon whose pursuit gives meaning and satisfaction to individuals and leads, at least sometimes, to significant social change.[40]

THE STRUCTURE OF THE BOOK

This book is divided into nine chapters that explore ideas about the definition, meaning, and value of humanness in a variety of traditions of thought. I do not discuss any of these traditions comprehensively; specialists in any one of these areas will find that I leave out many important issues. The purpose of this book is not to provide detailed knowledge about any single tradition but rather to reflect on the relations among conceptions of humanness, ideas about nature, and ethics. While respecting the complexity and distinctiveness of every tradition I mention, I explore each primarily in relation to problems in comparative ethics. This means that some significant issues and information relative to each tradition fail to emerge. However, this also makes it possible to ask a number of interesting and relevant questions that can arise only in a comparative context.

Following this introduction, the next two chapters examine conceptions of human uniqueness and the domination of nature in Western religion, philosophy, and social theory. Chapter 2 examines the established Christian and modernist narratives of human uniqueness. As noted earlier, these worldviews usually posit a definitive and unbridgeable gap between humans and all other species, justified most often by the possession of a soul or rational thought. These traditions have helped legitimize and expand not only instrumental attitudes toward nature but also hierarchies among humans. In later chapters I take up some of the critiques of these traditions; chapter 2 focuses on understanding the internal logic of Western anthropocentrism, and especially the particular ways in which Christian and modernist traditions define humans as unique and superior.

The third chapter explores a paradox: some recent social theories, while critiquing myths of progress and unity, reproduce the dominant tradition's anthropocentrism and its dismissive attitudes toward the nonhuman world. I focus in particular on approaches that stress the social construction not only of human experience but also of nature itself. Such theories, no less than those of Thomas Aquinas or René Descartes, harbor the danger of separating humanity from other, "biologically determined" creatures and of denying that nature has value independently of human attributions of meaning. In exploring recent social constructionist thinking, I seek to highlight the ways that very different visions of nature can also help generate dangerous attitudes and practices regarding nonhuman nature. In other words, while anthropological and ethical (including environmental) conceptions are closely linked, no single conception of humanness is uniquely and wholly damaging to the environment or anything else.

Nor, conversely, is there a single conception of humanness that is uniquely and wholly positive in this regard, as demonstrated in Callicott's exploration of multicultural environmental ethics. Rather, just as a range of different anthropologies might be harmful in particular ways, under certain conditions, so a variety of others might be helpful in their own ways and settings. I examine some of these potentially more positive visions of human nature in the next four chapters.

Chapter 4 looks at ways that two important Asian traditions, Buddhism and Taoism, have envisioned humanity's place in the world and relations to nature and other animals. I highlight Asian tendencies to define the self in terms of relationships and interdependencies, in contrast to the separate and autonomous anthropologies of most Western approaches. This chapter also explores a number of conceptual and practical problems raised by Western efforts to borrow or appropriate Asian philosophies of nature.

Some of these same issues arise in chapter 5, which examines ideas about nature and human nature in two Native American cultures, the Koyukon of Alaska and the Navajo of the southwestern United States. Native American worldviews, like Asian ones, offer important alternatives and challenges to established Western perspectives on the self and on the human place in the natural world. Native cultures also emphasize the importance of attachment to particular places in shaping and motivating efforts to protect nonhuman species. Both chapters acknowledge the problems inherent in trying to bring Asian or Native American worldviews, removed from their cultural and historical contexts, to bear on alternative narratives in the West. Still, it is helpful to look at the ways that other traditions have envisioned what it means to be human in relation to humanity's place in nature, in order to shed critical light on the perspectives that have most shaped our culture and to illuminate some aspects of the Western ethical tradition that might benefit from revision. For example, many indigenous and Asian traditions make the maintenance of right relationships and community, rather than adherence to abstract norms, central to moral judgments. This distinction stems from diverging notions of what it means to be human, as well as from the different cultural, political, and narrative contexts in which values are embodied.

Chapter 6 looks at internal challenges to the established Western moral tradition launched by feminist and ecofeminist theories. Feminist approaches are important to explore in relation to explicitly religious ethics because, like religious worldviews, feminism connects ethical ideas both to larger worldviews and to "real life." I do not contend that feminism is a "religion," but certain feminisms offer a fuller vision of the role of moral ideas in human life than do many secular philosophies.

An emphasis on ideas in context is, in fact, crucial to feminist critiques of male-dominated philosophical and theological traditions in the West. These traditions, feminists often argue, have ignored concerns with emotions, relationships, and community in favor of a rational, individual, and abstract understanding of moral value. This focus has encouraged definitions of nonhuman nature as being outside moral consideration because of its perceived lack of rationality. Male-dominated ethics have also tended to value domination and control—of nature as of other humans. A number of feminists have drawn on narrative as an important resource in establishing new ethical methods and concerns, insofar as narrative-based ethics highlight the importance of histories and relationships rather than abstract rules. The narrative interest of feminist ethics is tied to research on the differing moral priorities and perspectives of women and men, which in turn rest on different conceptualizations of what it means to be human.

Chapter 7 continues to explore the role of anthropological claims in ethics with a look at the ways the natural sciences might contribute to alternative narratives about humankind's nature and relations with the nonhuman world. Recent studies of animal behavior, for example, have revealed the enormous complexity of nonhuman species, including numerous parallels between the capacities of human and some nonhuman species. These findings, like the knowledge provided by contemporary evolutionary and ecological theories, challenge the notion that a wide, definitive, and unbridgeable gap separates humans from all other species. More generally, this research calls us to rethink established ideas about our own nature, the natural world, and correct behavior in it.

This has broader implications for the way we think about ethics, as well: if human nature is not so radically removed from the rest of nature, then human morality must also share some continuities with the non-human world. This insight need not degenerate into parodic sociobiological claims that all human behavior is biologically "determined." Understood in a more nuanced manner, it can help us understand the tremendous complexity of not only our own but also other species' perceptions and behavior. Ethics, then, might be understood not just as *reflection* upon our relationships and loyalties, our existence in a particular time and place, but also as a particular (and perhaps distinctively human, although some ethologists challenge this)[41] way of *being* in relationships, in the world. This points to the structural dimensions of lived ethics: just as our moral claims depend on how we see being human, this viewpoint in turn is shaped by what world we live in and how we live in it. An ethic, as Holmes Rolston writes, "is not just a theory but a track through the world."[42]

The final two chapters reflect on the potential for revision in mainstream ethics and, necessarily, in the anthropologies and narratives associated with them. Chapter 8 builds on the alternative traditions discussed earlier to flesh out the "chastened constructionist" approach to human nature suggested in chapter 3. I focus on five qualities of humanness: simultaneous shaping by both nature and nurture, this-worldliness ("being terrestrial"), embodiedness, relationality, and limitations. These qualities do not encompass all there is to humanness, nor are most of them exclusively human. However, they reflect dimensions of being human that need emphasizing in response both to the theoretical challenges of the alternative anthropologies discussed previously and to the practical and political demands of an ecologically damaged world. Chapter 8 also explores some of the possibilities of change in Christian theological anthropology, as articulated by the emergence of Christian eco-theology. Christianity's dominance in the United States and other powerful nations makes its worldviews and values especially influential, so that potential changes within the tradition hold great import for environmental attitudes and behavior and thus for the survival of global ecosystems. The potential for transforming Christian approaches to nature depends not only on the philosophical coherence but also on the practical and emotional appeal of new understandings of human nature and humanity's relationship to the nonhuman world.

The final chapter looks at the ethical correlates of the anthropology outlined in the previous chapter. This ethical project, which begins rather than ends here, involves a new understanding of a number of different natures: different human natures or ways of being human, the differences between humans and the rest of nature, and different understandings of nonhuman nature. The kind of ethic I begin to outline here (meaning not a single ethic but a *type* of ethic) must take all these different natures seriously, as credible critiques of established worldviews rather than simply as quaint reminders that other people are different. This means, for example, allowing certain indigenous understandings of nonhuman animals as persons to challenge our notions of agency as uniquely human. Even more radically, it might require us to take the knowledge that other species have of a landscape or a process as a source of insight that can alter our own ways of understanding the world. I highlight the value of a narrative-based ethic, including its valuation of embodiment, relationality, and utopian horizons as a framework for making sense and use of these diverse forms of knowledge. This approach suggests ways that new, recovered, and reworked narratives, building on the insights of religious, feminist, and scientific understandings of human and nonhuman nature, can contribute to the construction of a coherent ethical framework for understanding the different natures at stake, the relations among them, and the consequences of those relations.

CHAPTER TWO

Not of the World

Human Exceptionalism in Western Tradition

Do not be conformed to this world.

Romans 12:2

MAN IS THE ONLY ANIMAL

Man, writes Reinhold Niebuhr in *The Nature and Destiny of Man,* is the only animal that fears death.[1] This ambiguous (and empirically questionable) assertion follows centuries of similar statements in the West, usually beginning "man is the only animal that . . ." These claims reflect an ongoing effort to establish, once and for all, a singular and impassable barrier between humans, on the one hand, and the rest of creation, on the other. The actual trait that sets humans apart—the x that only humans have—varies for different thinkers, times, and cultures. As Daisie Radner and Michael Radner explain, "The value of x has to be changed from time to time as more evidence comes in, but there must be an x because humans are unique. Only human beings conceptualize and perform abstractions. They alone make and use tools; have reason; have a sense of humor; practice deceit; count; communicate about things not in the here and now; are aware of their own existence; anticipate their own death; have a sense of beauty; have an ethical sense; have speech. Darwin remarks that he once made a collection of such aphorisms and came up with over twenty, 'but they are almost worthless, as their wide difference and number prove the difficulty, if not the impossibility, of the attempt."[2]

While belief in a radical division between humans and the nonhuman world might be ubiquitous in Western thought, as Darwin's exercise suggests, it retains a particular place of honor in Christian theological anthropology. In the Christian tradition, human claims to uniqueness rest on the assertion that humans alone, as Augustine puts it, have a rational soul, the image of God and thus of the trinity.[3] The soul links humans' origins, capacities, and ultimate destiny to God and, thus, forever divides them from the "nonspiritual" part of creation. The soul performs the same function in Christianity that other human qualities, notably conceptual thought and language, fulfill for secular thinkers: the soul is not just an added piece of equipment but a singular dimension that transforms the meaning of humanness. While the nonempirical nature of the soul causes many secular thinkers to reject it outright, this very quality can support assertions of human uniqueness. While evidence might empirically show that a chimpanzee has learned a human language, there is no way to prove that one has a soul.

Christian thinkers most often turn to biblical narratives of human origins as the source of claims about the soul, which they usually identify as the "image of God" in humans. The first ("priestly") account of the creation, in Genesis 1:26–28, firmly anchors biblical understandings of human nature in assumptions of humans' radical difference from the rest of God's creatures. In Genesis 1:26–28, humans alone are created in God's likeness and, not incidentally, given dominion over the rest of creation. According to this version, creation proceeded thus:

> 26 And God said, "Let us make man in our image, after our likeness, and let them have dominion over the fish of the sea, and over the birds of the air, and over the cattle, and over all the earth, and over every creeping thing that creeps upon the earth."
>
> 27 So God created man in His own image, in the image of God he created him; male and female he created them.
>
> 28 And God blessed them, and God said to them, "Be fruitful, and multiply, and fill the earth and subdue it; and have dominion over the fish of the sea and over the birds of the air and over every living thing that moves upon the earth."[4]

Here the connection between theological anthropology and attitudes toward nature is clear, as the assertion of humanity's uniqueness is inextricably tied to humans' right to subdue and dominate other animals.

The environmental ethic that these verses suggest is especially powerful because it is embedded in a coherent narrative that ties together sacred and mundane history. A simple expository declaration about the distinctiveness of humans and their relationship to God would lack the motivating and staying power of the biblical version. The Genesis 1 account acquires potency because it locates the origins of human (and all other) life in a larger cosmic drama in which God enters into our time and space to create a special connection with a special species. This connection, the soul that all other animals lack, both defines humans and gives them transcendent value. The soul reinforces a logic that links value and exclusiveness: intrinsic worth stems not from shared features, such as life, creation by God, or residence in the garden, but from the qualities that are exclusively human.

The human soul and narratives about it bring together creation and salvation in Christian theological anthropology. In the end, the image of God implanted in the human creature returns to God. This means, crucially, that humanity's real home does not lie among the rest of creation but rather with God in heaven. It also means that humans' most important relationship is the vertical stretch to the divine rather than horizontal ties to other people or creatures. This interpretation defines humanity not in terms of relations among persons, physical embodiedness, or embeddedness in the natural world, but rather in terms of an invisible tie to an invisible God. This idea builds on Greek thought, especially the Platonic idea that the essences of things (or beings) are more real than physical bodies. In this tradition, as Gordon Kaufman summarizes it, "both man and that which was taken to be ultimately real were understood in terms of those features of man's being which most sharply distinguish us from other creatures."[5]

The Hellenistic tendency to devalue the bodily and look to the transcendent has emerged at different points and in different movements in Christian history. Some early Christians, for example, argued for a docetic interpretation of the incarnation, meaning that Jesus was not fully human but merely took human form, as a spirit temporarily housed in a frail and fallible body. One of the most extreme and best-known variants of this anticorporal tendency within Christianity was Gnosticism, a movement that thrived in the first three centuries C.E and peaked with the Manicheans, followers of the third-century prophet Mani. Gnosticism defined Jesus as pure spirit, and salvation as knowledge (gnosis) of the divine. The Manicheans and most other Gnostics, along with a number of other early Christian movements, rejected the notion that Jesus was fully human and had died a physical death. In their view, what was important about Jesus and every human being was the soul, which was trapped on earth but oriented toward heaven, its true home. The Gnostic God is alien to the material world, which God neither created nor governed. The world is a prison for the human soul, which is actually a segment of the Divine that fell into the created world. Humans, as carriers of this divine spark, are, like God, radically opposed to the created world. Believers in the Gnostic narrative await a savior who will descend and supply them with knowledge that enables individual souls to leave behind everything associated with the physical world and the body and reunite with divine substance.

The extremity of Gnostic dualism highlights the close ties between visions of nature and of human nature in Christian theology. In Gnosticism, what is valuable and distinctive in human life is what transcends the material body and earth. Just as God is radically other than the created world, so humans, as carriers of the divine spark, are other, not just more, than their bodies. On earth humans are lost travelers, imprisoned in nature and ruled by capricious powers that enslave humans, especially through the physical body. It is hard to imagine a more external vision of the relatedness between body and mind or between nature and humanity. While in an internal relation the terms mutually constitute each other, in an external relation the connection between things is "accidental" or subsequent to some prior constitution. In Gnostic Christianity, body and soul are not only externally related but actively hostile to each other. The human condition, in this view, includes a profound alienation from all that ties us to the earth and a longing for what might enable us to transcend it. In this view, humans, or at least Christians, are "strangers and pilgrims" wandering through the world, never at home in it.[6]

Emerging Christian orthodoxy ultimately rejected doceticism and Gnosticism in favor of a vision of Jesus as both fully divine and fully human and of the world, the valuable creation of a benevolent God. However, the dualism reflected in these movements has resurfaced again and again in Christian history. In thirteenth-century France, for example, the Cathari (or Albigenses) revived the Gnostic division between spirit and body. They again viewed the body as entirely negative, a prison for the soul, which was the only dimension of humanity that had value. Like the Manicheans, the Cathari embedded their theological vision in a narrative that began with a flawed creation and ended, at least for true believers, with a return to their true home with God in heaven. The Cathari so despised physical life that they condemned having children as a sin, since it trapped more souls. Like Gnosticism, the Albigensian heresy helped push mainstream Christianity to a fuller, though still ambivalent, endorsement of physical life, reproduction, and "the world" in general.[7] As a theological consensus began to emerge in the early Jesus

movement, tendencies to extreme body-spirit dualism vied continually
with more positive valuations of the physical world and human embodiment suggested by Christianity's Jewish origins and, in the view of many
interpreters, by the incarnation of God in Jesus.

Paul began the enduring Christian effort to resolve the tension between these two approaches by positing a vision of humans, or at least
Christians, as "in but not of" the world. For Paul, unlike the Gnostics,
the material world and the physical body have to be good, because they
are the creation of a benevolent God and the locus of redemption by an
embodied savior. Thus humans must be in the world, and not grudg-
ingly—but also not fully. For Paul, the world and the body in their
present forms are not evil, as Gnostics thought, but neither do they
comprise Christians' true or final home. "But you are not in the flesh,"
Paul writes; "you are in the spirit, if in fact the Spirit of God dwells in
you" (Rom. 8:9; see also 8:12–13).[8] Paul's primary concern is the salvific
meaning of Jesus' death and resurrection and the consequences of these
events for human life and history. Human redemption through Christ
creates the "new man" not through the transcendence of the material
world but via its actual recreation: a new earth to go with the new vision
of heaven made possible by the crucifixion and resurrection (as in, for
example, Rom. 8:18–23). In this context, the old earth is not evil, but
neither is it of permanent importance for human salvation, which alone
gives meaning to human life. Whatever value this world has is instrumental, insofar as it is the locus of salvation.

The ambiguity of Paul's references to the "present world" leads some
Christian thinkers to argue that Paul meant to reject only his own society
and its corruptions, not nature or the world in general. Some also contend that Paul's vision of the coming new creation does not render the
present creation valueless. In this view, Paul is expressing a notion of
"spiritual homelessness," a transcendence of the limitations of any particular human embodiment or setting. This can be distinguished from
what is, from an environmentalist perspective, the more problematic
concept of "cosmic homelessness," the inability of humans ever to be at
home on earth, as seen in Gnosticism. Certainly there are ambiguities
in Paul's vision, and we cannot place the burden for all, or even most,
of Christianity's anthropocentric tendencies on Paul. However, neither
can we absolve Paul of contributing to Christianity's ambivalence and
frequent hostility toward the created world. More important, we cannot
absolve the Pauline tradition; that is, the appropriation, circulation, and
reinterpretation of Paul's ideas since his death.

Paul's legacy for lived Christian ethics is not his "pure" ideas but the effective history of the symbols and concepts he wielded—the concrete ways ideas are embodied, worked out, and transformed in the course of human history. For example, Paul's preoccupation with Christians' spiritual homelessness has often been interpreted as a conviction that humans are never at home in the created world, which may or may not have been Paul's intention. The living out of religious ideas in concrete historical and political contexts results in what David Laitin calls "practical religion—the realm where theology and social and economic conditions meet."[9] Religious ideas, in this view, are not wholly determined by their context, but neither are they entirely autonomous. As Laitin points out, practical religion "can have an independent effect on political life, often quite different from the political or economic intentions of the original propagating group."[10]

Building on Paul's ambiguous legacy, Augustine also contended with the dualistic tendencies in his faith and its view of human nature. Also like Paul, Augustine sought a balance between a conviction that the highest good lay in heaven, on the one hand, and a positive valuation of God's worldly creation, on the other. Augustine was a Manichean prior to his conversion to Christianity, and his ongoing ambivalence about the body and nature reflect his and his religion's struggle with the seductive appeal of extreme dualism. Augustine explicitly rejects the Gnostic notion that the earth was essentially fallen. The Manichaeans are wrong, he writes in *City of God,* to despise earthly bodies as evil, as the Platonists are wrong to see the body's longing for "light" (i.e., escape from embodiment) as the cause of evil. Augustine devotes large sections of *City of God* (e.g., most of book 13) to his argument that sin results not from the fact of embodiment but from the wrong use of the will. What makes the body "heavy to the soul" is not "the body itself" but its potential for corruption."[11] All creation, including the human body, is a revelation of God's goodness, he writes in his *Confessions,* because God created "the earth which I walk on" as well as the human body, the "earth which I carry."[12] Thus the body cannot be the prison of the soul but is rather its partner, and to separate the two is unnatural.

Still, Augustine remains ambivalent about the body and about the material world generally. Soul and body are partners, but not equal ones: the body is not innately evil, but it is both secondary and ephemeral compared to the soul. More generally, all earthly goods pale in comparison to the supreme good of eternal life with God in heaven. Thus, in the mortal body, the Christian remains "a heavenly pilgrim."[13]

A pilgrim, of course, is looking for something better. The end of the journey, the true fulfillment of the divinely ordained narrative in which human life unfolds, is for Augustine the transcendence of physical existence by means of eternal life. Because only the fate of the soul is important ultimately, the nonspiritual created world lacks deep significance, and whatever significance and value it does have comes from its relation to God and eternal life. Ultimately, then, Augustine reinforces the idea that relations to all aspects of creation are, in the end, external, since what really gives value to humans is their link to the divine.

Since Augustine, a wide range of Christian theologians have attempted to hold body and soul together in productive tension. This tension is particularly evident in the Protestant tradition, beginning with Luther's reworking of Augustine's two-cities metaphor. For Luther, as for Augustine and Paul, humans must live in the "kingdom of man" and strive to improve it and obey its rules. However, they must also never forget that their true home and destiny lie in the kingdom of God. This dual citizenship, with its sometimes contradictory demands, stems from a deep anthropological dualism. In Luther's words, "Man has a twofold nature, a spiritual and a bodily one."[14] The former comes from and owes its allegiance to God alone, while the latter (and subordinate) nature results from the temporary human condition of embodiment in a flawed material world. Humanity's two natures never harmonize completely, either within individuals or in society more generally. In the not infrequent cases when they openly conflict, the believer's duty to God and the heavenly kingdom must come first. For Luther and for Calvin, as Michael Northcott writes, "it is not the relations between selves, and between humans and created order, which are salvifically and morally significant but the choosing of particular individual selves by the will of God to be objects of his eternal love and goodness."[15] Worldly ethical demands, in the end, can neither lead to nor modify the all-important goal of personal salvation and eternal life with God in heaven. In other words, while Christians' spiritual citizenship ought to make them better residents of the material world, their embeddedness in earthly social lives should not affect either their understandings of or the path to final redemption. Our spiritual and worldly natures remain separate, and residence on earth is, in the end, inconsequential to the meaning of human life.

The Reformation's ambivalence about the world resurfaces in complex and revealing ways in more recent Protestant theology. Reinhold Niebuhr, for example, asserts that human existence is distinguished from animal life not only by the fear of death but by humanity's "qualified participation in creation. Within limits it breaks the forms of nature and creates new configurations of vitality."[16] Humans, in other words, are not entirely subject to their "creatureliness" as are other animals; humans alone share something of God's creativity.[17] However, people rarely live up to their transcendent potential, in Niebuhr's view, since the inclination to sin shapes human behavior so powerfully. Thus Niebuhr is far from offering an unqualified celebration of human goodness and rationality. His ethics spring, rather, from his conviction that the tendency to selfishness is so powerful that it requires social and political, as well as rational and religious, constraints.[18] Still, at their core humans have an ethical potential—grounded in their unique participation in God's creative and transforming power—that is unavailable to any other creature. What defines human nature is precisely the tension within each person between the divine spark and the limitations of fallible, selfish embodiment.

Niebuhr does not simply reproduce the Lutheran dualism between God and the world, nor does he consider the material realm irrelevant to Christian theology. On the contrary, he takes life in the world very seriously and brings his theological insights to bear on a host of concrete social problems. Still, his ethics are shaped by a vision of human nature as divided between reason, on the one hand, and emotion and self-interest, on the other. Morality involves dominating what Niebuhr understands to be, literally, the baser instincts, through the combined efforts of rationality, religion, and social control. This approach refines the ambivalence evident in Augustinian and Lutheran theology: the world cannot simply be rejected as evil but must be confronted and improved as much as possible. Like Augustine and Luther, though, Niebuhr views the things of the world, including the baser parts of human nature, as separate from and ultimately detrimental to human reason, transcendence, and efforts to achieve the good and realize their intrinsic connection to God.

Niebuhr's ambivalence about the world reflects the deeply rooted Protestant assumption that human nature is divided between spirit and body. The spirit, the link to the divine, which provides both what is important and what is unique in human life, exists in constant tension with the physical existence shared with other creatures. Following Luther, Protestant thinkers including Niebuhr reject a simple identification of human sinfulness with the body or the created world, while remaining uneasy about the moral and spiritual status of physical creation. This ambivalence, which sometimes becomes open hostility, toward the world is evident in many, though not all, variants of Pentecostal Protestant theology. Latin American Pentecostal leaders, for example, frequently warn against the dangers of the things of the world *(las cosas del mundo),* which they see as radically opposed to the things of God.

The Roman Catholic tradition, in contrast, has generally viewed the created world in much more positive terms. While Protestantism has often seen human life on earth as radically separated from the spiritual realm or the reign of God, Catholicism has perceived greater continuity between the human and the divine and therefore between the material and the spiritual, creature and creator. This Catholic position was systematized in Thomas Aquinas's "medieval synthesis." Thomas wrote in the context of a revived interest, in the Middle Ages, in the notion of a "Great Chain of Being," which joined all creatures in a harmonious hierarchy. The medieval appropriation of the Great Chain of Being was tied both to growing confidence in humanity's mastery over nature, on the one hand, and to a grand vision of the hierarchy of being, on the other. Linking these two themes was the idea of the human creature as microcosm. Nature, as an ordered structure, reflected the human self and vice versa.[19] This perspective reflected a growing anthropocentrism but continued to define the natural world as the organic, living site of complex and valuable relationships among different kinds of beings.

Thomas summarizes the harmonious relationship between God and creation and among different aspects—human and nonhuman—of that creation in his notion of natural law. "The whole community of the universe," as Thomas proclaims in the *Summa Theologica,* "is governed by the divine reason." Thus the first key aspect of Thomas's thought in relation to understandings of nature is his insistence that "everything that in any way is, is from God," and that all aspects of creation are linked together because "all things partake in some way in the eternal law."[20] Rational creatures, meaning (male) humans and angels, partake in the eternal law through the imprint of eternal law upon them (or their participation in the eternal law), which is what Thomas terms specifically natural law (distinct from eternal and human law). Natural law frames human nature in optimistic terms, emphasizing human rationality and humans' capacity and inclination to act in harmony with God's will.

More generally, natural law refers to the entire system that links humans to God and to the other levels of creation. A second crucial aspect of Thomistic thought is that these linkages are not only harmonious but also hierarchical. God not only created and distinguished the creatures but also made them unequal. "In natural things," Thomas explains, "species seem to be arranged in a hierarchy: as the mixed things are more perfect than the elements, and plants than minerals, and animals than plants, and men more than other animals."[21] In other words, while God creates and rules all of creation, God is not equally near to all of creation, and it is crucial to understand the nature and proper place of every element in the divinely ordained hierarchy. Lower creatures can approach divine goodness only through their relationship to higher ones; and humans, as rational creatures, are superior to other animals and to all of inanimate creation. Their closer relationship to the divine makes humans not only more perfect than but also dominant over other creatures. This elevation stems from humans' possession of an eternal soul, which all other animals, as well as the inanimate features of creation, lack. In this view, as Thomas writes, "the subjection of other animals to man is natural."[22] Despite Thomas's conviction of the fundamental goodness of creation, he reinforces a hierarchical and human-centered ethic.

Subsequent Roman Catholic thought about nature, as about so much else, builds on Thomistic foundations. Recent Roman Catholic theology and ethics continue to affirm the goodness of creation and human embodiment and also the superiority of humans over other species. *Gaudium et Spes,* the final document of the Second Vatican Council, asserts that "man is the only creature on earth that God willed for itself,"[23] that is, the only creature that is an end in itself rather than a means for others. Here we see again Thomas's hierarchical vision, expressed in the claim that humans alone, of all creation, share the divine capacity to be an end for oneself and for others. Thus, the council declares, God made man "master of all earthly creatures that he might subdue them and use them to Christ's glory."[24] These themes find echo in John Paul II's 1980 encyclical *Redemptor Hominis,* which celebrates the "unrepeatable reality" of each person, chosen by God for "grace and glory" and given the earth to subdue and dominate.[25]

While modern Catholic humanism affirms human domination, it does so in the context of a cosmic hierarchy that assigns a purpose and value, however limited or subordinate, to all of creation. This valuation stems from the natural law assumption of continuity, in contrast to the Lutheran vision of a radical gap, between the divine and the earthly, spirit and body. This makes the Catholic (and Anglican) natural law tradition, in the view of some ethicists, a strong foundation for a Christian environmental ethic, particularly one centered on the notion of human stewardship over the rest of creation. As Michael Northcott points out, the natural law approach takes a more relational view of human nature, since it asserts that relationships among persons and among levels of creation, along with the human relationship to God, are necessary both to define and to fulfill human existence.[26] This builds on the social view of human nature in the Jewish tradition, in contrast to what some interpreters view as the Hellenistic and Reformation tendency to focus on the vertical tie between the individual person and the absolute as the defining relationship in human life. Human sociability is related in important ways to both human embodiment and human embeddedness in the natural world, as I shall discuss below. In all these ways, the natural law tradition can serve as an important resource for environmental ethics and, particularly, for the anthropology underlying it. Still, natural law ethics remain both human centered and hierarchical. The rest of nature has its own purposes, but those purposes are subordinate to—or harmoniously subsumed into—the human good.

HUMAN EXCEPTIONALISM AND MODERNITY

The theological assumptions that emerged so clearly in traditional Catholic and Protestant thinking about human nature went underground, in a sense, with the onset of the Enlightenment. Modern Western philosophy fused the Christian concept of an eternal soul (the image of God in humanity) with the more secular concept of the rational mind. As Callicott notes, the "divine spark" in humans was identified as human reason itself.[27] The exercise and study of reason retained a theological orientation for many Enlightenment philosophers and scientists, including Descartes, Newton, and Bacon, who understood their task as the discovery of the laws of God or universal reason. In this, their goals were similar to those of natural law theologians in the Middle Ages. However, unlike the medieval synthesis, the Enlightenment did not subordinate the exercise of reason to God's laws. Rather, it shifted the emphasis from reason as the transcendent source of human uniqueness to reason as the uniquely human expression of the transcendent. Modernist thinkers celebrated the autonomy and self-sufficiency of human reason, which increasingly was set free from theological and ethical moorings that bound both Luther and Thomas.

Escape from religion-imposed ethical constraints enabled Descartes and his peers to transform the natural law valuation of reason into an even more thoroughgoing anthropocentrism. Both Thomas Aquinas and Descartes viewed nature as something to satisfy human needs and aid the human quest for knowledge of God and God's creation. Descartes's followers, however, separated the divine spark within humans from anything outside humans that might be a source of and constraint upon reason. They also shed the organic view of nature in favor of the mechanistic model suggested by Baconian and Newtonian science. Anthropological dualism thus became linked to an individualism that contrasted sharply with the medieval Catholic view. Design of this new framework drew in part upon the "religious individualism" of Luther and Calvin,[28] which emphasized the capacity of each person to relate to God and achieve salvation alone, apart from the corporate body of the church or larger community. However, secular modernists, especially after Descartes, transformed the Reformation's emphasis on the individual's ultimate solitude before God into a doctrine of self-sufficient individualism that needed not even God for fulfillment. Reason, as an interior and universal trait, is by definition untouched by anything outside the mind (except of course its ultimate transcendent source). The Cartesian *cogito ergo sum* suggests, in the end, that the individual alone constitutes himself or herself and that all sense of relation and context remain accidental and external.

This philosophical anthropology, many critics argue, has had dire effects on attitudes toward nonhuman animals and nature more generally. For Descartes, nonhuman creatures lack not only rationality but even consciousness. Descartes finds proof for this claim in the use of language by humans. Since other animals do not use language, he argues, they are not conscious or sentient.[29] This assertion, in conjunction with technological and economic changes, undermined efforts to constrain human behavior toward the nonhuman world. While Descartes's belief that other animals are not sentient has been roundly rejected, his underlying supposition that human rationality is unique and superior continues to ground much thinking about human nature today. Many other assertions of human uniqueness, such as the ideas that only humans are self-conscious, only humans ask existential questions, and only humans are moral, represent versions of the Cartesian emphasis on rational thinking, with its narrow and anthropocentric definition of such terms as *rationality, consciousness,* and *morality.* Variations on this theme include Marx's claim that only for "man" is "his own life is an object for him"[30] and Durkheim's assertion that, because only humans conceive of an ideal and add something to the real, and because only humans have conceptual thought, "man is not merely an animal with certain additional qualities: he is something else."[31]

All these anthropological claims, despite their real and important differences in other contexts, rest on an assumption that is fundamental to the Western theological and philosophical traditions: human beings are not fully at home in the world. What is really important, really *human* about humanness is the extent to which it transcends its physical and social existence. As Durkheim puts it, humans must be "something else," radically other than the rest of the beings with whom they share the world. Different thinkers have offered up a range of qualities as constituting this something else, but there remains a broad and remarkably uncritical agreement that *something* sets human nature apart.

In the Christian tradition, as noted earlier, explicit human uniqueness emerges from biblical narratives. Christian theologians from Paul onward have relied on the stories of human creation in God's image and human "re-creation" (the emergence of the "new man") through Jesus' incarnation, death, and resurrection as the context for their assertions about human nature. Biblical narratives make the claims of theological anthropology accessible and authoritative to believers. The uniqueness of human nature is embedded in the larger biblical story of human origins and ends, and it neither can nor needs to stand by itself. It is not so clear, however, where the modernist philosophy of human exceptionalism finds coherence and legitimacy. Enlightenment claims are not obviously or explicitly embedded in narratives, until we look at the ways that philosophical tradition has rewritten biblical stories into a new myth of human self-creation. This creation, like God's, is ex nihilo: from nowhere, rational "man" constructs himself, like a Horatio Alger hero with only his own bootstraps for support.

In this story of heroic triumph over nature, emotion, the body, and other people, reason becomes its own raison d'être, as the rational mind draws its own image upon the blank paper of human bodily existence. This human nature is all the greater for its freedom from outside influence, not only from the physical body or nature but now from God as well. The progress narrative overcomes the "superstition" of cultures that believed in forces greater than the human mind and saw human life as part of a larger story populated by a range of beings, many of whom humans could not control. In the modern tale of never-ending human accomplishment, there are no forces humans cannot, in the end, understand and dominate. If God exists, it is to legitimize, rather than constrain, human domination. This humanism dissolves Christianity's "eschatological reservation," which insists that nothing but God is absolute. Pieces of the biblical narrative remain, but only insofar as they reinforce the assertion of human uniqueness and superiority.

DIFFERENCE AND THE LOGIC OF DOMINATION

The link between uniqueness and superiority is central to the relationship between anthropology and ethics in Western religious and philosophical traditions. For both Christian and secular modern thinkers, it is not incidental that humans possess an eternal soul or rational mind, as might be the fact that platypuses can lay eggs and also nurse their young, or that bats use echolocation to find their way in the night. The presumably unique qualities of humans, unlike the distinctive traits of other species, justify human domination. The Christian reading of human difference is, in other words, laden with both value and power. The ecofeminist philosopher Karen Warren highlights this point in her discussion of "oppressive conceptual frameworks." Such frameworks—in this case, readings of human uniqueness as superiority—share a "logic of domination." This logic begins with a perception of difference as value laden, which leads to the labeling of certain things—nature, animal, body, female—as inferior. Further, the logic of domination holds that this difference in value justifies subordination by others. In other words, what is important in traditional Western readings of nature or nonhuman animals is not just that they are different but that those differences are morally relevant, and that the relevant differences justify exploitative practices.[32]

Oppressive readings of difference between humans and nonhumans are intimately tied, in history and in theory, to readings of difference among humans and to justifications of power and privilege based on difference. Especially, but not only, in the West, the definition of humanness in terms of a single quality has legitimized the oppression of individuals or groups assumed to lack that quality. (This is one reason, Lynda Birke notes, that defining humanness by a particular trait "is asking for trouble.")[33] Only humans have reason, language, a soul, tools, and so on, the argument goes, and, inevitably, some humans have this supremely human capacity more fully. This logic underlies Aristotle's hierarchy of being, in which not only nonhumans but also certain humans were positioned lower and thus were subordinate to their "betters."[34] In many cultures, the same logic has led to subjecting certain members, such as children, the mentally ill, slaves, heretics, homosexuals, disabled persons, and women, among others, to treatment that full citizens, or full humans, would not receive.

Exclusive definitions of humanness have not only established hierarchies within particular societies but also shaped relations among cultures. Members of different social groups or nations have often seen each other as less than human. This is perhaps most evident in European and U.S. imperialism, which has conquered and destroyed whole cultures and ecosystems in the name of Western superiority. This usually has been justified not on biological grounds (although some imperialists certainly believed that other races were biologically different) but rather on the basis of cultural difference ("backwardness"), or, biologists might say, it has been based on the different ecological niches the groups occupied. Against this view, Western critics of colonialism, slavery, sexism, and racism have affirmed the value of all persons regardless of cultural and ecological differences. They have done this, for the most part, without fundamentally revising their underlying assumptions about what it means to be human. Rather than rejecting the notion that difference implies superiority, in other words, modern humanists deny that there are meaningful differences among humans, while still leaving intact or reinforcing the qualitative gap between human and nonhuman nature. Some critics have pointed out that assumptions of homogeneity among humans raise thorny conceptual and political problems, but few have explored the ways that both humanist universalism and the hierarchies it attacks depend on presumed differences between human and nonhuman nature.

EMBODIMENT, SOCIAL EMBEDDEDNESS, AND NATURE

Feminism has provided the primary exception to the general lack of theorizing about the connections between attitudes toward nature and human oppression. Ecological feminists in particular argue that human domination of nature is linked to male domination of women both conceptually, in the logic of domination, and historically, insofar as Western culture has understood women as more closely tied to, or determined by, nature and the physical body. Both theoretical and practical links center on women's inability to participate in humanity's distinguishing activity: escaping the body. Menstruation, pregnancy, and lactation continually recall women to the reality of physical embodiment. The Western tradition generally views this female bodiliness as a failure to transcend and, thus, a failure to become fully human. Many feminists, in contrast, argue that women's perceived inability to escape the body provides an important starting point for philosophical reflection and political activism.

Both traditional Western philosophy and feminist theory define the body and embodiment as subjective. Objectivism, a dominant approach in Western philosophy, insists that there is a single correct "God's-eye view" of the world. In this perspective, as Mark Johnson puts it, "there is a rational structure to reality, independent of the beliefs of any particular people, and correct reason mirrors this rational structure."[35] Correct reason, in other words, can achieve the God's-eye perspective, the view from nowhere. For Objectivism, as Johnson continues, "the humanness (human embodiment) of understanding has no significant bearing on the nature of meaning and rationality. The structure of rationality is regarded as transcending structures of bodily experience." In this view, meaning is objective insofar as it depends only on the relations between sign (symbol) and signified (things in the world). As a consequence, Johnson concludes, "the way human beings grasp things as meaningful—the way they understand their experience—is held to be incidental to the nature of meaningful thought and reason."[36]

Further, bodily experience not only is incidental to reason understood as universal, objective, and transcendent but actually subverts this reason, insofar as our bodies inevitably tie us to the particular and the concrete. One can be embodied only in *this* body, in *this* time and place. Our bodies are physical reminders that we are not abstract emanations of some universal essence, such as God or reason. For most Western philosophy and theology, however, what is important about humans is precisely their connection to that essence, and thus the body cannot be more than a temporary residence for the essential self or soul. The rational mind links us not to particular conditions or experiences but to the universal. Its purpose, in fact, is precisely to escape physical embodiment, as Johnson puts it, "by plugging into a transcendent rationality."[37] The body, on the other hand, seems to have nothing transcendent about it. It is messy, flawed, and finite, and, from the Objectivist perspective, it inevitably introduces into reasoning subjective elements that are (or should be) irrelevant to the objective nature of meaning.[38]

While the mind connects us to God, the body connects us both to nature in general and to nonhuman beings. While language, a soul, rationality, or any number of other features may divide us from other species, the physical body invariably reminds us of our links to them and to the material or created world. In theistic terms, our bodies show that we are part of creation and not the creator. Bodies make it obvious that we are similar to and dependent upon other species of animals and plants, the landscape itself, and, not least, other humans. (Mammals have a permanent reminder of human connectedness in our navels, into which Objectivist philosophers, presumably, prefer not to gaze.) The body is the outward and visible sign, as well as the vehicle (although that term suggests too external a relationship), of our social nature. It is difficult to conceive of a fully embodied person—defined as much by physical as by mental existence—as unencumbered by relations with other persons or an environment.[39] Bodies need other bodies in a way that souls or rational minds do not obviously need others. Only an individual defined primarily by what is "inside" can remain untouched by the body's inevitable relationality and embeddedness in the world.

Thus most definitions of humanness in terms of possession of the divine spark (or soul, or reason) view essential humanness as solitary, and vice versa. As Richard Schmitt notes, "The argument over individualism is an argument about the essence of human beings, over what human beings *are*."[40] The modern Western notion that relations among humans are necessarily accidental, voluntaristic, and external cannot be separated from the philosophical and theological conviction that the only internal or self-constituting relationship for "rational man" is with God or universal reason. If being human hinges on possessing a divine spark that separates us from the mundane, as Western philosophy and theology claim, then ultimate value cannot inhere in embodiment or relationships. This conviction has made a decisive impact on ideas about nonhuman nature. "Rational man," in this perspective, is capable of transcending not only embodiment and the demands of sociability but also nature itself. Like relations among individuals and between body and spirit within individuals, the relations between humans and the nonhuman world do not fundamentally shape human nature. We inhabit nature, as we live in our bodies and among other people, only accidentally. None of them impinge on us or constitute us in a substantive way, although any of them may constrain our actions. For the most part, we accept the limitations of our body and of human society, albeit sometimes with regret or annoyance. We know that the benefits of living in society must be countered by certain constraints, and that our bodies cannot leap over tall buildings, that in time they will get sick, age, and die (although we increasingly challenge the inevitability of aging and illness).

The limitations of nature, however, seem less acceptable. Nature appears not only separate from but radically other to us. Other species lack the essential trait or traits that make human life meaningful and valuable, and thus they exist merely as means to human ends. The mechanistic, reductive, and material view of nature constructed by early modern science in the West, under the influence of Bacon and Newton in particular, reinforced the idea that nonhuman nature had no intrinsic value, indeed no life of its own. The vision of a passive, soulless, even dead, nature constructed in modern science and natural philosophy has been the target of several influential critiques, first and most notably by Lynn White Jr. White focused on Western Christian ideas not only because of their content but also because of their power. In the context of colonialism and mercantilism, European culture and Christian belief spread around the globe, and with them their attitudes about how humans ought to live in nature. According to White, these attitudes shifted in the early Middle Ages, when Christianity spread throughout Europe and destroyed pagan animism, which had seen "spirits *in* natural objects, which . . . had protected nature from man." With the destruction of paganism, White writes, humans could "exploit nature in a mood of indifference to the feelings of natural objects."[41]

This indifference hinges on Christian theological anthropology. For Christianity, unlike paganism, "man shares, in great measure, God's transcendence of nature." Thus, with the triumph of Christianity "man's effective monopoly on spirit in this world was confirmed, and the old inhibitions to the exploitation of nature crumbled."[42] The collapse of pagan ideas about the spiritual value of nature in the Middle Ages opened the way, White argues, for the blending of science and technology, which meant that knowledge of nature was combined with domination of nature. Religious prohibitions against the exploitation of "natural resources" disappeared. As White puts it, "To a Christian, a tree can be no more than a physical fact. The whole concept of a sacred grove is alien to Christianity and to the ethos of the West. For nearly two millennia, Christian missionaries have been chopping down sacred groves, which are idolatrous because they assume spirit in nature."[43]

A number of Christian "ecophilosophers" concur with some aspects of White's critique while qualifying his condemnation of Christianity. (White's condemnation, in fact, was also qualified, since he found in Saint Francis a model of ecological consciousness.) They point to enduring alternative traditions within Christianity, notably mysticism, while agreeing that the dominant models have indeed devalued nonhuman

nature. Michael Northcott, for example, believes that exploitative attitudes toward nature are rooted in secularization and the decline of traditional Christian communitarianism and natural law explanations.[44]
Other contemporary Christian thinkers identify additional factors, such
as the influences of Greek or Enlightenment philosophy, as the reasons
that certain kinds of Christian culture in the West have contributed to
environmental destruction. Whatever its sources, Western "civil religion" has developed a view of human nature in which humans are separate from the rest of creation and, within humans, the body is separate
from reason. This split makes possible the devaluation of nature into
something that does not affect reason in any determining way. Only persons whose essence resides elsewhere can live in nature without being
touched by it. Nature, in this view, provides resources for our use and
sometimes threats to our survival, but it does not help constitute what it
means to be human.

THE END OF THE STORY

In Christianity's vision, the necessary end of human life in the world is
salvation. It is an end in two ways: in the narrative sense, as the close
to the story Christianity tells about human history and life, and in the
teleological sense, as the goal toward which believers move, or hope to
move. Salvation is necessary in two ways. First, salvation is required
conceptually, since without it Christian theology loses its meaning and
coherence: the whole story of creation, incarnation, crucifixion, and resurrection cannot hold together without redemption at the end. Second,
salvation is needed practically, for without its promise Christianity cannot resonate with and shape the lives of individual believers.

The conceptual and practical power of Christian ideas about salvation, as of Christianity's visions of creation and re-creation, comes from
its ability to link sacred and secular history. This connection generates
the power of religious narrative generally, and it is particularly potent
in the Christian tale of redemption. The two dimensions are joined in
at least two ways. First, the sacred can provide a model for believers'
actions in the world: as Jesus behaved, so should we behave; and our
actions will have the same consequences as his, since the structure of
sacred history parallels that of our own. Second, the sacred can shape
secular history more directly, insofar as God or other divine forces enter
our world. This is what happens in Christian notions of redemption, in

which divine grace transforms individual lives and perhaps larger histories as well. The importance of salvation in the Christian narrative underlines the vital role of eschatology in ethical narratives more generally. If Christians' main motivation and Christianity's chief purpose is the redemption of individual human souls, then the place of nature in salvation must be of central concern to Christian environmental ethics.

Mostly, Christian views of salvation seem to reinforce the tradition's negative attitude to nature. In a nutshell, Christian salvation theology provides the final, resounding answer to the question of where our true home lies. By emphasizing humanity's visitor (resident alien?) status in the created world, salvation reinforces the division between humans and nature decried by many critics of Christian anthropocentrism. This dualism, which excludes the nonhuman from questions of ultimate value, has dominated Christian thinking about salvation. Christian scriptures mainly focus on human salvation, as Paul Santmire notes, with the natural world as little more than a backdrop for the human drama of sin and redemption. The Gospel of John, for example, suggests that salvation means removal of believers to heaven, to a re-creation of the original time when the Word alone, disembodied and disembedded, was with God.[45] Thomas Aquinas does not go so far, but he does contend that salvation, the return of all things to God, is for rational creatures only. The world of nonhuman nature is not renewed, and in fact does not have to be renewed, since its purpose is to fulfill human needs on earth.[46] Again, in Thomas's hierarchical model, only spiritual beings are ends in themselves, and thus nonhuman beings or objects cannot have a final fulfillment of their own. The Protestant tradition has taken a similar line, even strengthening the central importance of individual salvation and the exclusion of nonhumans (and nonbelievers) from its glories.

A few Christian thinkers, however, have included nonhuman creatures, or nature generally, as more than just supporting players in the story of redemption.[47] Most notably, Francis of Assisi (and some earlier theologians, such as Irenaeus) suggested that the salvation of the human soul is linked to the spiritual renewal of creation more generally.[48] However, salvation can encompass nonhuman creation only for thinkers who, like Francis, refuse the dualism that separates the spiritual from the material, within humans and in the world more generally, and reserves ultimate value only for the former. Only in the context of a profound continuity between body and spirit, animal and human, can redemption encompass more than the individual human soul. Conversely, the denial of renewal to nonhuman nature both reinforces and reflects larger claims about humanity's peculiar nearness to God and unbridgeable distance from other creatures.

BECOMING NATIVE TO THIS PLANET

Critical analysis of Christian ideas about salvation highlights more general problems regarding the relations between environmental ethics and Christian theological anthropology. The first and most pressing issue is the claim that Christians are not of the world—the cosmic homelessness that may not be a necessary conclusion of Christianity's spiritual homelessness but has certainly been the dominant conclusion of Christian thinkers throughout most of Christianity's history as a practical religion. Humans' (or at least Christians') alienation from the created world begins with creation stories and runs throughout the tradition, but its most compelling justification is salvation: the final proof that Christians do not belong in the world is that, in the end, they go home to Jesus. Some of the problems posed by this core doctrine become evident if we look at it in relation to the growing emphasis, in environmental ethics, upon activism and analysis based on bioregions or "watersheds." Bioregionalism insists that the first step toward a more sustainable way of life is, as Wes Jackson puts it, "becoming native to this place"[49]—being grounded and fully at home in a particular place. Being "native" requires a profound knowledge of and attachment to a particular landscape and to the creatures and relationships (among humans and between humans and nonhumans) embedded in that setting. Only such attachments, bioregionalists contend, can undergird the attitudinal and practical changes necessary to generate more ecologically sustainable ways of life. Gary Snyder suggests the depth of the transformation required when he writes, "For the non-Native American to become at home on this continent, he or she must be *born again* in this hemisphere, on this continent."[50]

Traditionally, however, Christian theology (at least in its practical manifestations) has required that believers be born again apart from not only the hemisphere and the continent but the created world altogether. Thus in Christian theology and ethics, the bioregionalist demand for attachment to a particular place cannot be separated from attachment to "the world" in general. It is not clear which should come first. Bioregionalists argue that being rooted in a particular place is the precondition for a more encompassing attachment to the world. Thus, for Snyder we cannot simply "love nature" or "be in harmony with Gaia." Rather, he writes, "our relation to the natural world takes place in a *place,* and it must be grounded in information and experience."[51] Whether we are born again to the world in general or to a particular place in the world, a central question for Christian ethics is the extent to which Christian doctrine can enable and even encourage believers to be truly at home in—fully in and of—the world. A number of contemporary Christian thinkers, including Rosemary Radford Ruether, Shannon Jung, and Sallie McFague, have addressed this issue, which I will discuss in chapter 8. Despite the promise of contemporary eco-theologies, there remain both theological questions and the pressing problems of making symbols and doctrines *effective* in history. As Laitin's notion of practical religion emphasizes, laypeople do not always appropriate what theologians or religious founders consider central or correct.

Some environmental ethicists have focused on practical efforts to encourage ecologically sound behavior within the Christian tradition. Many point to stewardship ethics as evidence that a Christian environmentalism need not entail elaborate reworkings of theological anthropology. Stewardship ethics do not deny a special place to humans in the created order but use precisely that specialness as a call to responsible behavior regarding the rest of creation. Most stewardship ethics are marshaled, not accidentally, in defense of moderate environmental duties: humans are required to treat animals kindly, to farm responsibly, and to recycle but not to transform their entire relationship to nature. Obviously, widespread adoption of a moderate stewardship ethic would mark a great advance over present habits, and it would therefore be counterproductive to dismiss stewardship as too moderate. Its very moderation, in fact, is the key to its usefulness. It makes reasonable demands, asking humans not to give up their spot at the center of the universe but simply to take better care of those at its margins.

The practical value of moderate stewardship ethics, while real, might be limited in light of increasingly severe ecological crises, including global climate change, species extinction, loss of clean water and topsoil, and other conditions threatening the existence of all life. Many conservation biologists contend that current ecological problems demand a radical transformation in human attitudes to nature and not just a mitigation of the worst of present destruction. They argue, in relation to moderate environmentalism, that while a little change is better than no change, a little is still not enough. If they are right about the severity of the crisis, and if I am right that ethics are intimately tied to claims about human nature, then reflections on Christian theological anthropology are not simply abstract musings. Rather, hope for an adequate Christian environmental ethic depends on the possibility of transformation, practical as well as theoretical, in Christian notions of what it means to be human and, particularly, to live as a human being in the created world. In chapters 8 and 9 I discuss some efforts aimed at this transformation.

Moreover, this transformation has to take place not just in the context of Christian theology but within a larger Western capitalist, industrial, consumer culture. Today, Christian convictions of human uniqueness are deeply entwined with this culture and, to a considerable extent, freed from their original religious roots. Max Weber's analysis of the way a disembodied "Protestant ethic" contributed to the rise of capitalism in the United States represents the classic discussion of how ideas remain powerful even after they detach from their theological origins and the "religious capital" on which they first drew.[52] The disjunction between ideas and origins is evident in the fact that even contemporary critiques of Christian and Enlightenment thought reproduce some of the philosophical, ethical, and political problems of the traditions they reject. The next chapter turns to that paradox and to the perhaps unexpected dangers of deconstructing traditional Western ways of thinking about nature and human nature.

CHAPTER THREE

The Social Construction
of Nature and Human Nature

God made humans both different and better than other species, most Christian thinkers have insisted. By privileging humans with an eternal soul, which is the divine image within them, the creator permanently separated humanity from all other creatures. However, for many people, academic and otherwise, the monotheistic creation account no longer holds credibility. While religion remains a vital force in many people's lives and ideas, the contemporary world, in the West and elsewhere, is far too pluralistic, skeptical, and secular to adhere to a single religious worldview. (Of course, the world has always been too pluralistic for this, but most Western philosophers and theologians have recognized this fact only fairly recently.) In this context, making sense of humanity's nature and origins becomes more problematic. Some secularists turn wholeheartedly to physics, biology, and paleontology, but science-based accounts of the origins of life do not always provide a satisfactory answer to questions about culture and meaning. Rejecting both traditional religious myth and scientific empiricism, many contemporary thinkers highlight the importance of human culture, language, and social life. One of the most influential approaches to this problem comes from a sociological and philosophical genre often called social constructionism or constructivism, which encompasses various kinds of arguments for the unique and generative role of culture.

These arguments depend on a broader view of the ways that people constitute elements of their world in and through language, convention, and practice. This claim, in turn, builds on long-standing discussions in Western philosophy about the social meaning and shaping of reality. This approach can first be glimpsed in William of Occam's nominalism, which highlighted the lack of an intrinsic link between words and the objects or qualities to which they refer. What we call "a book" (or *un libro* or *ein Buch*) is such only because a group of people has agreed to call it that. The same holds for natural objects like trees and rivers, and different cultures assign not only different words but different meanings and valuations to these objects. For (a timeworn) example, the multiplicity of Eskimo words for snow suggests its central role in that culture, while English covers the frozen white stuff quite well with one or at most a few terms, and many cultures, no doubt, find no need to name it at all. Nominalism, insofar as it makes clear the disjuncture between things and the terms we use to describe them, provides the crucial insight for theories of the social construction of reality: there is no intrinsic, universal quality captured in the terms we use; rather those terms are conventions of particular cultures and times and are loaded with, and intelligible because of, the meanings and values of those cultures.

The contention that meaning comes only in and through particular settings has provided a starting point for a more extensive exploration of the degree to which other dimensions of our experience, and not just language, are human constructs. A number of thinkers have taken up these issues since Occam, including Hegel, Nietzsche, Wittgenstein, Saussure, Freud, and Durkheim. A classic statement of this approach is Peter Berger and Thomas Luckmann's *The Social Construction of Reality*, which contends that society is "built up by activities that express subjective meaning," although society also possesses "objective facticity." This facticity—the "world of things"—emerges through subjective, symbolic processes.[1] For Berger and Luckmann, this social construction of reality is the defining human activity: "Man is biologically predestined to construct and to inhabit a world with others. This world becomes for him the dominant and definitive reality. Its limits are set by nature, but once constructed, this world acts back upon nature. In the dialectic between nature and the socially constructed world the human organism itself is transformed. In this same dialectic man produces reality and therefore produces himself."[2]

This perspective allows for no essential human nature. If we can speak of a human nature at all, it must be characterized by an almost limitless plasticity resulting from its never-ending process of self-creation. Thus the anthropologist Clifford Geertz refers to human nature as "unfinished": we require culture to complete us, to make us fully human.[3] What it means to be human is largely or even entirely shaped by the interactions between individuals and their settings and between the natural and social worlds. Thus being human means something different in every different time and place that humans inhabit. There can be no universal human, no human species-being in any true sense.

Within this broad social constructionist framework, Geertz argues that culture, understood largely in terms of symbols and symbolic structures, defines and in fact determines what it means to be human. In this perspective, there is no humanity before or without culture. This is true, Geertz argues, because humans are born with so few instincts and so much flexibility in the ways we can live in the world and with others. We can be "completed" as human beings not by "culture" generally but only by a particular culture in a particular time and place. "To be human . . . ," he writes, "is not to be Everyman; it is to be a particular kind of man, and of course men differ."[4] This profound diversity in what it means to be human, for Geertz, stands in explicit opposition to the Enlightenment idea that "the great, vast variety of differences among men, in beliefs and values, in customs and institutions, both over time and from place to place, is essentially without significance in defining [human] nature." In this view, Geertz adds, culture "consists of mere accretions, distortions even, overlaying and obscuring what is truly human—the constant, the general, the universal—in man."[5]

This modernist essentialism or universalism, as Geertz and others have noted, has legitimized a variety of oppressive and simply inaccurate approaches to cultures other than that of the one doing the oppressing or approaching. Assumptions that there exists a single human essence have led to claims that a certain culture, such as medieval European Christendom, imperial Japan, or the capitalist United States, represents not just one culture but Culture itself. In this view, societies other than the one true Society (and people other than universal Man) must be distorted or incomplete, and as such they ought to be improved or eliminated by those who know better. This logic has justified imperialism, colonialism, and countless educational and development schemes that have caused great human suffering and the extinction of whole cultures and ecosystems.

Against this approach, assertions of the social construction of human identity and experience reinforce the various, contingent, and fluid nature of all human cultures and achievements. Put more abstractly, the claim that reality is socially constituted guards against the danger "of

[man] forgetting his own authorship of the human world," as Berger and Luckmann put it (acknowledging their debt to Marx).[6] In other words, once we insist that all our experiences are humanly constructed, we cannot attribute universal, divine, or eternal value to one over another. This insight, in various shapes, including Marxian, Foucauldian, deconstructionist, and feminist versions, among others, has been central to studies of the ways that such apparently universal categories as sex or race depend on particular cultural contexts for their meaning. In this light, to be female or homosexual or dark skinned does not have universal meaning and value but is determined by the history, language, and social conditions of particular times and places.

The feminist theorist Judith Butler has developed one of the most influential contemporary versions of this approach. Butler argues that a subject such as "the Arab" "is constructed through acts of differentiation that distinguish the subject from its constitutive outside."[7] The meaning of a particular term, in this case "Arab," requires a whole network of relationships, material conditions, and symbol and value systems. Butler's approach uncovers the ideological and partial nature of claims about Arabs or any other socially constructed subject. These claims have oppressive implications because identifying the essential qualities of "true" human nature leads, implicitly or explicitly, to efforts to reject or transform whatever does not correspond with this one true image. Postmodern feminists like Butler, as Joan Scott writes, "call universal categories into question and historicize concepts otherwise treated as natural . . . or absolute."[8]

Despite important differences among them, feminist critics like Butler and Scott join Geertz in seeking to demolish the "politically insidious" claim that there can be a subject preceding a particular context,[9] unchanging and unaffected by circumstances. Butler's, Scott's, and Geertz's approaches are all social constructionist insofar as they insist that there is no single, eternal way of being human (or of being Arab, or female, etc.). Instead, being a subject can have meaning only in and through particular cultural, social, or linguistic conditions or a combination of them. These critiques also share a conviction that great ethical and political harm often results from notions of an unconstituted, and thus universal and unchanging, self.

While the essentialism of Enlightenment approaches was the first and is still the most common target of constructionist critiques, since the 1970s another all-encompassing interpretation of human nature, sociobiology, has come under attack from similar quarters and for similar reasons. In *Sociobiology: The New Synthesis* (1975) and *On Human Nature* (1978), Edward O. Wilson argued, in sum, that "each living form can be viewed as an evolutionary experiment, a product of millions of years of interaction between genes and environment."[10] This approach explains most animal behavior, including that of humans, as the result of natural selection, which preserves certain traits and erases others over very long periods of time, according to their contributions to individual and species survival. Thus, for example, human parents nurture their children not because of moral or cultural superiority but because our early mammal, primate, and hominid ancestors who nurtured their offspring had more descendants survive and pass on their (nurturing) qualities than their negligent counterparts. We are good parents, in other words, not just because of our decisions or our education but mostly because natural selection rewarded our ancestors who were good parents. Other traits, such as aggression, can also be explained in this light, as Wilson writes: "Human beings are strongly predisposed to respond with unreasoning hatred to external threats and to escalate their hostility sufficiently to overwhelm the source of the threat by a respectably wide margin of safety."[11]

Such claims, not surprisingly, have encountered fierce opposition. According to critics, sociobiology's view of human nature was just as essentialist and potentially oppressive as any creationist or Cartesian account. According to the dominant critique, Wilson and like-minded thinkers, notably Richard Dawkins in his work *The Selfish Gene* (1976), portray humans as governed by genetically encoded drives to seek food, power, protection, sex, and so on.[12] Feminists in particular have attacked certain versions of sociobiology because they believe it promotes a biological determinism that legitimizes, even encourages, the oppression of women by portraying male domination of women as a natural and unalterable consequence of evolution.[13] According to this critique, sociobiology not only explains but also justifies behavior such as male aggression and even rape as the natural outcome of human evolution. Other critics point to the racist uses that have been made of biological interpretations of human nature. Stephen Jay Gould's influential book *The Mismeasure of Man* (1981) denounced the "scientific racism" that justified differential treatment based on "natural" (and supposedly quantifiable) variations in intelligence between races.[14]

Beyond sociobiology, other forms of biological determinism have been used to legitimize economic, as well as sexual and racial, differences. "Social Darwinism" applies a popularized version of the evolutionary principle of "survival of the fittest" to economic, and especially free-market, circumstances, with the goal of explaining all differences in socioeconomic status as the result of natural, and therefore legitimate and inevitable, variation in ability. Critics insist that this approach ignores the fact that humans do not begin on a level economic playing field and overestimates the freedom of the free market. In contrast, Marxist and other progressive analyses contend that economic structures and material processes in capitalism reward not the most capable but rather those who start out with more and who exploit others. While few supporters of capitalism accept the extreme versions of Social Darwinism, which advocate letting the poor die off as unfit specimens, Marxist critiques point to the theoretical and practical continuity between the crudest Social Darwinist approaches and more subtle defenses of the free market as a system that appropriately rewards those who are most able. All the positions on this continuum presuppose a more or less strict correspondence between inherent (biological) qualities and socioeconomic success, assume that market structures reflect humans' natural inclinations to seek their own (narrowly defined) self-interest, and move from innate differences to justifications of a particular way of organizing society. In sum, Social Darwinism, like scientific racism and sexism, uses supposedly natural qualities to defend the superiority of certain cultures, social groups, or individuals.

The history of such claims highlights the need for critiques of biological reductionism. While biological arguments have had less historical impact than Enlightenment understandings of human nature, both types of essentialism can lead, and have led, to justifications for denigrating, subordinating, and even exterminating certain individuals or groups. Amid the varied critiques of essentialism, I want to highlight several common claims that are especially important to my argument. Most crucially, anti-essentialist forms of constructionism insist that there is no true and universal human nature, whether it comes from God or biology. Thus there are no universals, only diverse and particular versions of being human that depend on the cultural or material circumstances at hand, or both.

While all forms of social constructionism deny that there is a single way of being human, few if any go on to deny that there is a distinctive quality we can call "humanness." Constructionism thus faces the problem of defining this generic humanness in a nonreductive way. Its supporters usually answer this question with self-referential logic: what makes us human is what humans do. We create culture (society) and culture (society) creates us. What comes before culture (or language, or society) is, in this light, irrelevant or nonexistent. This approach, in its general contours, is shared by theorists ranging from relative tradition-alists like Geertz and Berger to postmodernist innovators such as Fou-cault and Derrida. While these thinkers differ widely and disagree with each other in many respects, all reject biological, theological, and mod-ernist accounts of a universal or essential human nature in favor of local and historicized ways of being human.

Some versions of anti-essentialism are as reductive as their targets. The danger lies in the tendency of certain social constructionist argu-ments to suggest that human identity itself derives from human inter-pretation. In this view, there is nothing "out there," prior to human symbolization and naming, no universal human nature, no underlying reality of male and female (or white and black, heterosexual and ho-mosexual). There are only different ways of conceptualizing such qual-ities and attaching them to essentially empty human beings. In this light, to conceptualize a quality or a world is in fact to construct it. This construction, further, takes place upon an empty landscape. Instead of a divine spark, eternal reason, or selfish genes to determine what humans do and are, there is a void to be filled in by culture, language, social power, or other human-created forces. This is what Mary Midgley calls the "blank paper" theory of human nature, the claim that humans, un-like other animals, have no instincts or other internal forces shaping their behavior but instead are entirely determined by the circumstances in which they are born and develop.[15]

One of the most influential versions of this approach has been be-haviorism, which contends that animals, often including humans, can be explained and judged solely on the basis of observable behavior. In contrast to "subjective" psychology, behaviorism presents itself as ob-jective and rejects nonempirical and presumably nonverifiable assump-tions about inner states.[16] Behaviorism interprets all human activity as a series of reactions to stimuli, which can be predicted and controlled through conditioning. Prior to social and experiential conditioning, there is no inner self but only an infinitely malleable creature, predis-posed to nothing except, perhaps, to being conditioned. Behaviorism lost favor, in large part because it "lowered" humans to the same level as other animals.

A different kind of argument for human nature as blank paper emerges from the poststructuralist theory developed by Jacques Derrida and his interpreters. Building on and radicalizing the structuralist nominalism of Ferdinand de Saussure, Derrida claims that there can be no "signified" prior to signification and signifiers: "The signified always already functions as a signifier. . . . There is not a single signified that escapes, even if recaptured, the play of signifying references that constitute language."[17] For Derrida, not only the signified but also the author escapes into the play of language. Just as there is no essential or permanent relationship between words and the objects to which they refer, there is no essential or permanent subject that expresses itself in speech. Derrida's deconstruction of modernist understandings of language and selfhood implies, as Jean Baudrillard writes, that *"referential value is annihilated, giving the structural play of value the upper hand*. The structural dimension becomes autonomous by excluding the referential dimension, and is instituted upon the death of reference. The systems of reference for production, signification, the affect, substance, and history, all this equivalence to a 'real' content . . . all this is over with. Now the other stage of value has the upper hand, a total relativity, general commutation, combination and simulation."[18] As a consequence of this "emancipation of the sign," as Baudrillard terms it, meaning is not only fluid and contingent but also always humanly derived. Gilles Deleuze and Felix Guattari underline this notion when they write that "everything is production: *production of productions,* of actions and of passions[,] . . . of sensual pleasures, of anxieties, and of pain."[19] Everything is, more precisely, *human* production. Moreover, for Deleuze and Guattari, "Desire and its object are one and the same thing."[20] In other words, human desire, like human production and human language, lacks any reference outside itself. While this claim poses a radical challenge to what Derrida calls the "logocentrism" of Enlightenment notions of the self, it does not undermine its anthropocentrism. Poststructuralism's demolition of the Subject remains peculiarly blind to the imperial assumptions of human uniqueness. Human signification creates the world, and any world outside human signification is either meaningless or nonexistent.

Poststructuralism and behaviorism have little in common from many perspectives, and in fact poststructuralists explicitly reject behaviorism's claim to predict and determine human action through conditioning. I do not want to argue for similarities in the two beyond their shared assumption that human nature is blank paper prior to either social conditioning (behaviorism) or the play of language, production, and desire (poststructuralism). In fact, the very real differences between these two schools of thought in almost every other respect underline my point:

important and often destructive anthropological claims find their way into, and help constitute, widely varying philosophical positions. In portraying humans as blank paper inscribed only by culture, with no contribution from a realm beyond the human, both behaviorism and poststructuralism assert, as Kate Soper writes, that there is no "natural dimension at all to human subjectivity, bodily existence, or sexual disposition."[21] Humans are constructed by human constructions, be they the fluid and ever-present play of language or overt forms of social control.

While most philosophers today roundly reject behaviorism, poststructuralism and related approaches hold wide currency and are generally considered by their advocates to represent emancipatory improvements over the schools of thought they deconstruct. Without denying the important contributions of some postmodernist theories, here I highlight the damaging potential of poststructuralist notions of human and nonhuman nature. The problem arises with a shift in emphasis from Berger and Luckmann's assertion that "in the dialectic between nature and the socially constructed world the human organism itself is transformed" to their related claim that "man produces reality and therefore produces himself."[22] For Berger and Luckmann, the two propositions could not be separated. Their constructionism thus remains limited. However, extreme constructionist positions abstract the production of meaning from the natural and material conditions of human life. Humanness is defined not by the dialectical interaction between persons and the world but by the largely interior process of self-creation through culture and language.

This extension of social constructionism quickly runs into serious philosophical and ethical problems. In its emphasis on language and culture, on Derrida's endless play of signifiers, poststructuralism cannot do full justice to the influence even of human social relations—much less of physical embodiment or the natural environment—on human identity. The challenge to Enlightenment arrogance results, paradoxically, in a celebration of human cultural production as all there is or needs be. Thus, as David Harvey writes, in rejecting certain forms of determinism poststructuralists risk "rejecting all material and biological conditions of human behavior as irrelevant in favor of a triumphalist mode of thought in which human history, economy, and culture reign supreme."[23] Other critics point out that extreme versions of social constructionism undermine the basis for justifying critiques of existing practices or defending their alternatives. If there is no human nature defined by essential and specieswide needs or instincts, Kate Soper contends, people can neither be repressed by existing norms nor more fully realized under others.[24] Mary Midgley notes more concisely that the blank-paper theory cannot explain why people resist doing things they are culturally conditioned to do.[25]

Constructionist positions require a devaluation of the body that, paradoxically, has parallels to Gnostic approaches. If humans constitute themselves entirely through language and culture, then the body cannot help constitute human identity. Our physical bodies are the only things we do not construct ourselves (though of course, as more moderate versions of social constructionism remind us, we shape and redefine them constantly). Further, our bodies obviously and irrevocably tie us to other human beings as part of a species. Social constructionist emphases on language and culture necessarily make the body accidental, irrelevant to the real meaning and task of human nature, just as the Gnostic strains in Christianity and Cartesian modernism have done. All these positions radically undermine our grounds for resisting pain or distortions caused to the human body, as Soper notes, just as they reduce our possibilities for connection with other humans, other embodied creatures, or what Christianity more generally calls creation. Such conceptions not only lead to exploitative or indifferent attitudes toward nonhuman nature but also, as the ecofeminist philosopher Charlene Spretnak argues, diminish our notion of what it means to be human. Spretnak writes, "When deconstructive postmodernists conclude that there is nothing to life but arbitrary social construction and utter groundlessness, they continue and intensify the diminished conceptualization of the human that was begun by Renaissance humanism, the scientific revolution, and the Enlightenment. These foundational movements of modernity cumulatively framed the human story apart from the larger unfolding story of the earth community. Deconstructive postmodernists shrink the human story even further, insisting that it is entirely a matter of power plays and language games."[26]

The devaluation of the body and of nature in extreme social constructionism is not all that this approach shares with Christian theological anthropology. The vision of a human subject constituting itself through language also recalls biblical understandings of human special creation. For poststructuralists, as in the Genesis creation account and Saint John's vision of cosmic beginnings (when "The word was with God, and the Word was God"), naming wields constitutive power. While the mechanism differs—divine fiat versus the play of signifiers—the conclusion is strikingly similar: humans are alone among animals insofar as the clue to their origins lies not in the physical world and the body but in a realm of ideas or spirits. There may no longer be a Universal Man, but the multiple, contingent, and culturally shaped human is still the only animal that really matters.

SOCIAL CONSTRUCTIONS
AND CONSTRUALS OF NATURE

In its deconstruction of essentialism and universalism, social constructionism uncovers the source of certain ethical and political problems regarding social (intrahuman) relationships. In relation to nonhuman nature, however, social constructionist approaches frequently run into problems insofar as they argue that only humans have culture, that culture is the sole source of value and meaning, and thus that only humans can give value and meaning to nature. Not only are such clearly human phenomena as race and (human) sexuality constituted by social processes and conventions in this view, but nature itself—understood as wilderness, the nonhuman, the undomesticated—becomes, paradoxically, a product of human naming and practice.

Nature can be viewed as socially constructed in two distinct, though not contradictory, ways. First, individuals, groups, and societies "construct" particular versions of nature when they interpret it in different ways in and through cultural categories and values. This approach echoes the moderate version of social constructionism articulated by Berger and Luckmann, among others. The construction of nature in this sense is unavoidable, since we cannot experience nature except through the lens of meanings assigned to it by particular cultures and periods. The different meanings of nature affect attitudes not only toward the nonhuman but also toward other people, communities, politics, and much more. As Raymond Williams notes, "The idea of nature contains, though often unnoticed, an extraordinary amount of human history."[27] Williams's important, though relatively modest, point is that ideas about nature are historically and culturally determined. There is no single, essential "nature" that all individuals in all places and times would recognize as such or can access outside the mediations of human culture.

This basic insight has been elaborated on and illustrated in contemporary ethnographic work on the multiple meanings given to nature in different cultures today. Extensive documentation emphasizes that modern Western notions about nature, which are themselves complex and diverse, often make no sense outside the cultural contexts in which they arose. Philippe Descola identifies three main ways of "constructing" nature: totemism, in which nonhumans are treated as signs; animism, in which they are treated as the terms of a relation; and naturalism, which sees nature as an autonomous domain, essentially "other" to human culture.[28] While the last is clearly the dominant construction of nature in modern Western cultures, it is not the only way to construct it. As Tim Ingold points out, non-Western and especially hunter-gatherer cultures "systematically reject the ontological dualism of that tradition of thought and science which—as a kind of shorthand—we call 'Western,' and of which the dichotomy between nature and culture is the prototypical instance."[29] Signe Howell's work on the Chewong people in Malaysia illustrates Ingold's point. The Chewong, she writes, do not oppose a natural world with a cultural world, nor do they see oppositions between humans and animals, mind and emotion, or other dualisms common to Western thought. Thus they provide "an empirical counterexample" to the supposedly universal categories that we use to construct meaning and value.[30]

Challenging the notion of a universal nature is important for ethics, because the notion of "nature" or the "natural" has so often served as a common court of appeal for people seeking to enshrine or condemn certain practices or traits. In discussions of human sexuality, for example, repressive policies have been justified by reference to some supposedly universal and absolute notion of what is natural. For environmental ethics more particularly, revealing the conventional character of a particular vision of nature can make it possible to view nature, and our relations to it, in a different light.[31] With counterexamples that challenge the common Western idea that nature is radically other than human culture, environmental ethicists can argue more convincingly for alternatives to the dominant Western mode of treating the nonhuman world as a passive, essentially alien world to be exploited. These diverse ways of constructing nature might more accurately be described as ways of *construing* it. What is constructed in this sense is not the physical objects themselves, not the trees or animals or rivers, but their identities and worth in a particular context.

In a second sense, however, nature is literally physically constructed by human society. According to this view, not only do cultural concepts mediate our experience of nature, but most of what we refer to as nature, from city parks to rain forests, has in fact been shaped by human actions.[32] Thus very little of the world today remains natural, if that means free of human intervention. Such intervention has affected not only obviously inhabited areas but also many places commonly viewed as wilderness. For example, the earliest British colonists perceived North America as untouched by human hands. In reality, of course, humans had been living in North America for millennia and had helped form the forests and fields that the first European settlers saw as examples of nature untouched by civilization. Even the preeminent example of wilderness, the Amazonian rain forest, has also been shaped by human activities, particularly by indigenous agricultural practices.[33] Modern industrial cultures, of course, have affected environments even more extensively. This leads Kate Soper to write, "In our own time the human impact on the environment has been so extensive that there is an important sense in which it is correct to speak of 'nature' as itself a cultural product or construction."[34] For Bill McKibben, climate changes caused by the burning of fossil fuels have altered all global ecosystems so extensively that we can no longer speak of a nature free from human intervention: "the planet is utterly different now."[35]

This second understanding of the social construction of nature also carries important implications for ethics, environmental and other. First, acknowledging the human influences on "wild" areas such as the Americas prior to European settlement or tropical forests today challenges the erasure of native peoples, whose invisibility, evidenced by the apparent absence of marks of their habitation, helped (and helps) justify exploitation of the lands they occupied. (This erasure, of course, was effected by Europeans who saw indigenous people as part of a less-than-human nature.) Further, awareness of human impacts on the environment, including the less obvious effects pointed out by McKibben and others, marks the first step toward critical analysis of that impact and its ethical implications. It is important for environmental ethicists, ecologists, and activists to know if, for example, wilderness areas in national parks exist only because of human intervention, or if the extraordinary diversity in a tropical forest results in part from the careful work of generations of indigenous inhabitants. Only with such knowledge can we reflect on our responsibilities regarding what we call nature and its human and nonhuman residents. Finally, the recognition that even apparently wild areas have often been inhabited by humans can inform an evaluation of the varying environmental impacts of different lifestyles, ranging from those that remain invisible to outsiders, like the hunting, gathering, agriculture, and forestry practiced by pre-Columbian peoples in much of North America, to those with obvious, and undeniably negative, consequences for both humans and nonhumans, like the paving, clear-cutting, and burning by peoples of modern industrial societies. People have lived in most parts of the world and have always affected the places they live, but the effects vary widely in environmental and human cost. This knowledge can help environmentalists avoid a blanket condemnation of all human practices and point to precedents for more or less positive ways of acting in nature.

Just as awareness of the ways that nature is physically shaped by human cultures enriches environmental ethics, so does an understanding of the symbolic construction or construal of nature. Only a recognition that interpretations of nature are culturally mediated and varied can make us aware of alternatives to established ways of thinking about the nonhuman world and our relations to it. Thus, understanding the diverse ways that humans shape nature both physically and symbolically can help avoid dualistic visions of an eternal, universal, and unmediated nature as the realm of physical relations versus a human realm ruled by symbols. Most important, perhaps, both versions of social constructionism remind us that nature and culture in their myriad forms interact with each other, in our minds and also in the physical world.

Claims about the social construction of nature run into trouble, however, when they emphasize not the mutual shaping of culture and nature but a one-sided "invention" in nature by culture. In this view, the natural—that which is not humanly created—does not in fact exist, or exists, paradoxically, only as a human construct. Along these lines, Robert Harrison claims that culture is not an epiphenomenon of nature but is in an important sense more real than nature: "Human beings, unlike other living species, live not in nature but in their relation to nature. Even the belief that we are part of nature is a mode of relating to it."[36] In this perspective, humans, and humans alone, are first, foremost, and perhaps only products of culture. We live in culture, which includes our ideas about nature, and in the end there is no nature apart from those ideas.

If this is true, and there is no real nature—no nature not constituted by human interpretation or intervention—then we are left with no grounds on which to evaluate one environment as better or worse or to resist some forms of intervention and support others. This is a postmodern version of the old ethical dilemma of relativism. In its mildest form, it contends that since all interpretations of nature are partial, it is difficult, perhaps impossible, to judge among them. If nature means different things to different people, we cannot know who is behaving responsibly toward nature. Thus James Proctor, in a discussion of the struggle over ancient forests in the Pacific Northwest, writes, "It could be that there exist an infinite possible number of environmentalisms, each with its own nature to save. If so, how are we to choose among them?"[37] The forest that people work to protect "is as much a reflection of their own particular view of nature as it is some primeval ecosystem under siege by logging. Their ethic, their passionate sense of right and wrong, is only one of many possible ethics."[38] In the end, Proctor himself makes qualitative distinctions among these ethics, but he points to the possibility, realized by others, of simply casting all the alternatives into a single heap, with no defensible way to judge among them.

This sort of relativism regarding ideas, however, is less pernicious than relativism regarding practices. The latter can erase differences among ways of intervening in nature. William Cronon, for example, argues that wilderness "is quite profoundly a human creation" and "a product of civilization, and could hardly be contaminated by the very stuff of which it is made."[39] Cronon implies that because what we call natural or wild areas are shaped by human intervention, then anything goes. Since humans have already intervened, in this view, no sort of human interference or practice could harm or contaminate wilderness. This ignores the crucial insight of a more restrained approach to the social construction of nature, which points to the highly significant differences among ways that people not only apprehend but also live in their environments. This view would recognize, for example, that the hunter-gatherer transplanting fruit trees in one part of the Amazon and the logger clear-cutting another part of the same forest are both intervening in nature, constructing a certain vision and reality of it. Guided by these constructionist insights, environmental ethics must acknowledge that both of these practices represent human interventions in nature and that neither is completely innocent. Morever, it must go on to evaluate such interventions, to provide ethical guidelines for understanding the actions themselves and their consequences and differentiating between them. Instead of taking these steps, however, Cronon asks (rhetorically?) how we can accept one and not the other.

Stephen Budiansky makes similar arguments in his history of domesticated animals. He points out that primitive humans may have hunted some species to extinction and that early agriculturalists and some contemporary natives practiced slash-and-burn agriculture.[40] These facts, he suggests, should keep us from condemning current destructive practices, or at least we should condemn ancient and native practitioners as

well. Other scholars have also sought to demythologize indigenous conservation practices and spread the blame for environmental damage
more equally. According to Peter Coates, "Every culture has the capacity
not only to transform but to damage the natural world," and Native
Americans, although limited by technology and numbers, acted on this
negative capacity (for example, the presumed "Pleistocene overkill").
Thus, writes Coates, in evaluations of ecological damage, "Europeans
should be rendered less visible while Native profiles are raised."[41] It is
true that native people do not have only positive impacts on their environments. This fact, however, does not make irrelevant the differences
in the type and scale of the impact wrought by other societies. The
awareness that human cultures always intervene in their environments
and that our actions always have some consequences for the natural
world should suggest greater attention to the differences as a way to
learn about possibly reducing (though we cannot eliminate) our impact.
It should not lead us to lump all impacts together as essentially equiv-
alent. Nor should it lead us into the naturalistic fallacy of assuming that
whatever has been done is, by virtue of the fact that it has been done,
morally good.

ENVIRONMENTALISM AND
THE SOCIAL CONSTRUCTION OF NATURE

The erasure of difference in which some social constructionists engage
depends in part on their ability to set up straw figures against whom
they can argue. Their favored target is environmentalists, who are usually portrayed as naively or misanthropically trying to remove all human
traces from nature and return to some pristine, essential wilderness. This
is a repeated theme of Cronon, for example, and also Budiansky, who
argues, in a study of "nature management," that environmentalists have
falsely viewed nature as able to maintain a balance without human intervention.[42] Against the purported simplifications or mystifications of
the environmentalists they describe (but rarely cite), Cronon and Budiansky present themselves as uniquely able to understand the ways that
human culture shapes ideas about and practices affecting nature, and
thus are able to judge, or rather to avoid judging, among them.

A favorite claim is that the environmentalists and others who argue
for the preservation of wilderness areas live in isolation from nature.
Cronon, for example, writes, "Only people whose relationship to the
land was already alienated could hold up wilderness as a model for

human life in nature."[43] (It is worth pointing out the incoherence of this argument in light of Cronon's own belief that there is no correct or essential way of relating to nature. How can any way thus be alienated?) Environmentalists, Cronon asserts, are scornful of or even hostile to people who make their living from the land. Environmentalists want to preserve wild nature at the cost of both human well-being and accurate understandings of human needs and their ecological impact. Similarly, Richard White claims that "most environmentalists disdain and distrust those who most obviously work in nature."[44] (He, on the other hand, "cannot see my labor as separate from the mountains, and I know that my labor is not truly disembodied.")[45] Along the same lines, Budiansky lauds the knowledge of hunters and farmers, "the few . . . whose daily work still brings them into contact with animals."[46] Those who work on the land or with nonhuman animals, these authors suggest, have a more legitimate right to make descriptive and prescriptive statements about the nonhuman world than do environmentalists or animal rights activists, who presumably spend their days in offices attacking those "in the field" who understand the inevitability of human intervention in nature. It is worth emphasizing, again, the essentialist assumptions in these claims that some ways of relating to nature are more valid, less alienated, or less naive than others.

A number of constructionists reserve particular criticism for Bill McKibben, whose book *The End of Nature* argues that human practices have transformed ecosystems all over the world, effectively ending the possibility of a nature free from human intervention. McKibben acknowledges that ideas of nature as well as the physical realities of climates and ecosystems are at stake and that humans have long occupied most areas called wilderness. He critiques not all human intervention but a particular kind of human residence on earth, that which is grounded in urban and industrial European culture society and brought to other parts of the world through colonization. McKibben's book draws special hostility from Cronon and White, who reject his contention that there was once such a thing as nature or wilderness free from large-scale, destructive human impact. Thus White criticizes McKibben for failing to recognize that an independent nature, free of human influence, is "only an idea," "purely cultural." Somewhat confusingly, White then notes that McKibben "admits that his nature is only an idea." (More precisely, McKibben writes that nature as "a separate and wild province" is an idea, but nowhere does he call it *only* an idea.)[47] For White this qualification does not redeem McKibben but "only raises the question of why he is so upset over the end of an idea."[48] It is White, however, who has insisted that nature is only an idea. For McKibben, the death of the idea of a nature without humans is a symptom of the real deaths of countless plants, animals, and ecosystems.

Another favorite target of social constructionists is the supposed misanthropy of environmentalists, particularly those concerned with areas inhabited by indigenous groups in places like Brazil. Thus Cronon contends that rainforest activists in the United States and Europe want to protect the forests from the people who live there.[49] Candace Slater writes, "It troubled me that many of my students, friends, and neighbors did not seem aware of anything beyond The Rain Forest or particularly interested in how environmental questions impinged not just on trees and animals but on countless human lives."[50] Like Cronon, Slater assumes that concern for the environment precludes any concern for humans, as a result of the environmentalists' false vision of nature as that which is apart from the human. This critique fails to acknowledge the countervailing evidence that many environmental activists, in groups ranging from the mainstream Nature Conservancy to the more radical Rainforest Action Network, have joined with native groups in the United States, Latin America, and elsewhere in order to preserve both the wildlife and the cultures that inhabit threatened ecosystems. It also accepts and reinforces the common notion that human and nonhuman interests always conflict, that one cannot be truly concerned about both the animals and the people in the rainforest. Challenging this assumption, Mary Midgley writes, "Compassion does not need to be treated hydraulically[,] . . . as a rare and irreplaceable fluid, usable only for exceptionally impressive cases. It is a habit or power of the mind, which grows and develops with use. Such powers (as is obvious in cases like intelligence) are magic fluids which increase with pouring. Effective users do not economize on them."[51] We should value insights into the social construction of identity precisely because they enable us to question "givens" such as the presumed opposition between compassion for humans, on the one hand, and compassion for nonhumans or the environment, on the other.

Slater also implies that "trees and animals" inevitably matter less than human interests. This underlies many social constructionist critiques of environmentalists' ideas about nature. In the end, it is not just the supposed naïveté of the idea of nature without humans that bothers the critics but the idea that anything could have value apart from human inhabitation or discourse. Such anthropocentrism, in straightforward and unapologetic form, characterizes conservative critiques of environmentalism, which simply assert that the world (or deer or trees or rivers) was created for human benefit and that virtually any human use is therefore justified. The more traditional versions of these claims usually rest on theological notions, such as humanity's creation in the image of God. Social constructionists substitute a secular notion of human special creation: humans possess a special status in the universe, not because of divine intervention, this time, but because of our literally supernatural capacity, through discourse and symbolic practice, to invent and give meaning to both ourselves and the world.[52] (The usual corollary of this is a view of other animal species as passive and biologically driven.) While the constructionist argument is more complex and its language usually more obscure, it reaches the same conclusion as traditional theological anthropocentrism: something essential separates humans from the rest of the world (creation), and this something entitles humans to special consideration and privileges vis-à-vis that creation.[53]

ETHICS AND THE SOCIAL CONSTRUCTION OF NATURE

Some approaches to the social construction of nature, then, do not go far enough. In the end they challenge only part of the dominant perspective that they set out to deconstruct. They attack some elements of Western culture, mainly assumptions of an intrinsic tie between ideas (or words) and reality, but take for granted other, equally damaging assumptions. The multiplicity of perspectives and values upon which social constructionism insists ought to lead to serious consideration of alternative worldviews, not just as evidence of diversity but also as more constructive or appropriate ways of seeing humans and their place in nature. This in turn might encourage critics to question not only the notion that there is a pristine nature "out there" but other deeply held beliefs about nature as well. More dangerous than romanticized visions of Yosemite or Yellowstone, for example, is the idea that some essential quality (reason? naming? tool use?) separates humans absolutely from all other species or that nature is passive and other animal species are incapable of active intervention in their environments.

Social constructionist arguments would be more valuable for environmental ethics, and ethics more generally, if they considered alternative worldviews as sources not just of diversity but of actual knowledge about the world, taking seriously the critiques they pose to our accustomed categories and values. Then we might see some indigenous cultures' identification of other animals as persons not only as proof that human culture is endlessly varied but as equally—or even more— accurate understandings of those animals. For example, in the Amazon, the Huaorani people use the same term for woolly monkey and human (Huaorani) social groups, not simply because they have invented a likeness but because they have observed real similarities not present in other animals.[54] The Huaorani can perceive (not merely construct) such similarities because they see other animals not as ciphers on the opposite side of an unbridgeable us-them gap but as active agents sharing space, resources, and common traits. Similarly, Chewong people do not distinguish categorically between humans and animals or plants, but rather they understand beings "on the basis of presence or absence of consciousness." Consciousness makes one a "personage" *(ruwai)*, regardless of outer shape as animal, plant, or spirit.[55] Such views, based on close proximity to and observation of other species, challenge the predominant Western idea that humans are distinguished from all other species and natural objects by some essential trait like reason or consciousness. Most discussions of the social construction of nature, however, fail to take up such challenges. Instead, they dismiss all ideas as equally invented, except, of course, for the idea that humans exist in a uniquely cultural realm of discourse from which they give meaning to all other possible worlds. Thus, unquestioned assumptions of human separateness and dominion continue to ground social constructionist arguments.

In this sense, social constructionism does not go far enough for environmental ethics, because it fails to take seriously diverse ways of seeing nature that might challenge the anthropocentrism and dualism that dominate Western cultures. In other ways, however, social constructionism goes too far. The hostility to realism in many discussions of the social construction of nature undermines the coherence of its critiques. An emphasis on reality constructed by naming and human social processes can, and often does, lead to a denial of other realities, independent of human discourse. Thus Keith Tester rejects Mary Midgley's claim that "a fish is always a fish." For Tester, "a fish is a fish if it is socially classified as one, and that classification is only concerned with fish to the extent that scaly things living in the sea help society define itself."[56] What is important about a fish, in this view, is its relationship to human society. While it is true that any distinction we make between the reality of nature and its cultural representation is itself conceptual, as Soper notes, it does not thus follow that

> there is no ontological distinction between the ideas we have of nature and what the ideas are about: that since nature is only signified in human discourse, inverted commas "nature" *is* nature, and we should therefore remove the inverted commas.
>
> In short, it is not language that has a hole in its ozone layer; and the "real" thing continues to be polluted and degraded even as we refine our deconstructive insights at the level of the signifier.[57]

Soper argues that there is a nature out there, although she remains agnostic about our capacity to know this nature. Holmes Rolston III defends a harder realism regarding nature. While Rolston acknowledges that "all human knowing colours whatever people see, through our percepts and concepts,"[58] he believes that we can still know nature in a relatively and locally accurate manner. Thus, commenting on Neil Evernden's description of nature as "a category, a conceptual container," Rolston contends that we invent the category nature and put things into it because "there is a realm out there, labeled nature, into which things have been put before we arrive. . . . Nature is what is *not* constructed by the human mind. . . . 'Nature' is a generic word for these objects encountered and the forces and processes that produce them."[59] For Rolston, the word *nature* emerged, because of the need for a "container" to match the nonhuman "forces and processes" that existed before we arrived and that continue to exist even when we are not paying attention. Although terms like *nature* and *wilderness* are not historically or culturally universal, that does not mean they do not have real referents or that we cannot know those referents in a meaningful way.

It is true, Rolston admits, that we cannot escape our skins and our conceptual frameworks. However, "humans do not have to get out of their skins to reach what's really there; there are windows out and in— they are called eyes, ears, noses, hands. Life is a matter of transactions across semipermeable membranes."[60] Rolston offers a vital corrective to the solipsism and paralysis encouraged by hard versions of social constructionism, which too often contend that our incapacity to know the nonhuman world in any complete or final sense absolves us of responsibility for learning about or caring for it. This position often comes tied to a suggestion that our inability to avoid intervening in nature frees us from a duty to minimize the damage done by our interventions.

The hard dimension of Rolston's realism, and one that even some critics of a hard constructionism might find problematic, is his insistence that in our interactions with nature, at least in some cases, we "are registering natural forms" rather than just perceiving one possible version of them. There are many ways to construe nature, in his view, but some are more accurate than others. As many postmodernists would quickly and correctly point out, the dangers of absolutism, universalism, and ethnocentrism lurk in this assertion. So, however, does the very possibility of making ethical claims. As Rolston puts it, "We cannot correctly value what we do not to some degree correctly know." It is precisely the extreme constructionists' insistence that we cannot know nature that leads to their rejection of claims about intrinisc value in, for example, wilderness areas or nonhuman species. In Rolston's words, "We must release some realms of value from our subject-minds and locate these instead out there in the world."[61]

Advocates of a softer realism (or a softer constructionism), such as Soper, might amend Rolston's point to emphasize both the potential dangers of a strong realist position and the potential contributions of a nuanced reading of social constructionism. Ultimately, however, more unites than separates the two positions, at least in relation to the hard constructionist position they both critique. Rolston's insistence that natural entities "out there in the world" have value of their own, apart from human subjectivity, echoes Soper's point about the danger of thinking of nature as only a human construct. If nature is just a construction, they both emphasize, then we can hardly be concerned about harm due to ozone holes or other physical phenomena.

What Soper and especially Rolston find threatening in extreme constructionism is the way it undermines arguments in favor of protecting nonhuman species or wilderness areas. The potential for social constructionism to weaken arguments for conservation is exemplified in Cronon's and White's attacks on McKibben's lament for the end of nature. They contend that what has ended is merely an idea of nature (and ultimately a false idea, so good riddance to it).[62] In criticizing McKibben's realism, they fail to recognize the possibility that something real is in fact ending and is, further, worth lamenting. Their deconstructions of environmentalist naïveté thus lead away from appreciation of the nonhuman world, in all its various meanings, and toward "the radiant emanations of cynicism" against which Donna Haraway warns.[63]

WHAT REMAINS: A CHASTENED CONSTRUCTIONISM

Social constructionist attacks on realist approaches to nature ultimately fail to overcome the very dualism between nature and culture that they critique. They assert that notions such as human, animal, and nature are cultural constructs but also contend that humans are constructors of their environments who impose their own designs on the world. Claims about the social construction of nature rely, ultimately, on a conviction about the construction of human identity, which in turn rests on a self-contradictory assumption that culture is both a human invention and the basis from which everything else is brought into being. In addition to having logical flaws, this position runs into ethical and political problems insofar as it presumes that humans possess an essential quality, the capacity to construct meaning, which all other species lack.[64] In principle, social constructionist arguments hint at the possibility of deconstructing boundaries between humans and "a genuine Other"— nonhuman nature.[65] In practice, however, most constructionists shrink from that potential and instead enshrine discourse as something only humans can do. This reinforces a perception of humans "as ontologically privileged beings, set apart from, or even against, the rest of nature."[66]

In contrast, a naturalist position advocates an understanding of humans "as a species of natural being, as part of the order of nature."[67] This view makes possible ecological arguments based on our commonalities with other species or our need for healthy ecosystems, in which humans and nonhumans are materially interdependent. Ethics requires a naturalism of this sort, Ted Benton argues, in order to understand both the positive requirements of different species (including humans) and distortions of normal behavior. Such knowledge is necessary in order to know, for example, whether certain conditions meet basic needs or impose pain and, thus, to make ethical judgments. Holmes Rolston pushes the link between description and morality even farther, arguing that the "genetic set" of every organism enables it to distinguish "between what *is* and what *ought to be*. The organism is an axiological, though not a moral, system. . . . Every organism has a *good-of-its-kind*; it defends its own kind as a *good kind*." For Rolston, "These are observations of values which are at the same time biological facts."[68]

Rolston and Benton correctly assert that extreme antinaturalist or social constructionist approaches undermine efforts to attribute intrinsic value to nonhuman entities, places, or creatures. They are right, further, that environmental ethics requires some conception of intrinsic value in the nonhuman world. If language and culture not only interpret but somehow invent reality, then nothing can have value outside human attribution. In extreme versions of social constructionism, the initial insight that there is no essential relationship between signifier and signified degenerates into the claim that there is, in fact, nothing at all that is signified, merely the endless process of signification itself. This argument denies the reality of power that can harm things like human bodies, ozone layers, and nonhuman animals. Our power over such natural objects, as Lynda Birke reminds us, "extends to causing them hurt, real hurt, that does not disappear into webs of fancy narratives."[69]

The conceptual failures of extreme social constructionism and the ethical and political harm it causes lead some ethicists to dismiss all constructionist insights. Is such a rejection necessary? Put another way, can we achieve a balance between the social constructionist critique of the naive idea of an essential, universal nature, on the one hand, and a sense of the independent reality and value of nature, on the other? The question is, in Edward Reed's words, "How can we achieve an ontology that points to meanings without determining them, that denies scientific physicalism without adopting the sort of pseudo-scientific idealism that has always plagued the social sciences? . . . And how can we achieve all this without losing sight of the reality of socially created meaning?"[70]

These questions are not easy to answer. Perhaps the most promising approach, for environmental ethics, lies in Soper's and Katherine Hayles's call for a productive tension between realism and constructionism. Soper, following Benton, terms this approach a "non-reductive realism," while Hayles speaks of "constrained constructivism." This position strives to combine the constructionist insight that we can have no unmediated apprehension of nature with the realist claim that the world consists of more than human mediations and, linked to this, the naturalist insistence on continuities between human and nonhuman nature. In this view, as Donna Haraway summarizes it, "the world neither speaks itself nor disappears in favour of a master decoder." The natural world does not exist in pristine form, but neither is it "raw material for humanization."[71]

The constructionism that Hayles advocates is constrained because it asserts the existence of an unmediated real world. In another sense, though, Hayles pushes constructionism beyond its usual boundaries. She contends that not only humans "construct" worlds: all subjects, includ-

ing nonhuman animals, constitute different worlds through their embodied interactions with their environments, and every construction,
from a mouse's to a philosopher's, is "positional and local, covering only
a tiny fraction of the spectrum of possible embodied interactions."[72] This
view calls us to respect, take seriously, and seek out the viewpoints and
the worlds shaped and inhabited not just by other humans but by a
whole host of organisms sharing the planet. All these organisms are, like
humans, embodied and embedded in the physical world. However, in
various ways they are also all shapers of it, active agents and not merely
blank paper waiting for human symbols and discourse (and hoes and
bulldozers) to make something of them.

This approach echoes the beliefs of many indigenous groups that not
only humans are active agents or even persons. Many hunter-gatherer
groups, Tim Ingold notes, take "the human condition to be that of a
being immersed from the start, like other creatures, in an active, practical
and perceptual engagement with constituents of the dwelt-in world. This
ontology of dwelling . . . provides us with a better way of coming to
grips with the nature of human existence than the alternative, Western
ontology whose point of departure is that of a mind detached from the
world and which has literally to formulate it—to build an intentional
world in consciousness—prior to any attempt at engagement."[73] For
many hunter-gatherers, "apprehending the world is not a matter of construction but of engagement, not of building but of dwelling, not of
making a view *of* the world but of taking a view *in* it."[74] Ingold's "ontology of dwelling" reminds us that not only do we build worlds, we
live in them. We do so, further (paraphrasing Marx), not entirely in
conditions of our own choosing. We are residents and shapers, but not
masters and makers, of all we survey. We are also namers, as Adrienne
Rich notes:

> The Great Blue Heron is not a symbol. . . . it is a bird, *Ardea herodias,*
> whose form, dimensions, and habits have been described by ornithologists,
> yet whose intangible ways of being and knowing remain beyond my—or
> anyone's—reach. If I spoke to it, it was because I needed to acknowledge
> in words the rarity and signifying power of its appearance, not because I
> thought it had come to me. The tall, foot-poised creature had a life, a place
> of its own in the manifold, fragile system that is this coastline; a place of
> its own in the universe. Its place, and mine, I believe, are equal and inter-
> dependent. Neither of us—woman or bird—is a symbol, despite efforts to
> make us that. But I needed to acknowledge the heron with speech, and by
> confirming its name. To it I brought the kind of thing my kind of creature
> does.[75]

While naming might be the kind of thing our kind of creature does, as Rich suggests, we must keep in mind that our naming does not bring herons or any other part of nature into existence or under our exclusive power.

At its best, social constructionism offers environmental ethics several invaluable tools, beginning with humility about our own ways of seeing and being in the world and awareness of alternatives to them. More deeply, perhaps, constructionism suggests that nature "lies forever beyond the borders of our linguistic universe—that it does not talk back to us in a language we can easily understand."[76] However, the fact that we cannot gain knowledge of the nonhuman world easily or fully does not mean we cannot know it at all. We cannot step out of our skins, but at the same time, as Rolston reminds us, skins are not walls.

Further, if it is true, as Benton and Rolston contend, that proper valuation and care require knowledge, then we have not only the capacity but also the responsibility to gain some (always partial) knowledge of nature. This step is crucial: we are not off the hook just because something is hard. Put positively, the very difficulties inherent in knowing nature, the limitations of our own embodied and embedded particularity, can nourish rather than diminish our ethical commitments. Sameness, as constructionists above all should know, is not the only source of value. We can and must value the otherness of the natural world, the fact that it both exists apart from our theorizing and always remains to some extent out of our grasp. We live in the midst of multiple worlds, not all of them human, not all of them open to us. Sometimes, however, our trajectories cross, and "a piece of the universe is revealed as if for the first time."[77] Hope lies in the possibility of this crossing, of glimpses into lives, and goods, that are both real and fragile.

CHAPTER FOUR

The Relational Self

*Asian Views of Nature
and Human Nature*

The previous chapter suggests that even some apparently radical critiques of traditional Western thinking have not shed the notion that one unique element—be it the soul, the rational mind, language, or culture—defines and sets our species apart from other animals and the whole natural world. This conviction about humanity's discontinuity with the rest of creation is far from universal, though. A wide range of ways to conceive human nature exists, within and outside Western culture. This chapter begins an exploration of some of the most relevant and influential alternative visions of human nature and humanity's place in the natural world by examining Buddhist and Taoist traditions. This effort continues in the next chapter, on Native American views of nature and human nature.

In this chapter, I begin with what is, for Western environmentalism, the most important Asian tradition of thought, Buddhism, and then examine in less detail some relevant aspects of Taoism. I do not offer overviews of either tradition or comprehensive discussions of their importance for environmental ethics. Specialists have already accomplished both of these tasks much more thoroughly than I could. Instead, I concentrate on the ways each tradition conceives of human selfhood and the implications of these ideas for environmental ethics. Thus my first goal in this chapter is to uncover some of the elements of Buddhist and Taoist worldviews that have been most attractive to Western environmentalists and the reasons for their appeal. Second, and building on the first goal, I explore these traditions' anthropological claims and the relations between ideas about human nature and personhood, on the one hand, and social and environmental ethics, on the other. Third, I raise some broader issues concerning environmental ethics, comparative ethics, and the relations between ideas and practices. I begin with some of these issues in order to qualify and give context to the discussions that follow.

COMPARATIVE ETHICS

Before proceeding, it is worth highlighting several risks that arise in regard to comparative ethics. First, it is inherently dangerous to transplant ideas to foreign soil. As Gerald Larson points out, the notion that we can dig ideas ("conceptual resources") out of their own cultures and then process them for Western consumption mistakenly defines concepts and values as things that can be removed from their original settings and then made to fit ours. Greta Gaard calls this "cultural cannibalism."[1] Less picturesquely, Larson terms this the "fallacy of disembedded ideas," the failure to recognize that "conceptual frameworks are always embedded in larger conceptual frames."[2] This can lead to another danger, which Larson terms the "fallacy of misplaced symmetry," or thinking that ideas or practices from different cultures are the same.[3] For example, a Western observer might believe that personal identification with nature in European Romantic poetry is the same as the identification expressed in Taoism. This assumption neglects the extent to which ideas take their meaning from particular linguistic, historical, and conceptual contexts. Additional risks in Western borrowing of Asian and indigenous rituals and myths include romanticization, oversimplification, and the denial of particularity. Thus "Eastern" or "Native" philosophies are lumped together and represented by a selective sampling of ideas and practices, often resulting in a pseudogeneric worldview that obscures both the differences among cultures and the contradictions within particular traditions. Westerners have often perceived Buddhism to be a simple philosophy of harmony, for example, and collapsed the tradition into a "single flat circle of relatedness."[4] This perception ignores the spiritual disciplines and hierarchies vital to the tradition, as well as diversity and conflicts within it.

To avoid some of these problems, many scholars now advocate what Frank Reynolds and Robin Lovin term a "naturalistic" model for comparative ethics, which "treats a system of beliefs as a whole and refuses to isolate moral propositions for analysis apart from propositions about how things are in the world and how they came to be that way." This approach views ethics "not as isolated systems of moral reasoning but as activities integrated into a complex cultural whole that includes both moral beliefs and beliefs about reality."[5] These cultural wholes themselves often contain both inner conflicts and elements drawn from other cultures or traditions. Even well-integrated and coherent cultural wholes, in other words, are not undifferentiated or pristine.

All this makes comparative ethics an inherently messy and risky project. Still, it is worth examining other ethical traditions—and especially conceptions of humanity's place in nature—for several reasons. First and most basically, such an examination underlines the fact that ours is not the only perspective. The mere existence of other ways of seeing ourselves and the world can suggest how relative are our own visions. In this light, comparative perspectives help ethics become a critical enterprise, uncovering the ways in which persons and cultures "authorize the local as universal and the contingent as necessary."[6] Comparisons remind us that all ways of seeing the world are contingent and, thus, that ours is not the only way of seeing. Comparisons provide what Sandra Harding calls "categories of challenge" that can identify what is absent in dominant forms of thought and action, "what is relegated to 'others' to think, feel, and do."[7] This is a necessary first step toward self-critique and, perhaps, reconstruction. More specifically, consideration of alternative viewpoints and values can illuminate particular weaknesses of the Western ethical tradition that might benefit from revision. Viewing established Western conceptions alongside approaches from other cultures may throw into sharp relief the gaps or inadequacies in concepts that, standing alone, may have appeared quite satisfactory.

Further, although wholesale borrowing seems unlikely to succeed, there may be specific cases in which other cultures' values and insights can revise or replace ones that exist in our own. In other words, we may learn something from other cultures that is applicable, albeit in modified form, to our own. This possibility raises all sorts of problems for the naturalistic approach to comparative ethics, which emphasizes the study of ethics as part of larger worldviews and ways of life, as noted earlier. Still, the histories of individuals and cultures reveal time and again that learning and change are possible, and, further, that learning often results from contact (deliberate or accidental) with different ways of viewing and living in the world. (Of course, learning and change are not inevitable results of cross-cultural contact, nor are they always positive, at least not in the eyes of all observers or participants.)

In this perspective, knowledge about other ethical systems—"the very diverse ways of identifying, justifying, and living a good life that have been worked out in the course of human history"—can help our own efforts to "identify, justify, and live a good life."[8] Further, the comparative task may be more valid and more necessary given the present realities of multiculturalism and globalization, in which very few, if any, neighborhoods, regions, or nations are either homogeneous or self-contained. In other words, we are in constant contact with other ways of thinking and living, and we will be influenced by and will respond to them, one way or another. A deliberate and informed exploration of comparative ethical visions is, in this light, preferable to outright rejection of alternatives, among other possible reactions.

Theories of globalization contend that cultures, ideas, capital, and other tangible and intangible aspects of contemporary life are fluid and diffuse, crossing national boundaries time and again, no longer limited or limitable to particular geographic settings. Similarly, any number of environmental problems and possible solutions overflow national borders, including global climate change, pollution, and overfishing of oceans.[9] The fact that we can neither understand nor solve environmental problems within the confines of our own culture heightens the value of drawing on other traditions of thought in formulating environmental ethics. So does the apparently Western origin of many problems that are now global in scope, some observers suggest. As Baird Callicott and Roger Ames write, ecological problems are so "big, tough, and interrelated" that they seem to reflect "a fundamental misunderstanding of the nature of nature."[10] In other words, the present ecological crisis does not just reflect a few reparable flaws in Western attitudes toward the physical environment. Instead, the crisis reveals a profound inability—built into dominant ways of conceiving nature, the self, and the good—to build a healthy relationship between humans and the rest of creation. If this is the case, then even radical internal revisions of Western ethics may fall short, and a far-ranging search for "a more critical understanding of what it means to be human" is not just interesting but vital.[11]

Finally, a comparative study of ethics can help illuminate the ways conceptual frameworks function in concrete social settings. Uncovering the central doctrines and assumptions underpinning attitudes to the nonhuman world in different cultures brings us closer to an environmental meta-ethic, understood not as a universal prescription for human behavior but rather as a fuller (though never complete) understanding of the moral, philosophical, and ritual elements that shape values regarding nonhuman nature. I argue, for example, that understanding what it means to be human, including our origins and ends, is central to attitudes and practices regarding nature. Without comparative analysis, however, this contention remains culture bound. Perhaps anthropological assumptions are implicated only in mainstream Western attitudes to nature. While I can never survey all cultures and ideologies, I can and must make an effort to explore the foundations and dynamics of ethical approaches to nature in some cultures other than my own. Cross-cultural comparisons, in other words, are necessary to move beyond claims about ethics in specific contexts to an assessment of the nature and function of ethical systems more broadly (though never universally).

This approach differs from the formalist model of comparative ethics, which identifies a single, universal pattern of rationality (or something else) that underlies all ethical systems. I understand the "meta" project in environmental ethics, in contrast, as an exploration of the relationships between worldviews and the ethics they support. In a comparative volume on the links between creation stories and ethics, Robin Lovin and Frank Reynolds use a similar approach in order "to describe the relationships between worldviews and norms in ways that accurately reflect the tensions and controversies in a community's experience, in ways that reproduce the complexity of a tradition and allow the identification and meaningful comparison of the most crucial elements within it." The tension between recognizing particularity and making comparisons never disappears. Still, Lovin and Reynolds argue, even though "the ways that people seek to live well within the limits reality imposes are multiple," it is also true that "the constraints and the choices themselves are sufficiently similar that, over time, the effective ways of relating them will tend to reappear."[12] The common themes that Lovin and Reynolds discover lie not in abstract principles or structure of practical reason, they write, "but in the continual discovery and rediscovery of what we must do to live as we would in a world that is as it is."[13] This certainly holds true for environmental ethics, which must draw on diverse religious, philosophical, and scientific understandings of the ways the world is and of what, for better or worse, it might become.

NATURE AND NON-WESTERN
TRADITIONS OF THOUGHT

Of the countless alternatives to mainstream Western ways of thinking about human nature and humanity's place in the natural world, I have chosen to focus on only a few. As noted earlier, in this chapter I examine two major Asian traditions of thought, Buddhism and, to a lesser extent, Taoism. In the next chapter, I explore several indigenous North American cultures. I have selected these traditions for several reasons. First, Asian and Native American cultures are the most influential sources for countercultural and environmental movements in North America and Europe. Western environmentalists have been borrowing from Asian traditions of thought for decades, if not longer. Many of the movement's most influential thinkers, including E. F. Schumacher, author of *Small Is Beautiful,* and Arne Naess, the founding figure of Deep Ecology, draw heavily from Buddhism, Taoism, and other Asian philosophies. Native American traditions have also been seen as a major fount of "alternative" wisdom, especially since the late 1960s, when environmental campaigns began using the words and images of Native Americans in support of ecological causes. Because of the widespread popular appropriation of Asian and Native American traditions regarding nature, they are especially in need of careful examination in order to make clearer both the dangers and the possible fruits of cross-cultural borrowing. Given that borrowing is going on, in other words, we should strive to make it as well-informed, constructive, and historically and politically sensitive as possible.

Further, even though Western appropriations of Asian and Native American ways of thinking about nature pose various problems, the borrowing also reflects the fact that those traditions, despite romanticization and simplification, represent real alternatives to mainstream Western thought. A number of environmental ethicists have recognized the value of these alternatives in recent years, as reflected by the proliferation of books about comparative religious and cultural approaches to nature. These efforts suggest that the modern (and postmodern) West faces such profound problems, both philosophical and practical, in our relations to nonhuman nature that our search for a more adequate ethic must draw on all possible resources. This search should, of course, take into account the very real obstacles to conceiving, translating, and applying ideas from different cultures. These challenges render the task of comparative environmental ethics risky and always incomplete, but not without value.

Finally, my selection of cultures to examine is related to the meta-ethical task described above. Explorations of the appeal of Asian and Amerindian ideas about nature can help illuminate some of the larger requirements for revisions of environmental ethics, as well as social ethics more broadly, in our own culture. Put negatively, the aspects of Asian and Native American thought that hold the most attraction for environmental activists and ethicists may point to areas of weakness in our own tradition. These weaknesses are grasped, sometimes fuzzily, by those concerned about ecological crisis, who often look to other cultures for ways to mend or revise their inherited worldviews and values. Too often this search results in philosophical crazy quilts, pieced together with disembedded and often distorted ideas from around the globe. I hope to point to an alternative possibility, in which the strengths of other traditions help us identify certain conceptual requirements for a more adequate and effective environmental ethic, one grounded necessarily in local traditions, social conditions, and ecosystems. In sum, although specific environmental ethics must remain culturally embedded and particular, all worldviews, and particularly one as troubled as the Western conception of nature, can benefit from cross-cultural comparison and meta-ethical reflection.

BUDDHISM

Buddhism is at least as diverse, ideologically and culturally, as Christianity. Buddhism contains two major streams, the Mahayana and Theravada schools, and there is great variation not only among but also within schools that are spread across different cultural contexts. Still, it is possible to describe certain features that characterize Buddhism in general. Most basically, Buddhism asserts the wisdom of what is called *dhamma* in Pali (more familiar to Westerners as *dharma*, the Sanskrit term), which is translated most often as truth, doctrine, or way. Central to *dhamma* are the Four Noble Truths outlined by the Buddha in his first sermon. The first truth asserts the existence of suffering *(dukkha)*. The second truth is that *dukkha* has a cause, desire *(tanha,* or *trsna* in Sanskrit), also understood as thirst, attachment, clinging, or grasping. The third truth asserts that suffering can be ended, and the final truth is that there is a way to end suffering, through a "noble eightfold path," which requires spiritual training and discipline as well as correct behavior.

Related to the Four Noble Truths is the central Buddhist idea that, as Walpola Rahula puts it, "there is nothing permanent, everlasting, unchanging and eternal in the whole of existence."[14] Things are not merely *characterized* by flux and change, Buddhism insists; everything actually *is* flux and change. Thus "there is no unmoving mover behind the movement. It is only movement. It is not correct to say that life is moving, but life is movement itself."[15] The illusion that humans can halt or freeze this constant flow of change and movement is the root of attachment or desire, which in turn is the cause of suffering *(dukkha)*. Unenlightened humans want things, such as relationships, possessions, or patterns in their lives, to remain constant. When inevitably they change, the result is pain and confusion.

Continual change, according to Buddhism, results from an even more fundamental truth: everything is interdependent and relative. Nothing in human life or any other aspect of existence arises or continues by itself, and thus nothing can remain constant, untouched by the processes in which it is immersed. This insight is crystallized in the Buddhist doctrine of dependent co-origination *(paticca-samuppada)*, according to which "things exist only in interdependence, for things do not exist in their own right."[16] This means, further, that "each individual is at once the cause for the whole and is caused by the whole, and what is called existence is a vast body made up of an infinity of individuals all sustaining each other and defining each other."[17] In this context, parts and whole are inseparable, since neither would exist apart from the other. An image frequently used to illustrate this concept is that of the jeweled net of the god Indra, described in the Hua-Yen Sutra. Indra's net has a single jewel in each "eye" of the net, which is infinite in dimension, so that the jewels are infinite in number. Each jewel reflects all the other jewels in the net, and each of the reflected jewels in turn reflects all the other jewels, in an endless reflecting process. This image "symbolizes a cosmos in which there is an infinitely repeated interrelationship of all the members of the cosmos. This relationship is said to be one of simultaneous *mutual identity* and *mutual intercausality*."[18] Interdependence, also understood as dependent co-origination or mutual causality, leads to the idea of mutual identity, in which parts are identical to the whole insofar as the whole could not exist without all its causes (parts).

The notion of mutual causality, argues Joanna Macy, lies at the core of Buddhism's philosophical innovation. Macy insists that understand-ings of cause and effect shape the worldviews of cultures and individuals, "the ways we find the world intelligible and the ways we posit our re-lationship to it," and even "the relative reality we ascribe to ourselves and our world."[19] As notions of causality are central to philosophy gen-erally, the conception of mutual causality or dependent co-origination is central to Buddhism and constitutes its major innovation over both Western and traditional Indian (Vedic) philosophies. In contrast to the linear, unidirectional understanding of causality in these traditions, mu-tual causality views reality as "a dynamic interaction of mutually con-ditioning events," in which there is no prime cause or unconditioned absolute to which occurrences can be traced in linear fashion.[20]

Ideas about mutual causality and interdependence also ground Bud-dhist ideas about human nature. Macy writes, "Where all is process, so is the self, which by that token is neither categorically distinct from others nor endowed with any changeless essence." In contrast to the widespread assumption that the self is an entity that has experiences from which it is distinct, in Buddhism the self is "not separable from its experience nor isolable as an agent from the thinking, saying, and doing we attribute to it."[21] Like reality as a whole, in Buddhist thought, per-sons are "not alone but thoroughly relational, and the grounds for a relational nature must be found within man's own nature and not in something external, to which he must react on a one-to-one basis."[22] The profoundly relational character of the person leads to the crucial concept of no-self *(anatta)*. Just as there is no permanent, unchanging substance in all the cosmos, there is no separate, eternal soul or ego as commonly conceived in Western religious, philosophical, and psycho-logical traditions. Rahula summarizes: "What we call 'I,' or 'being,' is only a combination of mental and physical aggregates, which are work-ing together interdependently in a flux of momentary change within the law of cause and effect."[23] The doctrine of no-self should not be under-stood as the opposite of the Hindu or Western concepts of *atta (atman)*, or soul. Instead, *anatta* reflects and underlines the larger Buddhist chal-lenge to ego-based ways of viewing the world, the radicalness of inter-dependence. As Macy writes, in Buddhism "the belief in a permanent, separate self is a fundamental error: engendering greed, anxiety, and aggression, it is an illusion basic to the suffering we experience and which we inflict on others."[24]

Although Buddhism rejects the notion of a substantial self and the spirit-matter dualism behind Western ideas of the soul, it does not deny

a special place to humans. In Buddhism, the core of human distinctiveness lies in the claim that "a man and only a man can become a Buddha.
Every man has within himself the potentiality of becoming a Buddha, if
he so wills it and endeavors."[25] Because humans, and only humans, can
practice meditation and become enlightened, Buddhism places great
value on the good fortune of human rebirth. This valuation of human
life, however, is far from absolute. Buddhism sees all sentient beings as
fundamentally similar, in their urge to avoid pain and experience well-
being. While birth as a human is highly valued, it is also a birth into
"that vast universal web of interdependence in which what relates beings
to each other is much more fundamental than what divides them into
species."[26] Thus, as Rita Gross explains, the Buddhist term "precious
human body," which celebrates the special potential of human rebirth,
must always be understood in conjunction with the phrase "mother sentient beings."[27] The phrase "mother sentient beings" underlines the Buddhist insight that all beings have at some time been our mothers and we
theirs. Rather than feeling superior to other beings, we should feel com-
pelled to protect them from harm, because we know how much we do
not want to suffer and how closely related all beings are. In Buddhism,
then, "the preciousness of human birth is in no way due to human rights
over other forms of life, for a human being *was* and could again be other
forms of life."[28] The unique value of human rebirth makes sense only in
the larger context of the core doctrine of interdependence, which, as
Gary Snyder puts it, teaches "modesty in regards to human specialness."[29]

   The concepts of no-self and dependent co-origination (mutual causality) have enormous implications not only for metaphysics but also
for ethics, in practical as well as theoretical ways. As Gross notes, "The
reality of interdependence is sobering as well as poetic. Each of us feels
the effects of actions taken far away by people we do not know and
whom we cannot influence directly."[30] *Paticca-samuppada* is, in other
words, not just a mystical notion of interrelatedness but a concrete fact:
all beings affect others in their every action and are responsible for the
consequences of those actions. Thus, writes Gross, "any baby born anywhere on the planet affects the entire interdependent world, as does any
consumption of resources."[31] For Gross, this profound interdependence
leads to the conclusion that individual rights cannot "extend to the point
that an individual exercising his or her supposed rights may be allowed
to threaten the supportive matrix of life."[32] Accordingly, tolerance for
individual freedoms is less vital than the need to limit consumption and

reproduction in accord with the reality, not just the theory, of interdependence.

Other reflections on the significance of interdependence for environmental ethics emphasize its implications for understandings of human selfhood. Joanna Macy argues that ecological crisis "derives from a mistake about our place in the order of things. It is a delusion that the self is so separate and fragile that we must delineate and defend its boundaries, that it is so small and so needy that we must endlessly acquire and endlessly consume, and that it is so aloof that as individuals, corporations, nation-states, or species, we can be immune to what we do to other beings."[33] In her view, solutions to environmental and other ethical problems require full comprehension of the doctrine of interdependence and the "expanded" notion of self that it suggests. This extension of the self, asserts Macy, means that "virtue is *not* required for the greening of the self or the emergence of the ecological self. The shift in identification at this point in our history is required precisely *because* moral exhortation doesn't work, and because sermons seldom hinder us from following our self-interest as we conceive it."[34] What can modify our behavior is reconceiving self-interest itself, Macy believes. An expanded sense of self, as encompassing the rest of life, will lead to ecological restraint as a sort of enlightened self-interest. This echoes the often-quoted claim of the Deep Ecology activist John Seed that the statement "I am protecting the rain forest" means, for deep ecologists, that "I am part of the rain forest protecting myself. I am that part of the rain forest recently emerged into thinking."[35] Similarly, Arne Naess, founder of Deep Ecology, claims, "We need an expanded sense of self, one in which acting on behalf of others and the ecosphere is ultimately acting in terms of 'enlightened self-interest' and not out of some sense of moral obligation or duty, or even the rights of others perceived as separate from our own interests."[36]

A number of writers agree with and have elaborated on, with variations, this idea that the key to Buddhist (or perhaps, as Naess suggests, any) environmental ethics is the end of separation between an "I" and the "world." Rita Gross argues that the doctrine of interdependence challenges our identity as isolated, separated entities and calls us to forge a more inclusive and extensive identity, a "we-self." Writes Gross, "We do not simply stop at the borders of our skin if we are truly interdependent with our world."[37] Donald Swearer discusses this "we-self" in terms of an empathetic identification with all life-forms, which requires compassion as well as ethical restraint.[38] Similar arguments for an expanded self and identification with other life-forms come from Zen thinkers. According to Doug Codiga, "Ultimately, zazen is an unmediated identification with all life." For Codiga, zazen actualizes the idea that "the entire Earth—is our genuine human body."[39] Again, this echoes the philosophy of Deep Ecology, as expressed by Naess and Seed, among others.

The extended self and the ethical correlate that one acts for others not out of duty but out of an enlightened self-interest help illuminate some possible weaknesses in Western approaches to environmental ethics and even social ethics more generally. The emphasis in Western, particularly post-Enlightenment, ethics on rights and obligations rests on an assumption that a person's self-interest is inherently opposed to the interests of other persons (or beings) and of any larger human or nonhuman whole. Acting on behalf of others is perceived as "altruism," which suggests sacrificing one's own good for another's benefit. Underlying these assumptions is a definition of persons as not only separate from but antagonistic to each other and to larger (social or natural or both) communities. For Macy and other Buddhist thinkers, this anthropological assumption is fundamentally wrong. Instead, they begin with the Buddhist conviction that humans, like all beings, are inextricably constituted by and caught up in a web of mutual interdependence. In this perspective, one's own interests can never be cleanly or constructively separated from the interests of other beings or of the whole. The false dichotomy between the self and others lies at the root of mistreatment of the physical environment, other species, and other persons. Realizing that we do not stop at the borders of our skin leads to the logical conclusion that we should try to avoid harming other parts and wholes, since we are intimately related to them all. Thus, for example, Buddhism's first precept, nonharming, or nonviolence (ahimsa), emerges directly, even inevitably, from an understanding of the self as interdependent.

While most Buddhists agree on the need to extend or blur Western views of the self, some insist that Buddhist environmental ethics cannot stop there. A simple expansion of self-interest, they point out, may not inevitably lead to environmentally or socially constructive behavior. It might even become another way to justify destructive practices if it leads to the sort of expanded solipsism that links an extended self ("I am the rain forest") and personal preference ("I don't mind clear-cutting") to conclude that whatever does not bother the self is therefore morally right. Just as self-interest does not guarantee that all persons treat their own bodies well, expanded self-interest alone cannot ensure that persons treat their communities or environments well. An expanded self, in other words, is not necessarily an enlightened one.

Other critiques focus more specifically on the Buddhist dimensions of Macy's claims. Alan Sponberg takes issue with her argument that the "ecological self" that is emerging "is making moral exhortation irrelevant," so that "virtue is *not* required for the greening of the self." According to Sponberg, Macy wrongly assumes that rejecting an ethic of duty requires rejecting moral judgment, discernment, and cultivation of virtue. For Macy, writes Sponberg, "if one simply has 'self-realization' as one's goal, no further ethical effort is required."[40] This abdicates not only ethical responsibility for individual discipline and training but also the unique ethical potential of Buddhist spiritual training. Buddhism, in Sponberg's view, offers not just a message of relationality and a "green" self but also a method to achieve it: spiritual development in and through particular practices.[41] Interdependence, in this view, is not only a description of reality, Macy emphasizes, but also a goal to be sought through specific training and behavior.

This raises the question of the relationship between individual spiritual development, on the one hand, and ethical and political obligations, on the other. Some observers have charged that Buddhism, in stressing spiritual practices, such as meditation, which aim at enlightenment, is world denying. In response, Buddhists often insist that there is an integral relationship between spiritual and ethical practices. The goal of enlightenment, they contend, is resolutely this-worldly, since *nibbana* (Sanskrit, *nirvana*) is not a separate realm but rather *this* world free of desire and thus of suffering. Spiritual practices are not distractions from ethical concerns. Rather, they are the only way to free the mind from egoism and desire and to cultivate both the virtues and the actions that Buddhists should bring to ethical problems. Buddhist practice begins "with the impulse to purify the mind and cultivate one's own sense of self, through a sense of the self's interdependence with a network of all other beings, to a sense of affection and love for all existence."[42] The Vietnamese Buddhist monk Thich Nhat Hanh summarizes: "Meditation is not an escape from life . . . but preparation for really being in life."[43] In this perspective, meditation, mindfulness, and other elements of spiritual training and self-cultivation lead directly to appropriate ethical ideas and practices. The Western suspicion that meditation will lead to excessive focus on one's own spiritual fate misses the point entirely. The goal of Buddhist spiritual practices is precisely to realize the truths of interdependence and no-self and thus the ethical aims of compassion and empathetic identification.

The close link between spiritual and ethical aspects does not mean that Buddhism avoids all ethical tensions or difficulties. The doctrine that all aspects of existence are interrelated does not have only happy and harmonious implications. It also means, as Gary Snyder writes, that all beings need each other for survival, in a physical as well as metaphysical sense: "Everything that breathes is hungry." This insight leads Snyder to reflect on Buddhist attitudes toward eating, and especially meat eating, as a way to illuminate some of the ethical complexities implied in the notion of interdependence. "Food is the field in which we daily explore our 'harming' of the world," writes Snyder. No practice, even vegetarianism, can eliminate the suffering and loss caused by humans and other beings who must eat to survive. The inevitable harm caused by consumption of some life-forms by others, however, should not cause us to abandon efforts at right living, Snyder continues: "Clearly it will not do simply to stop at this point and declare that the world is pain and suffering and that we are all deluded. We are called instead to practice." Further, we must be humble in our expectations for this practice. "In the course of our practice we will not transform reality, but we may transform ourselves. Guilt and self-blame are not the fruit of practice, but we might hope that a *larger view* is. The larger view is one that can acknowledge the simultaneous pain and beauty of this complexly interrelated world."[44]

The ethical ambiguity that Snyder describes does not differ that much, ultimately, from the expanded self toward which Buddhism also points. An expanded self is aware not only of its identification with others, as Macy and Seed emphasize, but also of its dependence on others for its survival. Further, Snyder adds, because dependence has practical as well as mystical implications, we can never avoid all harming. Thus we can never justify self-righteousness. Practice, both spiritual and ethical, helps clarify these multiple implications of interdependence. While no being can avoid experiencing and causing pain, a mindful self can understand and take responsibility for both. Moreover, and crucially, the mindful self strives to minimize the pain caused. Snyder explains that although Buddhism recognizes the inevitability of harming, it never *justifies* harming. Rather, when a Buddhist kills or injures someone, "we can only say this was my decision, I regret that it happened, and I accept whatever results it may entail." And just as we should take responsibility for the harm we cause, we should also, as Thich Nhat Hanh explains, "be grateful for any little appearance of *ahimsa* wherever it is found in this world."[45]

The interdependent self in Buddhism thus has chastening as well as encouraging implications. Buddhist spiritual practice teaches the need to accept both pleasure and pain with equanimity, following the middle path between celebration and despair. Humans should accept the limits that stem from the basic reality of interdependence and identity. We are not the only actors, nor are we separate from other beings. Thus we cannot, as Snyder points out, save the world. This realization generates humility rather than ethical release. Realization of the inevitable limits of our action does not let us off the hook.

Snyder's argument echoes, in some ways, Sharon Welch's claim that we cannot achieve positive changes unilaterally. Welch refutes the dominant "ethic of control," which understands ethical behavior as action that attains its goal absolutely and without being influenced by other actors. This type of action is, in fact, immoral, because it presupposes severe imbalances of power and relations of domination and subordination rather than of interdependence. It assumes "that to be responsible means that one can ensure that the aim of one's action will be carried out. To act means to determine what will happen through that single action."[46] In place of the ethic of control, Welch proposes an "ethic of risk" that, like Snyder's Buddhist approach, accepts the limits of our capacity to effect change without consequently relinquishing responsibility to act. The key to the ethic of risk is a realistic assessment of the potential for present change, which may be extremely limited, with a commitment to creating "a matrix of love and respect" that might make further changes possible at some later point.[47] Welch's ethic is not Buddhist, but it shares with Buddhism an emphasis on interdependence and a recognition of the limitations that interdependence brings. Welch also agrees with Buddhist environmentalists such as Snyder and Gross that awareness of limits must go hand in hand with acceptance of responsibility. In Buddhism, interdependence means that individuals can never guarantee the results of their actions, *and* that individuals must not evade either mindfulness of their part in causing suffering or the need to mount a constant effort to minimize that suffering.

TAOISM AND TRADITIONAL CHINESE
UNDERSTANDINGS OF SELF AND NATURE

A relational view of reality is crucial not only to Buddhism but also to understandings of self and nature in many other Asian traditions of thought, including the major indigenous belief systems of China, Confucianism and Taoism. While Taoism and Confucianism differ and even conflict in significant ways, they share key concepts and values, including an emphasis on the continuity of the universe and the relatedness of all beings in it. Within this context, Confucianism is more "humanistic," stressing the ethical and philosophical dimensions of human society and relationships. Taoism de-emphasizes or relativizes the role of humans in the cosmos, emphasizing instead the value of "flowing with" the Tao, usually defined as the "way" of all things, a sort of law of nature, but also suggesting, in Roger Ames's words, the "natural environment of any particular."[48] Taoism's ultimate goal is harmony with this law or environment, rather than, as in Confucianism, the perfection of human character and society. *Wu-wei*, usually translated as nonaction or as effortless action, represents the achievement of this harmony with all entities and dimensions of the natural and social worlds.

Taoism assumes that the underlying reality of all life is continuity of being, in which all things are part of the same larger whole and thus interrelated and interdependent. Further, there is no outside creator that brought them into being. Tu Wei-Ming characterizes this model of the world as "an ordered harmony of wills without an ordainer."[49] What connects all these wills or modalities is the continuous presence of *ch'i* in everything. *Ch'i*, which Ames defines as "the hylozoistic vapors that constitute the process of existence," is dynamic, changing, and impersonal insofar as it is indifferent to us individuals.[50] However, we are not distant from it. Rather, as Tu Wei-Ming writes, "we are an integral part of this function; we are ourselves the result of the moving power of *ch'i*. Like mountains and rivers, we are legitimate beings in this great transformation."[51]

Another central concept in Taoism, and all traditional Chinese systems of thought, is that of yin and yang, usually defined as female and male, cool and hot, passive and active aspects of persons and, in fact, all beings and the entire cosmos. The relationship between yin and yang is not dualistic but polar. The notion of polarity indicates a relationship where each member requires the other as a necessary condition for being what it is.[52] Further, because Taoism insists that *ch'i* pervades all beings

and the cosmos itself, each member or part consists of the same substance as all others. What this suggests for personhood is that the human
being is irreducibly contextual, never autonomous in the Western sense.
In this light, personal cultivation is coextensive with cultivation of one's
environment. To reduce nature to a means not only compromises the
creative possibilities of nature but also impoverishes one's own. This
challenges dominant Western notions of personal responsibility, since in
Taoism one cultivates nature not as an other but as a dimension of
oneself. This leads to an understanding of humans not as the lords of
creation but as its faithful daughters and sons. "Filial piety," writes Tu
Wei-Ming, "connotes a profound feeling, an all-pervasive care for the
world around us."[53]

While in Taoism humans' responsibility to care for nature cannot be
understood as dominion, Taoism does suggest some form of human
exceptionality. Like Buddhism, Taoism views humans as the most sentient and complex beings in the universe. In Taoism, humans "are made
of the same psychophysiological stuff [ch'i] that rocks, trees, and animals are also made of," but humans are unique insofar as "our consciousness of being human . . . enables and impels us to probe the tran-
scendental anchorage of our nature."[54] Humans have a distinctive
spiritual capacity to enlarge and deepen their care for the universe, but
this is neither automatic nor absolute. Further, it brings not only privileges but also, and especially, responsibilities.

The understanding of human personhood in Taoism, as in Buddhism,
is a central part of its appeal to Western environmentalists. This is evident in Callicott's discussion of Chinese traditions. Dominant Western
thinking, Callicott contends, interprets the human being as characterized
by a fixed, underlying essence, either the image of God or the spark of
reason. Through the possession of this essence, humans participate in
something universal from which the rest of creation is excluded. This
"vertical" relationship is the only one that really defines humans; all
other relationships are "external" to the "real" self. In contrast, Chinese
traditions conceive of the self as socially constituted, fully defined by
natural and social relationships. In this light, the person is the sum of
his or her relationships, or "the sum of his or her relationships plus the
uniqueness, the individuality, that emerges from just this particular
blend of natural and social interactions."[55] This view of selfhood is important for environmental philosophy and ethics because the notion that
persons, like all beings, are constituted by relationships breaks down the
sharp distinction between oneself and other beings and the environment.

This has Buddhist echoes, or rather, Buddhism (particularly in China and Japan) has echoes of these older Chinese traditions.

The notion of socially constituted selves and the interconnected universe this presumes leads Callicott to describe Confucianism and Taoism as "East Asian Deep Ecology." Contemporary ecological science and Deep Ecology theory assert that organisms are shaped by their interactions with other individuals and species. This ecological worldview is holistic, Callicott claims, because it describes entities as being held together by myriad relationships, with each entity constituted by a particular location in a unique web of relationships. Chinese religions can help express and exemplify these ideas unfamiliar in the West.[56]

THE RELATIONAL SELF
IN ASIAN TRADITIONS OF THOUGHT

The risks inherent in any Western appropriation of other traditions only intensify when we turn to the possibility of discussing commonalities in different Asian views of nature. The dangers of disembedded ideas, false symmetry, and erasure of particularity arise not only in comparing Western and Eastern views but also in comparing two different Asian traditions, such as Buddhism and Taoism. Given these dangers, perhaps the best way to think about a possible pan-Asian (or pan-indigenous) worldview may be in relation to Western traditions. This means focusing not on the ways that Asian traditions are "the same" but on certain common ways that they differ from dominant Western ways of thinking.

In this context, understandings of personhood come to the fore. Callicott, Naess, and other environmental philosophers who look at Asian traditions, as well as scholars of Asian religions who turn to environmental ethics, often focus on the expanded or relational self as the decisive difference between post-Enlightenment Western perspectives and Asian traditions of thought. Anthropological claims, in other words, are central to the appeal of Asian thinking about nature, reflecting, again, the fact that anthropology is central to all ethics and particularly to ethical approaches to nonhuman nature. The main attraction in Asian thought regarding human nature is, as Callicott summarizes it, that East Asian traditions, especially Buddhism, Taoism, and Confucianism, "begin with the assumption that one is constituted by one's relationships."[57] The concept of the relational self offers a radical alternative to the individualism of the dominant Western anthropology. As pointed out in previous chapters, Western religion and philosophy usually conceive of the individual as self-sufficient and of relationships as accidental, added on to a preexisting self. In contrast, many Asian traditions understand persons as socially constituted. This view turns on the concept of internal relations, which Callicott summarizes thus: "Who or what one is, is defined not by reference to an essence, type, or universal but by one's natural and social relationships." In other words, to say that relationships are internal means that describing them is essential to describing the person. This conception of personhood appeals to environmentalists because it suggests that persons are intimately related not only to other humans but to nature more generally.

For Buddhism and Taoism, the relational self is not a distant goal to be attained but rather a reality of which persons can and should become aware. Interdependence has *descriptive* as well as *prescriptive* force. As Rita Gross and Gary Snyder emphasize, because we depend on other beings, our actions inevitably affect others beyond ourselves. Awareness of these connections should lead us to minimize the negative consequences of our choices (to choose the path of least harming, in Buddhist terms) and also to accept responsibility for these consequences. Thus a relational view of selfhood provides a strong philosophical basis for reducing consumption, population, pollution, species extinction, and other ecologically damaging practices. This behavior may stem from enlightened self-interest, as Joanna Macy and John Seed suggest, or from a sense of duty to the interrelated world and a desire to realize the virtues of compassion and empathy.

IDEAS AND PRACTICE

Whatever the theoretical contributions of Asian ideas about the interdependent self, it is still not clear that a *philosophical* basis for good behavior is sufficient to generate *practical* changes. Because the link between theory and practice is far from straightforward, we cannot assume that Asian notions of the self necessarily lead to less harmful ways of living in the world. This matter takes on particular urgency given the poor record of many Asian nations in terms of deforestation, industrial pollution, and cruelty to nonhuman animals. Some observers attribute all environmental failings in Asian nations to corrupting Western influences. This seems unlikely, however, given the evidence of deforestation in China and India well before contact with the West.

Several scholars have dug beneath the surface appearance of harmony and compassion to identify aspects of Asian worldviews that legitimize ecological harm. Yi-Fu Tuan contends that traditional Chinese attitudes toward nature are "quiescent" and "adaptive," leading not to harmony but to passivity, even fatalism, in relation to nature.[58] Stephen Kellert concludes, based on extensive survey evidence, that Japanese culture values not wild nature but rather nature that humans have transformed in particular ways, nature as "garden," as aesthetic object. The idealized perception of nature that predominates in Japan, Kellert argues, includes little empirical understanding of or interest in nonhuman species or ecosystems. It thus offers little explicit support for nature conservation beyond an abstract and generalized idea of compassion. He contends, further, that Japanese culture often portrays nature as all-powerful and beyond human capacity to grasp or control. This view can encourage passivity, even fatalism, toward environmental problems. Kellert argues that antienvironmental practices in contemporary Japan do not conflict with traditional East Asian, including Buddhist, views of nature. In this light, the seeds for environmentally destructive attitudes and actions emerge from Asian traditions themselves and not just from the influence of Western value systems.

Kellert and Yi-Fu Tuan both question the value of Asian traditions as a basis for an ecological ethic.[59] More broadly, they challenge the idea that a worldview "that regards man as simply a component in nature will entail a modest view of his rights and capabilities, and so lead to the establishment of a harmonious relationship between man and his natural environment."[60] In other words, they challenge the notion that ideas directly influence behavior. In the face of this argument, should we just throw up our hands and agree that no worldview prevents the possibility of environmental destruction? Peter Coates suggests as much: "Every culture has the capacity not only to transform but to damage the natural world." Identification or harmony with nature is no guarantee of positive practices: "It is particularly naive to assume that a world-view that includes humans within nature precludes the possibility of harm." Rather than worldviews, according to Coates, "human numbers and technological capacities are perhaps the key variable."[61] In this perspective, attitudes toward nature matter much less than pragmatic considerations. Thus, in Japan and other parts of Asia, centuries of intensive agriculture, sophisticated technology, and high population density have led inevitably to deforestation, air and water pollution, and other environmental ills. Buddhist notions of interdependence are not only powerless against the force of population and industry but perhaps

can, like any worldview, be read to justify humans' pursuit of a decid-
edly unenlightened self-interest.

I believe that this argument is just as inadequate as its mirror image,
the naive supposition that attitudes of interdependence and kinship necessarily lead to environmentally or socially constructive practices. The
links between theory and practice are not straightforward or unilateral,
but neither are they insignificant. Part of the task of environmental philosophy and ethics is precisely to uncover the complex, variable, and
often unpredictable ways that ideas shape behavior. Certainly, people—
individually or collectively—do not simply act out ideas. They reinter-
pret, select, reject, and ignore some ideas, sometimes but not always
deliberately, and their actions, experiences, and conditions (social and
natural) in turn shape ideas. Although this claim is hardly novel, it is
worth restating at this point because it points to some underappreciated
challenges in the comparative study of environmental ethics.

First, comparisons of ethical systems risk overestimating the causal
importance of ideas. To guard against this, we should avoid assuming
causality whenever particular ideas and practices coexist. A causal link
may exist, but in dilute or circuitous form, or both, subject to a host of
other variables; or it may not exist at all. The presence of a belief or
value presumed to cause certain behaviors may even mask other, more
important causes. Of course, philosophers and ethicists cannot conduct
controlled experiments, isolating all other factors, to pinpoint causal
relations. We can, however, take care not to make conclusions about
causality based merely on coexistence. In particular, we can recognize
that ideas influence behavior only in and through the mediations of
countless other factors, including but not limited to political and economic conditions, individual and collective histories, ecological locations, and personal relationships and loyalties.

Further, the fact that all these factors influence the ways ideas shape
action (and vice versa) means that when a causal relation does exist, we
can often be wrong about its consequences. Ideas, including religious
images and stories, mean different things to different groups, even within
their "original" cultural setting. Reynaldo Ileto explains this in his history of protest movements in the Philippines. Wealthy Filipinos, Ileto
writes, assumed that certain "folk religious traditions and cultural values
. . . promote passivity and reconciliation" among the poor, while many
poor people found in their faith latent and sometimes revolutionary
meanings.[62] Whether certain rituals "encouraged subservience or

defiance, resignation or hope" was "not fixed, but rather depended on social context," which varied widely *within* the Philippines.[63] The same is true for ideas about nature. We might assume that a particular concept or belief system necessarily has certain consequences in its own culture and thus fail to discern the complex, often problematic social roles of ideas. As Calvin Martin argues in his controversial study of Micmac Indian culture during European colonization, ideas that seem appealing to a Western environmentalist, such as respect for animal powers or identification with nature, do not necessarily have consequences that that environmentalist would expect or endorse.[64]

In relation to Taoism and Buddhism, then, we cannot conclude that ideas about continuity among species and the relational self lead directly or even indirectly to environmentally sound ethics. It remains to ask, however, whether such ideas may be capable of generating such ethics in particular settings. This has, indeed, been the case in a variety of places in Asia, including Thailand, where Buddhist monks have ordained specific trees to prevent logging, and Sri Lanka, where economic development has included environmental considerations based on Buddhist principles. Possibly, however, the relationship between these movements and Buddhist values and ideas is merely accidental. In other words, just as any culture has the capacity for environmental harm, perhaps any culture has the capacity for environmental protection. Local factors, including the efforts of charismatic leaders, may determine whether worldviews are interpreted in constructive or destructive ways. In that light, the differences among worldviews seem insignificant.

Against this conclusion, I argue that while local conditions and interpretations are crucial, there are also "elective affinities," to use Weber's term, between certain theories and certain practices. While Calvinist Protestantism did not inevitably support capitalism, Weber contends, in the right (or wrong) circumstances it had a special capacity to justify capitalist practices such as the accumulation of wealth for its own sake. Further, Weber believes, other religions, including Catholicism, did not by themselves prevent the rise of capitalism, but their worldviews and values did limit the expansion of attitudes and practices necessary for the full development of market economies.[65] Weber argues for a complicated, fluid, but still potent relationship between ideas and practices mediated, again, by a variety of other factors.

Building on this approach, we might hypothesize that certain worldviews and values have a greater "affinity" for environmental care or harm than others. In other words, as Baird Callicott suggests, while humans always consume and modify the environment, ideas about nature affect the type and extent of consumption and modification. Some worldviews, then, have a moderating effect on human interaction with the nonhuman world, while others, such as the dominant European mentality, shaped by Christianity and by Greek culture, accelerate the "inherent disposition" to consume and modify. For Callicott, European worldviews provided the decisive ingredient, the sine qua non, that led to a quantum leap in the damage humans caused to the natural world.[66]

As Callicott cautions, no simple deterministic model can accurately uncover whether or not cultural attitudes and values really affect collective behavior. Further, testing hypotheses about the relations between ideas and practice is problematic. While complete isolation of variables is impossible, future research may provide more clues regarding the complicated relations between ideas and behavior by examining, in diverse settings, both the content of the ideas and their effective histories—their apparent role in actual places and events. Pending the results of such studies, the best approach to the practical impact of ideas is a cautious one that neither asserts complete linear causality nor rejects ideas as "mere entertainment, epiphenomena of the mind," in Callicott's words. As he argues, ideas about nature (and, I add, about human nature) define the possibilities and the limitations that circumscribe human behavior.[67]

In the cases of Buddhism and Taoism, central ideas, especially concerning the relational self, not only provide a basis for greater awareness of human dependence on the natural world but also shape foundational assumptions and set goals that do, in many instances, guide human behavior. This, in turn, can inspire and legitimize efforts to preserve the delicate web of social and natural relationships in which we all exist. The effective histories of these traditions are murky, however, and complicated by post-Buddhist and post-Taoist innovations. The most powerful of these later developments, capitalism and colonialism, both emerge from Western worldviews that have tremendous tendencies toward ecological destruction, as has been made clear by examinations of both the ideas involved in colonialism and capitalism and their environmental consequences in Asia and elsewhere.

CHAPTER FIVE

Person and Nature
in Native American Worldviews

Asian ideas and practices raise important questions but offer no clear-cut answers regarding the links among human nature, nonhuman nature, and ethics. To clarify the questions, raise further issues, and suggest some tentative and partial answers, I turn now to indigenous cultures, particularly in North America. Though Native American cultures were never without internal and external conflicts and complications, prior to European contact most indigenous Americans managed to make a living off the land without seriously harming the possibilities for other species, plant and animal, to live on it as well. This claim, of course, should not obscure the fact that Amerindian traditions of thought and ways of life are extremely diverse. Scholars believe that before European colonization, four to twelve million people lived in the area north of the Rio Grande alone, and millions more to the south, including the great Mexica (Aztec) and Inca civilizations. North American natives spoke about 550 distinct languages and dialects, traceable to nine different linguistic stocks.[1] These cultures varied widely not only in language but also in political and economic organization, religion, and ways of making a living in the different ecosystems they inhabited. All this means that generalizations about "Native American culture" are rarely accurate. Such assertions are also dangerous, for some of the same reasons noted earlier regarding Asian traditions, including the fact that they can lead to the fallacies of disembedded ideas and misplaced symmetry, and because of the particular political conditions facing most indigenous groups in the Americas today. A long history of oppression and even genocide by colonial and postcolonial governments in North, Central, and South America has left most indigenous groups fragile culturally, politically, and economically. Distortions and misrepresentations of their cultural traditions, ideas, and practices further weaken Native Americans' struggles for identity and autonomy.

Given this context, Bron Taylor identifies three main approaches to environmentalist appropriations of Native spirituality. One perspective holds that appropriation of Native American religion is simply impossible because once non-Natives "borrow" ideas, symbols, or rituals, the result can no longer be called Native American. In this light, ethical questions are largely moot, since the borrowed features are so far removed from indigenous cultures. A second view contends that however well intended, borrowing is a form of cultural genocide that destroys Native American traditions.[2] Along these lines, George Tinker, an Osage-Cherokee theologian, argues that the New Age interest in Native American spirituality is damaging for a variety of reasons, especially because it exposes Indian culture, particularly young Indians, to the individualism and commercialism of the dominant culture. Further, writes Tinker, cultural borrowing alters "the thinking of the 'traditional' people in an Indian community. Little by little, usually without them even perceiving it, their language about spiritual practices changes both to accommodate the participation of whites and to translate discrete cultural idiosyncrasies for an alien culture in ways that can be more easily understood and appropriated (or rather, misappropriated)."[3] In the end, borrowing distorts both the values of indigenous people and the expressions of indigenous culture itself.

Another perspective holds that blanket opposition to cultural borrowing relies on a mistaken belief in a pristine culture of origin that remained untouched until powerful European groups began exploiting and distorting it. Such an *Urkultur,* however, does not exist, in this view. Rather, as Swedish scholar Ake Hultkrantz puts it, "all cultural life inevitably undergoes continuous transformation,"[4] not only in episodes of deliberate imperialist appropriation. No cultures or groups are entirely self-contained. If the mixing of myth, symbol, and rite occurs among all cultures, it becomes more problematic to dismiss such development as exploitative. This approach does not exonerate all instances of borrowing. Rather, it insists that since different cultures are always interacting, in varied circumstances, then a case-by-case moral assessment is preferable to blanket condemnations.

In this light, as Taylor points out, scholarly insights about syncretism (the blending of elements of two traditions) and bricolage (the amalgamation of many bits and pieces of diverse cultural systems) can help make sense of the meetings between ideas espoused by Natives and Western whites. Theories of syncretism challenge the notion that in all cross-cultural borrowing, the dominant cultures prevail and destroy the pure traditions of minorities. Instead, some scholars argue, there are no pure religions in the first place—even precontact Amerindians were shaped by contact with other native cultures. Further, even meetings between indigenous and European cultures are often contested and subject to negotiation, characterized by a mutual rather than unilateral process of influence. Natives are agents, not just victims, in these processes. Perhaps, then, certain instances of cultural borrowing can strengthen respect, solidarity, and reciprocity between Native Americans and whites. Some Native Americans argue, in fact, that the extension of indigenous cultural practices might improve the well-being of Native communities and the lands to which they are tied.[5]

In the end, Taylor suggests that despite the very real dangers, there may be some benefits for both Natives and non-Natives in permitting the latter to study and even share some aspects of Native American cultures. This process can be healthy only under certain conditions, however, including respect for the distinctiveness of each group and its ideas. In this spirit, I will not attempt an overview of Native American beliefs about nature. Instead, I will discuss (necessarily briefly) two particular traditions: those of the Koyukon of interior Alaska and the Navajo of the southwestern United States. These are not more typical or representative than any other culture, but they do provide some well-articulated and challenging understandings of self, community, nature, and ethics. After discussing these specific cases, I will look at some of the common themes that surface in these two traditions and, according to other accounts, also in some other indigenous American cultures. I will then address some of the important issues that Native ideas about persons and nature raise for comparative approaches to environmental ethics.

A KOYUKON VIEW OF
THE FOREST AND HUMAN LIFE

The Koyukon people live in the northwestern interior of Alaska. Their language is part of a family called Athapaskan, widespread in many variants throughout northwestern North America and even, as a result of long-ago migrations, found in parts of the southwestern United States. Athapaskan people have been in the region now occupied by the Koyukon for at least a thousand years. The Koyukon first came into contact with Europeans—in their case Russians—in 1838, although Western items such as iron pots and tobacco and Western diseases such as smallpox had already reached the interior Koyukon lands as a result of trade with coastal Inuit (Eskimo) people.[6] The Koyukon remained relatively isolated from white society, however, until around the turn of the twentieth century and the beginning of the Alaskan gold rush. From that point, as Richard Nelson summarizes it, "forces of change grew steadily and affected all aspects of the traditional culture and lifeway."[7] Christian missions, schools, hospitals, trade, and other facets of Western culture came to Koyukon territories and entered into their ways of seeing and living in the world. Still, the Koyukon have managed to retain to a great degree their traditional ideas and knowledge, to continue inhabiting "a distinctly Koyukon world," in Nelson's words.[8]

Most Koyukon people today still subsist, as they have for centuries, primarily by hunting, especially large animals like caribou, moose, and bear and, to a lesser extent, by fishing. The Koyukon also trap fur-bearing animals, mainly beaver but also rabbits, foxes, wolves, and wolverines. Koyukon culture and attitudes to nature have been publicized through Nelson's sympathetic and influential ethnography, *Make Prayers to the Raven,* and a series of documentary videos about the Koyukon that Nelson helped make. Nelson emphasizes the specificity of Koyukon culture and warns against generalizations about Natives. Still, he finds in the traditional Koyukon way of life and ideas about nature and selfhood a powerful resource, or at least inspiration, for environmental ethics. Nelson summarizes this worldview thus: "Traditional Koyukon people live in a world that watches, in a forest of eyes. A person moving through nature—however wild, remote, even desolate the place may be—is never truly alone. The surroundings are aware, sensate, personified. They feel. They can be offended. And they must, at every moment, be treated with proper respect. All things in nature have a special kind of life, something unknown to contemporary Euro-Americans, something powerful."[9]

This view of the natural world as personified, conscious, and demanding of human respect is grounded on a close relationship not only between human and nonhuman realms but also between the natural and the supernatural. This relationship means that just as human actions affect the natural world, so events in nature are shaped by spiritual

forces. Consequently, Koyukon culture contains numerous rules for behaving toward nature, governed by understandings of the spiritual
power of animals, plants, and even the landscape itself. Hunting, in
particular, requires adherence to elaborate rules before, during, and after
the kill, varying according to the different nature and power of particular animals. In traditional Koyukon culture, obedience to these rules
makes possible humans' continued survival. Failure to behave properly
can have immediate impact on the violator's well-being, leading to disease, hunger, bad luck, and even death.

These rules, the Koyukon believe, stem from the relations between
humans and other beings in the "Distant Time." During that time, the
subject of most of Koyukon oral history, "the animals were human,"
meaning they had human form, lived in human society, and spoke human language. Some of these protohumans died and became animal or,
in a few cases, plant beings, still possessing "a residue of human qualities
and personality traits." Thus the Koyukon identify a host of shared
characteristics among species, primarily behavioral, which are not those
usually emphasized by Western taxonomists. For example, ravens' wit,
ego, genius, love of play, and guile make them similar to humans; and
like people, wolves cooperate in pursuit of prey and share the spoils.[10]
In this context of shared characteristics, common origins, and constant
mutual influence, the distinction between humans and other animals
lacks the clarity and absoluteness it possesses in dominant Western models.

Further, explains Nelson, the similarity between humans and other
species "derives not so much from the animal nature of humans as from
the human nature of animals": their emotions, personalities, and capacity for communication both among themselves and with humans.[11] This
view contrasts with the dominant Western perspective, which sees any
attribution of shared traits between humans and other animals as anthropomorphism, the extension of essentially human qualities to
"lesser" beings. For the Koyukon, shared qualities of both human and
nonhuman animals stem from shared origins. Such qualities are not the
original or exclusive property of humans. Nelson adds that nonhuman
animals are even ethical actors in the Koyukon world, sharing "a spir-
itually bound moral unity" with humans. The attribution of morality,
language, and emotions to other species reflects more generally the Koyukon belief that "no animal is just that and nothing more," Nelson
writes. "Even the least imposing of creatures, those that seem insignificant from the lofty perspective of humanity, have dimensions of being

that extend far beyond the realm and power of the senses. It is not a world where humans may become too proud, for nothing that lives is truly humble, regardless of how it may appear."[12]

According to Koyukon tradition, humans are distinctive in their possession of a soul that differs from animal spirits. However, humans' role is not to dominate but rather to serve a natural universe that is nearly omnipotent and demands propitiation for humans to survive. Because spiritual power is everywhere in nature, a moral system must guide human behavior toward the nonhuman world. Nelson identifies this moral system as a "conservation ethic," which includes several key elements. First, Koyukon culture prohibits wasting anything from nature or killing for recreation. Further, the Koyukon intentionally limit "resource harvests" in order to encourage high population levels. For example, they do not kill young animals and plants and they carefully monitor the populations of fur-bearing species that they trap. They also prohibit caging or otherwise harming or humiliating animals for human amusement.[13] All these specific rules harmonize with what Nelson identifies, in a later work, as the Koyukon's "fundamental canons of restraint, humility, and respect toward the natural world."[14]

Nelson emphasizes the links between specific conservation-oriented practices and Koyukon beliefs about human dependence on nature, the finite dimensions of natural resources, and the human capacity to overexploit resources. The Koyukon understanding of human and nonhuman nature, in his view, leads them to impose and abide by intentional limits on their behavior.[15] Thus Nelson argues for a strong correlation between ideas and behavior: the Koyukon live lightly in the northern forest precisely because of their religious and cultural traditions, he believes. Further, these traditions are for the most part strong enough to guide Koyukon behavior even in the face of cultural and economic change. Thus he shows how Koyukon people apply the same traditional ideological restraints to new technology (high-power rifles, snowmobiles) as to old.[16] As a direct result of their conservationist practices, and thus as a result of their ethic, even today the Koyukon environment functions much as it would if no humans inhabited it, Nelson contends. While the Koyukon have not left the north woods completely unaltered, few outsiders can perceive the transitions from utilized to unutilized environment. This contrasts strikingly with Western ideas about the inevitable consequences of human habitation of wilderness. As Nelson writes, "The fact that Westerners identify this remote country as wilderness reflects their inability to conceive of occupying and utilizing an environment without fundamentally altering its natural state. But the Koyukon and their ancestors have done precisely this over a protracted span of time."[17] For Nelson, this experience makes the Koyukon world-view a powerful potential source of information about how to live without causing great harm to the natural environment. I will discuss the Koyukon "land ethic" in more detail below, after exploring another Native American culture.

PERSON AND NATURE IN NAVAJO CULTURE

The Navajo or Dine (or Dineh) people constitute a much larger population than the Koyukon—in fact, theirs is the largest native nation in the contiguous United States. Most of the approximately two hundred thousand Navajo people in the United States today live within a twenty-seven-thousand-square-mile reservation spanning parts of Arizona, New Mexico, and Utah.[18] This is part of an ancestral homeland at which they probably arrived between 1300 and 1500 C.E., a remnant group of Athapaskan hunters (thus connected, remotely, to Koyukon culture). Many changes since that time have affected the Navajo and their neighbors, including the arrival of Spanish conquerors in the 1500s and the consequent introduction of horses, metals, and tools, as well as Navajo mixing with Pueblo Indians, especially after the Spanish reconquest following the Pueblo revolt of 1680. Navajos have adapted many Puebloan practices, including dry farming and loom weaving, and cultural traits such as a female-centered social structure, a system of clans, and certain religious rituals and narratives.[19] Later Western introductions, such as guns and sheep, also profoundly affected Navajo worldviews and ways of life, as did their encounters with the U.S. military, their forced removal from many areas, and the institution of trading posts, Christian missions, boarding schools, and the Native American Church.[20] Presently, the dispersal of young people, partly due to the difficulty of making a living on the reservation, is a major cause of change and concern.

As a result of these ongoing changes, the Navajo nation today, like other Native American groups, is religiously and ideologically pluralistic. Navajos belong to many different Christian churches and also the pan-indigenous Native American Church. However, Karl Luckert argues, these do not necessarily compete with traditional cultural ideas and practices, since identification as a Navajo usually involves allegiance to at least some traditional beliefs and knowledge. Traditional beliefs are "social identifiers, markers, part of that which sets the Navajo people apart," Luckert explains, beliefs valued by many Navajo people even if they regularly attend a Christian church, for example. Thus even "acculturated" Navajos believe the maintenance of traditional religious knowledge and values to be important to retaining a separate Navajo identity. (Traditional religion and knowledge also mark subgroups within the Navajo nation.)[21]

Overall, most observers agree, the Navajo have succeeded more than the majority of indigenous peoples in North America in retaining their traditional culture and language. Despite many outward changes in Navajo lives, the most important Navajo values have remained substantially the same over the last century.[22] Still, Navajos have suffered greatly, particularly as a result of their forced relocation from native lands. In these respects, the Koyukon in their more remote homeland have fared better than the Navajo. The Navajo, though, in turn have fared better than indigenous groups in what is now the eastern United States, who confronted European settlers much earlier and, in many cases, who were almost completely removed from their tribal lands or exterminated by European diseases and military incursions, or both. Still, like other Native American peoples, the Navajo face enormous obstacles, including 45 percent unemployment and a 56 percent poverty rate (per capita income is $5,600). Despite these socioeconomic problems, the Navajo nation has pioneered bilingual education and other programs to retain and promote traditional culture. As a result, more young Navajo today speak their native language than do youth in most tribes, and overall the Navajo nation has retained traditional myths and rituals at a higher rate than most other Native American peoples in the continental United States.

In Navajo culture, as in Koyukon and many other indigenous cultures, practices and ideology are shaped and passed on by oral history. Navajo stories, as Maureen Schwarz asserts, "constitute a philosophical system that underlies the cultural construction of every aspect of the Navajo world."[23] This cultural world is an integrated whole, as the Navajo anthropologist Harry Walters emphasizes in relation to interpretations of Navajo art. The Navajo language has no word for art, Walters explains, because "art is not seen as separate from other cultural components like music, philosophy, religion, or history. To study Navajo art, one must study the whole culture."[24] According to Navajo oral history, this culture originates as a result of the activities of the Navajo Holy People and the emergence of different life forms on earth. A crucial moment in this generative time was the creation of humans ("Earth

Surface People") by Changing Woman (so-called because she repeatedly ages and rejuvenates in a seasonal cycle), the most revered of the Holy People. Changing Woman, the mother to all Navajo people, provides the image in which Navajo culture molds and constructs persons. This process of construction means that all members of the Navajo nation are related to each other as kin, pointing to the relational definition of what it means to be a "person" in Navajo culture. Mamie Salt, a Navajo elder, summarizes these relationships: "The Holy People put us here and the people considered all things sacred, the land, plants, and animals— we are their children."[25]

Salt points to the central position of the mother-child relationship in Navajo culture.[26] The culture defines a mother as one who gives and sustains life, and the life and sustenance that mothers provide for their children are the primary symbols of kinship solidarity in Navajo culture. This relationship is not one of voluntaristic, reciprocal exchange but of unconditional giving, in which life, sustenance, and care are offered without desire or expectation of the same in return. This image of the mother-child bond represents the highest form of solidarity, the ideal relation between and among all people, as Gary Witherspoon emphasizes: "All one's kinsmen are simply differentiated kinds of mothers; and . . . everyone is treated and addressed as a kinsman."[27] This kin relationship is described by the term *k'é,* understood as affective action and solidarity, encompassing love, compassion, kindness, friendliness, generosity, and peacefulness.[28] As Witherspoon writes, "The *k'é* that exists between mother and child provides foundational concepts and norms for all relationships in Navajo social life. Moreover, this foundational bond of kinship is not limited to people, for the earth is called mother, the sheep herd is called mother, corn is called mother, and the sacred mountain soil bundle is called mother. The symbols of motherhood and the *k'é* solidarity which they symbolize pervade Navajo culture and provide the patterns and sentiments which order Navajo social life."[29]

Because of these "patterns and sentiments," Schwarz writes, the Navajo world encompasses "a network that makes every human part of and dependent on the kinship group and the community of life, including plants, animals, and aspects of the cosmos."[30] Affirming one's place in this network is the key to well-being on individual, collective, and environmental levels. According to Sam Gill, "Navajos believe that suffering results when one does not have a proper relationship with the surrounding world [,] and consequently that relief is acquired by reestablishing relationships with everything in the environment."[31] The goal

of rituals such as the rain ceremony, Gill asserts, is to restore these relationships. In the rain ceremony, "It is not rain which is actually sought,
rather it is the reinstatement of the order of the world, characterized as
an environment of beauty, *hozho*."[32]

Moreover, Witherspoon points to an additional facet of Navajo understandings of the relational world. Actions, such as giving birth or
sharing sustenance, determine Navajo kin relations, in contrast to the
predominant Western definition of relationship in terms of shared substances (e.g., "biology," genes). Western cultures qualify any extension
of kinship terms outside the biological family with terms like *step-, fos-
ter,* or *-in-law.* This view of relationship leads white observers to identify
the Navajo use of kin terms beyond the circle of biological relatives as
fictive or metaphorical.[33] This interpretation, Witherspoon insists,
misses the point for the Navajo. Motherhood is based on the provision
of life and sustenance. Thus not only women who give birth biologically
but also the earth, sheep, the cornfield, and other entities in the Navajo
world are literal, not metaphorical, mothers because Navajo people rely
on them for survival.[34] Even a tool can be a mother, as the Navajo
scholar Wesley Thomas points out: "My grandmother constantly tells
me that my weaving tools are my defenders, my weapons against hunger
or any form of 'hard times.' They are never to be used as weapons to
cause physical harm to a human or animal because weaving tools provide for and protect life. They are nurturing tools, mothers."[35]

This understanding of motherhood, and of relationship more
broadly, helps explain the widely documented practice in Navajo culture
of applying not just kin terms but the concept of person to nonhuman
entities, including nonhuman animals and aspects of the natural landscape, such as mountains; elements of the built environment, such as the
hooghan or traditional Navajo house; and artifacts, such as woven
rugs.[36] Through stories, rituals, and other aspects of everyday life, as
Schwarz explains, "Navajo people are taught from earliest childhood to
consider phenomena such as the earth, sky, sun, moon, rain, water,
lightning, and thunder to be living kin."[37] Just as human persons have
inner forms, "in-standing wind soul," nonhuman persons such as earth,
sky, sun, moon, rain, water, lightning, and thunder also have inner
forms—they are *bii'asti,* "an animate being lies within."[38] Thus Navajo
stories, as Klara Bonsack Kelley and Harris Francis point out, assume
that "the land and everything on it are alive, permeated by a life essence
of mingled air, light, and moisture. Each 'thing' in this system, including
landforms, individual plants, animals, natural forces, and so forth, has

its own immortal humanlike 'inner form' (Holy Person), which interacts with the other 'things' in the system. There are also other Holy People, who move freely about the earth and sky."[39]

This definition of life is, as Schwarz emphasizes, inseparable from the Navajo attachment to particular places and landforms. When Schwarz asked Harry Walters what defines "being alive" in Navajo philosophy, he answered, "For living beings it is to have your foot, to have your feet, planted into the earth and your head in the sky. In your Mother Earth and Father Sky. Everything that is alive has its feet planted in the earth and its head in the sky. Birds, plants, animals, insects, people. So this is what determines what life is."[40] The attachment to place is not taken for granted but is carefully established and reaffirmed throughout a (human) person's life, beginning before birth and "reaffirmed at every step on the path to full Navajo personhood." It is solidified shortly after birth through the burial of the umbilical cord, which "anchors an individual to a particular place," as Schwarz writes.[41] Thus Navajos often refer to the place where their umbilical cord is buried as their home. This attachment to the land, Schwarz adds, "goes beyond mere sentiment to actual physical and social connections that are components of personhood."[42]

Navajo culture decrees that humans depend on the land not only for physical well-being but also for their identity. Navajo culture, including narratives, art, rituals, and other aspects of collective identity, loses much of its meaning and enduring power if separated from the Navajo homelands and their particular geographical features, animals, and plants. In particular places—and especially in the stories associated with those places—the histories and present relations of Holy People, natural objects, and humans come together and gain meaning. In their study of Navajo sacred places, Kelley and Francis emphasize the strong links between landscapes and stories:

> The landscape provides a material anchor for those stories and thereby stores them. The land is a physical link between people of the present and their past. The landscape and the stories that go with them depend on each other. In a sense, the landscape is part of the "text"—usually you can't grasp all the connotations of a story without knowing how the places in the story line up with each other, with other storied places, or with locations of other human events and natural processes like the movements of celestial bodies. . . . Places with stories, being part of the land-based life, are integrated into larger, living landscapes, just as the stories that go with each place are integrated into larger, living narratives.[43]

Without this storied landscape, Navajo narratives, and Navajo culture more generally, lose their power. Thus in a real sense, Navajo people need their traditional homelands not only for subsistence but for the perpetuation of their cultural identity. The disturbance of these landscapes, Kelley and Francis emphasize, will inevitably speed the loss of Navajo stories and culture because "the stories and the land are not only powerful symbols, but also constituents of Navajo ethnicity."[44] This suggests that Navajo people must keep control of the land if their stories, customs, and way of life are to stay alive.

Conversely, however, the land also relies on human care for its well-being. Ceremonies conducted at sacred sites and matrilineal homes rejuvenate these locations. "The dependency between Navajo and the earth is reciprocal", says Schwarz; "the health and well-being of Mother Earth is dependent on the care of those people who have been given stewardship over particular locales just as Navajo people are dependent on the continuing nurturance of their mother, the earth."[45] This notion of the earth as mother and the need for the Navajo to nurture it bring us back to the fact that relationships are the center of Navajo culture. As Witherspoon explains, for Navajo people "it is impossible to have order and harmony among unrelated entities. K'é terms refer to forms of social harmony and order that are based in affective action. Rather than seeking to emphasize their independence, self-reliance, and separateness, and rather than seeking to escape bonds with others that involve continuous obligations of assistance and generosity, Navajos seek to relate themselves to others in their world, and seek to join in the vast system of interdependence that characterizes the social harmony and order of their world."[46] While this vision of harmony may gloss over some conflicts, the deeply relational nature of Navajo understandings of the self is real. This sense emerges also in Harry Walters's explanation of why one should not conduct protection ceremonies that oppose close relatives: "What you say to them, you know, they are a part of you, you know, you are saying [it] to yourself. . . . If that man [at whom the ceremony is targeted] is your relative, you're also working against you [yourself]." When Schwarz asks, "If you send evil towards a relative you're working against yourself because you're part of the relative?" Walters replies, "You're part of that. You're part of that."[47]

Of course, even among the Navajo not all relations are harmonious. When positive relationships are not possible, Navajo culture uses the concept of control, especially ritual control of potential evil powers.

Control, Witherspoon emphasizes, "is something one utilizes only in relating to malevolent or potentially malevolent beings with whom an affective and harmonious relationship is impossible." In other words, control contradicts the ideal model of kinship *(k'é)* relationships, which is based on the paradigmatic mother-child bond. Thus, he continues, "Navajos abhor the idea or practice of controlling other beings in the normal course of everyday life. This attitude is most poignantly felt in relationship to other Navajos, but it also extends to animals and plants as well."[48]

Because the Navajo strive to maintain harmonious *k'é* relations with all other persons in their universe, human and not, Witherspoon explains, "Only real and immediate need justifies the killing of an animal or the cutting down of a tree. On such occasions a prayer is said to the plant or animal, explaining one's need and asking the pardon or indulgence of the plant or the animal."[49] Navajo elder D. Y. Begay elaborates this point: even in cultivated gardens "we pay respect to the plants that we take from the earth by blessing them with corn pollen."[50] This echoes the importance for the Koyukon (and many other Native American cultures) of expressing gratitude and regret for the gifts that nonhuman persons make for the continued survival of humans. For the Navajo, particularly, ritual expressions of sorrow and gratitude formalize the recognition that perfectly harmonious relations between humans and nonhumans cannot always be achieved.

This does not mean, however, that Navajos accept all less-than-ideal relationships with human or nonhuman persons as inevitable. The Navajo rejection of avoidable conflict and suffering is exemplified in their resentment of a government stock reduction program that caused thousands of sheep to die in pens or en route to railroads. "Such behavior, perfectly understandable in white economic terms, was viewed as utter barbarism by the Navajo and is still spoken of in Piñon," according to James Downs.[51] This resentment makes sense in light of the Navajo view that nonhuman animals are persons and, further, that sheep, who provide sustenance, are kin, mothers to the Navajo people. This attitude toward nonhumans not only contradicts the dominant Western understandings of animals and nature generally but also poses dilemmas even within Navajo culture. A recent conflict regarding a Navajo zoo in Window Rock, Arizona, the capital of the Navajo nation, reflects the contradictions that arise when Navajos seek to interpret their traditions in the light of present circumstances.

The controversy began when two Navajo women told the outgoing president of the Navajo nation, Milton Bluehouse, that Holy People had appeared to them and warned them that "the Navajo people were not living according to tradition and that they were upsetting the natural order by keeping animals caged." The sighting of the Holy People, according to Harry Walters, requires the Navajo to ask: "Are we going the way we should?"[52] Bluehouse responded to this message on January 11, 1999, his last day as president, by ordering the zoo closed and its animals set free. However, his successor, Kelsey Begaye, reversed the order in the face of protests from many Navajos, mostly children, and also questions from wildlife experts about whether the zoo animals would be able to survive in the wild. (The zoo contains only species traditionally known to the Navajo, although some, such as bears and wolves, are absent or very rare in Navajo territory today.) While the zoo remains open, the controversy has raised questions for the Navajo about their cultural values and traditions generally and especially their attitudes toward nonhuman animals. The existence of the zoo conflicts with the Navajo rule against keeping animals, even pets like cats and dogs, enclosed (a precept shared by the Koyukon, among other indigenous groups).[53] Further, the Navajo tradition of respect for nonhuman animals prohibts using them for human entertainment, so that sport hunting, for example, is also unacceptable. Some Navajos argue, however, that given contemporary threats to Navajo traditions, the zoo serves as a vital resource for education about native species and native traditions regarding those species. For most young Navajos, the zoo is the primary, even only, place to see the nonhuman animals that for centuries shared their land. Further, some traditional Navajo healers have used zoo animals, especially eagles, for traditional rituals.

The zoo controversy throws into sharp relief the dilemma of preserving ancient traditions in contemporary contexts.[54] More specifically, the debate reflects the gap between the context in which traditional Navajo myths and attitudes regarding nonhuman animals emerged—the Navajo hunting culture focused on native wild animals—and present conditions, in which hunting is rare and most Navajos rely on herding, wage labor, or government support, or a combination, for their subsistence. This gap leads to a paradox: even though the most prominent nonhuman animals in the Navajo world for generations have been domestic species, cultural values still emphasize rare game animals. As Gladys Reichard writes, "The belief that wild animals are helpers of human beings has not been laid aside now that game has been supplanted by the more easily obtainable sheep, goat, or steer."[55] Even though most Navajos today know relatively little about the wild species native to their lands, many value the traditions of respect and correct treatment for them. Thus the Navajo nation's Hataali Advisory Council, a group of medicine men, told the new president, Begaye, that it would be disrespectful to discuss the animals' fate while they were sleeping or hibernating, so the discussion was postponed until spring. Respect for nonhuman persons continues to pervade Navajo culture, even though few Navajos still practice the way of life in which those values emerged.

As the zoo dilemma emphasizes, Navajos today face the challenge of maintaining traditional attitudes toward the nonhuman world, including having respect for other animals' freedom and autonomy, on the one hand, while meeting the contemporary need for education and the preservation of Navajo knowledge and culture, on the other. This is a dilemma that the Koyukon do not face, at least not in such acute terms, since their ancestral homeland is still populated by the same species that lived there centuries ago, and since hunting remains a major, though no longer exclusive, source of subsistence for most Koyukon. The situation of the Navajo, however, is more typical of indigenous peoples in North America today. The Navajo struggle to interpret traditional values regarding nature in light of changing circumstances, and vice versa, throws into sharp relief the problems facing traditional lifeways and traditional ideas. Clearly, many traditional Native Americans, including the Navajo and Koyukon, value nonhuman nature and limit human behavior in order to protect that nature. It is less clear, however, to what extent and to what ends those values can survive in the absence of traditional subsistence activities that joined native peoples in intricate relations of dependence on native species.

CULTURAL DIVERSITY, BIODIVERSITY, AND BEING NATIVE

For the Navajo and many other native cultures in and outside North America, the decline of traditional means of subsistence has in turn diminished traditional knowledge about native lands and species. This loss of cultural diversity, some observers argue, threatens the preservation of biological diversity as well. Among the most articulate defenders of this claim is Gary Paul Nabhan, a biologist who works in the Sonoran desert region south of the Navajo nation, traditional homeland of O'odham and other native peoples. In the course of his efforts to preserve biodiversity, especially indigenous plants, Nabhan realized that this task could not be separated from the preservation of cultural diversity and traditional cultures. This realization become more urgent when a colleague pointed out the striking overlap between regions with a high incidence of endangered plant and animal species, on the one hand, and the high mobility of human populations, on the other. Nabhan writes, "Where human populations had stayed in the same place for the greatest duration, fewer plants and animals had become endangered species; in parts of the country where massive in-migrations and exoduses were taking place, more had become endangered."[56] Thus, he concluded, stable human communities are better able to protect native plants and animals from otherwise pervasive threats. This reinforces the claim of conservation biologist Michael Soulé, who contends that "the most destructive cultures, environmentally, appear to be those that are colonizing uninhabited territory and those that are in a stage of rapid cultural (often technological) transition."[57] Other writers, including Wes Jackson, have also argued that cultures of "conquest" are the most damaging not only to indigenous human cultures but also to native ecosystems.[58]

This idea, in turn, led Nabhan to reflect on the evolution of culture and, more broadly, on the traditional Western distinction between nature and nurture. Long-term residence in a particular place, amid a particular set of nonhuman species and landscapes, shapes a culture's development. Thus, Nabhan suspects, "a stable human community may have both genetic and orally transmitted cultural adaptations to place that often escape the eye," and these adaptations may offer a greater capacity for conserving biodiversity.[59] Because of the conservation values of cultural adaptation to particular places, "ultimately, the most potent way of conserving biological diversity may be to protect the diversity of cultures that have stewarded the plant and animal communities on which our agriculture is based."[60] This insight accords with one of the basic tenets of the bioregionalist movement, which seeks to build "sustainable human societies in harmony with the natural world and consistent with the flourishing of all native species."[61] The construction of such societies, bioregionalists argue, must rest on the knowledge and attachment that people within a given ecological region have for the land and its nonhuman inhabitants. Wes Jackson summarizes a central claim of bioregionalism: "The majority of solutions to both global and local problems must take place at the level of the expanded tribe, what civilization calls community."[62] In short, bioregionalists argue, ecological preservation depends on becoming native to a particular ecosystem.

Nabhan insists that the capacity of indigenous people to live in relative harmony with, or at least without great destruction of, native species does not stem from a "conservation gene." Rather, indigenous populations learn both the value and the practical means of conservation
the hard way, by having to make a living in a particular place over long
periods. It takes time "for any culture to become truly 'native,' if that
term is to imply sensitivity to ecological constraints." It takes time, but
it is possible, and not just for people whose ancestors lived for generations as hunter-gatherers in a place. In fact, Nabhan suggests, "indigenous cultures probably learned to manage vulnerable habitats and plant
populations in response to earlier episodes of overexploitation."[63]

Shepard Krech III is sharply critical of any romanticization of Native
Americans as ecologists or conservationists, and, in an effort to demolish
the myth of the "ecological Indian," he points to many examples of
overexploitation of natural resources by indigenous peoples. However,
ultimately he draws a conclusion very similar to Nabhan's. Based on
physical dependence on the land, Krech writes, "Native North Americans were close to the environment in ways that seem foreign today to
urban dwellers and nonindigenous Westerners. Their origin stories and
histories tell about long-ago eras when significant boundaries between
humans and animals were absent. Animal-human beings like raven, coy-
ote, and rabbit created them and other things, and then tricked them.
People modeled relationships with sentient other-than-human beings on
human relationships, and toward many acted with respect (culturally
defined) and in expectation of reciprocity; or expressed kinship or alli-
ance with them in narratives, songs, poems, parables, performances,
rituals, and material objects."[64]

Thus despite their different starting points, both Nabhan and Krech
argue that long experiences in and dependence on particular places and
their native species led many Native cultures to develop what Nabhan
calls "conservation traditions," which preserve biodiversity and native
species in the course of protecting human subsistence. This accords with
Nelson's portrayal of Koyukon attitudes toward nonhuman nature and
the relation between these attitudes, on the one hand, and their knowledge of and history in the northern forest, on the other.

Nabhan focuses, as does Nelson, on the places where "diverse natural
habitats and indigenous cultures coexist without one overwhelming the
other," a terrain Nabhan calls "the Far Outside."[65] The Far Outside is
characterized by constant interactions between humans and nonhuman
nature, an experience familiar to few contemporary people, even few

Native Americans. "Ecological illiteracy" is the norm today, Nabhan writes, because "only a small percentage of humankind has any direct, daily engagement with other species of animals and plants in their habitats."[66] This loss of experience with and knowledge of the natural world leads to both cultural and ecological harm, particularly but not only for native people, whose traditional identities are tied to specific places, landscapes, and the species among whom they have lived. Just as native people need contact with these nonhuman forms and creatures for their cultures to flourish, ecosystems may need native people who will protect habitats and species diversity. It is not clear, however, what it takes for non-natives to become natives in this sense. Nabhan asks whether Mennonite and Amish farmers are now native to their adopted Midwestern homelands, and conversely, whether urban Sioux living in Minnesota are no longer native to their places of origin in what is now the southeastern United States and the Great Plains.[67]

Some answers to Nabhan's questions come from Richard Nelson's effort to apply certain Koyukon practices and ideas about human interactions with the nonhuman world to his own life. Nelson recognizes the inherent difficulties in this task: Koyukon practices, rituals, stories, and ideas are deeply embedded in a particular ecosystem and history, an entire world, in fact, of which he cannot become a full citizen. Thus, he writes, "I have not aspired to adopt the feathers of another people but to bring certain principles that have guided them into my life as a citizen of North America." This is, he continues, "a matter of personal choice based on direct experience with [Koyukon] traditions, not an attempt to achieve orthodoxy or enlightenment or even sophisticated mimicry, nor an effort to encourage wider adoption of these practices. I have chosen the Koyukon way, as one among many, to express the fundamental canons of restraint, humility, and respect toward the natural world."[68] His own application of these principles is embodied particularly in his life in a wilderness area, in which hunting is a central feature not only of his subsistence activities but also of his understanding of the natural world. He recalls that one of his Koyukon teachers "treated meat as a sacred substance, a medium of interchange between herself and the empowered world in which she lived."[69] He celebrates the meat of a deer he kills as "pure food, taken from a clean, wild place, and prepared by our own efforts. There is a special intimacy in living directly from nature, nourishing my body from the same wildness that so elevates my spirit. . . . When we eat deer, its flesh becomes our flesh. Each time we eat we should remember the deer and feel gratitude for what it has given us.

And each time, we should carry a thought like a prayer inside: 'Thanks to the animal and to all that made it—the island and the forest, the air, and the rain . . . ' "[70]

What Nelson takes from Koyukon culture and values regarding nature is, most of all, the idea of gratitude to and dependence on the nonhuman world. He also takes the idea of commitment to a particular place, and from this generalizes about the need for such attachment as the grounding for a respectful relationship to nature. This stems from his belief that "Koyukon people's extraordinary relationship to their natural community has emerged through . . . careful watching of the *same* events in the *same* place, endlessly repeated over lifetimes and generations and millennia. There may be more to learn by climbing the same mountain a hundred times than by climbing a hundred different mountains."[71] It does not matter *which* place he has chosen, but rather what matters is "the fact that I'd chosen a place and focused my life around it." No place is more inherently beautiful or meaningful than any other. Instead, "every place, like every person, is elevated by the love and respect shown toward it, and by the way in which its bounty is received." In this spirit, Nelson writes, "my hope is to acclaim the rewards of becoming fully involved with the near-at-hand, of nurturing a deeper and more committed relationship with home, and of protecting the natural community that sustains all who live there."[72] Thus, the Koyukon environmental ethic that Nelson identifies rests on a deep knowledge of and commitment to a particular place. Other people cannot become Koyukon, but they can, he believes, adopt a similar approach to the natural world by choosing a place and becoming native to it.

SHARED THEMES
IN NATIVE AMERICAN TRADITIONS

Nelson and Nabhan both suggest that environmentalists can learn from Native American attitudes toward nature not just because they are Native but because they are native, a cultural and not an ethnic category. This notion may help refocus explorations of common ideas about nature in Native American cultures, especially the questionable effort to abstract general principles from cultures that are, like any culture, idiosyncratic and deeply embedded in particular landscapes. We cannot separate out a land ethic from the particularity of Navajo or Koyukon or any other indigenous experiences and practices in particular places, in the context of particular history. We can, however, identify some common experiences, or types of experiences, that not only link Native Americans but also distinguish them from white inhabitants of the Americas.

This approach accords with Catherine Albanese's suggestion that the best way to think about common themes in Native American worldviews is not by trying to identify how they are all like each other but rather by trying to see the shared ways in which they differ from the European traditions they came into contact with at the time of conquest. Albanese writes, "In one way, to speak collectively of native North American tribal cultures is to do violence to the subjective sensibility of many different peoples. On the other hand, cast beside the European invaders, Amerindians and their religious ways shared much in common."[73]

Albanese identifies the first of these common themes as the fact that Native Americans "saw a world peopled with other-than-human persons."[74] This clearly applies to both Navajo and Koyukon cultures. It is also emphasized in studies of many other indigenous cultures in North and South America. For example, Joseph Eppes Brown notes that the Oglala Sioux of the Great Plains refer to nonhuman animals as nations or peoples (e.g., winged peoples, four-footed peoples).[75] Along the same lines, A. Irving Hallowell writes that "in the universe of the Ojibwa [in Manitoba] the conception of person as a living, functioning social being is not only one which transcends the notion of person in the naturalistic sense; it likewise transcends a human appearance as a constant attribute of this category of being."[76] Similar themes emerge in Adrian Tanner's study of Mistassini Cree hunters, who conceive of their relations with game animals in terms of reciprocal, personalized ties. These relationships are possible because the animals themselves, in Cree perspective, live in social groups like humans (Cree) and share a number of human qualities.[77] The multiplicity of such examples leads Paula Gunn Allen to conclude that Native American cultures view "the very nature of being" as "intelligent in and of itself" and, further, they assume that "the earth is alive in the same sense that human beings are alive."[78] Vine Deloria summarizes: "In the religious world of most tribes, birds, animals, and plants compose the 'other peoples' of creation."[79] This respect for the personhood and spiritual power of nonhuman animals has guided many traditional Native American hunting practices and rituals. In sum, a wealth of ethnographic and historical documentation supports

Albanese's claim that many indigenous cultures in North America have defined personhood in a way that encompasses a variety of nonhuman animals and entities.[80]

Further, a number of these cultures understand some nonhuman entities not only as persons but even as kin. This is strikingly evident in traditional Navajo identification of sheep, mountains, and other non-human entities as mothers, as described earlier. Similarly, Hallowell notes, traditional Ojibwa culture applies the term *grandfather* to both human and other-than-human persons. Echoing Witherspoon, Hallowell contends that we misunderstand these cultures if we perceive the use of such terms only in the Western sense; that is, as metaphors or expressions of fictive kinship. The Ojibwa categorize and construe the natural world in thoroughly social terms, Hallowell argues, such that "the concept of *impersonal* 'natural' forces is totally foreign to Ojibwa thought."[81] The Ojibwa and many other native peoples see nature not as an abstract force "out there" but as the society in which human and nonhuman persons live in intimate mutual understanding and dependence.

This leads to another of Albanese's general claims about Native American understandings of nature. In contrast to European conceptions, she writes, "Amerindians' view of their world was fundamentally relational."[82] Albanese bases her argument primarily on materials about Native Americans in what is now New England, but a similar relational emphasis appears in Koyukon and Navajo cultures, as we have seen. Brown also contrasts the Oglala Sioux emphasis on relationships with the dominant white understandings of personhood. For the Oglala, he writes, "a series of relationship reaches further and further out from the individual to the immediate family, the extended family, the band, the clan, and the tribal group. Relationships do not stop with the human realm, but extend out to embrace the environment: the land, the animals, the plants, the elements, the sky, the wind, the clouds, the heavens, and the stars. Ultimately, relationships extend to embrace the entire universe."[83] Paula Gunn Allen makes a similar point in her discussion of Native American oral literature: "The notion that nature is somewhere over there while humanity is over here, or that a great hierarchical ladder exists . . . is antithetical to tribal thought. The American Indian sees all creatures as relatives (and in tribal systems relationship is central), as offspring of the Great Mystery, as cocreators, as children of our mother, and as necessary parts of an ordered, balanced, and living whole."[84] The continuous, extensive, and varied *social* interactions among humans and between humans and nonhumans help define, even constitute, all parties involved.

This does not mean, however, that Native American cultures fail to recognize or value individuality. Rather, the existence of powerful alternative visions of what it means to be an individual challenges established Western notions of individuality, which may be neither as universal nor as inevitable as we have assumed. This parallels Sam Gill's argument about the relationship between formality and creativity in Navajo ritual. Gill contends that "formality is the very key to the Navajo idea of freedom and creativity."[85] This, he adds, should prompt a rethinking of dominant Western white ideas about freedom and creativity, especially the tendency to see formality and freedom as being opposed to each other and mutually exclusive. Similarly, the relational view of the self in Navajo and other Native American and Asian traditions can challenge us to rethink what it means to be an individual and, in fact, to be human.

Native cultures' relational view of personhood and the world, Nabhan might add, is firmly grounded on experience, especially years of making a living in a particular ecosystem and landscape. The links among extensive knowledge of and experience in a particular place, expanded conceptions of personhood, and a sense of relationship with the nonhuman world are clear in the worldview of the Huaorani, a group indigenous to the Amazon. Laura Rival argues that Huaoranis' continual engagement with nonhuman agents sharing their environment enables them to recognize capacities for will and purpose, social organization, and other "human" qualities in nonhuman animals. Awareness of these similarities, Rival writes, leads the Huaorani "invariably" to describe animal behavior by means of "anthropomorphic" expressions.[86] For the Huaorani, as for many other indigenous peoples, "humans and animals are social beings mutually engaged in each other's world."[87] In these "societies of nature," plants, animals, and other entities belong to a larger community of persons; they are part of the social domain, according to Huaorani beliefs, in sharp contrast to Europeans' tendency to establish clear and impassable barriers between the "cultural" (human) and "natural" (other than human) realms.

For native peoples such as the Huaorani the fluidity of species boundaries does not meant that they view humans as being identical to other animals. Rather, these cultures recognize differences but interpret and evaluate them differently than do dominant European cultures. This is often difficult for non-native peoples to understand: Western cultures generally insist that the difference between humans and other species must be absolute and, further, must posit human superiority. Attempts by some to understand species differences in other ways often draw charges that they have erased the idea of difference altogether. Such accusations may reflect, more than anything, the narrowness of established Western models of thinking about both personhood and nonhuman animals. In contrast, many indigenous cultures acknowledge that difference exists—not only between humans and other species but also among nonhuman species—without automatically positing superiority and without perceiving shared features as threats. Perhaps long-term shared inhabitation of a particular ecosystem, along with the mutual dependence and the knowledge that it engenders, enables natives to perceive a continuum of shared traits rather than opposition. These common qualities are expressed in many cultures in stories of common origins, human-animal communication, and animal-human metamorphosis. In this light, qualities like social organization, consciousness, spirit, or personhood do not become less desirable or less fitting for humans just because they are evidently shared with other species.

An emphasis on relationship to, similarity to, and dependence on nonhuman persons is linked, for many indigenous peoples, to social definitions of human personhood. This is especially clear for the Navajo. Witherspoon, Schwarz, and other ethnographers have amply documented the extent to which Navajo culture understands human personhood as constructed and fulfilled in and through relationships with both human and nonhuman kin. Achieving full Navajo personhood, as explained by Sunny Dooley, one of Schwarz's consultants, means "we're going to be good relatives, we're going to be good nurturers, we're going to be good parents."[88] Speaking of Native American cultures in general, Vine Deloria puts it more bluntly: "The concept of an individual alone in a tribal religious sense is ridiculous."[89] A relational understanding of personhood helps ground an ethic in which reciprocity, nurturing, and gratitude, not only toward other humans but also toward nonhuman persons and entities, take center stage.

This highlights again the ways in which conceptions of human nature ground ethical claims. Conceptions of human nature, of course, exist and make sense only in the context of larger conceptions about how the world works and how humans relate to other elements and residents of the world. However, definitions of what it means to be human are central aspects in these larger understandings and, often, microcosms of them. For many native cultures, definitions of humanness rest both on an expanded understanding of personhood, which encompasses shared traits and intimate relationships with other species, and on life experiences in a particular place. As Albanese writes, "For native North Americans the numinous world of nature beings was always very close, and the land itself expressed their presence. Indian peoples created religious geographies in which specific sites were inhabited by sacred powers and persons."[90]

This is clearly true for the Navajo, who identify particular mountains as persons, as kin (mothers), and as the sites of crucial events in sacred history. Klara Kelley and Harris Francis write that when they began their study of Navajo sacred places, they expected people to answer their questions—about what local places are important—with lists: "Instead, people told stories, or at least alluded to them, about Navajo origins, about Navajo encounters with colonialism, and about their own personal encounters with immortal beings. The names of places are embedded in these stories, which explicitly tie many places together into landscapes or allude to or imply other, related stories that involve other places and landscapes. The people we talked with simply do not think of these important places as isolated locations. A place usually is important because it is part of a larger landscape constituted by a story, customary activities, or both."[91] Kelley and Harris note that of 164 Navajo sacred places their study identified, three-quarters are significant because they are linked to Navajo stories, Navajo customary activities, or both. In sum, "most significant places . . . are important because they are where people have performed the activities that keep Navajo life going and because stories go with them."[92]

These connections link land not only to Navajo culture generally but also to particular individuals and families. As Schwarz writes, "The connection between individual and place is reaffirmed in the action and process of contemporary living," beginning with the burial of the umbilical cord, after it falls off the newborn baby, in the matrilineal family home.[93] The cord anchors a person to a particular place, tying her or him to that landscape in relations of mutual dependence. In Navajo philosophy, both land and person depend on this relationship for their well-being. "As part of Mother Earth, each use area is dependent on the nurturing of members of the Navajo family given stewardship over that location who are intimately connected with that place," says Schwarz.[94] This intense connection heightens the tragedy of the forced relocation of Navajo people from their ancestral homes.

Similarly, the Navajos' neighbors, the Western Apache, define person and community in the context of particular places and the histories of those places. Keith Basso's account highlights the ways that connections to places ground social norms of correct behavior. Traditional Apache stories tell of what happened in specific places in order to provide models of good behavior and to comment on unacceptable behavior. After the story is told, the place and the place-name serve as concrete and permanent reminders of the group's values and expectations. For the individual who has been "stalked" by a particular story, for whose benefit a moral tale has been told, the place takes on a special meaning. In summarizing this, Basso notes that in Western Apache culture, "oral narratives have the power to establish enduring bonds between individuals and features of the natural landscape, and . . . as a direct consequence of such bonds, persons who have acted improperly will be moved to reflect critically on their misconduct and resolve to improve it. A native model of how stories work to shape Apaches' conceptions of the landscape . . . is also a model of how stories work to shape Apaches' conceptions of themselves."[95]

The landscape of the Western Apache territory serves as a repository of distilled wisdom, a keeper of tradition, and an ally in the efforts of individuals and communities to live out their own standards for social living. "In the world that the Western Apache have constituted for themselves," Basso writes, "features of the landscape have become symbols of and for this way of living, the symbols of a culture and the enduring moral character of its people."[96] The links between place and story for the Western Apache underline the importance of narrative as a key means to inculcate native values. Francis and Kelley make a similar argument regarding Navajo culture. Stories, they claim, interrelate "the speaker, his home, the Navajo social structure, the land, the origin of the present world, various Navajo deities, and the idea that these relations are morally imperative." Traditional narratives show how a speaker "can make a statement, simply by naming places, events, people, and other things dense with unspoken cultural meanings that speaker and listeners share."[97] Further, in efforts to instill social norms the landscape complements and strengthens stories' motivating power. Particular geographical features embody key moral lessons, and people's ties to their culture and its values are interwoven, in relations of mutual reinforcement, with their ties to the nonhuman world and stories about their shared history.

IDEAS AND PRACTICES REVISITED

Few individuals or groups in the United States have the kind of long-standing, intimate ties to specific places that the Koyukon and Navajo have. That sort of connection comes only when a people has had many generations of residence in a particular place and knows the land, its features, and the history of the communities (human and other) who have lived there. In other words, places can reinforce moral values only for those who are *native* to their land. Further, stories may wield motivating power only for those who are native to the culture that gives birth to those stories. The ethical power of narratives, in other words, requires an intimate relationship between tellers and hearers, as well as close ties between the story and the present situation.

What does this mean for people, such as the dominant Anglo-European, industrial, urban population in the United States today, who are native to no place? The inherited stories of this culture reinforce its lack of rootedness by celebrating a vision of individual liberty that requires (or feigns) an absence of limiting ties to places and the nonhuman world. We need a new story, as Thomas Berry puts it, a story "that will educate us, a story that will heal, guide, and discipline us."[98] However, the kind of stories that stalk the Western Apache, stories that shape personal identity, sustain relationships, and direct behavior, cannot simply be invented or borrowed.

Thus we return to the dilemma of becoming native to a place, which seems to undergird effective environmental ethics both practically and symbolically. From a pragmatic perspective, the Koyukon, Navajo, and many other native groups have deliberately limited their actions, imposing ethical restrictions on themselves because of their dependence on and knowledge of a limited ecosystem—because, in short, they are native to a particular place and cannot (or do not wish to) exhaust its resources and then move on. This makes behavioral constraints necessary to ensure survival. The need for such constraints is less obvious for human groups that are newly arrived or temporarily resident in a place.

On a symbolic and ideological level, being native means that one's personal and cultural identity is tied up with a particular place, with its geographic features and, as many Native American traditions suggest, the well-being of the nonhuman persons that share it. Thus, being Navajo, being a full person in the Navajo world, requires recognizing and nurturing connections to the place where one's umbilical cord is buried.

Being Apache means living amid the places that narrate and embody Apache values.

Most contemporary Western cultures have lost their links to particular land areas that define communal and individual identity. Reestablishing such traditions—becoming native—requires a sort of cultural evolution, which takes time. However, Western cultures may not have generations to learn how to live sustainably on our adopted homelands. Is there a way, as Val Plumwood asks, that the West can come to see in native cultures "some fuller and better possibilities for reworking its own world view and traditions"?[99] Can we learn something from indigenous cultures' experiences of living lightly in places as diverse as the Alaskan boreal forest and the Arizona desert? Put another way, is it possible to speed up cultural evolution in the present condition, not only to conceive of but to *live by* an environmental ethic that makes long-term survival possible? And can we do so by learning from conservation-minded cultures whose development has taken millennia? If so, what do we borrow from those cultures?

One thing many indigenous cultures emphasize, both practically and ethically, is *relationships* both among persons (of the human and non-human sort) and between persons and the land. The fundamental canons of restraint, humility, and respect toward the natural world, as Nelson emphasizes, rest on such relationships. This echoes Buddhist and Taoist conceptions of interdependence, suggesting that ethical action will always be limited and partial because single actors lack the power to achieve (single-handedly) their goals. Relationships, in other words, limit one's ability to achieve predetermined goals or even to decide or pursue those goals alone. This emphasis on relationship is crucial not only to non-Western cultures such as those that guide Koyukon and Navajo life but also to some *internal* critiques of Western ethics and attitudes toward nature. The next chapter turns to the feminist critiques that represent perhaps the most powerful internal challenges to dominant Western ethical and anthropological claims.

CHAPTER SIX

Relationships, Stories, and Feminist Ethics

If the imagination is to transcend and transform experience it has to question, to challenge, to conceive of alternatives, perhaps to the very life you are living at that moment.
Adrienne Rich, "When We Dead Awaken: Writing as Re-vision," On Lies, Secrets, and Silence: Selected Prose, 1966–1978

Cross-cultural critiques and comparisons show that our ideas about the self, nonhuman nature, the good, and a host of other crucial issues are not exclusive, inevitable, or universally valid. These external critiques provide alternative, sometimes radically different, standpoints and perspectives that highlight the weaknesses and gaps in our established ways of thinking and acting. Without such critiques, it is difficult, sometimes impossible, to question the "givenness" of our own ways of thinking and living. Taking seriously the claims and insights of other systems of thought broadens our moral vision, as Sharon Welch contends. Building on an argument of Michel Foucault, Welch writes that "we can see foundational flaws in systems of ethics only from the outside, from the perspective of another system of defining and implementing that which is valued."[1] Finding another perspective is especially useful when it comes to ideas as deeply embedded as conceptions of what it means to be human and how we should live with and in nature.

The external nature of cross-cultural comparisons, however, can also limit their influence. The possibility of not just critiquing but also reconstructing established ideologies requires challenging a culture from within as well as from without. *Inside* and *outside,* of course, are relative and fluid terms. Ideas about who or what counts as being inside a culture vary as widely as do definitions of what it means to be an American, a

Buddhist, a Navajo. These identities are socially constructed, thus neither inevitable nor unchangeable. Further, an individual or a community
can have various identities in different contexts, and these identities,
along with the relationships they encompass and the responsibilities they
carry, may overlap or conflict with each other.

Speaking broadly, though, critiques perceived (by criticizers and crit-
icized) as coming from within a culture, tradition, or group will share
some, though probably not all, of the foundational assumptions, language, and histories of the positions they challenge. Such critiques,
therefore, may be easier for other insiders to hear, understand, and take
seriously. Consequently, they may be more likely to generate changes in
attitudes and behavior. Debates within American Protestantism, for example, were crucial in convincing a number of white Christians to support the civil rights movement of the 1950s and 1960s. Similar discussions helped move many individuals and congregations to support the
movement to offer sanctuary to Central American refugees in the 1980s.
These debates succeeded in changing some people's attitudes and behavior because they relied on shared principles, language, and goals,
which, advocates for civil rights and sanctuary argued, were more fully
realized by some approaches than by others. The participants, in other
words, shared a commitment to Christianity, and internal critiques of
dominant institutions and attitudes succeeded in changing, for many,
what being Christian meant. Arguably, such internal dialogues and challenges are more effective than efforts to win over people who do not
share any foundational assumptions or values.[2]

Internal critiques also underline the fact that not all members of a
group or heirs of a tradition are equally committed to its currently dominant ways of conceiving or living in the world. Christian civil rights
and sanctuary activists successfully argued, for example, that not all
Christians believed or acted in accord with dominant or stereotyped
images. Critiques of this sort may not only influence the critics' direct
targets or conversation partners but also show others the possibility of
alternative, equally or even more valid ways of being Christian. Internal
challenges also underline the fact that not all members of a group are
equally responsible for dominant attitudes and institutions. A number
of writers, for example, have explored the differential involvement of
white Southern women and men in slavery and racism. Further, such
studies show that not all members of a group benefit, equally or at all,
from the oppressive or damaging practices of their traditions. These
issues are central to studies of the intersections between gender and race

and also to some environmentalist approaches. In particular, environmental justice movements point out that poor and minority populations share fewer of the benefits and suffer more of the costs of air, soil, and water pollution, disposal of toxic wastes, and other forms of ecological damage. Philosophical efforts in social ecology analyze the connections between environmental damage and social, economic, and political structures.

Recent decades have seen a wide range of internal critiques of Western philosophical and theological traditions, which point to the complex and crosscutting dynamics of race, sexuality, and a host of other human characteristics. Many of these critiques can deepen our understandings of the connections among conceptions of humanness, attitudes toward nature, and ethics. I focus here on the work of feminist scholars and activists, for several reasons. First, feminist scholars and activists have addressed the links between social and environmental ethics in detailed and diverse ways. Any analysis of the relations between attitudes toward nature and other issues in social ethics, then, must confront the challenges of feminism and ecological feminism (or ecofeminism).

Further, feminism is among the few nonreligious philosophical systems that have profoundly and intentionally influenced the ways people live and the shape of political institutions. In other words, feminist worldviews, like religious ones, seek and often achieve a link between ethical ideas and real life. I do not contend that feminism is a religion (nor, in defining feminism as nonreligious, do I discount the work of religious feminists). The point is that feminism offers a fuller vision of the role of moral ideas in human life than do many secular philosophies. This emphasis on ideas in context is in fact crucial to the feminist critique of male-dominated philosophical and theological traditions in the West. Exploring feminist moral philosophy, then, can help us discern possible structural similarities in feminist and religious ethics that make both types effective. These parallels include the relational and narrative dimensions of feminism and, especially, its concern with ideas about human nature. Reconceptualizations of what it means to be human lie at the heart of feminist ethics.

FEMINIST THEORY AND WOMEN'S EXPERIENCES

Feminist philosophies usually begin, chronologically and logically, with the distinctive and diverse life experiences of women. The notion that personal experiences legitimately enter into moral judgments and behavior is, in fact, one of feminism's distinctive contributions to ethics. This approach challenges the presumption that only impersonal, universal forces, such as reason or God, can grant or determine value. Thus an exploration of what is distinctive about feminist ethics, particularly in relation to ideas about human nature, ought to begin with feminist analyses of what is distinctive about women's life experiences. The literature on this topic is vast, diverse, and continually evolving. However, in relation to the particular ethical issues at stake here, feminist thinking about mothering is especially important and provides a good starting point for further reflection. Feminists usually begin with the claim that motherhood is a social, not just biological, fact. It is, as Adrienne Rich puts it, both "experience and institution."[3]

This is the underlying assumption of Nancy Chodorow's influential 1978 study, *The Reproduction of Mothering.* Chodorow acknowledges that biology, especially women's unique capacities for childbearing and lactation, plays a role in women's primary responsibility for child and especially infant care. However, she insists, biological factors alone cannot explain women's mothering practices. Further, she claims, feminist and sociological arguments that girls and boys are taught appropriate behaviors and feelings are also insufficient.[4] In her search for fuller explanations of gender arrangements and especially mothering, Chodorow concentrates on early childhood and particularly on the different ways girls and boys relate to their female and male parents. Because of the predominance of female care for young children, both girls and boys receive their all-important first experience of relationship and care, models of behavior, and images of what it means to be human from women, usually their mothers. Boys, however, eventually define themselves as male, in opposition to female caregivers. Thus they develop what Chodorow defines as an Oedipal tension between desire for and alienation from the mother. Girls, in contrast, continue to identify with the mother and thus do not experience the same fundamental alienation from the first parent and the experiences and images she provided. This process, for Chodorow, fundamentally shapes women's and men's self-definition as well as their relations to both parents and to the "opposite" sex in general.

Chodorow suggests that experiences of maternal care in early childhood are formative not only for gender identities and ideas of humanness but also for ethics. Early childhood experience, she claims, "entails a relational complexity in feminine self-definition and personality which is not characteristic of masculine self-definition or personality. Relational capacities that are curtailed in boys as a result of the masculine oedipus complex are sustained in girls." Because of their early care by women, "girls come to experience themselves as continuous with others; their experience of self contains more flexible or permeable ego boundaries." In contrast, early experience of maternal care leads boys "to define themselves as more separate and distinct, with a greater sense of rigid ego-boundaries and differentiation." The end result is that "the basic feminine sense of self is connected with the world; the basic masculine sense of self is separate."[5]

These primary models of selfhood remain as women and men grow up. Women's self-understanding and view of the world tend, Chodorow claims, "to be particularistic and affective—embedded in an interpersonal relationship with their mothers." For boys, however, self-identification is embedded not in relationships but rather in the rejection of relationship with their mothers. Thus male psychological development tends to be "more role-defined and cultural, to consist in abstract or categorical role learning rather than in personal identification."[6] What women learn in early childhood about sex roles is reinforced by their adult experiences, particularly as mothers. Dorothy Dinnerstein asserts that women's primary responsibility for babies and small children makes them "specialists in the exercise of certain essential human capacities, capacities crucial for empathic care of the very young and for maintenance of the social-emotional arrangements that sustain everyday primary-group life."[7]

Feminist scholars like Chodorow and Dinnerstein contend, in sum, that female experiences of mothering and being mothered reproduce a characteristically female sense of self. This sense of self is relational in two senses. First, women's relationality is descriptive insofar as relationships help define women's personal and cultural identities. Relationality is also prescriptive for women, however, because they make the maintenance of relationships a primary goal. The focus on relationships is central to feminist challenges to mainstream philosophy. Most of Western philosophy and ethics relies heavily on the notion of an autonomous, rational, self-interested moral actor, which, feminists claim, turns out not to be universal at all but rather male (and probably well-educated, white, and heterosexual, among other traits). More precisely, this autonomous self is a male invention and a male ideal, to which most women do not aspire and which most men do not, in fact, achieve. Men may think themselves independent when they are covertly in relation and dependent on others, especially women, for countless forms of material, social, and moral support that enable their survival. Feminist theorists have pointed out that dominant Western ideas about human nature are both narrow—they masquerade as universal when they really apply only to (certain) men—and illusory, insofar as they assume a self-sufficiency that does not exist. The characteristic experiences of women present both an alternative and a more realistic way of conceiving human life as social, interdependent, and embodied. This "feminine" understanding of human nature generates different ways of interacting with others, of building community, and of understanding and judging ethical priorities.

The most influential exploration of women's different moral approaches is Carol Gilligan's 1982 book, *In a Different Voice*. Gilligan, an educational psychologist, argued that from childhood on, girls and boys, later women and men, base moral decisions on very different patterns of reasoning. Boys, Gilligan writes, characteristically establish hierarchical orderings to resolve conflicts between desire and duty, while girls base their decisions on their participation in and commitments to various relationships.[8] Gilligan illustrates this approach with a female college student's vision of abortion "not as a contest of rights but as a problem of relationships, centering on a question of responsibility which in the end must be faced. If attachment cannot be sustained, abortion may be the better decision, but in either case morality lies in recognizing connection, taking responsibility for the abortion decision or taking responsibility for the care of the child." In this context, Gilligan argues, "morality and the preservation of life are contingent on sustaining connection, seeing the consequences of action by keeping the web of relationships intact."[9] This approach does not exclude considerations of rights, but it does place the discussion of rights within the context of relationships.

Gilligan terms these two differing moral approaches the "justice" and "care" perspectives. In a more recent essay, she explains the contrast between the two perspectives as one of priority and emphasis: "From a justice perspective, the self as moral agent stands as the figure against a ground of social relationships, judging the conflicting claims of self and others against a standard of equality or equal respect . . . From a care perspective, the relationship becomes the figure, defining self and others."[10] These shifting emphases lead to different moral questions and different ways of answering these questions. In the care perspective, the central issue is not "What is just?" but rather "How should I respond?"[11] Further, this response takes place in a particular context, and detailed knowledge of this context is crucial to making proper moral judgments and decisions. The necessary details of this context are known through coherent narratives. In a care perspective, moral decision-making is personal, concrete, contextual, and narrative, in contrast to the abstract, general, and formal approach of justice approaches.

Gilligan agrees with Chodorow that both care and justice approaches to ethical dilemmas have their roots in fundamental orientations toward the world and, especially, in definitions of the self and even of humanness. Gilligan illustrates the contrasting definitions of self by describing how, in one study, the male participant "places the world in relation to himself as it defines his character, his position, and the quality of his life," while the female "places herself in relation to the world and chooses to help others." This represents a more general "contrast between a self defined through separation and a self delineated through connection, between a self measured against an abstract ideal of perfection and a self assessed through particular activities of care."[12] These images, which Gilligan terms "hierarchy" and "web," are not mutually exclusive, in individuals or in cultures, and in fact they can and should be complementary. Gilligan argues for an expanded developmental theory that includes the characteristically female voice of care and relationship as a complement to the typically male emphasis on rationality and abstract principle. The goal is not only to understand women's development but to understand what might for both sexes constitute a fuller conception of moral maturity.[13]

FEMINIST ETHICS: RELATIONSHIPS AND CARE

A central question raised by Gilligan's research is, as Virginia Held puts it, "how to count the experience of women."[14] In other words, if it is true that women differ characteristically from men not only in life experiences but also in moral perspectives, then what can and should ethicists make of these differences? Gilligan, as noted above, insists that adequate moral theories must incorporate both justice and care rather than raise one above the other, as traditional Western ethics have elevated the justice perspective. Like Gilligan, a number of feminist thinkers view care models primarily as an effort to correct past philosophical emphases on justice and universal principles. They advocate an ethical pluralism in which various moral approaches can and should coexist, complementing and correcting each other in different situations.

Other feminists, however, have suggested that women's moral approaches ought to replace, rather than coexist with, justice-oriented ethics. In this perspective, characteristically female concerns with relationships and care and women's tendency to interpret moral problems in terms of detailed contextual frames are often, perhaps even always, superior to the traditional male emphasis on justice, rights, and the application of universal, abstract principles. One of the earliest efforts to work out the explicitly ethical dimensions of women's experiences, especially maternal care, was Sara Ruddick's 1980 article on "maternal thinking." By *maternal,* Ruddick means a social category, not the merely biological dimensions of motherhood. She is interested in mothering as a discipline or practice that prioritizes particular questions and particular ways of judging the truth, relevancy, and adequacy of proposed answers. According to Ruddick, maternal practice values above all the preservation, growth, and development of acceptability in children. These interests sometimes conflict, and mothers typically know that they cannot realize all their goals with unqualified success. This unavoidable conflict of basic interests leads, in part, to the importance of humility as a maternal virtue. Humility is "a metaphysical attitude that one takes toward a world beyond one's control," characterized especially by "a profound sense of the limits of one's actions and of the unpredictability of the consequences of one's work."[15] While isolated moral actors may entertain the illusion that unqualified success or total control is possible, Ruddick argues, mothers are continually reminded of the various constraints on their efforts to achieve important goals. On the one hand, mothers strive to control themselves, their offspring, and the world, in order to protect their growing children. On the other hand, mothers must relinquish some degree of control. Successful mothers learn both that they cannot control every aspect of their children's environments and that children are individuals who require certain freedoms in order to develop into mature adults.[16]

Maternal humility, Ruddick emphasizes, does not simply entail obedience to authority. While obedience also involves the recognition of limits, it differs from humility in the kinds of limits each respects. Maternal humility entails acknowledgment of indifferent nature, the supernatural, and human fallibility, aspects of experience that clearly lie beyond our power to change or remove. Obedience, in contrast, involves submission to the control and preferences of dominant people.[17] This echoes Sharon Welch's argument about the ethical and political significance of the distinction between genuine, unmovable limits and those that are socially imposed and changeable. Welch contends that while activists should not deny that some real limits do exist, they must also question "what a social system has set as 'genuine limits.'"[18]

In addition to humility, Ruddick identifies "attention" as a central maternal virtue. Drawing on the work of Iris Murdoch, she celebrates mothers' particular capacity for "attentive love," exemplified in the question "What are you going through?"[19] The notion of attention highlights the ways that maternal thinking values concrete, particular others, distinct from the generalized, abstract other of formalist moral theories. This resonates with Gilligan's claim that women typically demand more detail about an ethical dilemma than men do: rather than make an important moral decision on the basis of sketchy information, women often consider the histories, needs, characteristics, and potentials of the persons involved relevant, even necessary, for an adequate answer to the problem. For women, in other words, individual particularity matters greatly in evaluating whether an action is morally justified. This emphasis on particularity and concreteness is a central theme that feminists often distinguish from the tendency in male-dominated moral philosophy to speak of abstract others who share generic human features and lack specific needs, interests, or relations.

Ruddick, like Gilligan and Chodorow, explicitly grounds her moral theory on a different conception of human nature. Maternal ways of thinking about moral problems—which are concerned with concrete persons and relations, not formal structures and general principles—stem from different visions of the human condition. "Out of maternal practices," Ruddick writes, "distinctive ways of conceptualizing, ordering, and valuing arise. We *think* differently about what it *means* and what it takes to be . . . a person, to be real."[20] In a later essay, Ruddick elaborates the anthropological claims in her earlier argument. Maternal thinking, she explains, sees selves not as "centers of dominating and defensive activity trying to achieve a stable autonomy in threatening hierarchies of strength" but as persons connected to other humans and to nature, able to give and receive.[21]

Maternal models of personhood and of ethics offer not an alternative or complement to traditional male models but rather a replacement for them, in Ruddick's view. She does not seek a gender-neutral culture, in which there will be no mothers, only parents. She hopes for a society in which there are no "fathers," by which she means no people who have power over their children's lives without having done "the work of attentive love." Instead, there will be "mothers of both sexes."[22] Maternal ethics provides a new and superior conception of what it means to be a good person, what counts as a virtue, what would constitute a good society.

A similar conviction that "feminine" ethics are superior to the established male-dominant ones guides Nel Noddings's influential 1984 book, *Caring*. Noddings argues that ethical behavior relies on close personal relations, with the mother-child relationship as paradigmatic. This relationship is the fundamental model for what Noddings calls "natural caring," which is based on a response built on "love or natural inclination" of the "one-caring" for the "cared-for." Natural caring, Noddings explains, is "the human condition that we, consciously or unconsciously, perceive as 'good.' It is that condition toward which we long and strive, and it is our longing for caring—to be in that special relation—that provides the motivation for us to be moral. We want to be *moral* in order to remain in the caring relation and to enhance the ideal of ourselves as one-caring. . . . This ethical ideal, this realistic picture of ourselves as one-caring . . . guides us as we strive to meet the other morally."[23] In short, being ethical means acting "with special regard for the particular person in a concrete situation."[24] Again, the themes of concreteness, particularity, and contextuality take center stage in feminist critiques and reconstructions of moral philosophy.

Like Ruddick, Noddings intends for her ethic of caring not to correct or supplement male-dominated ethical systems but to replace them. She firmly rejects ethics based on principles and universalizability, because she is interested not in guidelines for particular acts but in "how we meet the other morally." This meeting of the subjective and widely varying experiences of those involved in ethical encounters is the only foundation of ethics she acknowledges. Its paradigm is the behavior of mothers, while rule-based, "universal" ethics are associated with fathers' styles of parenting.[25]

From natural caring emerges ethical caring, which rests on a deliberate "evaluation of the caring relation as good, as better than, superior to, other forms of relatedness." Natural caring, in other words, becomes an explicit ethical ideal, one we must strive to make possible and to enhance. This ethical ideal springs, first, from the natural sympathy humans feel for each other and, second, from the longing to maintain, recapture, or enhance our most caring and tender moments. Thus, although an ethic of care rests on natural foundations, it requires effort to perfect and sustain. As Noddings explains, "We must recognize our longing for relatedness and accept it, and we must commit ourselves to the openness that permits us to receive the other. The effort required to summon ethical caring is greatly reduced by renewed commitment to the sentiment from which it springs. For if we commit ourselves to receptivity, natural caring occurs more frequently."[26] The experience of relatively effortless, natural caring in parent-child and other close personal relationships leads to an ideal of caring that we can then cultivate and apply to other relationships.

The chief contribution of feminist care ethics comes from the fact that it makes relationships central to epistemology and ethics. However, some versions of care ethics rest on a very limited understanding of relationship. The relationships that matter, argues Noddings, are those that involve face-to-face contact and reciprocity ("completion"). Ethical caring, she insists, cannot be generalized outside of this type of personal relationship, because then it loses its distinctive character and force: "We cannot care for everyone. Caring itself is reduced to mere talk about caring when we attempt to do so."[27] Nodding's version of care ethics explicitly excludes from moral consideration the many realms of human experience that do not involve close personal relationships, ranging from international politics to the status of nonhuman animals. In her words, "Our obligation is limited and delimited by relation. . . . I am not obliged to care for starving children in Africa, because there is no way for this caring to be completed in the other unless I abandon the one to which I am obligated. I may still choose to do something in the direction of caring, but I am not obliged to do so."[28]

While Noddings insists that people are social beings, ultimately she fails to recognize the many ways we depend on and affect those distant from us: the connection, for example, between the hunger of a child in Africa and the affluence of a college professor in California. Noddings also insists that moral obligations do not extend to nonhuman animals (except in special cases, such as pets) or nonsentient natural objects. This vision elevates certain kinds of relationships at the cost of denying relatedness and, thus, obligation outside a narrow realm of face-to-face contact. This contrasts with the larger sense of relationship and responsibility generated, for example, by Buddhist understandings of mutual causality or by ecological science. While the care ethic that Noddings has pioneered offers a valuable corrective to justice perspective, this type of caring cannot serve as a basis for an adequate political or environmental ethic. We need an ethic that appreciates the intense and distinctive ethical character of personal relationships without making them the only locus of moral insight and responsibility.

THE POWER AND PROMISE OF FEMINIST ETHICS

A number of feminist theorists have built on, revised, and critiqued the early work of Chodorow, Gilligan, Ruddick, and Noddings. Today, feminist ethics is a diverse and dynamic field encompassing various forms of care ethics as well as many approaches that reject care as the only or primary basis for adequate moral decisions and behavior. I will not discuss in any detail the field or the controversies it encompasses, since numerous articles, books, and anthologies provide excellent introductions to feminist moral philosophy and its controversies. Instead, I will highlight several of the most relevant aspects of feminist ethics taken as a whole: the emphasis on concrete relationships, attention to the importance of context to ethical thinking, explorations of the narrative dimensions of ethics, and reconceptualizations of human nature. All these themes are central to environmental ethics in general and especially to ecological feminist approaches.

First, feminist ethics make *relationships*, rather than principles, rules, or rights, central to moral thinking. Building, maintaining, and improving relationships constitute primary ethical objectives. Gilligan, Chodorow, and others contend that women value relationships, and work to nurture and preserve them, a contention that contrasts with liberal philosophy's emphasis on isolated moral agents acting in accord with principles. Further, it is not just relationships in general that should be preserved but relationships with "concrete others," in Seyla Benhabib's term. Most male-dominated Western moral theories emphasize the "generalized other," in which we must "view each and every individual as a rational being entitled to the same rights and duties we would want to ascribe to ourselves."[29] In contrast, according to Benhabib, the standpoint of the concrete other "requires us to view each and every rational being as an individual with a concrete history, identity, and affective-emotional constitution."[30]

The concrete others of feminist ethics are not always the equal, rational peers upon which traditional liberal (contractarian and utilitarian) ethical theory depends. Feminist theory brings relations between persons who are unequal or dissimilar into the realm of moral significance. This clearly diverges from traditional theories of justice, which assume "that relationships between equals or those who are deemed equal in some important sense, have been the relations that morality is concerned primarily to regulate."[31] In such models, Benhabib writes, "the *other as different from the self* disappears. . . . Differences are not denied; they become irrelevant."[32] In contrast, Benhabib claims, attention to concrete others means that "differences complement rather than exclude one another."[33] Relationships between people who differ from each other in significant ways, including in the amount of power each wields, become important subjects for moral theorizing. Feminists' attention to difference stems, as Ruddick notes, in part from the importance that the private sphere, especially the family, holds for women. Because family relations, especially those between parents and children, are usually constituted in terms of difference and inequality, traditional theories of rights and justice cannot encompass all the types of moral dilemmas that arise in those contexts.[34]

Family relationships, further, are often what Annette Baier terms "unchosen relations,"[35] which receive little if any attention in liberal and formalist ethical approaches. The significant relationships in dominant theories are not only between similar and equal parties but also between consenting individuals, as in the social contract model. In contrast, feminist theory insists that many of our ethically significant relationships are unchosen. We are born and grow into relationships in the family and larger communities, which we can neither choose nor avoid and which are significant both for constituting our identities and for generating moral obligations. This feminist contention echoes environmental ethicists' insistence that human relations to nature, while often unequal and unchosen, nonetheless have moral significance.

Second, in feminist ethics the importance of relationships is linked to an emphasis on *context*. Feminist ethics generally reject universal, abstract principles as guides for ethical decision making, principally as a result of the conviction that moral judgment and action require knowledge of the "whole story," its history, characters, their relations, and likely outcomes of different actions. Abstract and highly general principles, in striving to fit all occasions, often fail to accommodate the particular needs and interests involved in any concrete occasion in people's actual lives. Feminist ethics emphasize the importance of context in ethics and also in epistemology, questions of how we know what we know. Feminists usually reject the objectivist and universalist epistemology of traditional Western moral theory, its presumption that it is possible to have a "God's-eye view" of moral problems. Instead, feminists aim for an embodied objectivity. "Feminist objectivity," Donna Haraway writes, "means quite simply *situated knowledges*."[36] This approach insists on the particularity and concreteness (embodiment) of all perspectives, since the notion of an objective, impartial, infinite vision is a "god-trick."[37] This means that all our knowledge, including the knowledge on which we base moral decisions, is partial because it is contextual, located in specific times and places, seen from particular vantage points, and witnessed and interpreted by concrete individuals. Our knowledge, in short, is always limited. Elizabeth Bird summarizes the problem: in light of theories of the social construction of knowledge, and especially in light of Thomas Kuhn's work of scientific paradigms, we can no longer claim, or even aim for, complete, objective truth, about nature or anything else. Rather, the most we can claim to know is a *relative* truth, seen "only in partial terms through a particular lens at any one time." The partiality and contingency of any given view poses the ethical and political problem of finding "grounds for choosing one as a more accurate representation than another."[38] Some construction-ists conclude that no such grounds are possible, that all representations are equally true or false. Many feminists, however, argue that while accepting the impossibility of an all-seeing, impartial view, we still must strive, through dialogue and interaction with others, to achieve a fuller vision, to construct what Haraway terms "better accounts of the world."[39]

Knowledge is not only contextual but also *bodily:* shaped by physical experiences as well as reason. The body has been so problematic for women and women's theorizing, Adrienne Rich writes, that "it has often seemed easier to shrug it off and travel as a disembodied spirit" or, in other words, to "think like a man."[40] Rich, along with other feminist theorists, seeks "not to transcend this body, but to reclaim it. To recon-nect our thinking and speaking with the body of this particular living human individual, a woman."[41] In this view, not the body in general but the concrete, particular body in particular circumstances becomes the grounds from which women can speak with authority *as women.* Ac-cording to Rich, feminist theory should explore the possibility for women "to think through the body, to connect what has been so cruelly disorganized" by male-dominated philosophies that count particularity and physicality as moral and intellectual defects.[42] The feminist insis-tence on reclaiming the bodily as a sphere of ethical discourse and value echoes and complements environmentalist efforts to think ethically about nonhuman nature.

A third dimension of feminist ethics, in addition to its relational and contextual-bodily emphases, is its tendency to take the form of *narra-tives.* Ethical narratives present both concrete individuals and their re-lationships with each other as, in Margaret Urban Walker's words, "nodes of a story (or of the intersection of stories) that has already begun, and will continue beyond a given juncture of moral urgency."[43] Further, narratives help make sense not just of the individuals and the relationships involved but also of the moral dilemmas at hand, which have specific histories and characteristics. Thus the desire of many female participants in Gilligan's study to know more details about the moral dilemmas reflects an understanding of the dilemmas as stories in which the characters' and the situations' past histories and possible future outcomes become crucial to reaching valid decisions. Women, in this view, seek to make judgments on the basis of an ongoing story rather than a snapshot, as it were, that tells nothing about the characters and their problems outside the moment in which a decision is required.

Finally, and related to the previous points, feminist ethicists have put concepts of personhood at the center of ethical thinking. Beginning with Ruddick and Gilligan, feminist theorists have emphasized that their moral theories rest on particular ways of describing, or redescribing, human nature. Benhabib summarizes this: "The contextuality, narrativity, and the specificity of women's moral judgment is not a sign of weakness or deficiency, but a manifestation of a vision of moral maturity that views the self as being immersed in a network of relationships with others."[44] For feminist moral philosophy, relationships both constitute the ethical self and serve as a primary goal of ethical practice. Like religion in Clifford Geertz's classic definition, relationships constitute both models *of* reality—that is, maps or descriptions of the way things are— and models *for* reality, that is, principles to be followed, goals to be sought.[45]

Relationality describes the reality of how women understand themselves and others: the relationships in which they participate are not external or accidental to the real person but constitute at least in part the individuals themselves. For feminists, in other words, "the 'solitariness' that Hobbes speaks of is a myth; we are never in a totally unrelated 'state of nature.' "[46] Relationships are also, as noted above, not always or even usually chosen. This has important implications for ethical thinking and action. Gilligan argues, for example, that women view moral actors "not as opponents in a contest of rights . . . but as members of a network of relationships on whose continuation they all depend."[47] In this light, protecting one's perceived individual autonomy often takes second place to nurturing relationships among individuals, including those in larger communities as well as personal contacts.

While Western feminist accounts reject the image of a separate, self-made moral actor, they usually do not posit as all-encompassing a relationality as do many Asian traditions. Buddhism, for example, views the self as wholly constituted by its relationships, so that we cannot identify a self apart from those relationships. In contrast, Western feminists usually attribute a degree of individual autonomy and stability to selves. However, feminist theory departs radically from Western, male-dominated versions of autonomy by insisting that the self, and human nature generally, cannot be understood outside its history, context, and relationships. The idea of the separate, rational, self-interested moral agent interacting voluntarily with similarly and equally separate, rational, and self-interested others is a myth, feminists claim, and a damaging one at that. It masks the extent to which supposedly autonomous selves depend on others, and it can obscure the consequences of individual moral decisions on others. Further, it reinforces the myth of objectivity, insofar as the solitary moral actor is understood as separate not only from relationships but also from concrete situations and interests that shape his decisions and actions.

Feminist thinking about human nature has generated a number of debates that help clarify the significance of anthropology in ethics. One important set of questions concerns the gender-specific character of the self described in feminism. Does the relational self describe a distinctively female way of being, or rather a female insight into a larger pattern? Gilligan, Chodorow, and Noddings, among others, assume that the relational self, along with a moral emphasis on caring for others and on nurturing relationships, is primarily and typically, though not exclusively or essentially, feminine. Gilligan believes that this view of humanness, just like the moral commitments and styles it engenders, ought to complement but not entirely replace the emphasis on autonomy and rights that a traditionally male anthropology supports.

Other theories contend that women's relational understanding of human selfhood represents a more accurate vision of *general* human nature, not just one aspect of that nature. In this view, human beings are always social animals, although not all individuals (or cultures) give equal weight to the ways we are shaped and defined by our relationships with others. Richard Schmitt argues that humans generally and not just women are social beings, but that the conviction of separateness is a characteristically male illusion. What men consider their autonomy, Schmitt claims, ultimately depends on women's support. Thus it is not really independence but a covert, unacknowledged, and often exploitative relationality. This autonomy relies on the toleration of others, especially women—on their willingness to do the work and allow the autonomous person to make decisions and take actions separately.[48] In this light, men's autonomy, and the very world in which men act as though they were autonomous, is made possible by "woman's work," which Adrienne Rich describes as "the activity of world-protection, world-preservation, world-repair, the million tiny stitches . . . the invisible weaving of a frayed and threadbare family life, the cleaning up of the soil and waste left behind by men and children." Because those in power rarely value or even notice these activities, Rich explains, "women are not described as 'working' when we create the essential conditions for the work of men; we are supposed to be acting out of love, instinct, or devotion to some higher cause than self.[49] This false separateness is exploitative and dishonest, Schmitt contends, and thus "separateness is rarely a morally admirable quality."[50]

It is also not a common one, since even the illusion of autonomy is open to only a small part of the population, mainly financially secure white men. Most people in the world cannot deny the reality of interdependence, along with the vulnerability and constraints it brings. The maternal humility that Ruddick describes, for example, is not just a virtue to be sought but a common consequence of being a mother (or, in Ruddick's gender-neutral term, a mothering person). The participants in maternal practice—mothers and children—experience in an especially powerful way the extent to which human identity, well-being, and even survival are inseparable from dependency on and responsibility to other persons. Perhaps, however, this experience simply makes explicit a more universal feature of the human condition or human nature. Much feminist theory suggests precisely this: human beings cannot live as islands, and attempts to mask or deny our interdependencies with others lead to dishonesty, exploitation, and often unhappiness.

Feminists have pointed out, however, that even if we are all inescapably social and ethics ought to be concerned with nurturing relationships, it does not follow that all relationships are morally equal. Some feminists argue that relationality alone is not enough to guarantee ethical treatment of others, human or not. As Marti Kheel writes, "The *quality* of relation is more important than the fact that a relation of some kind exists."[51] This is tied to the issue of whether just being relational can suffice for ethical thinking and practice. A relational emphasis, as Joan Tronto points out, can undervalue autonomy, especially for women, and can also fail to appreciate the degree to which relationships, even caring ones, might also be power laden and oppressive.[52] Intimate relationships, especially but not only in the family, can be far from ethically (or psychologically) sound. Some feminist anthropologies also risk portraying relationships or care as essentially female preoccupations, thus limiting women's sphere of activity and exempting men from the responsibility of building and maintaining healthy relationships. Another weakness is the failure of many feminist philosophers, like the vast majority of their nonfeminist counterparts, to examine the ways that human beings are both natural and social, in relationships with and dependent upon not only other people but nonhuman animals and the natural world in general.

FEMINISM, NATURE, AND ETHICS

Ecological feminism directly addresses this gap in feminist philosophy as well as the failure of male-dominated environmental ethics to take gender into account. Ecofeminism is not just a hybrid of feminist and environmental philosophies, however, but a distinctive, though heterogeneous, approach to the relations between humans and nature and among humans. It provides a new "conceptual framework," defined as "a set of *basic* beliefs, values, attitudes and assumptions which shape and reflect how one views oneself and one's world. . . . [A] socially constructed lens through which we perceive ourselves and others."[53] The conceptual framework proposed by ecofeminism replaces existing frameworks that have been oppressive because they have helped explain, justify, and maintain oppressive relationships through what Karen Warren calls the "logic of domination." As described in chapter 2, the logic of domination begins with a recognition of differences—for example, between women and men, humans and nonhumans, or white and black people. These differences always carry moral weight: one is always superior to another. Finally, this superiority carries political weight: it justifies subordination.[54] In this way, the powerful use differences, such as those based on gender or race, to legitimate prejudices and hierarchies.

The logic of domination resembles what Val Plumwood terms "centrism"; both of these models are challenged by the ecofeminist insistence on linkage among different forms of oppression, especially against women and nonhumans. Oppressive centrisms, including racism, sexism, and anthropocentrism, include several common characteristics: radical exclusion, which marks an "otherized" group as both inferior and radically separate; homogenization, which erases or ignores differences within the other group; denial or backgrounding, which represents the other as inessential; incorporation, which defines the other in relation to the self, especially as lacking in relation to the self; and instrumentalism, which denies the other's independent agency.[55] Like the logic of domination, oppressive centrisms begin with the fact of differences based on gender, race, species, or other factors and then move to justifications for the objectification or exploitation of those seen as different others.

Many liberal philosophers, including some feminists, have sought to end oppression by denying the existence of important differences among humans. They class all persons together as essentially similar on the basis of highly general characteristics, such as intrinsic dignity or reason, which then justify equal treatment, often conceived of in terms of rights. Ecofeminism, in contrast, takes seriously the differences between women and men, among ethnic groups, and between humans and other animals, while also denying that these differences carry the moral and political weight perceived by the logic of domination. Ecofeminists, says Warren, seek to build a world in which "difference does not breed domination."[56]

Warren and other ecofeminist theorists argue that the logic of domination provides a framework for understanding the relationships and parallels between exploitation of nature and of women in Western culture. This relationship is not only conceptual but also historical and empirical. Carolyn Merchant's 1980 book, *The Death of Nature*, strongly influenced ecofeminism, documenting as it did the links between the objectification of women and of nature in the West, especially with the rise of mechanistic science, Enlightenment philosophy, and economic modernization. Merchant highlights the gendered features of Western definitions of both nature and humanness. She asserts that emerging modernist views understood nature as female and women as natural and both as possessing common features, such as passivity or irrationality, that made them suited to, even in need of, domination by men. The rise of mechanistic science, especially as conceptualized by Bacon, Newton, and Descartes, represents a historical example of the logic of domination, which "transformed the body of the world and its female soul, source of activity in the organic cosmos, into a mechanism of inert matter in motion."[57]

Based on the work of Merchant and others, a number of scholars have pointed to tangible connections between treatment of women and treatment of nonhuman nature. Vandana Shiva has demonstrated empirical links between environmental degradation and violence against women in India, for example. More generally, Shiva shows how "women's impoverishment has increased and their status decreased relative to men as the environment has been degraded, exacerbating prior gender inequities."[58] Shiva argues that since the domination of women is linked to that of nonhuman nature, struggles for women's survival are also struggles to protect nature. Using such examples, some ecofeminists argue that, as Sallie McFague puts it, the status of women and that of nature are "historically commensurate: as goes one, so goes the other."[59]

While there certainly are connections between the oppression of women and the exploitation of nature, the link might not be as universal as McFague suggests, particularly outside the West. Huey-li Li argues, for example, that Chinese culture does not include the notion of "transcendent dualism" that ecofeminism views as central to the logic of domination. This has not, however, precluded the oppression of women in China: "There are no parallels," she writes, "between Chinese people's respectful attitude toward nature and the inferior social position of women."[60] The increasingly multicultural and international character of ecofeminist theorizing has helped clarify the complex and diverse relationships between women and nonhuman nature in different communities and parts of the world.

Insights into these connections give ecofeminism distinctive ways of conceiving and elaborating on the central themes of feminist moral theory I described above: its emphases on relationships, context, narratives, and anthropology. Ecofeminism, like other forms of feminist philosophy, holds relationality up as a guide for ethical action and an ideal to be sought. However, it also expands moral relationships to encompass those with nonhuman animals, natural objects, landscapes, and nature in general. This can be seen, in one light, as consonant with the general feminist claim that morally significant relationships are not limited to those with persons who are equal or similar or both, or to those that are freely chosen. For feminist philosophers, seeing these relationships as morally considerable poses a fundamental challenge to mainstream moral theories. Feminism calls not just for a simple expansion of existing theories to encompass other types of persons and relationships (the "add women and stir" approach)[61] but for a reconceptualization of key philosophical categories such as ethics, epistemology, anthropology, and ontology. Understandings of what qualifies as an ethical agent or ethical behavior tend to change when applied to unequal, unchosen, and often nonreciprocal relationships, such as those between parents and children.

Ecofeminism sharpens and radicalizes this challenge by calling philosophy to take seriously the human relationships to nature. This does not mean erasing differences between humans and nonhuman animals; rather, it requires understanding those differences in a way opposed to the logic of domination. This means, first, paying careful attention to differences between humans and natural entities and to the particular needs and interests of nonhumans, just as feminists recommend in regard to human others. This sort of individual attention makes possible the special relationships that, Noddings and other feminists contend, form the basis for much of our moral life and concern, in contrast to the traditional emphasis on abstract, formalized, and voluntaristic definitions of what counts as a moral relationship. Ecofeminists apply this approach to relationships with nonhuman nature, which also must be personalized, at least as a starting point. That is to say, rather than loving or caring for nature in general as some sort of broad category (akin to universal humanity in liberal philosophy), we must begin our moral relationships to the natural world with concern for particular places, trees, or animals.[62] They need not stop there, just as, many feminists argue, ethical caring ought not to stop with intimate personal relationships. Because, in fact, relationality is prescriptive for feminists and ecofeminists both, the fundamental moral task can be seen as creating, sustaining, and broadening moral communities. In this context, ethical issues are about correct relationships rather than about claims of competing interests or rights or who has moral standing.[63] However, moral communities can be built only upon knowledge and experience of specific relationships with concrete human and nonhuman others.

Ecofeminists, like feminist theorists more generally, emphasize not only relationships but also context. As we saw earlier, feminist ethicists building on Gilligan's work insist that moral dilemmas cannot be understood or evaluated without knowledge of their context. Ecofeminism broadens this assertion by arguing that not only historical and social but also ecological context matters. In this sense, ecofeminism incorporates insights from ecological science as well as from feminist theory. As Karen Warren and Jim Cheney put it, "The ecological dimension of ethical reflection stems in large part from the fact that ecology is context . . . dependent."[64] Contemporary models in ecology, like feminism, provide no single universal model for viewing any, let alone every, ecosystem. Instead, observations always depend on particular conditions and perspectives, including scale as well as time and space. Conceptual frameworks help determine not only how but what an observer sees.

Ecofeminism thus challenges mainstream approaches to knowledge, as well as to human nature and ethics. Ecofeminists insist that all human knowledge, and even the very possibility of knowing, is relational and contextual. Further, every given object of knowledge "is in part a function of *where* it is, a function of the relationships in which it stands to other things and to its history, including (where applicable) its evolutionary history."[65] Thus ecofeminism, and particularly its attention to ecology, sharpens the feminist notion of embodied objectivity. Much of contemporary ecological science, like feminist theory, rejects the idea that there is one ahistorical, context-free, neutral view from nowhere. Instead, it incorporates multiple frames of reference, standpoints, and scales, without privileging one over another. In this light, ecosystems, like human relationships and moral dilemmas, embrace multiple understandings—all of which help contribute to a fuller and thus more objective picture, and none of which can stand alone.[66]

The emphases on contextuality and relationality point many ecofeminists to the narratives involved in philosophy and especially ethics. Narratives can give center stage to relationships, including relationships with nonhuman entities and creatures, in ways that analytic ethics do not, as Warren argues. Narratives also help show the ways ethics emerge out of particular contexts in which moral agents find themselves, in contrast to traditional models of moral guidelines imposed from above. The situation, history, and relationships of the characters become central to the ethical values and judgments that emerge from or are reinforced in particular stories. Further, narratives make central not only context and relationship but also the idea of ethical pluralism, another important theme for many ecofeminists. Ethical narratives involve multiple voices, perspectives, and values, all of which may be valid or helpful, at least in some ways or situations. Narratives' capacity to portray diverse attitudes and behaviors can suggest important ethical contrasts between the different types of relationships people may have with natural objects and shed new light on what counts as an appropriate ethical solution.[67] In many Native American cultures, as discussed earlier, narratives and oral histories help strengthen and transmit people's sense of connection to and dependency on the land and nonhuman species. Some feminist theorists have adopted a similar approach to literature, especially postmodern stories, as "a way of knowing the natural world."[68] Stories make possible the investigation of new meanings and values in nature or the recovery of old ones. For many ecofeminists, as well as for other feminist theorists, narratives and mythic thinking and language can be transformative as well as expressive.[69]

For ecofeminism, as for feminist philosophy more generally, narrative approaches help present a view of relationships as both a goal of moral behavior and a constitutive dimension of humanness. Ecofeminists contend, however, that humans have defining relationships not only with other humans but also with other animals, with landscapes, even with nature in a general sense. We are natural and ecological, as well as social, animals, partially constituted by historical and social relations and conditions, including those tied to gender, and by relations with nonhuman nature. One of the central questions for ecofeminism is how to understand the ways these different relationships and circumstances interact in the exploitation and potential liberation of both women and nonhuman nature. As Catherine Roach puts it, "How can we think about and live out the differences and commonalities of being female and male and the complexities of being self-conscious, prolific builders within the environment, in order that we may, on the one hand, be more just and more supportive of one another and, on the other (connected) hand, be more environmentally sound?"[70]

The relations between ethics and anthropologies raise concerns for ecofeminists, as for other feminists. Some ecofeminists contend, for example, that a relational self does not by itself guarantee good-quality relationships. Just as love and closeness in a marriage do not guarantee equality or respect between the partners, intimate relations between humans and nonhuman species do not ensure nonexploitative treatment of the natural world. It is possible to justify selfish and exploitative behavior on the basis of a relationship with nature (or a particular tree or animal or mountain) just as it is possible to justify exploitation in interpersonal relationships. Roach points out, for example, that in light of the meanings and functions traditionally associated with mothers in patriarchal culture, seeing the earth as our mother will not necessarily lead to behavior that is more environmentally sound. It may, in fact, help maintain exploitation of both mothers and the environment.[71] Claims about the relational character of the self and about our dependency upon nonhuman and human others and ecological processes are necessary but not sufficient elements of an adequate environmental ethic.

FEMINISM, BIOLOGY, AND ETHICS

Anthropological assertions based on human connections and similarities to nature and nonhumans run another risk that concerns many feminists. The emphasis on our physical, animal natures can suggest that nature is destiny, that biology imposes gender-specific limits on humans' potential capacities and roles well beyond the constraints of exclusively female pregnancy and lactation. Similar dangers arise in the more general feminist emphasis, seen in the work of Ruddick, Noddings, and Chodorow, on experiences of mothering as at least partially constitutive of female experience. Some interpretations of this work conclude that mothering is a natural fact, self-justifying and self-explanatory. This can help legitimize, for example, the conservative arguments that women, and only women, are meant to be parents and only parents. To avoid such conclusions, Chodorow warns, feminists "must question all assumptions which use biological claims to explain social forms," especially given the ways some sociobiologists have attempted to justify sexual and racial inequities on the basis of presumed "biological differences."[72]

As Chodorow suggests, sociobiology, which uses evolutionary theory to explain social characteristics and behaviors of humans and other animals, is a particular target of feminist critique. Feminists have attacked sociobiology, when applied to humans, as both essentialist and determinist. They argue that it ascribes particular traits, such as nurturance or passivity, to women, and others, like aggression or dominance, to men and claims that these traits are evolutionary adaptations and, as a consequence, unchangeable. Zuleyma Tang-Martinez summarizes the general feminist critique: "Human sociobiology is biologically deterministic and serves only to justify and promote the oppression of women by perpetuating the notion that male dominance and female oppression are natural outcomes of evolutionary history. Further, [feminists] argue that reliance on questionable evolutionary scenarios can be used to rationalize and exonerate obnoxious male behavior," such as middle-aged men's abandonment of their wives in favor of younger women.[73]

Undoubtedly, evolutionary theories can be and have been used to help legitimize sexist and racist attitudes and behaviors. In consequence, some feminists have rejected all biological approaches as at best irrelevant and at worst oppressive to women. They identify culture as the main or even sole determiner of human behavior, rejecting the notion that humans have a nature—as do other animal species—based on biological factors. Behind this rejection of biological and evolutionary arguments is an assumption that culture, as a shaper of human character and action, can be changed through social reforms and different child-rearing practices, while biology is out of human control.[74] Many ecofeminists, however, argue that humans, including and perhaps especially women, are part of nature, dependent upon and connected to it in multiple, often positive, ways. This implies a rejection of at least the strong-est versions of social constructionism, because, as I argued in chapter 3, hard constructionist arguments presume a hard and fast division be-tween humans and the rest of nature. Feminist rejections of sociobiology can, intentionally or not, strengthen an image of humans as radically different from all other animals in both their evolutionary origins and their present relations with other species and with their own ecosystems.

This issue has led to debates between ecofeminists and culturalist feminists. Carol Adams criticizes feminists who fail to see the oppressive consequences of the perceived divide between humans and all other spe-cies. "While feminism has liberated white women and people of color from the onerous equation with animals and otherness," Adams writes, "it has not disturbed the equation of animals with otherness." Thus feminism remains "a species-specific philosophical system, in which an (expanded) humanity continues to negate the other animals precisely because their otherness is located in the natural sphere."[75] Adams crit-icizes, in particular, Nel Noddings, who sees nonhuman animals "as being dependent on their relationship to us, as literally existing (only) for us."[76] For feminists like Noddings, challenges to the liberal philo-sophical dualisms between men and women, reason and emotion, and mind and body do not lead to questions about the divide between human and animal, culture and nature. Ecofeminists argue that those opposi-tions are all related, through the oppressive logic of domination. An integral liberation for women requires challenging exploitative attitudes toward nature, including claims, even by other feminists, that humans are radically other than nature.

Thus many ecofeminists adopt a soft constructionist position, which acknowledges the complex mutual shaping between humans and nature. As Stephanie Lahar writes, "There is not a place in the world that does not reveal the touch and bear the consequences of human hands and minds. . . . At the same time, there are no people who have not been shaped by the effects of landscape and water, the climate and natural features of the area in which they live."[77] This position strives to inte-grate scientific (ecological and evolutionary) and social-cultural insights about human character and history and, particularly, about humans' impact upon the nonhuman world. It strives not just to understand hu-man nature better and to improve relationships among humans but also to find ways of relating to nonhuman nature in less damaging ways.

Feminist theorists insist that we need to learn from women's distinc-tive experiences and perspectives in order to create more just human

societies. Such societies would value both our common human traits and
the differences between women's and men's experiences. Ecofeminists
add an insistence that we recognize the intimate links between humans
and nonhumans, our similarities to and dependencies on the natural
world. This means, as Adams argues, learning about and taking seriously the "ontological integrity" of nonhumans: "As much as men's
accounts of women's lives have been partial, false, or malicious lies, so
too have humans' accounts of the other animals' lives."[78] The next chapter takes a look at some different accounts of other animals, in the larger
context of the ways humans are shaped by evolutionary and ecological
relations with nonhumans, as a necessary step toward making sense of
the complex relations among ideas about human nature, attitudes toward nonhuman nature, and ethics.

CHAPTER SEVEN

Evolution, Ecology, and Ethics

The preceding three chapters have documented both external and internal critiques of the dominant Western view of human nature as individualistic, rational, and disconnected from the rest of life. I now turn to an even more internal challenge: the evidence provided by Western science—the presumed pinnacle of what human reason can achieve—that we are related to, dependent upon, and similar to the rest of nature in countless ways. This is not merely one of many possible critiques internal to a diverse and ever-changing Western culture but a challenge from within the heart of reason itself. The very capacity to reason, which has seemed to divide us from other species and from nature in general, now provides evidence that we are not so separate after all. In this chapter I explore some of this evidence, beginning with evolutionary theory, which underlies all the biological sciences. I spend most of the chapter on evolution because it is so fundamental and so controversial in its implications for human nature and humans' place in nature. Within the context of evolution, I look at the increasingly rich picture of nonhuman behavior provided by studies of animal behavior. Finally, I turn to ecological knowledge and its role in ideas about human nature and environmental ethics.

EVOLUTION BY NATURAL SELECTION

Feminists' frequent discomfort with biological explanations of human behavior, noted in the previous chapter, points to some of the ethical and political dangers of biological determinism for women. Further, not only women have suffered, as shown by the results of various efforts over the past century to classify certain races, social classes, and ethnic groups as inferior based on supposedly scientific grounds.[1] In the late 1800s, Social Darwinists sought to legitimize class divisions as a result of evolutionary processes that elevated those with inherent intellectual and moral capacity. (Thus one Victorian Social Darwinist claimed, "The millionaires are a product of natural selection.")[2] Some conservatives in Britain and the United States used versions of evolutionary theory to argue for neglect (often not very benign) of the poor. The eugenicists of the early 1900s went further, advocating deliberate selection to ensure that those they deemed less fit did not reproduce, at least not as quickly as the more fit. Nazi scientists infamously applied eugenics to their efforts to preserve the purity of the "Aryan race."[3]

The obvious dangers of Social Darwinism and eugenics have encouraged, since the 1930s, a strong bias in the social sciences and humanities toward a vision of human nature as "blank paper," endlessly malleable by culture. In this model, humans differ from all other animals in being shaped only by nurture and not nature, in lacking, in fact, a nature at all. This assumption underlies many contemporary theories of gender, race, and even nature itself. Constructionist or culturalist approaches so dominate the social sciences now that almost any claim about biologically shaped aspects of human behavior meets with scorn, fear, or aggressive counterattacks. Are these attacks justified? Do all applications of evolutionary theory to *Homo sapiens* start us on the slippery slope to Social Darwinism and eugenics? Behind these questions lurks the larger issue of whether evolutionary theory should be limited to other life forms, applicable to humans only in relation to our distant origins. More to the point for this book, if ethicists must think clearly and carefully about humanness, should they take evolution into account? Or does something about humans justify setting our species outside the framework of natural selection?

This rephrases the question about human distinctiveness raised at the beginning of this book and lurking behind much of the discussion throughout. Different perspectives on what it means to be human— alternatives to the vision of rational, self-sufficient, cultural "man"— must be put in the context of larger questions about whether and how humans diverge from the rest of the natural world. More generally, thinking about what humans are like and should be like, in any cultural or ideological context, requires considering humans' relations to the rest of nature. This necessarily points us to the natural sciences and especially to evolutionary theory. We return, then, to the question of whether evolution can be applied to human nature and, if so, what are the ethical implications of the anthropological understanding thus gained.

To begin to answer these questions, we need to understand the process of evolution by natural selection, as first described by Charles Darwin in *The Origin of Species* in 1859. Natural selection is a three-part process, which begins with natural variation among individual organisms. All species will tend to reproduce at a greater rate than can be sustained, which leads inevitably to a "struggle for existence." In this struggle, some individuals possess traits that enable them to survive and reproduce while others fail. The survivors pass on to their progeny the qualities that had helped them succeed, and, over many generations, "the population as a whole progressively changes to resemble the successful types."[4] For example, natural variation gave some ancestral giraffes longer necks than others. As giraffes carved out their niche among other savannah herbivores, those with longer necks could reach food unavailable to shorter-necked ones. The longer-necked giraffes had an advantage, especially when food was scarce. These successful giraffes had offspring that shared their longer-neck characteristic, and eventually the species as a whole came to be long-necked. As Darwin summarizes it: "Every slight modification, which in the course of ages chanced to arise, and which in any way favoured the individuals of any of the species, by better adapting them to their altered conditions, would tend to be preserved."[5]

Natural selection explains not just the ways that certain traits become emphasized within a species but also how new species emerge. The process of speciation is central to Darwin's theory, as the title of his major book suggests. He needed to explain how evolution by natural selection could generate distinctive species, since creationists insisted that only an intentional designer could make so many different species, each fitted precisely to its environment. Darwin contended that all the various species of animals and plants have emerged from common ancestors under the pressure of natural selection. Small variations in individual animals and plants, such as minute differences in the shape of a finch's beak, enable some to survive and reproduce where others cannot. Distinctive traits that lead to greater success are exaggerated in succeeding generations, leading eventually to the development of separate species. (Speciation can also result from the physical separation of species, e.g., through migration.)

Darwin's studies of the tremendous diversity among finches, barnacles, and other species convinced him that the divisions among varieties within a species and among species were much less clear-cut than traditional classifications suggested. He concluded that "no line of demarcation can be drawn between species, commonly supposed to have been produced by special acts of creation, and varieties which are acknowledged to have been produced by secondary laws."[6] Different subspecies exist within a given species' range, and when many similar individuals are competing in the same niche, the ones that differ in some useful way will tend to flourish, as will their descendants who share this difference. In an island population of finches mostly adapted to eat seeds, for example, individuals that can also eat insects will thrive, especially in times of scarcity. Eventually natural selection will split these neighboring varieties into distinct species, in what Darwin called the "principle of divergence."[7] Thus "natural selection literally organizes life," as Jonathan Weiner summarizes it.[8] In Darwin's own words, "It may be said that natural selection is daily and hourly scrutinising, throughout the world, every variation, even the slightest; rejecting that which is bad, preserving and adding up all that is good; silently and insensibly working, whenever and wherever opportunity offers, at the improvement of each organic being in relation to its organic and inorganic conditions of life. We see nothing of these slow changes in progress, until the hand of time has marked the long lapses of ages, and then so imperfect is our view into long past geological ages, that we only see that the forms of life are now different from what they formerly were."[9] This implies, Weiner says, that "one species can shade into one another: that there is no species barrier."[10] This conclusion, as Darwin himself recognized, has radical implications, particularly in regard to human origins.

For these and other reasons, Darwin's ideas did not meet with immediate widespread acceptance. Not only creationist but also alternative evolutionary theories held sway in the late nineteenth and early twentieth centuries. (The most popular competing theory of evolution was Jean-Baptiste Lamarck's idea that traits acquired during an individual's lifetime could be inherited by its offspring.) A variety of factors helped Darwinism emerge from its relative obscurity during the late 1800s. Most important in scientific terms was the growth of genetics. As Darwin knew, the theory of evolution by natural selection was incomplete without an understanding of the mechanics of inheritance that showed how traits were passed down from parents to offspring.[11] Darwin's theory required not only that variations in behavior or physical attributes lead to variations in an individual's success in its environment but also that these variations be passed on to offspring, who would then share their parents' success. However, Darwin did not know exactly how this heredity worked. Beginning in the 1920s, the new Mendelian genetics provided this understanding by showing that "in the absence of per- turbing factors (such as mutation, selection, drift, migration, or nonran- dom mating), variance remains constant from generation to genera- tion."[12] This approach replaced the earlier idea that inheritance "blended" maternal and paternal factors. With blending, variance would decrease in each generation, contradicting natural selection's need for continued diversity. Mendel's confirmation that inheritance pre- served genetic variation provided the link between heredity and fitness that was required by the theory of natural selection. The connection between Mendelian genetics and Darwinian natural selection led to the now dominant "evolutionary synthesis."[13]

Just as the theory of evolution depends on certain facts, it implies others. One important conclusion is that all plants and animals alive today descended from one ancestral life-form.[14] All current species are related not in a linear progression but rather in the form of a "tree of life" that begins with a single trunk, the primordial life-form, and branches out again and again, as Darwin sketched in *The Origin of Species*.[15] All species are related by virtue of this original ancestor, and many species are related through more recent common ancestors. The closeness of the relation is determined by the length of time since species branched off from a common ancestor to continue their evolution along separate paths. (Not infrequently the paths are very short, since a great number of incipient species die out quickly.) Contrary to some popu- larized notions of evolution, few species alive today descended from other living species. Instead, closely related species are like cousins, shar- ing common ancestors. If we go back far enough, we find that all forms of life today are our cousins, more or less removed.

NATURAL SELECTION AND HUMAN EVOLUTION

Darwin was reticent about his own species in *The Origin of Species,* devoting only one sentence to the likelihood that the theory of natural selection would shed light on human origins. Not until 1871 did he produce his full-length work on human evolution, *The Descent of Man.* He waited, in part, because he knew that any application of evolutionary theory to humans would generate tremendous controversy. Darwin believed that *Homo sapiens* shared common ancestors with other primates, especially the African great apes, to which humans are very close in both physiology and behavior.[16] This relationship challenged the prevailing conviction about humanity's radical divergence from all other species. Confirming Darwin's fears, most attacks on his theories focused on the links between humans and apes. (*The Descent of Man* was popularly termed the "monkey book.") Even many people who accepted that nonhuman species emerged through gradual evolution rather than special creation denied that humans could be yet another result of natural selection. Others accepted that physical structures evolved but denied that intelligence, morality, or culture could have emerged through natural selection. Thus the evolutionist Alfred Russel Wallace, a contemporary of Darwin, held that "the body of man is indeed a biological structure, clearly descended from the apes, but his culture, which stems from his extraordinary and unique mind, is on a new, higher hierarchical level of its own; evolutionary biology has nothing to tell us about this higher level."[17] This idea still holds sway among many scholars in the social sciences and humanities.

Well after evolution gained general acceptance as the story of human origins, scientific debate continued over the timing and nature of divisions among humans and other members of the primate "superfamily" of hominoids, which encompasses present and ancestral humans and apes. In regard to the timing, recent fossil and molecular evidence suggests that the first great ape to diverge from a common primate ancestor was the orangutan, which split off around twelve million years ago. The African great apes and ancestral humans went their separate ways about five or six million years ago, perhaps later for chimpanzees and humans than for gorillas.[18] The diverging hominids (ancestral humans) eventually evolved into the genus *Homo,* which includes two extinct species and our own, *Homo sapiens. H. sapiens* probably emerged, about five hundred thousand years ago, from *H. erectus,* which had evolved around two million years ago from *H. habilis.* Because of gaps in the fossil record in Africa for the period between two and three million years ago, scientists do not know if *H. habilus* evolved from the earlier genus *Australopithecus* or from a still unidentified intermediate species.

A central issue throughout the study of human origins has concerned the qualities that separated early hominids from the common ape ancestor. What set our earliest ancestors on the path to humanness? Darwin speculated that the key was upright posture, which freed the hands for toolmaking, in turn stimulating the growth of intelligence.[19] Most

Victorian evolutionists argued the reverse, insisting that the expansion of the brain, not bipedalism, was the driving force behind human evolution. In their view, as Grafton Elliot Smith wrote in 1912, "it was not the adoption of the erect attitude that made Man from an Ape, but the gradual perfecting of the brain and the slow upbuilding of the mental structure, of which erectness of carriage is one of the incidental manifestations."[20] These claims depended less on fossil evidence than on a conviction that greater intelligence makes *H. sapiens* distinctive and thus must mark our chronological as well as logical separation from other creatures.

Advances in genetics and fossil findings have forced a redrawing of this boundary. In South Africa in the mid-1920s, Raymond Dart discovered the remains of a small-brained but bipedal hominid he called *Australopithecus africanus.* Mainstream anthropology challenged Dart's claim that our direct ancestors had walked upright while still having ape-sized brains, but over the next several decades new evidence confirmed his theory. This evidence also shows that human evolution has not followed a straight line. *Australopithecus* includes not one but several species, some of which coexisted in Africa for various periods before dying out. Older than Dart's *A. africanus,* and apparently longer lasting as a species, is *A. afarensis,* the first specimen of which was uncovered in Afar, Ethiopia, in 1974 (the famous "Lucy"). Even older is *A. ramidus,* discovered in 1992, also in Afar. While the fossil evidence is incomplete, it suggests that *A. ramidus,* dating to about 4.4 million years ago, was bipedal. *A. afarensis*—Lucy and her companions, whose remains have been found throughout East Africa and dated at 2.5 to 4 million years old—certainly walked upright. It seems, then, that Darwin was correct in his speculation that upright posture marked the first key step in human evolution, with growth in brain size secondary. We should not, as anthropologist Adam Kuper warns, exaggerate the decisive nature of this break, since hominids remained well adapted to tree climbing for another two million years. Still, "hominids were the only primates that walked upright for much of the time," and most anatomical differences between *Australopithecus* and other hominoids, such as the shape of the pelvis, stem from upright posture.[21]

If bipedal locomotion was a key evolutionary step, two questions arise. First, why did it emerge? Most researchers believe that one major factor was climate change. Cooler temperatures reduced forests and opened savannahs in the early hominids' African environment, pushing them out of the trees and onto the plains, where upright posture and free hands provided adaptive advantages. The second question concerns the consequences of bipedalism. Darwin and many scholars since have connected upright posture, which freed the hands, with the beginning of tool use. However, current evidence suggests that even the most rudimentary tools did not appear until after *H. habilis* emerged, several million years after *Australopithecus* began walking upright. What about intelligence: did bipedalism spur growth in brain size? If so, the effect was gradual. The brain of *Australopithecus* was ape-sized, while that of *H. habilis* was larger but still not within "human" range. Brain size started to increase notably with *H. habilis* (2.5 million years ago). *H. erectus*, living about 1.8 million years ago, was probably within "human" range for brain size, and the anatomically modern humans who emerged about a million or a million and a half years later, *H. sapiens,* certainly were (and are) within that range.

All this suggests that the emergence of distinctively human qualities was gradual, nonlinear, and certainly not inevitable. As Stephen Jay Gould puts it, "*Homo sapiens* is not the foreordained product of a ladder that was reaching toward our exalted estate from the start. We are merely the surviving branch of a once luxuriant bush."[22] The elements distinguishing our branch, guiding it farther from the trunk, did not appear all at once, as a neat package. Upright posture preceded tool use by millions of years, and tool use emerged before fully human cranial capacity. Further, symbolic culture, of the kind that seems uniquely human, arose 45,000 to 20,000 years ago, some 450,000 years after *H. sapiens* achieved its current anatomy. As Kuper summarizes it, "Physical evolution and cultural evolution did not march hand in hand. The physical capacity for culture had been in place for millennia before modern human culture began its explosive development."[23] This raises, again, questions about the definition of humanness: Is it tied to the common biological characteristics of *H. sapiens,* or does it depend on the much later emergence of culture? If prehistoric *H. sapiens,* with our brains but without culture, were not human, then what were they? What, in short, does it mean to be human?

SOCIOBIOLOGY AND EVOLUTIONARY INTERPRETATIONS OF HUMAN NATURE

Since Darwin, many scholars have tried to answer this question in terms of evolution. If humans evolved via natural selection, they reason, then human behavior, like anatomy, should be explicable in terms of the adaptive advantages they provided during evolution. Human nature, in this view, is neither mysterious nor extraordinary. Rather, as Robert Wright puts it, "if the theory of natural selection is correct, then essentially everything about the human mind should be intelligible in these terms."[24] It is implausible that evolution would slowly, painstakingly shape fish gills, bat wings, and human hands but have no bearing on behavior and the senses. In evolutionary terms, humans, like fish and bats, are integrated wholes, whose brains no less than the rest of their bodies have emerged from, and carry the marks of, earlier forms of life.

The study of nonhuman behavior in evolutionary perspective came to be known as ethology (from the Greek *ethos,* meaning character), a field pioneered in the early 1900s by European researchers, notably Nico Tinbergen, Konrad Lorenz, and Karl von Frisch. Their basic premise was that "instincts, like organs, were inherited and had been formed by natural selection."[25] This approach caused little comment when applied to geese, fish, and other nonhuman species. However, enormous controversy exploded when, in the 1970s, prominent scientists sought to explain human behavior by reference to natural selection. This approach, which became known as sociobiology, was first presented in three books: Edward O. Wilson's *Sociobiology: The New Synthesis* (1975) and *On Human Nature* (1978) and Richard Dawkins's *The Selfish Gene* (1976). Wilson summarizes their "genetic hypothesis": "the traits of human nature were adaptive during the time that the human species evolved and . . . genes consequently spread through the population that predisposed their carriers to develop those traits."[26]

An important application of sociobiology's genetic hypothesis is the effort to explain male and female mating strategies. In most nonhuman animals, researchers contend, males are eager to mate as often as possible, while females tend to be selective ("coy"). This stems, sociobiologists claim, from variations in "parental investment," in Robert Trivers's term.[27] Females usually make much greater investments in mating and child rearing, because they produce fewer eggs than males produce sperm and, in species with parental care, because females devote a great deal of time and energy to pre- and postnatal nurturing of offspring. It makes sense for females who literally put all their eggs into one basket to ensure they are the best possible eggs, fertilized by high-quality males. It makes equal sense for males who can spread their sperm around to do so, since engendering more offspring usually means that more survive. The pattern of female coyness and male eagerness varies according to relative parental investments, reaching its extremes in species where men invest nothing more in offspring than sperm, and moderating when males share responsibilities for nurturing young. Applied to humans, the pattern suggests that men will tend to be slightly promiscuous, as befitting a species in which males typically invest a great deal, though still less than females, in rearing young. Women will be somewhat more monogamous and will seek partners who make good prospective fathers, both in the genes they pass down and in their likely contribution to infant care.

Parental investment seemed fairly straightforward to many sociobiologists, but other behaviors did not seem to lend themselves so easily to evolutionary interpretations. Chief among these anomalies was altruism, defined as behavior that does not further the individual's own interests. Neo-Darwinism presumes that because the primary selective force in evolution is genetic self-interest, the behavior of humans, like that of all species, should aim at surviving and getting one's genes represented in the next generation. Evolution teaches, in Richard Dawkins's words, that "we are born selfish," or at least our genes, the "replicators" for which we are mere vehicles, are innately selfish.[28] However, neither humans nor other species always act in selfish ways. The problem, as Wilson framed it, was "How can altruism, which by definition reduces personal fitness, possibly evolve by natural selection?"[29]

Efforts to answer this question reveal the problems and the possibilities of sociobiology. For many culturalists, Wilson's question exemplifies sociobiologists' unhealthy desire to explain complex human behaviors in terms not of free will and conscious decisions but of impersonal evolutionary processes. The question reflects, in other words, a desire to reduce human behavior to its biological grounds. For sociobiologists, however, altruism posed a fascinating problem, whose resolution could illuminate the capacity of evolutionary theory to explain the most intricate human behaviors. They found the first step toward solving the evolutionary mystery of altruism, in humans and other species, in the theory of kin selection. Kin selection rests on the concept of "inclusive fitness," in William Hamilton's term, which explains how an individual's genes may achieve greater representation in succeeding generations not only through the individual's own offspring but also through close relatives, especially siblings, nieces, and nephews, who share many of the same genes. Individuals who sacrifice their own interest, in reproducing or even in surviving, in order to benefit close relatives may further their own genes' long-term survival.[30] Thus *conscious* emotions that motivate deliberately altruistic behaviors, such as affection for close relatives, may emerge because they provide *unconscious* advantages. As Robert Wright explains, "Natural selection tends to work underground, by shaping human feelings, not by making humans conscious of its logic."[31] The logic of natural selection that shapes feelings, just as it shapes anatomy, is the logic of inclusive fitness. In scientific terms, kin selection occurs when a gene (or a complex of genes) "*happens* to make its vehicle behave in ways that help the survival or reproductive prospects of other vehicles likely to contain a copy of that gene." In such cases the gene itself may thrive "even if prospects for *its* vehicle are lowered in the process."[32] In lay terms, kin selection is exemplified by wolves who do not reproduce but stay with their pack of close relatives and help rear their nieces and nephews.

Canine sociobiology may account for the altruism of wolf aunts and uncles, but what about the equally well-documented human habit of altruistic behavior directed at nonrelatives? Giving one's life for one's country or rushing into a burning building to save a stranger's child harms the individual's chances of reproducing, but without helping any close relatives preserve their shared genes. Sociobiologists and ethologists often explain such practices with the theory of reciprocal altruism. This holds that natural selection will favor non-kin altruism if help provided to others is sometimes reciprocated. In short, individuals who maximize friendships and minimize antagonisms will gain an evolutionary advantage.[33] This thesis gains support from studies of nonhuman animals who provide reciprocal favors, such as sharing food with individuals who have previously shared with them.[34] Computer simulations also show that a reciprocal strategy (called "tit for tat") benefits its "vehicles" more efficiently than either consistent niceness or consistent meanness.

This narrowly focused reciprocity, however, is not the same as more generalized risks on behalf of others, which we can call heroism. Heroic behavior is not limited to humans. For example, in many social species, including different birds, monkeys, and prairie dogs, individuals call loudly to alert their companions to the presence of a predator, even though the alarm calls might help the predator locate the noisy individual. One explanation is that the animal is simply so alarmed by the predator that she or he calls out stupidly, oblivious to personal danger. Natural selection, however, would not have preserved simple stupidness, at least in life and death situations, for many generations. Stupidness is also contraindicated by studies that show, for example, that vervet monkeys have different alarm calls for different kinds of predators and respond to each call with appropriate behavior, heading for the trees at the leopard alarm and descending at the eagle alarm.[35] Such examples suggest that at least in some species, we must explain altruistic risk taking in terms that account both for intelligence and for the unforgiving process of natural selection. The best explanation of risk taking, like other complex behaviors, must account for both genetic factors (evolved through natural selection) and external or cultural factors such as intelligence, learning, and choice, in nonhuman animals as well as *Homo sapiens.*

Mary Midgley suggests a modified theory of non-kin altruism based on the model of parental care developed by ethologist Irenaus Eibl-Eibesfeldt.[36] All animals who behave altruistically, Midgley points out, already care for and protect their young. Non-kin altruism simply supposes the extension of this sort of care to other adults. Midgley elaborates:

> Now the development of sociability proceeds in any case largely by this extension to other adults of behavior first developed between parents and young—grooming, mouth contact, embracing, protective and submissive gestures, giving food. In fact, wider sociability in its original essence simply *is* the power of adults to treat one another, mutually, as honorary parents and children. It is enriched later with other patterns largely drawn from the interactions *between* parents and infants: hence the enormous importance of play as a source of social sophistication. But quasi-parental interactions come first. They work well because they are adapted to soothe, to conciliate, to forge a bond. Once forged, why should this bond not carry its usual consequence of protectiveness?[37]

In other words, once a tendency or behavior emerges, it can extend beyond its original context as long as this extension does not damage the individual's adaptive advantage. Midgley does not insist that this extension be genetic. Richard Dawkins, though, suggests that extensions of altruism could have a genetic basis, in small genetic changes in an already complex, gradually evolved pattern of behavior, such as parental nurturing.[38] Another possibility, as J. L. Brown and E. R. Brown contend, is that altruistic behavior might sometimes originate as a byproduct of selection in some other context. For example, "cooperative breeding, by allowing birds to coexist within social units, enables and ultimately capitalizes on the 'mistake' of feeding unrelated offspring." Helping behavior, then, might persist in species in which the initial mistake benefits the helper or the individuals helped or both.[39]

Various kinds of non-kin altruism, then, might represent extensions or by-products—genetic or cultural or both—of parental nurturing. As Midgley points out, parental care must be a very strong motivation in order to inspire the great effort and sacrifice required to raise young. It is thus likely to shape individuals' behavior outside the context in which it originally emerged. Genes, as Robert Wright puts it, are imprecise in "turning on and off our emotional spigots."[40] These explanations of non-kin altruism need not conflict with the tit-for-tat theory. Rather, they suggest the multifaceted ways in which complex behaviors might evolve and spread and the need for pluralistic explanations of such behaviors. This pluralism is necessary not only for nonhuman species but also for understanding human behavior, which in the light of sociobiology appears distinguished in degree but not in kind from the rest of the natural world. Evolutionary theory does not exclude the possibility that quantitative differences in human biology, especially in the size and structure of the brain, can be so great that they lead to qualitative differences in behavior. It does, however, exclude any notion of human special creation, of an absolute divide between humans and the rest of life.

THE SOCIOBIOLOGY DEBATE

Sociobiology faced a barrage of critiques from the moment Wilson's book of that title appeared. Some attacks came from conservatives who insisted that humans were the result of special creation and that God, not genetic fitness, determines our behavior. These arguments need not concern us here, except as interesting examples of the ways that moral and political agendas depend on specific understandings of human nature and origins.[41] More important here are the critiques by people who accept evolutionary theory in general but reject its application to modern human behavior and culture. Many of the challenges came from feminists who interpret sociobiological theories of parental investment as justification for male philandering and female domesticity, among other things. Human sociobiology, in this view, explains negative or stereotyped behavior as the result of biologically determined forces that cannot be altered. In response to these concerns, sociobiologists often insisted that descriptions of biologically shaped behavioral tendencies do not justify those tendencies. As Wilson wrote in 1975, "The 'what is' of human nature is to a large extent the heritage of a Pleistocene hunter-gatherer existence. The demonstration of any genetic bias [for a behavior] cannot be used to justify a continuing practice in present and future societies."[42] Sociobiologists have responded similarly to charges that evolutionary explanations of human aggression and territoriality legitimize war making.

Other critics have argued, as Adam Kuper puts it, that sociobiologists only guess at "the unconscious, ecological consequences of customs and pay no attention to the meaning of the customs for the people who practice them."[43] In focusing on the adaptive benefits of behaviors, in other words, evolutionary approaches dismiss the role of conscious decisions in cultures and in individual lives. This charge, like feminist critiques, reflects a fear that biology is destiny, that genetically shaped traits must be immutable, and thus, as Midgley puts it, that "any notion of inborn active and social tendencies . . . threatens human freedom."[44] If our behaviors are biological adaptations, in this view, then individual decisions count for nothing. To preserve freedom, human behavior must be learned and thus, presumably, open to intentional change. In metaphysical terms, freedom seems to demand that minds be autonomous, determined neither by forces outside nor by genes inside. As the physicist Paul Davies puts it, consciousness, intelligence, and free will can be "no trivial detail, no minor by-product of mindlessly purposeless forces."[45]

What evolution says about human intentionality and consciousness is central to the capacity of Darwinism to contribute to understandings of human nature. Daniel Dennett and Edward Wilson have taken on this problem directly, from different angles. Dennett focuses on the *origins* of consciousness. He asks, in response to Davies, why does the fact that consciousness is "a byproduct of mindless, purposeless forces make it trivial? Why couldn't the most important thing of all be something that arose from unimportant things? Why should the importance of *anything* have to rain down on it from on high, from something more important, a gift from God?"[46] Quoting John Dewey, Dennett argues that evolution shifts interest "from an intelligence that shaped things once for all to the particular intelligences which minds are even now shaping."[47] Minds, in other words, are an effect rather than a "First Cause." However, the fact that mental qualities evolved, that they are (partially) shared with other creatures, does not diminish the worth or excellence of human intelligence or intentionality. As neuroscientist Antonio Damasio writes, "The partial explanation of complexity by something less complex does not signify debasement."[48]

Edward Wilson also argues that evolution does not make freedom a self-delusion. He does argue that an evolutionary perspective makes human behavior, like the behavior of other animals, predictable to some extent. Humans are not fully self-created blank paper, capable of any and every action or feeling. However, this does not eliminate free choice, because, within the broad parameters of predictability, humans are capable of a wide variety of behaviors, shaped (in part) by an intelligence that is far too complex to be predicted in advance.[49] More generally, Wilson points out that biology merely provides the constraints within which learning, socialization, and intentionality determine specific behaviors. Such biological constraints, Wilson readily admits, are very broad. He insists, however, on a bottom line: within these broad constraints, the behavior of humans, like that of all species, is biologically determined and thus can be predicted if categories of behavior are made general enough.[50]

The categories have to be extremely general, critics point out, to allow for the existing range of cultural variation in everything from the ways people make a living to their ideas about how to raise children. This problem leads Stephen Jay Gould to reject Wilson's suggestion that traits such as homosexuality, aggression, and spite, among others, have a genetic basis.[51] Instead, Gould contends, specific behaviors and customs represent not biological but cultural adaptations. He rejects "adaptationism," the "reverse engineering" central to sociobiology, in which researchers try to determine "what Mother Nature had in mind," why a trait was beneficial in the ancestral environment.[52] Even those who accept some applications of adaptationism often criticize those sociobiologists who argue that *all* traits that are widespread in a species must have an evolutionary basis. For example, Daniel Dennett critiques Wilson's assumption that territoriality must be biological because it is so common. Dennett points out that cultural transmission could provide an equally plausible explanation: "The ubiquity of territoriality in human societies is *by itself* no evidence at all for this, since territoriality makes so much sense in so many human arrangements."[53] Thus it could have emerged in many different cultures through trial and error rather than genetic predisposition. Dennett calls such advantageous learned behaviors "Good Tricks." Other species have their own tricks. For example, Carolina wrens often build nests in hanging plants. This may imply not a genetic attraction to flowerpots but simply the capacity to find good nesting sites. If wrens can come up with Good Tricks, so can humans, and much more easily because language and other aspects of culture facilitate transmission even to those who do not come up with a Good Trick by themselves. Dennett puts it bluntly: "If you are not totally idiotic, you don't need a genetic basis for any adaptation that you will pick up from your friends in any case."[54] Thus, different human cultures can reinvent the wheel, literally or figuratively, without any genetic basis for wheel making other than general intelligence or inventiveness.

Sociobiologists argue that even if genes code only such general capacities, evolutionary approaches still illuminate human nature. Wilson, for example, suggests in a recent book that human nature has evolved to favor innovation, learning, and choice, which is why culture adapts to environmental changes so much more rapidly than biology does.[55] Despite these caveats, Wilson, among others, holds out hope that many complex behaviors can be traced ultimately to fairly straightforward genetic factors. Wilson explains that he hopes and believes "that all tangible phenomena, from the birth of stars to the workings of social institutions, are based on material processes that are ultimately reducible, however long and tortuous the sequences, to the laws of physics."[56] It is possible to reject Wilson's search for all-encompassing scientific explanations and still accept the core thesis of sociobiology: many human behaviors have evolutionary, thus biological, roots. This deceptively simple claim directly confronts the belief, dear to constructionists and creationists alike, that an impassable divide separates *Homo sapiens* from other animals and from our own animal roots.

ETHOLOGY

Maintaining this divide requires assumptions on both sides. On one side stand humans, who possess qualities found nowhere else in creation. On the opposite side stand all other animals, united by their lack of the quality or qualities that make humans valuable. Evolutionary theory, especially in its sociobiological manifestation, challenges the presuppositions on the human side, insisting that we are not purely cultural (self-) inventions. Ethology, which studies nonhuman animal behavior, sheds light on the other side, by showing that our presumed opposites are far more complex and diverse than exceptionalist anthropologies allow.

While ethologists are far from unanimous, research on species ranging from chimpanzees to octopuses has discredited the assumption that other animals' lives "are wholly made up of blind, innate responses to the world around them," as Marian Stamp Dawkins puts it. Rather, "the more we learn about animal behaviour, the more it seems that such stupidly simple responses are the exception and that a far more complex assessment of the animal's environment is the rule."[57] Studies of a wide variety of species confirms this conclusion. Some are well-known, notably the capacity of great apes to learn symbolic language, use tools, hunt cooperatively, and pass information on "culturally" (through learning and example rather than natural selection). Other species, however, also reveal much greater flexibility, complexity, and subtlety in their behavior than permitted by mechanistic, instinct-driven images.

Of countless possible examples, I will mention only a few here. A number of bird species feign injuries, leading potential predators away from their nests or offspring. Many of these species demonstrate flexibility in their injury-feigning behavior, modifying it in relation to factors such as the type of intruder (is it a fox who will eat eggs or young, or a cow who might crush them by accident?) and the type of terrain (might hiding work better than distraction?). Reductive accounts of animal behavior, which interpret injury-feigning as a rigid instinct, cannot fully account for this flexibility. A more adequate account, as Carolyn Ristau argues, might incorporate both genetic factors (which, for example, predispose some species and not others to feign injuries) and intention or consciousness, such as the capacity to make decisions based on past experience and assessment of a particular situation. Her research leads Ristau to conclude that "it is highly unlikely given all the continuities between humans and other organisms that humans alone should be aware or conscious and have thoughts, purposes, beliefs, and desires. It is more likely that creatures other than humans should have a mind."[58] While this conviction is not universal among ethologists, it is much more widespread than a few decades ago and is constantly being reinforced by new research.

Not only the mental but also the emotional and social lives of non-human animals have revealed much greater complexity than previously thought. Parental nurturing, alliances between individuals (biologically related or not), reciprocity, and other complex social behaviors are well-documented in a range of mammal and bird species. Fascinating evidence that some of these behaviors are socially shaped emerges from a study, coordinated by Frans de Waal, in which researchers placed monkeys from two very different species together in order to explore the possibility of changing characteristic modes of social interaction. The researchers put adolescent rhesus monkeys, usually very aggressive, together with slightly older stump-tailed macaques, described by de Waal as an easygoing species that rarely fights and that reconciles readily after conflicts. The stump-tails typically display tolerance or indifference in situations where rhesus monkeys would respond aggressively. When the two species were placed together, the stump-tails' peaceful behavior confused the rhesus monkeys at first, but eventually the latter adopted some of the traits of their stump-tail "tutors." After five months of cohabitation, as de Waal concludes, the experiment "infused a group of monkeys of one species with the 'social culture' of another."[59] De Waal hypothesizes, further, that the rhesus monkeys suppressed aggression or made peace not just because they were imitating the macaques but because they valued their relationships with them: "Rather than a blind process, primate reconciliation is a learned social skill, sensitive to the social configuration of which individuals are part and wielded as an instrument to preserve precious ties."[60] Other studies have revealed complex social arrangements and interactions not only in primates but also in wolves, dolphins, elephants, and ravens, among other animals.

The accumulated impact of ethological research, as Marian Dawkins puts it, has been "a general change in perception of animal behaviour brought about by detailed studies of animals that have revealed far more complexity than was initially imagined."[61] Ethologists seek to explain this complexity in evolutionary terms. Perhaps the most complex behavioral phenomenon that evolution might explain is consciousness, defined as the capacity for intentionality, choice, and flexible behavior. When animals face new and difficult challenges, evolutionary theorists argue, and when stakes are high, conscious evaluation may offer significant adaptive advantages.[62] The piping plover who responds differently to a fox than to a cow, for example, can improve her chances of preserving her offspring. So can the monkey who tailors his social skills to a new context and the wren who makes creative use of novel nesting sites. In these and other cases common in the everyday lives of many species, cognitive skills offer crucial evolutionary advantages. As Colin Allen and Marc Bekoff put it, conscious cognition might "enable organisms to react appropriately *in a variety of circumstances.*"[63] This challenges the behaviorist notion that behavior is more efficient if it is automatic and uncomplicated by conscious thinking, so that there is no reason for consciousness to evolve. Many ethologists now believe that when different options appear, as they do on a daily basis in the lives of most creatures, cognitive abilities to anticipate and choose will help one individual succeed over another who lacks such capacities. Behavioral evidence reinforces the evolutionary or adaptionist suspicion that consciousness appears in many species. Human consciousness may be the most complex manifestation, but it is not unprecedented.

Detailed research also reveals just how much the lives of other species differ from one another. Far from the image of a unitary animal nature, ethology reveals, as Midgley puts it, that "every existing animal species has its *own* nature, its own hierarchy of instincts—in a sense, its own virtues."[64] It makes no sense, in evolutionary, behavioral, or physiological terms, to lump all nonhuman species, from oysters to chimpanzees, together on one side of a line, on the other side of which stand humans alone. Rather, as Dale Jamieson and Marc Bekoff write, ethology increasingly portrays "a world of creatures with different subjectivities leading their own individual lives."[65] The message of ethology, we might summarize, borrowing from Midgley once again, is that many nonhuman animals are "much less different from men than we have supposed. (There is still plenty of difference, but it is a different difference.)"[66] The difference in the difference, we might say, is the shift from a clear and impassable wall to a continuum with fuzzy boundaries and innumerable areas of overlap.

EVOLUTION AND ETHICS

Thus we return once again to the question of humanity's specialness, our supposed capacity to escape the biological "leash," in Wilson's term, that constrains all other species. This issue is intimately tied to the ethical implications of evolutionary theory and especially of human evolution. How is the "is" of human life, as evolution explains it, related to the "ought" of ethics? One possible answer comes from Social Darwinism and eugenics, which see evolution's message for human morality and society as, in essence, might makes right, with the mightier being those deemed fitter by natural selection. A subset of Social Darwinism contends that humans as a whole, rather than a particular group of humans, represent the pinnacle of natural selection ("the top of the food chain") and thus can justify any treatment of those below.[67]

A fundamental problem with these approaches is simply that they get evolutionary theory wrong. Most often they misinterpret the crucial term "fitness." It is true that the core principle of natural selection, as Darwin writes, is unforgiving: "Multiply, vary, let the strongest live and the weakest die."[68] The strongest, however, do not possess any intellectual or moral superiority over all species. Rather, they are the individuals best adapted to a particular niche. Evolution selects for survival and reproduction in specific contexts, not for abstract excellence. Any species that survives and reproduces over many generations, including cockroaches and bacteria as well as lions and humans, proves itself fit for its particular circumstances. Thus, Midgley writes, we cannot insist that it is better to be "a wolf than a polar bear, a jackdaw than a wandering albatross, or a human than any of them."[69] Such assertions lead her to ask "What test have the lives of these creatures failed? The answer, though embarrassing, seems simple—they have failed to become more like ours."[70] Understanding *fit* as a synonym for *human*, in short, grossly misreads evolutionary theory. It is Social Darwinism on the scale of species rather than economic classes.

Another problem with Social Darwinism stems from the move from descriptions of what *is* to prescriptions about what *ought to be,* usually dismissed as the "naturalistic fallacy." This step is clearly problematic when the "is" is inaccurate, as is so often the case in various forms of Social Darwinism. Millionaires do not result from natural selection; Homo sapiens is not the king of beasts. Social constructionists insist that such inaccuracy is inevitable, since any description of "the way things are" is inevitably biased by the describer's own experiences and interests. In this view, the limitations of human perception—the fact that we always shape the reality we interpret—prevent us from ever drawing a truly objective portrait of reality as a whole.

What about a softer constructionism, one that acknowledges that a more accurate reading of evolution, or at least of the latest evidence, is possible? Even in this perspective, naturalistic ethics remain problematic. Critics of the naturalistic fallacy contend that, even if we could correctly describe a particular reality, such a description does not tell us anything definitive about how things ought to be. Human life, *all* life, is fraught with enormous pain. As Richard Dawkins writes, "The total amount of suffering per year in the natural world is beyond all decent contemplation."[71] This suffering, further, is not incidental to the process of natural selection, since "let the strongest live," as Darwin knew, means letting others die. A purely naturalistic ethic would have to find good in pain and death. It would need to draw a moral from the Ichneumonidae wasp's practice (which horrified Darwin) of capturing and paralyzing a caterpillar, then laying its eggs inside the body. The wasp larvae eat the immobilized but still living caterpillar as they develop.[72] Any accurate description of human life would similarly give countless examples of emotional and physical suffering. Like the caterpillar and the wasp, we struggle to survive, avoid pain, and prosper. Evolution, however, has no such goals in mind but blindly selects the fortunate few who are fit enough to engender the next generation.

Evolution is unforgiving, but it is the best story we have about how life developed on earth. We cannot hold that humans are outside its compass without affirming special creation. And if humans are not outside its compass, then evolution must bear on philosophical anthropology and on ethics. The theory of natural selection is too big, too compelling, too implicated in what it means to be human to remain on the sidelines as we think about the Good and the good life for our species. This means we cannot dismiss evolutionary naturalism as an irremediably fallacious resource for ethics. We need to find ways to move from evolutionary theory, as a general description of how the world works, to ethical reasoning and judgment. We must step cautiously, hedging our bets and taking the long way around, but we must look for a way.

In this effort, the work of Mary Midgley is invaluable. In *Beast and Man* (1978; revised 1995) and *The Ethical Primate* (1994), Midgley explores sociobiology's claims about human nature, the opposition to these claims, and the philosophical implications of this debate. She begins with a conviction that evolutionary theory, including sociobiology and its parent field of ethology, makes "very useful contributions to the enquiry about the difficult subject of human motives." Most social scientists and humanists, however, react defensively and "retreat from the whole subject behind the species barrier" at any suggestion that evolution bears on their disciplines.[73] Midgley acknowledges that this retreat stems in part from the crude and provocative language used by some sociobiologists, their apparent celebration of the endless competition among "selfish" organisms making "investments" for their own individual advantage.[74]

Opposition to "biological Thatcherism," however, is not the only reason so many intellectuals object so passionately to sociobiology. Many resist, above all, its challenge to human exceptionalism, to "our unwillingness to accept continuity between ourselves and nature," in Stephen Jay Gould's terms, "our ardent search for a criterion to assert our uniqueness."[75] This uniqueness fades in light of the strong evidence that human beings, no less than other animals, inherit behavioral tendencies as well as anatomical features. If we accept the evidence, a number of implications for philosophy follow. Midgley's reflections provide a good starting point for exploring the ways evolutionary theory can shed light on ethical anthropology.

First and foremost, Midgley writes, evolution tells us that "we are not just rather like animals; we *are* animals."[76] This is the simplest and most self-evident but also the most profound and disturbing claim of Darwinism. It upsets centuries of thinking that humans are something more, something else, something better. Behaving "like an animal" is bad, folk psychology tells us. Philosophers from Aquinas to Descartes to Marx devote pages to explaining just how humans differ from animals. Emancipatory political movements resist the categorizing of some humans—women, natives, blacks—as animals. Evolutionary theory suggests that the problem lies not in categorizing *certain* humans as animals (and understanding *animal* in pejorative terms) but rather in failing to categorize *all* humans as such (and to make *animal* a neutral category). We cannot differ from animals in general any more than a squirrel or a salmon can. This does not mean that we do not differ from *other* animals, just as squirrels and salmon differ from each other, and both from dragonflies. However, opponents of evolutionary interpretations of human nature often seem to prefer binary oppositions—human or animal—to the continuum (or series of overlapping continua) suggested by evolution.[77]

A second claim of evolutionary theory, also with important ethical and philosophical implications, is that whatever humans are, we are all the same kind of animal. This unity stems from our relatively short history as a species. The six million or so years since humans diverged from other apes is brief in evolutionary terms, so that humans as a species are biologically homogeneous. On average, two humans on different continents differ genetically less than two gorillas in the same forest, because, as Chris Stringer and Robin McKie explain, humans "simply have not had time to evolve significantly different patterns of genes."[78] Thus evolutionary theory, despite its misuses in eugenics, can undergird powerful arguments against racially based discrimination.

This counters the constructionist fear that sociobiologists not only wish to blur all differences between humans and other animals but also, paradoxically, to harden the differences *among* humans; for example, among races or between women and men. Without absolving all sociobiologists, it is worth noting that most believe they are proving "the psychic unity of mankind."[79] Thus Edward Wilson argues, in terms that might surprise his critics, that "it is futile to try to define discrete human races. Such entities do not exist." Although certain traits such as height and skin color vary genetically by locale, he explains, additional variation within regions means that we cannot identify separate races. He concludes that "almost all differences between human societies are based on learning and social conditioning rather than on heredity."[80] Without denying the significance of Wilson's "almost," the cause of so much sound and fury, it is hard to read this as crude biological determinism.

A third inescapable conclusion of evolution is that we are kin to all species and life forms. Darwin hinted at this with his idea of a single primordial ancestor and his rejection of the notion of fixed, discrete species. This continuity not only denies humans the distance and exceptionalness that mainstream Western thought has accorded our species but also highlights the complexity of other forms of life, especially other animals, our more or less close relatives. Other species are also intricate, marvelous constructions, shaped by and shaping our shared environments and our shared genes. An evolutionary perspective need not deny human distinctiveness, but it also insists, first, that our continuities with the rest of life are as important as our differences and, second, that other species are just as distinctive, just as fit to their own lives, as we are to ours. Evolution teaches, further, that we are not only related to other life-forms but also dependent upon them and on the processes and substances of our common environments. The philosophical and ethical implications of this claim are clear: the vision of humans as atomistic and unprecedented lords over a distant "nature" cannot survive evolutionary science's portrait of the complex, intimate relations among humans, other species, and the physical environment.

ECOLOGY

The scientific study of these complex and fragile interdependencies among organisms and between organisms and their physical environments is known as ecology. The term *ecology* (*Oecologie* in German) was first coined in 1866 by the German evolutionist Ernst Haeckel, who drew on the Greek *oikos,* meaning household, also the root of "economy." Ecology, then, is the study of nature's economy. As a science, it rests heavily on evolutionary theory. As Donald Worster argues, Darwin is "the single most important figure in the history of ecology over the past two or three centuries."[81] Evolution explains not only how but why organisms are connected to each other in such varied, intimate, and necessary ways. In Darwin's own words, "The structure of every organic being is related, in the most essential yet often hidden manner, to that of all other organic beings, with which it comes into competition for food or residence, or from which it has to escape, or on which it preys."[82]

This quotation emphasizes competition, a major theme not only for Darwin but for many ecologists, who place antagonistic contests at the center of present ecological relations among and within species, as in the evolutionary history of these relations. Competition is the key, for example, to the well-known idea of the food chain, introduced by Charles Elton in the 1920s. The food chain defines relations among different species in an ecosystem in terms of the intrinsically competitive relationship between predators and prey (including most plants in the latter category). Elton also introduced the important concept of niche, meaning a particular organism's lifestyle, "the group of strategies it employs to obtain the food, water, shelter, mating spots, and other necessities that it must have to survive."[83] Species generally divide up niches within a given habitat or region, and competition ensues if two or more different species (or individuals of the same species) seek to occupy the same niche. Elton believed that each species required a completely separate niche, a principle he termed "competitive exclusion."[84]

The heavy emphasis on competition assumed a fixity in nature that the theory of evolution, with its continual expansion of diversity, contradicts. Another Darwinian theme, the principle of divergence, helps clarify the immense variety of life on earth. Worster writes, divergence is "nature's way of getting round the fiercely competitive struggle for limited resources." If all organisms are fixed types, each seeking the same resources, conflict is inevitable. In contrast, "deviance from the norm could open a more peaceful route and a well-rewarded one; the organism that was born different and found a way to use its uniqueness might establish itself without the need for competition. One might, that is, create one's own special place that none had ever occupied before—and not at the expense of another's survival." Darwin saw the principle of divergence in action in the Galapagos when different varieties of finches did not just fill stereotyped places that had no occupants as yet but actually created "new places for themselves in a new environment. Similarly, the evolution of a new kind of grass may create a series of new niches for animals still undeveloped, and they in turn may someday serve as prey for new species of predators—all occurring without competition."[85]

Building on the idea of divergence, a number of scientists have claimed harmony and balance rather than strife and death as the guiding principle of ecological relationships. This emphasis, no less than the stress on competition, often assumed that the laws of nature somehow embodied guidelines or moral values that human society should emulate. This raises again the specter of the naturalistic fallacy, what Worster calls the often-recycled idea that "the 'Is' of nature must become the 'Ought' of man."[86] For example, many socially progressive ecologists of the 1930s, rejecting the brutality of monopoly capitalism, looked to nature for a model of harmonious collective existence. From this perspective, as Walter Taylor declared in 1935, ecology shows "there is little rugged individualism in nature," but rather the natural community acts as "a closely organized cooperative commonwealth of plants and animals . . . [which] is more nearly an individual organism than any of its parts."[87]

Taylor links the emphasis on cooperation rather than conflict to another important debate within ecology, that between organismic (or holistic) and reductive models. The view of nature as a whole greater than its parts, an organism in itself, has existed for centuries, as seen in the Romantic writings of the nineteenth century as well as in scientific models. The pioneering ecologist Frederic Clements, for example, understood ecological relations as progressing toward a "climax community," which he saw as a kind of superorganism, greater than its parts. Presently the Gaia hypothesis advanced by James Lovelock and Lynn Margulis holds that the earth itself is a living organism, with its own regulatory mechanisms.[88] While these organismic models have not disappeared, for the past few centuries they have competed with models based on the physical sciences. A major contemporary challenge has come from approaches that identify physical processes, especially the recycling of energy, gases, and nutrients, as the core of ecological relations.

Debates continue within ecology regarding competition versus cooperation and organistic versus physics-based paradigms, among other issues. One common emphasis in all the models, however, is interdependence among organisms and between organisms and the physical environment. Ernest Callenbach summarizes this theme in the first two of four often-cited "laws" of ecology: "All things are interconnected" and "Everything goes somewhere."[89] The precise nature of these connections, exactly where things go, and what consequences they have when they get there are what contemporary ecological science continues to explore and debate.

Complicating the process is the application to ecology of chaos theory, which first emerged in physics. According to this approach, disturbance and randomness, rather than order and balance, characterize ecosystems. This is exemplified by the "butterfly effect," the idea that "a butterfly stirring the air today in a Chinese park can transform the storm systems appearing next month over a North American city." This means that "tiny differences in input might quickly become substantial differences in output." However, we cannot know "every one of the tiny differences that were occurring at any place or any point in time; and even if we could, we still could not know which tiny differences would produce which particular substantial differences in output."[90]

The butterfly effect has profound implications for ecology. How can ecologists possibly know about all the forces impinging on any community of organisms? Which forces should they ignore and which should they study? While chaos theory thickened the plot, however, most ecologists did not conclude that all natural systems are totally random. An emerging approach known as "complexity theory" brings together different models to demonstrate that nature includes chaos and disorder as well as order. Further, order is more difficult to locate and describe than had been thought, and will "always have an unruly element of indeterminacy in it." Ordered and chaotic states, in addition, are "all connected in a continuous spectrum."[91] Thus even emerging scientific theories of chaos and complexity, which challenge previous assumptions about the essentially stable and ordered nature of ecosystems, share the emphasis on interdependence that is probably the single most important theme of ecological science.[92]

ECOLOGY AND HUMAN NATURE

What does ecology tell us about human nature or the self? First and foremost, it insists that we depend upon other animal and plant species and upon the physical environment and its processes. This interdependence means not only that we are affected by changes in climate, for example, or loss of species diversity but also that our actions affect other species and the environment as a whole. As the "laws" of ecology put it, in nature not only does everything go somewhere, but "there's no such thing as a free lunch."[93] All our actions, all the actions of any organism, have impacts and costs.

Beyond a general assertion of interdependence, a number of environmental philosophers argue that ecological science leads to specific conclusions about human nature. Baird Callicott has articulated a strong challenge to Western individualism based on contemporary ecology, especially field ontology. This model, which draws heavily on contemporary physics, describes living natural objects as subordinate to events or flow patterns. In this view, as Harold Morovitz explains, "each living thing . . . does not endure in and of itself but only as a result of the continual flow of energy in the system."[94] Thus, Morovitz adds, "the reality of individuals is problematic because they do not exist per se but only as local perturbations in this universal energy flow."[95] Individual organisms, including human beings, are moments in the network or pattern, inconceivable apart from the larger field in which they exist. Callicott ties this approach to evolutionary explanations of the ways species adapt to niches in particular ecosystems: "A species has the particular characteristics that it has because those characteristics result from its adaptation to a *niche* in an eco*system*."[96] The nature of the part, in other words, is determined by its relationship to the whole.

Callicott concludes that the self, in ecological perspective, "is a nexus of strands in the web of life. More formally, any entity (oneself included), from an ecological point of view, is a node in a matrix of internal relations."[97] This notion is taken even further in Deep Ecology, which insists that individuals must be understood in light of the "relational field," or, in Arne Naess's terms, "the totality of our interrelated experience" in general. This implies, Naess argues, that relationships "define the thing conceptually."[98] As Callicott points out, Naess's Deep Ecology revives the metaphysical doctrine of internal relations, the idea "that a thing's essence is exhaustively determined by its relationships, that it cannot be conceived apart from its relationships with other things."[99] According to Naess, we cannot even speak of the interactions between organisms and their environment or milieu, because "an *organism is interaction*. Organisms and milieu are not two things—if a mouse were lifted into an absolute vacuum, it would no longer be a mouse. Organisms presuppose milieu." This holds true not just for mice but also for human beings: "A person is a part of nature to the extent that he or she too is a relational junction within the total field."[100] This represents, perhaps, the logical extreme of the more general ecological insistence that humans, like all other individual organisms, exist only within tightly connected webs of interdependence. This challenges not only individualism but also forms of social constructionism that accept the fluidity and contingency of persons only in relation to society and culture. Ecological and evolutionary science show that humans are also the product of ecological flows and forces, which are as variable, fluid, and unpredictable as social processes. Understanding humanness in relation to nature, this suggests, need not lead to the static, reductive portrait that some constructionists fear.

ECOLOGY AND ETHICS

Ecological understandings of human nature, like their evolutionary counterparts, yield important ethical implications. According to Naess, ecology demands that humans strive for a process of increasingly wider self-identification, "in which the relations which define the junction expand to comprise more and more."[101] In this view, as I will discuss in the next chapter, no sense of duty is required, for an expanded self will recognize that preserving the natural world and other species is in its own self-interest. Many other environmental philosophers also use some version of ecological science to ground ethical claims. Ecofeminists Karen Warren and Jim Cheney, for example, argue for the philosophical relevance of hierarchy theory, which focuses on the idea of an observation set, "a particular way of viewing the natural world." An observation set "includes the phenomena of interest, the specific measurements taken, and the techniques used to analyze the data."[102] Warren and Cheney contend that hierarchy theory in ecology shares a number of features with ecofeminism. Ecofeminism and ecological science agree, for example, that the context of knowledge "will quite literally shape and affect what one sees; both provide a context for theorizing." Thus there can be no single best point of view or any most accurate description of "reality." Both ecofeminism and hierarchy theory also value pluralism and relate various analyses to each other in "a unity which does not erase difference." Further, Warren and Cheney contend, hierarchy theory and ecofeminism agree that there are no "degrees of reality." Neither individuals nor wholes are less real than, or reducible to, the other. Rather, both are real and are intimately tied together.[103]

Warren and Cheney insist that ecofeminism, while rejecting the possibility of an ahistorical, context-free, neutral observation stance, still values empirical research and makes good scientific sense. The effort to ground philosophy on ecological science has also motivated other environmental philosophers, such as Aldo Leopold, Baird Callicott, and Holmes Rolston. Leopold drew on his experience as a naturalist and wildlife manager, as well as on his studies in the natural sciences, to develop an ethic based on a view of "land as a biotic mechanism."[104] Leopold rejected predator control, for example, because of his growing conviction that a healthy ecosystem requires the presence of all native species. He drew on ecological knowledge as the source of guidelines for human interactions with other species. Rolston makes the relation between ecological knowledge and environmental ethics even more direct: "A morally satisfactory fit must be a biologically satisfactory fit. What *ought to be* is derived from what *is*."[105]

This naturalism has led Callicott, Rolston, Leopold, and many other environmental philosophers to argue against efforts to reduce individual suffering in the natural world. Their naturalistic ethics rest not on a romantic notion that nature is always kind but on the conviction that even though nature is often "red in tooth and claw," it is as it should be. Humans should not interfere, not even by trying to reduce suffering. Thus Callicott asserts that pain, worry, and death are "the way the system works. If nature as a whole is good, then pain and death are also good. Environmental ethics in general require people to play fair in the natural system."[106] The efforts of "humane moralists" (by which he means especially animal rights advocates) to project human social values (such as preserving life against the odds) onto the nonhuman world are mistaken. Rolston agrees: "That [suffering] ought not to continue is a tender sentiment but so remote from the way the world *is* that we must ask whether this is the way the world *ought* to be in a tougher, realistic environmental ethic."[107] This "tougher" ethic takes not the elimination of pain but rather "satisfactory fitness" as "a criterion for some moral judgments." It leads us, Rolston says, to "endorse a painful good."[108]

This painful good is tied to the holism of ecosystems, which some environmental philosophers take to be a necessary conclusion of ecological science (although others, like Warren and Cheney, explicitly reject this form of holism). As Callicott summarizes it, "From an ecological perspective, relations are 'prior to' the things related, and the systemic wholes woven from these relations are prior to their component parts. Ecosystemic wholes are logically prior to their component species because the nature of the part is determined by its relationship to the whole."[109] In ethical terms, this holism suggests that individual organisms must sometimes be sacrificed for the whole, that individual "specimens can claim no legitimate right to life in an economy of nature in which one being purchases life only at the expense of the life of others."[110]

While individuals might have few claims in the economy of nature, most ethicists, environmental and other, reject this sort of holism as a rule for human social life. Thus Rolston sidesteps the question of human social relations: "Nature is not a moral agent; we do not imitate nature for interhuman conduct."[111] It is not clear, however, on what grounds we can justify this move. If humans are intimately related, in evolutionary and ecological terms, to the rest of nature, then why do entirely different sources and scales of value operate in the human and social realms? Faced with this question, Callicott is one of the few environmental ethicists who has, at least partially, been willing to extend holistic naturalism to the human sphere. He writes that we ought to "reaffirm our participation in nature by accepting life as it is given without a sugar coating. . . . accept and affirm natural biological laws, principles, and limitations in the human personal and social spheres."[112]

Such an extension inevitably raises hackles, and even charges of fascism, from many quarters.[113] How can we justify accepting limits, such as premature (or even mature) death, among human beings? To many, "accepting life as it is given without a sugar coating" echoes Social Darwinist arguments in favor of letting the poor die off to "improve the species." However, Rolston's avoidance of the question is no less problematic, if we take seriously what evolution and ecology tell us about human life. If we are related to and dependent on the rest of nature, where and on what grounds do we draw a line between environmental and social ethics? Why are we allowed, or even required, to separate suffering and death in nature from suffering and death in human social life? Are biological laws suspended in the case of a premature human infant who will die without extraordinary medical intervention, but not in that of an injured baby squirrel? Are some features of natural ecosystems, such as interdependence and diversity, relevant values for human social life, while others, such as suffering and death, are not and should be rejected? Are there ever occasions on which we might accept pain and death in human life? (Just-war theory claims that under certain conditions even Christians might justifiably kill.) Are there ever occasions on which we should struggle against pain and death in nonhuman life? These questions are crucial at many levels, from the very practical (setting policies, making individual lifestyle decisions) to the very abstract (what kinds of beings have intrinsic value?). They are also questions for which evolutionary and ecological knowledge make a difference.

The problem is understanding the kind of difference they make. Because humans are cultural animals, and ethics are cultural products, we cannot move simply or directly from nature to human value. One reason naturalism is so often seen as fallacious by definition is that many philosophical naturalists have tried to make the move from *is* to *ought* look straightforward, when in reality it is always a messy and subjective process. It requires a number of intermediate steps and decisions—about which facts to consider important, where we look for them, who is authorized to identify them, and so forth. However, because we are products not only of culture but also of nature, simply rejecting naturalism suspends or displaces certain facts that might be important to keep front and center. For example, both natural selection and the survival of ecosystems require that most organisms produce far more offspring than can survive to reproductive maturity. This fact is unproblematic for environmental ethicists, who immediately recognize that if, say, all the deer ever born in a given forest survived, the forest itself and all the species that depend on it, including the deer, would soon die. Thus many, perhaps even most, young deer *must* die before reproducing, and many others must die before the end of their "natural" lives.

Applied to social ethics, this logic is far from unproblematic, for most environmental ethicists no less than "humane moralists." The consensus, expressed in secular notions of universal human rights and the religious idea that every person is precious to God, is that every individual *human* life should be saved, at almost any cost. While this principle is very far from consistent in application, efforts to improve infant mortality, along with increases in consumption, technology, and other factors, have succeeded so brilliantly that we are now crowding the planet and threatening all the species that depend on it. No environmental ethicist argues for culling humans the way "nature managers" routinely cull deer (in the absence of nonhuman predators that earlier managers eliminated). Few environmentalists advocate forced human sterilization, although many hope for voluntary contraception. In the light of ecological science, though, it is not self-evident why, for example, population control for the good of the whole should be voluntary for humans but mandatory for deer. Environmentalists are deeply divided on these questions. Most believe that having one child is acceptable; some accept two, others any number at all. Most argue that it would not be acceptable to kill the last remaining Florida panthers in a "recreational" hunt. However, most would accept killing a panther (the last panther?) attacking a child (though not one killing a deer). Other environmental issues raise equally thorny moral questions. Is it acceptable to drive a sports utility vehicle, given what we know about their contribution to global warming? Is it acceptable to drive at all? What sorts of limits, in short, can and should be placed on human behavior in order to preserve healthy ecosystems? Which human values take precedence over healthy ecosystems?

These questions have no easy answers. However, they are not merely rhetorical. Again, if we take evolution and ecology seriously, we must accept that humans are both natural creatures and obviously cultural ones. Sorting out the relations between natural and cultural dimensions of human life is a difficult but necessary task for ethics. In many cases, the goals of social life conflict with the "laws of nature" as understood by evolutionary and ecological science. This conflict leads some ethicists to reject naturalism entirely. Among environmental philosophers committed to ecological and evolutionary knowledge, the conflict usually leads to a split, exemplified by Rolston, between the painful good of nature, which is to be accepted, and the pain in human social life, which by definition is *not* good and should not be accepted. Only a few philosophers, notably Callicott, are willing to extend naturalism to social ethics. I do not argue that any particular type of naturalism is the best conclusion in the face of the moral problems posed by ecology and evolution. However, we cannot reject all forms of naturalism out of hand if we are to face these questions head-on. In ethics, as in anthropology, we need to continue pressing for a nonreductive naturalism capable of taking seriously both the natural and the cultural dimensions of our lives.

CHAPTER EIGHT

In and Of the World

Toward a Chastened
Constructionist Anthropology

This chapter sketches some qualities of humanness that undergird the ethical vision presented in the next chapter. These qualities include the following: humans are both natural and cultural animals; we are terrestrial; we are embodied; and we are relational. Moreover, all these characteristics must be viewed in the context of limits, especially our dependence on fragile ecosystems. Although these claims appear simple, they hold tremendous, often radical implications for the way we think about being human. Before proceeding, I offer some caveats. Most important, these characteristics do not encompass all that humans are. Nor are all, or perhaps any, of the features I describe exclusively human. For example, we are also rational, conscious, playful, and willful, among many other things, and other animals are some of these things also. Contrary to the traditional pattern of defining humanness in terms of uniqueness, I contend that qualities need not be exclusive to be important. In fact, some of our most important traits are important precisely because they are shared—with other people or other species or both. (This does not, however, deny that some human characteristics may be quantitatively or even qualitatively distinctive.)

In sketching this anthropological framework, I draw on the approaches discussed in earlier chapters—namely, social constructionist, Asian, Native American, feminist, and scientific perspectives—without attempting to synthesize or unify them. I approach the traditions for the light they shed on ethical anthropology generally and for their perspectives on particular issues: for example, the ways Asian traditions help us understand relationality and the ways feminists rethink the body. I also look at several of these issues in relation to Christian theological anthropology, especially the work of contemporary eco-theologians. Despite the negative aspects of traditional Christian thinking about nature and human nature, as discussed in chapter 2, I believe that Christianity can play an important role in the construction of an alternative ethical anthropology. First, Christianity's damaging influence in the past suggests that if even Christianity can change, there is indeed hope for new attitudes toward the natural world. Further, Christianity's global compass means that its changes might have far-reaching effects. However, Christianity's influence stems not just from its scope but also from its character as a lived or embodied ethical system, an issue I explore in more depth in the next chapter. Looking at the ways, often incomplete and tentative, in which contemporary Christian theologians are trying to rethink their tradition in relation to some of the themes I highlight here can illuminate not only Christianity's possibilities but also ethical anthropology more generally.[1]

NATURE AND NURTURE

Evolution tells us that humans are animals and, further, that we are animals of a particular and unified kind. If we are to take evolution seriously, these assumptions hardly seem debatable, despite all the controversy they cause. They constitute the minimal, necessary starting point for any discussion of what it means to be human, at least in relation to environmental ethics. A look at our evolutionary history shows, further, that as animals we have many overlapping bonds of kinship with other species: we possess many generally mammalian traits, other distinctively primate characteristics, and still other specifically human qualities. The last category, of course, generates all the debates about what separates humans from other animals. A more realistic and productive question asks what distinguishes us *among* animals. Humans have physical traits such as bipedalism, opposable thumbs, and color vision, none of which are exclusively human, but which combined help define our nature. Another defining feature is, of course, culture. The interactions between nature (genes, biology) and culture (nurture, learning, socialization) construct us as distinctively human creatures. Few observers, from evolutionary biologists to postmodernist anthropologists, disagree with this general statement. Many also define culture as a distinctive second evolutionary path in which learning and social memory, rather than genes, carry information, and in which humans adapt to their environment, often very quickly, rather than adapting to it slowly and biologically. However, the specifics of the interactions between biology and culture, their respective influences and the paths they take, are far from settled. The debate over these issues provides, in some ways, an overarching framework in which to understand many other aspects of humanness. I will examine here two influential and in some respects characteristic positions on the nature-nurture relationship: social constructionism and sociobiology. These do not, of course, exhaust the continuum, but they shed light on some central issues at stake in rethinking our nature, our naturalness, and the ways nurture and nature combine to define and create humanness.

As noted in chapter 3, the anthropologist Clifford Geertz is one of the most influential and articulate defenders of the constructionist position. Geertz rejects the notion of a universal human nature, either as reality or as heuristic device. We do not need and should not want, he writes, a "lowest-common-denominator view of humanity" that holds that "what it means to be human is most clearly revealed in those features of human culture that are universal rather than those that are distinctive to this people or that." The only kind of people, Geertz insists, are distinctive ones, and they are distinctive all the way to the core, not merely in their surface adornments. Thus Geertz decisively rejects the Enlightenment quest for a "common" human nature beneath the trappings of culture. He summarizes by saying, "Men unmodified by the customs of particular places do not in fact exist, have never existed, and most important, could not in the very nature of the case exist." More concisely he states, "There is no such thing as a human nature independent of culture."[2]

Geertz bases his argument on a further claim. Humans, unlike other animals, depend upon culture for their completion, both as individuals and as a species. For individuals, Geertz argues, culture provides a set of "control mechanisms," akin to plans, recipes, instructions, or rules, which govern behavior. Humans are "desperately dependent upon such extragenetic, outside-the-skin control mechanisms, such cultural programs, for ordering [their] behavior."[3] Geertz defines this dependence as a biological fact: humans are unable to develop or to survive in isolation from public symbol systems—in short, from culture.[4] This is because humans, in contrast to all other species, have only very general instincts or innate behaviors. This allows for great plasticity and complexity but leaves our behavior very imprecisely regulated. As a result, without the direction of culture, or "organized systems of significant symbols," human behavior would be "virtually ungovernable, a mere chaos of pointless acts and exploding emotions." Culture, again, "is not just an ornament of human existence but . . . an essential condition for it."[5] The unfinished character of human nature makes culture both possible and necessary: "What sets [man] off most graphically from nonmen is less his sheer ability to learn (great as that is) than how much and what particular sorts of things he *has* to learn before he is able to function at all."

This biological incompleteness, in turn, stems from the distinctive character of human evolution, which, Geertz insists, is not only cultural and physical but *simultaneously* cultural and physical. In other words, he believes that mental evolution and cultural evolution were not two separate processes, with the first completed before the second began, but that "the transition to the cultural mode of life took the genus *Homo* several million years to accomplish; and stretched out in such a manner, it involved not one or a handful of marginal genetic changes but a long, complex, and closely ordered sequence of them." Thus "culture, rather than being added on, so to speak, to a finished or virtually finished animal, was ingredient and centrally ingredient, in the production of that animal itself." As culture developed step-by-step, encompassing tools, hunting and gathering, family organization, fire, and symbol systems, humans created a new environment, which in turn gave a selective advantage to the individuals most able to take advantage of it: "Quite literally, though quite inadvertently, [man] created himself."[6] This view of evolution demonstrates, according to Geertz, that *Homo sapiens* as a species required cultural evolution to complete its transition into modern humanity, just as individual humans require culture—in the form of nurturing, social learning, public language, and symbols—to complete their development.

Geertz does not deny that physical evolution and biological structures play a role in shaping humanness, but he contends that these natural features and culture are separated by a long and twisted path: "Between the basic ground plans for our life that our genes lay down—the capacity to speak or to smile—and the precise behavior we in fact execute . . . lies a complex set of significant symbols under whose direction we transform the first into the second, the ground plans into the activity."[7] On the face of it, this claim need not contradict Edward O. Wilson's insistence that biology helps determine human nature. For Wilson, "What is truly unique about human evolution, as opposed say to chimpanzee or wolf evolution, is that a large part of the environment shaping it has been cultural." In other words, "to genetic evolution the human lineage has added the parallel track of cultural evolution, and . . . the two forms of evolution are linked." Wilson also contends, again in accord with Geertz and other constructionists, that virtually all of human behavior is transmitted by culture. Geertz might agree, further, with Wilson's claim that human biology has an important effect on the origins of culture and its transmission—that genes and culture together helped select for the traits that came to define *Homo sapiens*. Both ask, as Wilson puts it, What "joins the deep, mostly genetic history of the species as a whole to the more recent cultural histories of its far-flung societies?"[8]

Despite their agreement on the importance of this question, Geertz and Wilson offer answers that reveal significant differences between the two positions, culturalist and naturalist, that they represent. Geertz insists that culture finishes both human evolution and individual human development, while Wilson argues for a stronger and more specific role for genetic factors, as expressed in his understanding of gene-culture coevolution. Gene-culture coevolution begins when genes prescribe epigenetic rules, "the regularities of sensory perception and mental development that animate and channel the acquisition of culture." Then culture helps determine "which of the prescribing genes survive and multiply from one generation to the next." Successful new genes change the epigenetic rules of populations, and these altered epigenetic rules, finally, change "the direction and effectiveness of the channels of cultural acquisition."[9] What this last step means is that biologically based epigenetic rules connect genes to culture by biasing cultural evolution in one direction and not another.

To clarify this process, Wilson offers an example of the ways an epigenetic rule for innovation might have evolved. First, over thousands of generations of human evolution, people's varying capacities for innovation caused individual differences in survival and reproductive success. Second, this variation was, at least in part, passed on to offspring, so that people varied in their "hereditary propensity to learn certain things." Genetic evolution inevitably ensued: natural selection favored the "gene ensembles" that made some individuals more innovative. Ultimately, "universals or near universals emerged in the evolution of culture." For Wilson, these universals include not only innovativeness but also a tendency toward certain forms and themes. This bias is not total, Wilson insists: it only sets broad parameters, within which art and other

forms of culture are freely constructed. Similar processes of natural selection, reinforced by culture, led to epigenetic rules such as fear of
snakes, mother-infant bonding, basic taste preferences, color vision, bi-
narism, the tendency to reify concepts, basic facial expressions, and pho-
neme constructions.[10] Even the most hardened constructionists could
hardly object to some of these, such as color vision. However, some of
Wilson's other suggestions, such as the tendency to think in binary terms,
face challenges even from committed evolutionists.

Wilson argues that many of these challenges, along with more sweep-
ing rejections of biological imagery of origins of human nature, stem
from a misunderstanding of gene-culture coevolution that confuses it
with "rigid genetic determination."[11] It is possible, Wilson insists, to
combine a conviction that biological evolution (genes, epigenetic rules)
helps determine human behavior and a sophisticated understanding of
complex, tortuous, and multiple links between genes and culture. Geertz
would agree both that human nature, in individuals and in the entire
species, emerges from interactions between biological and cultural factors and that these interactions are far from simple or straightforward.
Again, however, he and Wilson approach this complexity, and the ultimate meaning of these interactions, with very different assumptions
and emphases.

These differences become clearer when we look at the ways Wilson
and Geertz respond to the paradoxical fact that, as Wilson puts it, "At
the same time that culture arises from human action, human action
arises from culture."[12] Both acknowledge the truth of the paradox, but
their efforts to resolve it reveal fundamental disagreements. Geertz answers the paradox with a straightforward assertion of human exceptionalism: humans, and only humans, "create themselves," becoming
"artifacts" of the environment they themselves have created. This claim,
as noted in chapter 3, suffers from serious internal contradictions. While
Geertz and hard constructionists claim to avoid defining human nature
by some essential feature, in the end they merely redescribe the vital
principle. For Geertz, human exceptionalism results from a unique biological and evolutionary incompleteness that requires humans to invent
themselves, as individuals and as a species. Our unique need and ability
to finish ourselves, Geertz explicitly states, make us human. Our "des-
perate" dependence on culture "is what we really have in common."[13]
Ultimately, lack becomes the essential character of humanity, or, as Carl
Esbjornson puts it, "absence" replaces "essence."[14]

In addition to the internal contradictions of hard constructionism,

Geertz's position suffers from a failure to take seriously the biological grounds of human behavior, the reality of biological universals as well as cultural particularities.[15] This stems, perhaps, from the common culturalist fear that both the worth and the freedom of human beings would be undermined, even destroyed, if we did not completely transcend our biological moorings. This fear rests on a series of assumptions: first, value requires uniqueness, so shared traits cannot be intrinsically valuable; second, biological features are unchangeable and thus limit our freedom; and finally, culture and genes (nurture and nature) are opposed to each other, so we must choose one or the other as being definitive of human nature. All these assumptions are faulty, and together they lead to the erroneous but widespread conclusion that taking human distinctiveness seriously requires divorcing human behavior and culture from biology and physical evolution.

Wilson points to an alternative way of resolving the paradoxical relationship between culture and human action and, thus, of rethinking human distinctiveness. He notes that countless species, from termites to elephants, help construct the environments in which they live. There exist, in other words, various forms of reciprocity between environment and behavior, from the relatively simple ways that certain insects create the kind of soil in which they need to live to the infinite complexity of human societies. While human culture is by definition unique, Wilson argues, the underlying principle of gene-environment coevolution is the same.[16] This argument is tied to another revealing area of difference between him and Geertz: their attitudes to nonhuman behavior. Geertz radically distinguishes humans from "lower animals," whose behavior is largely determined by "genetic sources of information" and constrained within "much narrower ranges of variation, the narrower and more thoroughgoing the lower the animal."[17] Despite his sharp critiques of Enlightenment rationality on some topics, on this point Geertz echoes Descartes: other animals all have "instructions coded in their genes and evoked by appropriate patterns of external stimuli: physical keys inserted into organic locks."[18]

Geertz's mechanistic and reductive portrayal of nonhuman species contrasts sharply, as it is meant to, with the endless possibilities of human behavior. It also clashes with Wilson's claims of continuity among humans and other animals. Wilson argues that all animals, including humans, are innately prepared to learn some behaviors and predisposed to avoid others.[19] He calls this "prepared learning," a subset of epigenetic rules of behavior. The particular things that humans are prepared to learn, such as speaking a language or making and using tools, distinguish us among animals. However, we share with other species the more general or underlying fact that we are prepared to learn some things and not others. Cats, for example, are prepared to learn to hunt small rodents, and songbirds are prepared to learn particular tunes. However, the fulfillment of these innate potentials, like the acquisition of language by human children, requires external conditions or triggers, which range from intensive training by parents to environmental factors such as sufficient territory.

It is important to keep in mind here that, as noted in chapter 7, not all things that are universal or nearly so need to be biologically grounded, at least in the specific sense that Wilson often suggests. Whereas many species-typical behaviors, like hunting in cats, might have genetic bases while still depending upon external conditions, other equally typical behaviors might represent what Dennett calls Good Tricks, which individuals and groups discover with the help of their general capacities or preferences. Members of a species or population may invent a trick again and again in each new generation, or a group may discover a trick once and transmit it through teaching or socialization.[20] Conversely, the existence of Good Tricks does not mean that all shared human characteristics are simply tricks of individual ingenuity or cultural transmission. In other words, we do not need to choose between biology and culture in making sense of human nature. Acceptance of this false dualism weakens both hard constructionist and hard naturalist positions.

How far apart are the arguments of constructionists, represented by Geertz, and the naturalists, represented by Wilson? Is there any way they might be reconciled, or at least made to seem less distant than they appear? Geertz himself offers some clues when he asserts that it need not be "contradictory to say that one and the same occurrence is governed by mechanical laws and moral principles."[21] In other words, we can and must allow multiple explanations for complex behaviors and phenomena. Geertz adds that we should approach the relations between various aspects of human existence not in a "stratigraphic" way, in which different aspects (physical, mental, cultural) are seen as layers one upon the other, but rather within a synthetic framework that identifies various factors as variables within overarching systems of analysis. In sum, says Geertz, "We need to look for systematic relationships among diverse phenomena."[22] This suggests (although Geertz himself does not follow through) that thinking about human nature requires diverse sources of knowledge and types of analysis. No single feature can define what it means to be human, and no single principle can explain all the different aspects of humanness, including cultural diversity and biological universals.

One attempt at this pluralism is the "nonreductive physicalism" articulated by various philosophers, theologians, and scientists. While these thinkers differ among themselves, they share a commitment to biological explanations of human behavior and life generally without restricting all explanation to biology. Francisco Ayala chooses the example of ethical behavior as a distinctively human trait that has both biological and cultural explanations. He contends that biological evolution generated distinctive intellectual capacities in humans, specifically the ability to anticipate the consequences of one's actions, the capacity to make value judgments (seeing some objects or deeds as more desirable than others), and the ability to choose among alternative courses of action. These in turn made possible ethical behavior, which he defines (rather narrowly) as "the proclivity to judge human actions as either good or evil." Ayala concludes that "the proclivity to make ethical judgments, that is, to evaluate actions as either good or evil, is rooted in our (biological) nature, a necessary outcome of our exalted intelligence," but "the moral codes that guide our decisions as to which actions are good and which ones are evil are products of culture, including social and religious traditions." He sees ethical behavior as analogous to language: the general capacity (to learn language or to make ethical judgments) rests on biological grounds, but the specific content (a particular language or ethical norm) results from culture.[23]

The nonreductive physicalism articulated by Ayala and others takes biological evolution seriously as a factor in human behavior while also accounting for distinctively human features, especially those associated with culture, such as ethics, art, science, literature, and religion. It tries to balance the sociobiological interest in the evolutionary bases of behavior with the constructionist attention to cultural diversity and free will. A number of Christian theologians have contributed to this effort to identify the systematic relationships among diverse aspects of human nature, and particularly to rethink the nature-nurture relationship in light of evolutionary theory and contemporary scientific knowledge. One of the most detailed approaches is that of the Lutheran theologian Philip Hefner, who seeks to articulate "a theological anthropology that takes seriously a biocultural evolutionary model within the physical ecosystem." Hefner argues that humans are thoroughly natural creatures who have emerged in and through biological evolution, which has given us a constitution informed by both genetic and cultural material. We are, as Hefner summarizes it, "biologically formed culture-creators,"[24] or, in theological terms, "created co-creators."

Hefner's anthropology rests on the model of biocultural evolution, which sees humans as the result of two streams of information, one inherited and genetic, the other cultural. Although the notion of two streams is common, in basic terms, to both Wilson and Geertz, Hefner offers a distinctive analysis of the relationship between the two. Like Wilson, he emphasizes evolutionary processes, agreeing with the sociobiological claim that "natural selection has built us, and it is natural selection we must understand if we are to comprehend our own identities."[25] Hefner's approval of this thesis suggests the greater weight he gives to biological factors compared to constructionists like Geertz. Like Wilson, Hefner identifies biology as the ultimate factor that constrains and enables human possibilities: "For humans the genetic agent has both mandated the necessity and provided the possibility for cultural reality, just as it holds the final cards in the game of life." Hefner specifically rejects "supernaturalism," which denies the significance of natural selection and posits "that the destiny of the human being lies elsewhere, in a realm outside the order of creation, in such a way as to devalue the evolutionary realm in which selection occurs."[26]

Hefner's characterization of humans as created suggests not only the genetic components of a two-natured creature but also our dependence on an ecosystem. For humans to be created, he writes, means that "they exist within, and for the sake of, the matrix of creation within which they have emerged."[27] Humans depend not only on their genetic inheritance but also on the physical world in which they live. This dependence, however, does not deny humans a significant and distinctive degree of independence. In this sense, Hefner insists that humans are not just created but are also "cocreators" with God. The two aspects are inescapably tied together in his model: neither term adequately describes humanness in the absence of the other. Thus, despite his emphasis on evolution, Hefner differs from both Wilson and Geertz in his description of evolution and of the unique creativity that marks human nature in theological terms. For Hefner, we are created proximately by natural selection but ultimately by and for God.

His conviction about humans' special purpose shapes Hefner's insistence that humans are cocreators, not just creative. While other species might also be creative in various ways, "human beings are God's created co-creators whose purpose is to be the agency, acting in freedom, to birth the future that is most wholesome for the nature that has birthed us—the nature that is not only our own genetic heritage, but also the entire human community and the evolutionary and ecological reality in which and to which we belong. Exercising this agency is said to be God's will for humans." In exercising their agency, their distinctive kind of freedom, humans are meant "to participate in the intentional fulfillment of God's purposes."[28]

Hefner acknowledges that some critics will find his model too anthropocentric because it classifies us as cocreators, while other species are, presumably, simply created. Others, he admits, will believe it demeans humans by emphasizing our biological nature.[29] Still others will reject Hefner's approach because it is explicitly theological. Despite its limitations, Hefner's model helps illuminate the nature-nurture dilemma and the possibility of incorporating insights from both the naturalist-evolutionary and constructionist approaches into an integrated anthropology. Like Ayala and other nonreductive physicalists, Hefner reinforces Geertz's claim that we do not have to choose between explanatory devices. We can understand humans as the products of biological *and* cultural evolution, not of just one or the other. Further, it is plausible to argue that biological and cultural evolution require each other in shaping humans as a species, just as nature and nurture require each other in the development of every individual person. In other words, we can do away with the model that layers one factor on top of another in favor of an approach that finds "systematic relationships among diverse phenomena." Even though Geertz argues for this approach, the hard constructionist model he supports fails because, in the end, it does not take biology seriously enough. Despite his interest in physical evolution, Geertz ultimately enshrines culture as the defining factor. Conversely, hard naturalist positions fail because, as Ayala puts it, they make biology a sufficient, and not just necessary, factor in explaining human behavior.

The relative influences of nature and nurture in developmental processes vary greatly among individuals, populations, historical periods, cultures, and ecosystems. Further, different factors, such as genes or environmental conditions, often have multiple effects, which are multiplied even further when genes and environment interact. For these and other reasons, we may never be able either to pinpoint the causes of many traits or to predict the consequences of particular genes, environmental conditions, or their interactions. Resolving the nature-nurture dilemma, then, does not mean achieving full knowledge of what nature and nurture each contribute, either in general or in any given situation. Resolving the dilemma may just mean understanding that it is not a dilemma. We can aim at understanding the various factors and their interactions more fully, and we do not have to choose one or the other as the single or preeminent influence. This is the point of the nonreductive physicalist position and the similar models of constrained constructivism and nonreductive naturalism.

This is also the bottom line for the chastened constructionist anthropology I outline here. Humans are natural and cultural animals, created both as individuals and as a species out of the interactions between these features. The interactions of nature and culture in humans have parallels and continuities with the interactions of biology and environment experienced by other species. To speak of interactions between nature and culture or environment means that not only do these factors affect us separately, but they affect us most of all by working together, as suggested by the model of gene-culture coevolution. Many species shape their environments even as those environments shape them, and humans do this to a greater extent than other animals. In this sense, we construct ourselves, as any understanding of humanness must acknowledge. However, this constructionism must include the recognition that we do not create ourselves ex nihilo, or in isolation, or just as we please. We face limits, of varying sorts, in our efforts to build identities and reshape our environments. (The consequences of our frequent refusal to recognize these limits is an issue for ethics, discussed in the next chapter.) Biology and culture help determine each other, and neither one alone can explain what it means to be human.

THE TERRESTRIAL SELF

Biology and culture shape each other, moreover, in a particular setting: on earth. As discussed in chapter 2, the degree to which humans are truly at home on earth has long been a subject of debate in Western philosophy and especially in Christian thought. Dominant philosophical and theological traditions have asserted that humans, or at least the essential, defining dimension of humans, usually understood as the mind or soul, belong elsewhere. Often this is tied to religious convictions that we came from somewhere else and will return there after death. However, secular worldviews, including those that emerged from the Enlightenment, have also propagated the notion that what is really important in humanness is somehow alien to the world in which we live. This belief is often accompanied by denials of our dependence on the natural world, and by denials of the unity of mind and body, as well as of the body's ultimate worth and its capacity to influence reason.

In contrast to these dominant strands in Western thought, a number of alternative approaches argue that humans are fully and inescapably terrestrial, as Mary Midgley puts it.[30] These challenges come from within Western philosophy, theology, or science, notably ecology, and, as I will discuss in more detail below, some revisions of Christian theology. Some of the most powerful non-Western understandings of humanity's belonging on earth are articulated by different Native American traditions, examined in chapter 5. Few of these traditions view humans as waiting for some other world to reveal their true identities. While indigenous cultures do not lack ideas about other worlds or human connections to these worlds, they generally do not understand human beings as aliens on earth. Instead, the Navajo, Koyukon, and many other Native American peoples view humans as belonging to the earth: they depend on it for sustenance, identity, and meaning and return to it after death.

Most native cultures do not view these intimate relations of interdependence and belonging in the abstract, however. Rather, being at home on earth means being at home in a particular place. This may be as specific as the Navajo tie to the place where one's umbilical cord is buried, or more general, as in the Koyukon sense of belonging to the vast northern forest. In each case, however, the human community is fully embedded in and committed to a particular place, and, through that specific relationship, to the earth more generally. People do not need to look elsewhere for identity, completion, or redemption.

This sense of belonging, of being at home, is summarized in the notion of being native to a place, as discussed by bioregionalist writers such as Wendell Berry, Wes Jackson, Richard Nelson, and Gary Snyder. In chapter 5 I quoted Nelson's praise for "the rewards of becoming fully involved with the near-at-hand, of nurturing a deeper and more committed relationship with home, and of protecting the natural community that sustains all who live there."[31] In ethical terms, I suggested, bioregionalism proposes a native (though not necessarily or usually Native) approach to replace the supernaturalism of the Enlightenment and most Christian thought. However, challenges to otherworldliness have also arisen within Christianity, especially in the work of contemporary theologians struggling to understand humans as both *in* and *of* the world and, at the same time, to retain central elements of Christian theology.

These theologians recognize the ways the "sojourner sensibility," as Sallie McFague terms it,[32] has contributed to harmful environmental attitudes and behaviors. Summarizing traditional understandings, the Catholic writer Thomas Berry contends that Christianity has taught that "we somehow did not belong to the community of earth. We were not an integral component of the natural world. Our destiny was not here. We deserved a better world, although we had not even begun to appreciate the beauty and grandeur of this world or the full measure of its entrancing qualities."[33]

In contrast to this alienation, contemporary eco-theologians often emphasize belonging or being at home on earth. Philip Hefner, for example, insists that despite humans' distinctive telos as cocreators, we "share the common destiny of one planet and the systems that constitute its life."[34] More concisely, Rosemary Radford Ruether writes that "we have no home outside the earth."[35] Thomas Berry advocates adopting a Christian bioregionalism in order to restore human understanding of, respect for, and participation in natural communities, and especially to celebrate the "numinous mystery of the universe expressed in the unique qualities of each regional community, [in which] the human fulfills its own special role."[36]

Another Christian theologian, Shannon Jung, has elaborated a detailed vision of human and natural flourishing as being connected to each other and to their homes in a given place. Like Berry, Jung contrasts his argument with the traditional Christian "fiction that human beings [are] not constitutionally part of the world of nature."[37] This erroneous belief has generated many of our current environmental problems, Jung notes, and is closely tied to consumerism and other economic factors. To improve both environmental conditions and the quality of human life more generally, we need to understand that "the earth is not an external home; we are part of the home. We are part of the earth. The whole web of life that is the earth cannot be externalized from us. We are all part of God's home; we constitute nature. *We are not at home; we are home!*"[38] Being our own homes on earth requires being at home in the body. Jung takes a new look, through an ecological lens, at Augustine's idea of the body as the "earth we carry." "Each of us," Jung writes, "is an environment. Our local environment is our body. It is a body connected with other bodies—animal, human, celestial. . . . We have a connection to every other environment; the environment moves through us; we modify the environment. All of us are part of the environment."[39]

These claims, the Protestant theologian Sallie McFague emphasizes, draw support from contemporary science, including evolutionary theory and postmodern physics, as well as ecology. The sciences tell us "that the universe is a whole and that all things, living and nonliving, are interrelated and interdependent." This organic model predominated for most of human history, but modern science and philosophies, including much of Christian thought, have replaced it with a mechanistic model. Environmental ethics gains, McFague argues, from a reconsideration of the organic model. This approach invites Christians in particular, "who have been made to feel that we do not, in a fundamental sense, *belong* on the earth (for our home is in another world)," to be at home on earth.[40] Thus McFague ties the sense of being at home on earth to a particular model of the earth and its history, rooted in the "common creation story" of evolution.

McFague's attention to evolution is important for contemporary understandings of human belonging on earth. Midgley also highlights this connection: "We are at home in this world *because we were made for it*. We have developed here, on this planet, and are adapted to live here. . . . We are not fit to live anywhere else."[41] We have no home anywhere else; we are not merely passing through but are here for the duration. This conviction, the rootedness on this planet and in particular parts of it, pervades many Native American and other traditional cultures; it is what the bioregionalist movement hopes to generate or rekindle. This approach challenges not only mainstream Western ways of life but also dominant anthropological claims: it replaces the notion of humans as supernatural beings, accidentally or temporarily on earth, with a vision of humans as inseparable from the planet, inseparable from the landscapes in which we emerged and on which we continue to depend.

AT HOME IN THE BODY

Mainstream Western attitudes toward humans' terrestrial nature have close links to ideas about our bodily nature. Specifically, as I noted in chapter 2, many scholars argue that mechanistic understandings of nature are tied to a dualistic vision of the body as separate from and inferior to the mind or soul. Human bodies connect us to nonhuman animals, the earth, and natural processes over which we have little control. Western thought often identifies women with the body and men with the rational mind that is somehow separate from and superior to it. This identification has prompted a number of feminist thinkers to reflect on embodiment. Especially since the early 1970s, feminists have sought to rethink "the woman in the body," in Emily Martin's phrase, or more directly, "our bodies, ourselves," like the title of a popular and influential guide to women's health.[42]

The poet and essayist Adrienne Rich has developed an especially articulate and influential feminist approach to embodiment. Rich argues that the mind-body dualism of modern Western culture has made the body "so problematic for women that it has often seemed easier to shrug it off and travel as a disembodied spirit."[43] This acquiescence to dualism and to the degradation of the body, however, ultimately harms women, since "the struggle of women to become self-determining is rooted in our bodies."[44] Shrugging off our bodies means relinquishing the possibility of an integral liberation for women, which would allow women to determine the shape of their lives and to embrace their identity as a whole rather than a fragmented polarity. Instead of adopting the mind-body dualism of the dominant culture, feminist thought needs to integrate body and mind, to "think through the body."[45] This means feminists should seek "not to transcend this body, but to reclaim it. To reconnect our thinking and speaking with the body of this particular living human individual, a woman."[46] Thus, she adds, we ought to speak of "my body" rather than "the body."[47] We should define humans, including women, neither as only bodies nor as separate from bodies. No free-floating essence, such as mind or soul, defines the person. Rather, we are bodies that include brains and that can think and feel (and that, in the case of women, contain both a uterus and a brain and can use both, even at the same time, as Representative Pat Schroeder once said).

The integration of mind and body emerges as an important theme in Christian interpretations of human embodiment as well, many of which have been influenced by feminist work on the topic. The most thorough exploration of embodiment in eco-theological perspective may be Sallie McFague's book *The Body of God*. McFague seeks to help people "to think and act as if bodies matter. They are not all that matters but they do, and if we believed they mattered and understood in detail what that belief entailed, how might that change our way of being in the world?" Like Rich, McFague contends that thinking through the body would change our ideas about a range of issues. First, it would alter our thinking about the human person or self, discarding dualism for a holistic view. In this perspective, McFague writes, "the body is not a discardable garment cloaking the real self or essence of a person (or a pine tree or a chimpanzee); rather, it is the shape or form of who we are. It is how each of us is recognized, responded to, loved, touched, and cared for—as well as oppressed, beaten, raped, mutilated, discarded, and killed. The body is not a minor matter; rather, it is the main attraction."[48] McFague thus rejects the view of humans as accidentally encased in bodies that do not shape their true identities and argues instead for a fully incarnational model, in which all dimensions of human being are embodied. Nothing we do or are, nothing we hope to be, exists in isolation from the fact that we are embodied creatures existing alongside, and dependent on, other bodies. Focusing on the body, McFague writes, provides "a way, a lens, a glass, by which we might see ourselves more clearly, see where we belong in the scheme of things—not as a spirit among bodies, but as a spirited body among other spirited bodies on our planet."[49]

Thinking through or taking seriously the body not only shapes our view of human nature but also alters the way we understand humans' relations to and understandings of our physical environment. To be truly at home on earth, McFague argues, we need to be at home in our bodies. This in turn requires a new understanding of human nature and especially of human embodiment. As McFague puts it, the body is the most basic, primary notion of space, the central category for relations to the land: "Each life-form is a body that occupies and needs space."[50] By viewing not only humans but also other creatures and natural objects as spirited bodies, she attacks the human-nature dualism from both sides of the divide.

Finally, taking embodiment seriously transforms ways of thinking about God. McFague proposes understanding the earth as the body of God. This model, she argues, takes incarnation seriously, in a way that mainstream theology has not. Seeing the universe as God's body, writes McFague, radicalizes the incarnation "beyond Jesus of Nazareth to include all matter." If the world is God's body, nothing happens to the world that does not also happen to God.[51] This redirects Christian attention away from its dominant focus on relations with God and personal salvation and toward human and nonhuman bodies and the embodied earth itself.

Just thinking through and about the body is not enough, however. McFague emphasizes that we need not only to affirm our embodiment but to think differently about it as well. Simply expanding or transferring traditional models of the body will not suffice. Rather, we need to understand both the radical interdependence and the radical diversity of all the bodies and embodied lives on earth. Influenced by feminist thought, McFague argues that "the particular, concrete, situated differences among humans, who at the same time exist together within the body of the planet, must be the starting points for knowing and doing, for embodiment *is* radically particular."[52] Bodies, no less than minds or souls, are heterogenous; to have a body is not to be reduced to a mass term but rather to be a particular, unique being. Bodies are also, as discussed below, inescapably related to other bodies; this relationality does not contradict or eliminate radical diversity.

Much more can be and has been written about the philosophical and ethical implications of thinking through the body. A number of writers, for example, have explored the links between bodies and emotions, arguing that mind-body dualisms parallel dualistic conceptions of rationality and feeling. This issue is tied to the larger claim, central to the ethical anthropology I sketch here, that the human body is an integral whole. In this light, the body, and specifically the brain, provides the indispensable frame of reference for what Antonio Damasio calls "the neural processes we experience as the mind." Our body, not some external or supernatural reality, constitutes the reference point and yardstick for our constructions of the world and our sense of subjectivity. Damasio summarizes this: "The mind exists in and for an integrated organism; our minds would not be the way they are if it were not for the interplay of body and brain during evolution, during individual development, and at the current moment. The mind had to be first about the body, or it could not have been."[53]

For a chastened constructionist anthropology, the importance of being at home in the body revolves around the integration of mind and body, the insistence that there is no "I" placed accidentally in the body, no essential self looking out. In evolutionary perspective, this means that humans have developed no special quality, no x that is more than, or apart from, the human body. Mind, consciousness, sentience, and subjectivity are not extra phenomena but are fully embodied (and not merely fully "embrained," as Damasio writes).[54] As bodies have evolved, so have minds.[55] Mind is not some unprecedented trait marking humans off from all other species. Rather, mental qualities come in every imaginable grade and intensity. As Dennett puts it, there is no threshold of mind or subjectivity to discover, no morally significant step but rather a "ramp."[56] Dennett's image of a ramp suggests a continuum in which humans are connected to all other species, in varying ways and degrees. This approach emphasizes the unity of different mental qualities with other dimensions of the body, the embodiedness, again, of *all* the ways in which we are human.

RELATIONAL SELVES

The importance of embodiment for a chastened constructionist anthropology suggests not only that humans are embodied unities but also that we are relational or social. Bodies, as McFague notes, relate to and depend on other bodies, in ways that the disembodied mind or soul might not. While bodies are diverse and particular, they are also connected to each other in myriad and inescapable ways: in their shared evolutionary heritage, which leads to behavioral similarities, and in their common dependence on ecosystems and on each other. Many critics, feminist and other, have pointed out the ways that divisions between culture and nature and between mind and body both parallel and reinforce a binary view of individual and society. Conversely, a relational view of personhood represents a common point of many alternatives to and critiques of the Western philosophical tradition. For example, as noted in chapter 6, many feminists identify and affirm a female tendency to define the self in terms of relationships, in contrast to the abstract, individualistic conceptions of self typical to (Western) men. As Sandra Harding summarizes it, "For women, other people and nature tend to be conceptualized as dependent parts of relational networks. Humans and nature are continuous with each other."[57] To Harding, this "feminine" worldview looks "suspiciously similar" to those of many Africans, Asians, and Native Americans. Similarity should not obscure the important differences among cultural understandings of individuality and of the relationships that define the self. We must guard against homogenized, often idealized visions of non-Western cultures and indeed of Western culture itself, since many feminists, among other critics of mainstream thought, are embedded in and shaped by Western traditions of thought. Still, attention to diversity need not and should not lead us to ignore the real contrasts between the individualism of dominant Western, especially U.S., models of personhood and other approaches.

Relational conceptions of humanness generate several crucial ethical questions. First, is a relational self simply another alternative to mainstream Western anthropologies, or is it a more adequate vision of humanness? Second, if this model is more adequate, is that because it is truer or because it might have better ethical consequences?

In response to the first question, hard constructionists would answer that the relational models of self articulated by feminists, Buddhists, and others are simply various constructions among others, none with a greater claim to truth or objectivity. The constrained or chastened constructionist approach I advocate would acknowledge that different visions of humanness do depend to some extent on cultural processes. However, this does not mean that all are equally accurate portrayals of human nature. (Hard constructionists, of course, deny that there is such a thing called human nature in the first place.) Constructionists argue that we always see through the lenses of history, culture, social class, gender, religion, and other particularities of our condition and location. Thus we cannot achieve the transparent vision that hard realists seek, at least not of anything as controversial and close to home as human nature. However, the fact that we see through a glass darkly, or rather through many dark glasses all at the same time, does not mean that we cannot see at all.

In contrast to the dominant Western notion of objectivity as a view from nowhere, feminist theorists such as Donna Haraway insist that all visions are particular and embodied, that no knowledge is "innocent." While understanding all knowledge as partial and constructed, however, Haraway and other feminists do not deny either that knowledge is possible or that some kinds of knowledge are better than others. This approach is reflected in feminist studies of science, which, as Joseph Rouse points out, differ in important respects from what he terms sociological studies of science. While both approaches challenge many of the choices and claims of mainstream Western science, Rouse shows, sociologists of science rarely hope to resurrect "contingently defeated" points of view. In contrast, feminists often urge reconsideration of the merits of less dominant views, rather than simply discrediting all perspectives as equally partial. Feminists seek, in other words, to show how "one story is not as good as another," as Haraway puts it.[58]

The question is, how to know which story is better, or how to achieve the limited objectivity that is possible, in order to generate better stories, more adequate accounts of the world? This goal, Haraway argues, requires taking seriously the standpoints and knowledge of the subjugated: not only marginalized persons and cultures but also perhaps nature itself. Seeing from below, of course, is not simple or straightforward.[59] Perspectives from the underside are not necessarily or always more accurate than those from above, and different perspectives from the underside sometimes contradict each other. Still, seeking them out is necessary to achieve the goal of a fuller, more objective vision of reality. This effort poses not only an intellectual but also a moral challenge. Haraway writes that knowledge implies both risk and responsibility; it demands that we "become answerable for what we learn how to see."[60] Objectivity requires not disengagement but involvement in the world and acknowledgment of that involvement, of the mutual and usually unequal relations among persons and between persons and nature, of our power and also of the fact that this power is not total.[61]

What might an embodied objectivity tell us about the self? First, it would acknowledge that all anthropologies are socially constructed, that there is no single way of being human or of interpreting humanness. Nonetheless, the views from below, in this case alternatives to mainstream Western culture, differ substantially from the views from above. And they differ in similar ways: Asian, Native American, and feminist approaches all portray humanity as shaped and even defined by relations to a host of other beings, including people, animals, plants, and natural processes. In fact, post-Enlightenment culture stands peculiarly alone in its vision of the autonomous, isolated individual. The idiosyncrasy of this perspective is underlined by evolutionary and ecological science, which reveals how intimately and inescapably related we are to the rest of life in myriad ways: in the history of our species, in our physiology and behaviors, in our shared dependence upon both particular landscapes and planetary processes. The message of evolution, as Midgley argues, is that individualism and competition must always be understood in relation to nurturing and cooperation. Darwin himself noted that the social instincts are "always present in proper balance against the waste and cruelty of natural life."[62] Midgley puts it concisely: natural history, like human history, shows that "love is not a lie."[63]

In sum, the cumulative impact of the partial views of non-Western cultures, feminist critiques, and the natural sciences is to suggest that, among various possible visions of humanness, that of the individual as an island is the least objective and least plausible of all. Further, while all worldviews, including all anthropologies, are ideological, meaning that they are tied to the interests of particular groups, the Western emphasis on autonomy is ideological in a particularly insidious way, reinforcing ecological, political, and economic practices that marginalize and exploit other persons and other species.

A situated objectivity, then, supports a relational view of humanness while also acknowledging the partial, embodied, and incomplete nature of this perspective. This still leaves us with the second question I posed several pages back: is the relational model better because it is truer or because it might have better ethical consequences? Despite my wording, these possibilities are not mutually exclusive. This model might be both more accurate *and* better ethically. I phrased the question in either/or terms, however, to emphasize that accuracy does not necessarily lead to better ethical consequences, as noted in the previous chapter regarding naturalism in evolution and ecology. Accurate understandings and moral value are related in complex ways, and there can be no simple step from *is* to *ought*. Nor, however, are connections entirely lacking.

Part of the answer to this question is that the relational model is more accurate, objectively speaking. Humans are social animals, not the isolated monads imagined by Hobbes and Locke and enshrined in modern Western philosophy, folk understanding, and political and economic institutions. However, this is not the only answer to the question. I also argue that a relational view of humanness is closer to what contemporary Western, especially U.S., society needs ethically, at least here and now. This does not mean that an emphasis on relationships should always take precedence in ethics or politics. For example, as some feminists have pointed out, women who have suppressed their own interests and independence in deference to or under coercion from men may benefit from an individualistic understanding of the self. In our present culture generally, though, the dangers of individualism far outweigh those of sociability. Warren Copeland notes, in relation to economic justice, that we can at the same time value different goods, such as individual agency and relatedness, and also recognize the need in a given time and place to press for one good over another. Copeland argues compellingly that equality and solidarity receive short shrift in contemporary U.S. economic life and thus ought to be supported, in ethical analysis and in policy decisions, over the legitimate but overemphasized value of individual liberty.[64] Similarly, I believe that the view of humans as separate individuals, independent from both other persons and the natural world, has contributed to grave environmental damage. Thus we now need to understand and appreciate the ways in which humans are related to and dependent on human and nonhuman others.

IS A RELATIONAL SELF ENOUGH?

Some thinkers contend that a relational understanding of self, by itself, will lead us all or most of the way to ecological responsibility. In this view, if we understand ourselves as parts of a continuous whole, then we cannot easily distinguish between self and other. This vision of continuity makes the classical problem of moral philosophy—of how to manage or overcome egoism—irrelevant, as Callicott notes.[65] The notion that revising or expanding one's sense of self is sufficient for a correct relationship to nature (or other people) is central to some versions of Deep Ecology, including the Buddhist version espoused by Joanna Macy. As noted in chapter 4, Macy argues that an expanded understanding of the self means that "virtue is *not* required. . . . The shift in identification at this point in our history is required precisely *because* moral exhortation doesn't work, and because sermons seldom hinder us from following our self-interest as we conceive it."[66] Thus we need to reconceive our self-interest as tied to the interest and well-being of all of life, which will lead to ecological restraint as a sort of enlightened self-interest. The concept of enlightened or expanded self-interest is central to Deep Ecology, particularly as articulated by Arne Naess, and is embodied in John Seed's claim that to say "I am protecting the rain forest" really means "I am part of the rain forest protecting myself." For Deep Ecologists, environmental responsibility is a form of expanded self-interest rather than a moral obligation imposed from outside.[67]

Some critics argue that the expanded self of Deep Ecology does not necessarily lead to ecologically superior behavior. According to Val Plumwood, Deep Ecologists believe that "once one has realized that one is indistinguishable from the rain forest, its needs would become one's own." However, Plumwood argues, "there is nothing to guarantee this—one could equally well take one's own needs for its."[68] She contends that the "expanded self is not the result of a critique of egoism. Rather, it is an enlargement and an extension of egoism. It does not question the structures of possessive egoism and self-interest; rather, it tries to allow for a wider set of interests by an expansion of self."[69] The expanded self recognizes others morally only to the extent that they are incorporated into the self and their differences denied.[70] Simply being in relation to an ecosystem or seeing its good as attached to one's own does not guarantee that one will preserve that ecosystem. An expanded self might, in fact, become an even stronger reason to exploit nature, if its good is seen as inseparable from one's own narrowly conceived self-interest. Perhaps the rainforest with which I identify wants me to have teak garden furniture, for example. Expansion, in other words, might unleash an imperial, not an enlightened, self. In light of this danger, the notion that morality is irrelevant, that we should just expand our Selves and then trust enlightened self-interest to fix things, falls short. More generally, we could argue that anthropological claims underlie ethical guidelines and values but do not make them irrelevant or unnecessary any more than ethics make legal, economic, and legislative changes irrelevant or unnecessary.

What about a modified version of the expanded-self argument? If a relational self is not sufficient, is it at least necessary for ecologically or ethically correct behavior? Here Buddhism offers a valuable insight. Mental attitudes, including understandings of humanness, are connected to behavioral changes, but the relationship between them is complex, variable, and mutually reinforcing, rather than univocal and unidirectional. Increases in wisdom and compassion can reinforce improved behavior, but certain practices, such as meditation and vegetarianism, also contribute to wise and compassionate mental states.[71] This suggests that we need not and in fact should not wait for the achievement of the proper mental attitude, be it Buddhist mindfulness or Deep Ecology's expanded self, as a necessary, let alone sufficient, prerequisite for proper behavior. Practice can help us achieve right mindfulness, compassion, and wisdom, including wise understanding of human nature. We lack the Kantian luxury of limiting morality to that which rational adults do entirely voluntarily and with full understanding and right intention. Sometimes we must do the right thing for less than the best reasons, and sometimes understanding the "right" reasons comes later as a result of behaving in a responsible and compassionate manner and being part of a larger community that models and supports such behavior. This view of spiritual and moral training contradicts the Enlightenment notion that morality and faith require prior, complete understanding (evident in different form in some Reformation thought, e.g., in the rejection of infant baptism). "I think, therefore I am" gives way to a mutual dependence between thinking and acting.

It may be most helpful to think of the goals of expanding or revising notions of self, on the one hand, and achieving ethical and political change, on the other, as not identical but rather interdependent, demanding simultaneous effort on all fronts. A relational vision of the self is both more accurate *and* ethically required in our time and place. This does not mean that relationships are the only dimension of humanness that is important, nor does it imply that a relational view of humanness is sufficient in and of itself to generate ethical and political change. It does, however, reinforce the central argument of this book: how we envision humanness is deeply and inescapably intertwined with our understanding of ethical behavior.

LIVING WITH LIMITS;
OR, TOWARD A CHASTENED CONSTRUCTIONISM

It should be clear by now just how the anthropology I outline here is constructionist, insofar as it is partial, embodied, and culturally shaped. In affirming the truth of constructionism, however, I do not want to reinforce the claims to human uniqueness and superiority that often accompany culturalist positions, as discussed in chapter 3. This means acknowledging that the building of identities and worlds is not limited to humans. As Katherine Hayles argues, many nonhuman animals also construct worlds, insofar as they constitute and transform the space and relationships they inhabit, in and through embodied interactions. This interpretation is also implicit in Wilson's argument, noted in chapter 7, that many species help create the conditions in which they thrive. Different species also perceive and construe these worlds in distinctive ways: they see in black-and-white or in color, from high above or underfoot, by means of sonar or by touch. The wolf's world is dominated by smells, that of the owl by tiny sudden movements. Each of these constructed worlds, as Hayles points out, is "positional and local, covering only a tiny fraction of the spectrum of possible embodied interactions."[72] This reinforces the importance of not simply taking seriously, but also seeking out, the worldviews and worlds made and inhabited by a whole host of organisms sharing the planet. This accords with Haraway's notion of situated knowledge, in which greater objectivity is gained by considering a variety of partial knowledges, especially those from "below." This approach also extends Sharon Welch's challenge to liberal ethics. Welch argues that ethics should not simply encompass new viewpoints but should allow them to transform our own. Hayles suggests that not only the worlds and worldviews of other humans but also those of other species must enter into our own worlds.

How do we learn about the worlds that other species construct? Some ethologists have made this question explicit, as suggested in the titles of Dorothy Cheney and Robert Seyfarth's book *How Monkeys See the World* and Thomas Nagel's article "What Is It Like to Be a Bat?"[73] Even asking these questions, let alone trying to answer them, requires an openness to the possibility that nonhumans can be conscious agents, makers, shapers, and interpreters of their worlds. This perspective is implicit in many indigenous notions of nonhuman agency, often dismissed as anthropomorphism or animism or, in more liberal views, tolerated as evidence of diversity among human cultures. If we take

seriously the views from the underside, then the knowledge of indigenous peoples and even that of nonhumans can help contribute to a better
understanding of the world.

This approach, Haraway argues, makes possible a fuller, more objective understanding of our own worlds and the many other worlds
that coexist and overlap with them. It also engenders a healthy sense of
humility, which leads us to the "chastened" part of my model, a revision
of Katherine Hayles's term "constrained constructionism." I underline
the constraints we face, due both to the limited capacities of our own
bodies, including that of our brains, and to the limitations imposed by
our necessarily particular location in the world, described by our ecological niches as well as by our gender, ethnic, and social positions. I
also emphasize the limits to constructionism itself: humans' social constructions do not create the world, any world, out of nothing. Our constructions of reality are in an important sense construals, as I argued in
chapter 3: they encounter a world that preexists us and our interpretations. Even the constructing subject is not blank paper, since humans
are shaped by nature as well as nurture. The self-made man is as much
a biological as an economic fiction.

Humans, then, face a range of limits, notably in our knowledge of
our world and in our ability to shape it. Today we also face the limits
of the earth's carrying capacity, of the fragile ecosystems on which our
lives depend. The recognition of constraints can lead to the idea of restraint, imposed from within or outside the self. Being chastened implies,
more specifically, that we not only restrain ourselves but that we do so
with humility and gratitude.

A number of religions emphasize human limitations. Christianity
stresses the fragility and ambivalence of human nature, its capacity for
both good and evil. Protestantism highlights humans' frailty and tendency to sin; Roman Catholicism places emphasis as well on the possibility of repentance and reconciliation. Buddhism teaches that we cannot
control our lives or the lives of any other beings, and especially that we
cannot eliminate suffering or change. Nor will we achieve complete purity in our own practices or character, as Gary Snyder points out, so we
should not indulge in what would be seen, in a Buddhist perspective, as
self-righteousness.[74] This does not mean we must approve of any and
all behavior. Rather, Buddhism insists on continual discipline and practice. Although perfection is not possible, improvement is. A Buddhist
environmental ethic, as Alan Sponberg explains, is a virtue ethic that

asks not just which specific actions are required but the deeper question "what are the virtues . . . we must cultivate in order to be able to act in such a way[?]"[75] We can and should cultivate virtue; at the same time, we ought to recognize the limitations in our capacity to achieve perfect virtue.

An emphasis on limits and constraints, in religious or other world-views, carries the risk of resignation to injustice. The chastened dimensions of an ethical anthropology must be balanced with a willingness to test boundaries, to question whether limits are truly inevitable. While bodiliness and partiality, for example, impose constraints that we cannot finally remove, other limitations, such as many unjust social structures, may in fact be changeable, even though we sometimes see and are encouraged to see them as natural and inevitable. We should also keep in mind that biological constraints are not always less changeable than cultural ones. Social learning can be just as rigid as genetic programming, something that opponents of biological determinism often fail to see. Again, a chastened constructionism recognizes that we face limits in our capacity to understand the world and to change it, but that those limits are not always complete. Ethics, as Sharon Welch emphasizes, must ask whether some harmful limitations can be changed and then must seek to change them, without expecting or demanding complete fulfillment.[76]

A chastened constructionist view of human nature accepts, to a certain extent, the "always already" of postmodern constructionism: the awareness that we are always interpreters and shapers of our selves and our worlds, that there is no original purity waiting to be discovered. This anthropology also acknowledges the "not yet" of Christian eschatology: we never quite get where we want to go. Just as there is always *some* construction, there is never *complete* construction. Something always escapes human efforts to know and control. Christians attribute this "more" to God, while some environmental thinkers point to the irreducible otherness of nature, the extent to which it always lies just outside our grasp. The emphasis upon constraint and its ethical correlate, restraint, points to a balance between recognizing our real power to construct and change the world, on the one hand, and the equally real limitations of that power, on the other. Maintaining this balance, or tension, has high ethical stakes. Overemphasizing the constructionist dimension can nurture the triumphalist notion that humans, and only humans, are makers and shapers of all we behold. Overemphasizing limits, however, can lead to resignation, to acceptance of social injustices or ecological deterioration as being beyond our control. Being chastened suggests recognizing that some limits are real without resigning oneself to inaction and failure. This points to the need for a fuller discussion of the ethical correlates and implications of the anthropology I have been sketching.

CHAPTER NINE

Different Natures

And this is the meaning of ethics: to express the ways in
which love embodies itself and life is maintained and saved.

Paul Tillich, *The Protestant Era*

This book describes many different natures: diverse human natures or
ways of being human; different constructions of nonhuman nature; and
the differences as well as connections between humans and the rest of
nature. In this final chapter, I explore some important ethical and meta-
ethical questions raised by these differences and relationships. In the first
section of this chapter, I look at one of the key substantive issues at stake
in the book as a whole: how do we reconceive the relationship between
value and difference? Is it possible to unlink uniqueness and intrinsic
worth? I then turn to some structural and methodological issues in
ethics. I focus on the place of narratives, especially utopian narratives,
and on the relations between stories and attachment to place, revisiting
some of the questions regarding being native that I raised in chapter 5.
Finally, I explore the connections between ideas and practice, especially
the ethical and political implications of alternative ways of conceiving
and construing human nature. The chapter seeks, overall, not to settle
any of these questions once and for all but to clarify how my earlier
discussions of particular traditions and issues might help sharpen what
is at stake and what remains to be done.

RETHINKING THE HUMAN DIFFERENCE

"We are both similar to and different from other animals," Stephen Jay
Gould argues. "In different cultural contexts, emphasis on one side or

the other of this fundamental truth plays a useful social role." In Darwin's day, according to Gould, it was most important to emphasize continuity in response to the dominance of creationism. Presently, however (or at least in the mid-1970s when he wrote that sentence), Gould believes we need to emphasize differences. This results from his fear of eugenics and Social Darwinism and his desire to distance questions of human social justice from notions of survival of the fittest and biological determinism.[1] We ought to discount neither these fears nor the increasingly urgent demands of interhuman justice. However, at this point in our history it is not just useful but also vital to emphasize human continuity with the rest of nature, or at least to avoid dichotomizing, to insist on continuity as much as on difference. The need for this emphasis stems both from the predominant emphasis on human exceptionalism in academic and folk models and from the severity of environmental problems.

Many different people find assertions of continuity between humans and nature threatening. The sense of threat often stems from the erroneous assumption that we must choose between nature and culture, biology and free will. This dualistic vision leads many people to conflate continuity with denial of all difference and thus to believe that preserving difference requires rejecting continuity.[2] To respond to these points, at least in part, we need to examine the relations between difference and value. Popular and scholarly opinions alike link value to uniqueness. In mainstream Western thought, the intrinsic worth of individuals rests in large part upon their nonrepeatability. (This assumption underlies some of the concerns about human cloning: how do we value persons who are *not* unique?) The value of general qualities of humanness also seems to depend on their exclusiveness. Intelligence, consciousness, intentionality, morality, and other important human features are somehow diminished, in this view, if they are shared with other species. Further, the moral worth of uniqueness is tied to autonomy. Post-Enlightenment thinking in particular has defined humanity in general, as well as every individual human, or at least every man, as an island, needing no one and nothing else for completion. Social relationships, ecological conditions, and the vagaries of physical embodiment do not impinge on the essence of humanness, in this perspective. All relations are external to a predefined, discrete, and absolutely unique identity, for individuals or the species in general.

This vision, I have argued, loses plausibility in light of the undeniable interdependence, continuities, and similarities among humans and between humans and the rest of nature. These realities require us not merely to embrace ambiguity but to rethink both how humans are different and how we are similar to other animals. In considering difference, we need to avoid confusing being particular with being exceptional. Every natural object—every human, every plant, every animal—is particular. Each one possesses a distinctive combination of characteristics (shaped by both biology and environment-culture), and each is concretely embedded and embodied in a particular setting, particular relationships of interdependence, and a particular history. Continuity, interdependence, and similarity, in other words, do not deny particularity. They *do* deny that a certain kind of natural object, and only that kind, stands absolutely apart from and above all the rest. Mainstream understandings of human nature have, paradoxically, insisted on uniqueness while denying the embodiment and ecological embeddedness that shape our particularity. Our uniqueness is supposed to stem from abstract qualities such as mind, spirit, or soul, that disembody and disembed us. They separate us from the rest of the natural world at the same time that they make us its center, its reason for being.

Challenging exceptionalist anthropologies and the domination and exploitation they legitimize does not require us to erase or ignore difference. We need, rather, to reconceptualize and revalorize difference, to move away from dualistic understandings that generate value hierarchies. As ecofeminists emphasize, we need to find ways to take difference seriously without breeding domination. A number of contemporary Christian theologians have undertaken precisely this task in relation to their tradition's understanding of human dominion over the rest of nature.

STEWARDSHIP ETHICS

As noted in chapter 2, some Christian theologians have proposed replacing models of human dominion with an ethic of stewardship, in which humans are still special but accept that their superiority carries responsibilities as well as privileges. I suggested that moderate versions of this approach may not go far enough, especially insofar as they reconfigure but do not challenge the idea of human superiority. A number of Christian eco-theologians have begun redefining stewardship to encompass human distinctiveness but not (necessarily) human superiority or dominion. This is what Philip Hefner, for example, intends with his notion of humans as God's created cocreators. In his model, humanity's "purpose is to be the agency, acting in freedom, to birth the future that is most wholesome for the nature that has birthed us—the nature that is not only our own genetic heritage, but also the entire human community and the evolutionary and ecological reality in which and to which we belong. Exercising this agency is said to be God's will for humans."[3] This model maintains a privileged place for humans but makes them stewards responsible for seeking a better future while still dependent on ecological and evolutionary processes. Humans possess special features, including a unique degree of freedom, but we cannot employ these qualities for arbitrarily chosen ends. Rather, God has granted us freedom so we can "participate in the intentional fulfillment of God's purposes."[4] This is a theocentric, not an anthropocentric, ethic. Humans may be superior to the rest of creation in certain respects, but in equally profound ways we remain dependent upon God and nature. We are God's vice-regents, as the Muslim form of stewardship puts it, always subordinate to divine power.[5]

Like Hefner, a number of contemporary eco-theologians seek a balance between recognition of human distinctiveness and power, on the one hand, and attention to our continuities with and dependence on the natural world, on the other. Sallie McFague contends that we must view humans as particular kinds of beings with special gifts as well as distinctive limitations. In light of evolution as the common creation story, McFague suggests, humans are "*decentered* as the point and goal of creation and *recentered* as God's partners in helping creation to grow and prosper in our tiny part of God's body."[6] Humans are distinguished from the rest of creation not by our superiority but by our "peculiar form of individuality *and* interdependence," she writes. "We are the responsible ones, responsible for all the rest upon which we are so profoundly dependent."[7] Shannon Jung frames the question of human distinctiveness explicitly in terms of our ends: "What are people for?" Our purpose, he replies, is linked to our capacity for responsibility.[8]

Many theologians attribute this responsibility to our greater degree of consciousness. For McFague, the difference that makes all the difference is that "we are, to our knowledge, the only creatures on our planet who not only participate in it but *know* that they do." We possess information about who we are in the scheme of things and how much we depend on the rest of nature. This knowledge gives us a choice: "We can choose to be at home on our planet, learn to follow its house rules, value its fragility and beauty, share in its limited resources with other human beings and other life-forms. We may decide not to do so, but we will not be able to say 'If only we had known.' We *do* know."[9] Our knowledge, further, is complemented by a capacity for intentional action. We have the option of deciding differently, of changing intentionally, through culture, and not exclusively through biological evolution. Stewardship ethics provide guidelines for these decisions, which must be based on awareness of our distinctive features, including technological power and scientific knowledge, and of the limitations placed on us by nature and, in theological perspective, by God's will for the world.

The emphasis on limitations in contemporary models reflects an effort to remove the arrogance of traditional understandings of stewardship, which often relegated divine power over humans to a distant background while human lordship over nature took center stage. In contrast, contemporary eco-theologies emphasize the limitations upon human stewardship. Land, for example, is a gift of God and is always ultimately referred back to God, as Holmes Rolston points out: "In legal terms, land ownership is imperfect and does not carry the right irreplaceably to destroy. In theological terms, land ownership is stewardship."[10] This echoes the Roman Catholic insistence on the common purpose of created things. Catholic social thought has long asserted, as the Second Vatican Council reaffirmed in *Gaudium et Spes,* that "God intended the earth and all that it contains for the use of every human being and people." Thus all people have the right to necessary material resources, and the better-off are obliged to help the poor and "not merely out of their superfluous goods. If a person is in extreme necessity, he has the right to take from the riches of others what he himself needs."[11] In this perspective, God and the community have prior claims to all forms of property. Individuals may use property only as long as they serve the common good and are not denying the basic needs of others. *Gaudium et Spes* declares, "By its very nature private property has a social quality deriving from the law of the communal purpose of created goods."[12] Rolston and Christian eco-theologians add to this social quality an ecological quality, so that not only human needs but also environmental concerns place constraints on the ownership and use of property.

We face limits not only in our right to control nature but also in our capacity to do so. We are powerful and thus responsible, but we are neither all-powerful nor all-responsible. Interpreted in theological terms, this means, Jung writes, that "no single individual is responsible for the state of the natural world. Only God sustains, oversees, and renews the world. God has chosen to work through individuals and communities to do this. *I am* responsible for my contribution to the health of the environment individually and through my communities."[13] This puts stewardship within a theocentric framework that challenges what Sharon Welch calls the ethic of control, the illusion that individuals can achieve unilateral, total solutions to problems. Theocentric revisions of stewardship ethics aim to avoid both arrogance and fatalism, two dangers of thinking in terms of an ethic of control.

Despite the increasingly radical tone of contemporary stewardship ethics, some Christian environmentalists argue that they still fall short. George Kehm contends, for example, that a stewardship ethic "inevitably falls into some form of utilitarianism with respect to extrahuman creation."[14] In other words, stewardship ethics persist in seeing nature as a resource that is subject to human interests. Paul Santmire elaborates on this notion, concluding that the Protestant theme of human dominion over the earth cannot encompass the radical revisions required. Dominion reinterpreted as stewardship can suggest how humans might manage the productivity of the earth wisely, but this model still fails to see nature as "a world with its own life and its own value[,] . . . its own history with God."[15] Santmire argues that Christian eco-theology must find a way of showing that "God has a history with nature that is independent of God's history with humanity, although the two, nature and humanity, are also intimately interrelated and interdependent."[16] To replace the stewardship notion of special responsibility, Santmire proposes cooperation as the best model for human interaction with and use of nature.[17]

These concerns echo those I raised in chapter 2. Still, stewardship models do address several problems that are difficult for environmental ethics. Some of the most important of these issues involve understandings of human nature. First, how can we see humanness as intrinsically valuable if we conceive of it as continuous with and dependent on other life-forms and ecosystems? The models proposed by Hefner and Mc-Fague address this question directly. Humans retain intrinsic, even unique, worth, but their value is sharply redefined in the light of ecological and theological dependencies. Value no longer requires, and may not even permit, the assertion of radical difference and autonomy. Our identities and our intrinsic worth are tied up with our embodied, embedded, fragile coexistence with the rest of life on earth.

Another anthropological issue concerns the fit between ethical demands and the realities of human nature. Stewardship models are helpful insofar as they acknowledge human weakness and ambivalence. As Midgley puts it, Christianity allows for, even insists on, conflicting motives, in contrast to the "streamlining" of minds and motives demanded by the Enlightenment tradition.[18] Christian stewardship ethics do not demand the total consistency required, for example, by Kant. Instead, stewardship acknowledges, first, that human beings have needs that require the use of nature. It does not ask people to become completely innocent in their dealings with nature. Second, stewardship provides not only guidelines for using nature but also a reason for following these guidelines: the demands of a personal relationship with God. Failure to follow these rules requires repentance and humility, enforced by the divine will that ultimately creates value for both humans and the nonhuman world.

This establishment of theistic grounds for the intrinsic value of nature is a further contribution of stewardship ethics, in addition to its revised understanding of humanness. As Baird Callicott notes, environmental ethics requires some objective source of intrinsic value to counter the danger of seeing nature in terms of either subjective human preferences or economic "resource value." As various secular environmental ethicists have argued, the source of intrinsic value need not be suprahistorical and divine. However, even though theism it is not the only possible foundation for nature's inherent worth, it is an especially powerful one. In stewardship ethics, as Callicott puts it, God steps in as a "disinterested valuer" to fill an "axiological void." Belief in God also helps environmental ethics resolve the dilemma of moral reciprocity posed by ecological holism or egalitarianism. If people are "plain members and citizens" of the biotic community, in Aldo Leopold's words, then why do other members not have the same responsibilities as humans? Why should we not hold elephants responsible for deforestation, cats for endangering songbird species? In stewardship ethics, human uniqueness provides a "moral asymmetry" that solves the problem. Finally, Callicott adds, stewardship ethics are "eminently practicable," insofar as they attribute intrinsic value to nonhuman entities and to nature as a whole while still permitting humans to use natural resources to meet their needs.[19]

The main practical difficulty Callicott sees is that stewardship ethics require belief in a transcendent God, which obviously diminishes their credibility for people who are not monotheists. Callicott tries to resolve the practical problem by eliminating God: "Purged of its literal elements, the Judeo-Christian stewardship environmental ethic powerfully speaks to the present condition of the relationships of human beings to nature."[20] This condition encompasses the facts that humans are the dominant species on the planet, that we hold the fate of the earth in our hands, and that we are moral beings in a largely amoral world. Callicott appreciates these anthropological implications but wants them without their associated theology. However, purging God from stewardship ethics is not so simple. The revised ethic does not look the same and, crucially, likely will not function the same—that is, it may not provide convincing motivation to nonbelievers. Stewardship ethics, like all theological ethics, work to the extent that they do precisely because of their literal elements. Without those elements, and especially without God, we are left with gaps of meaning, authority, and credibility.

This dilemma reflects the problems generated by many philosophers' attempts to understand religious ethics as a subset of philosophical ethics. This approach makes "literal elements," such as belief in God or convictions about salvation, accidental to the system of beliefs and values. I suggested in chapter 4, however, that religious ethics do not constitute "isolated systems of moral reasoning," as Robin Lovin and Frank Reynolds put it. Rather, religious ethics are "integrated into a complex cultural whole that includes both moral beliefs and beliefs about reality." Thus we cannot "isolate moral propositions for analysis apart from propositions about how things are in the world and how they came to be that way."[21] Ideas about God are crucial to theistic models of the world. This is especially true for models of nature, which depend heavily on accounts of divine intention and creation.

This points us again to the question about what makes religious ethics especially efficacious. Clearly, many factors contribute, including the solidarity of the religious community, the emotional and aesthetic satisfactions of ritual, and intellectual agreement with the logic of religious rules and values. The content of belief, however, carries particular weight. Thus we cannot purify a tradition, at least not a monotheistic one, to remove theological references and then repackage it as a new, improved version acceptable to believers and nonbelievers alike. The content of belief not only defines religion for many people but also provides the primary motivating force behind ethical guidelines and goals. While faith without works may well be dead, for many religious people works without faith are empty. In monotheistic traditions in particular, we cannot understand what it means to do good outside the context of believers' relationships with God and the loyalties, obligations, and satisfactions those relationships bring. In sum, we ought not to mistake the literal idea of God as tangential or accidental to religious stewardship ethics.

Accepting the unity of morality and theology in stewardship ethics, though, leaves nonbelievers still facing an axiological void. Filling this gap remains a central dilemma for secular environmental ethicists, just as generalizing their own answers remains an issue for theistic ones. While there is no single or simple way to resolve these problems, some of the structural dimensions of religious ethics, such as their narrative character, can point to partial answers. Before turning to these questions in more detail, however, I will discuss another approach to the problematic relationship between value and difference.

RETHINKING THE SOCIAL
CONSTRUCTION OF NATURE

Perhaps the chief contribution of stewardship ethics is their effort to rethink the relationship between difference and value on the human side. They pay substantially less attention, as critics note, to the nonhuman world. Stewardship ethics leave largely unanswered some crucial questions for environmental ethics: Are continuity and similarity the only grounds for valuing the rest of nature? Can we value other organisms if, or even because, they are radically different from us? What if humans never encounter them, never even know they exist? How do we even begin to understand this sort of difference? These questions hinge upon our understanding not of human nature, and not even of nonhuman nature in relation to human nature, but of the ways in which nonhumans, especially animals, are agents, constructors, and residents of worlds. These worlds often overlap with ours, but not always, at least not in readily discernible ways. In the tension between kinship and otherness, difference and relation, all these terms demand respect. Neither similarity nor difference means the same, once we begin taking these other worlds seriously.

This insight is central to many indigenous and traditional cultures, which have attended carefully to the mental capacities, histories, and emotional and social lives of other species, apart from their interactions with and usefulness to humans. As noted in chapter 5, for example, a number of Native American cultures understand nonhuman species as other tribes or other peoples, with their own languages, talents, defects, social structures, and even moralities. The rich Koyukon portrait of ravens, as contradictory and complex as the humans with whom they continually interact, exemplifies this approach. So does the Navajo conviction that nonhuman animals can both be kin, even mothers, to humans and still have radically different needs and desires. Thus, for example, forcing nonhuman animals to live under a roof would be as wrong as depriving humans of their homes. Western observers have often called these cultures and their ideas "animistic," singling out their attribution of agency to nonhuman others as a defining and inferior ("primitive") feature. Perhaps it is possible to recover the term animism, to define it not as a derogatory term indicative of a foolish, naive, and even sinful misreading of the natural world but rather as descriptive of a careful and realistic reading.

I do not argue that industrial (or postindustrial) Westerners should try to adopt Koyukon, Navajo, or any other culture wholesale. Rather, I propose that we strive for an embodied objectivity in our vision of nature. This requires taking indigenous constructions of nonhuman nature as substantive critiques of our view of nature and not just as quaint reminders that some people are different. We might allow Native viewpoints to challenge our deeply held assumptions, for example, that qualities such as agency, consciousness, mind, or morality, to name only a few, are uniquely human. Too often, constructionists fold serious challenges into their own overarching framework. This technique, as Sara Ruddick explains, places "differences within a governing theory without recognizing its challenge to the theory's fundamental assumptions."[22] In contrast, Seyla Benhabib cites the ways that Carol Gilligan takes seriously the differences between what ethical reasoning is supposed to look like, according to Kohlberg's model of moral maturity, and the ways women actually respond to moral dilemmas. Because Gilligan confronts discrepancies instead of ignoring them or explaining them away in the terms of the established model, she has to—and can—redefine moral development to accommodate anomalous results. This extension allows her to see other problems in a new light, leading to fundamental revisions in theories of moral development.[23]

A similar paradigm shift might result if we attend seriously to the divergences between, on the one hand, established Western conceptions of nonhuman nature as passive, homogeneous, and mechanistic and, on the other, the evidence of both indigenous cultures and natural sciences, which portray nonhuman animals, even other natural objects, as intentional agents. If many Westerners find it difficult to take seriously indigenous perspectives such as animism, taking nonhumans seriously seems nearly impossible. An honest constructionism, however, should examine not only native worldviews but, even more radically, the worldviews of other species—their knowledge of a given landscape, their own constructions of reality—as sources of insight and change for our own knowledge.[24] We ought to ask whether there are nonhuman ways of being conscious, of having a mind, of acting morally. Perhaps our human ways are unique, but are they the only ways? Are they even the best ways, in terms of the Darwinian notion of fitness as adaptation to a particular niche and way of life?

More radically, we might consider whether our world is the only world. If different individuals and cultures really do construct as well as construe their own realities, perhaps other natural agents do the same. The fact that we cannot enter fully into their worlds does not mean that such worlds do not exist. "The world in which the kestrel moves, the world that it sees, is, and will always be, entirely beyond us," Midgley writes. This otherness, however, does not make other species or their worlds irrelevant to us: "That there are such worlds all around us is an essential feature of our world."[25] We cannot know their worlds fully but we can reach toward them. In fact, we cannot really know what it means to live as humans in our world without recognizing and valuing the worlds created and inhabited by other species. This task requires expansiveness and imagination, which we should not forget even as we recognize the value of limitation and restraint. Again, rethinking human nature means not only dethroning humans but also liberating other animals from their passive and mechanistic portrayal by Western rationalism. This tradition, no less than animistic ones, presents a nature that is always already interpreted through specific cultural and ideological lens.

NARRATIVES AND ETHICS

Recognizing the socially constructed character of all thinking, Raymond Williams wrote, regarding nature, that "we need different ideas because we need different relationships."[26] I would bracket Williams's sentence with two additions: We need different stories because we need different ideas. We need different ideas because we need different relationships. And we need different relationships because we need different ways of living in the world. Unpacking these sentences can illuminate two issues that are central to this book and to ethics. The first theme concerns the relationships between stories and ideas, the ways ideas are embedded in narratives and receive their coherence and force from them. This is a meta-ethical question, concerned with the structural dimensions of at least some ethical systems. A second theme, taken up later in this chapter, involves the relations between theory and practice. These two themes are connected, since ideas and relationships, stories and ways of living in the world, interact with and shape each other in multiple ways.

I have been arguing that ethics rests on notions of what it means to be human, images of what we are really like. Further, I contend that many of our ideas about humanness, about nature, and about right and wrong are embedded, explicitly or implicitly, in narratives. I discussed some general aspects of the narrative dimension of ethics in previous chapters. In particular, I have highlighted the ways that narratives can provide a meaningful and coherent framework for people to think about the relations among understandings of the world, values, and actions. Because narratives embody rules and goals in concrete images, they help make ethical systems practicable, livable. Further, as feminist scholars have pointed out, stories often tie moral decisions to significant relationships, thus reinforcing a social view of human nature and drawing on the motivating power of loyalties and personal ties. For these and other reasons, narratives are central to various sorts of moral thinking, including evaluations of nonhuman nature.

Several environmental ethicists have suggested that stories can play a central role in shaping attitudes toward nature. Karen Warren has laid out a systematic argument in favor of an explicitly narrative style in environmental and ecofeminist ethics, reinforcing several points I have made so far. First, Warren notes, narratives take seriously relationships and the relational character of the self, which, as I have argued, are central to environmental ethics. Further, because narratives tend to portray the self in relationships, they can point to the moral and epistemological significance of relations with the nonhuman environment. Second, a narrative form makes it possible to express and reflect upon diverse ethical attitudes in ways that mainstream Western philosophical styles do not permit. Narratives may, for example, present an indigenous or even nonhuman voice as that of a moral actor whose perspectives and interests demand serious consideration. At their best, stories can help us recognize difference without legitimizing subordination. Thus narratives might be specially suited for the kind of engagement with alternative constructions of reality that, I have argued, is necessary for environmental ethics. I have also proposed that ethics ought to take into account the concrete, embodied, and particular dimensions of humanness. Warren suggests that a narrative form is uniquely able to provide this contextual framework. In stories, ethical values and conclusions emerge out of particular situations in which moral agents find themselves, rather than being imposed on those situations.[27]

Narratives can also help us imagine and evaluate the practices that accompany the ethical visions they embody. Narratives have a powerful capacity to mobilize people, as is evident, for example, in Christian stewardship ethics, which receive force from their embodiment in biblical stories of creation and of humanity's unique relations to both God and other creatures. Even the notion of God itself is compelling in part because of the stories of the history of divine intervention in the world and of the meaningful relationships between God and creation. The evident risk that such tales can breed domination leads some thinkers to reject both theistic ethics and the narrative form in which they are often embedded as inherently oppressive. This may amount to throwing out the baby with the bath water. In seeking an alternative to stewardship and other theocentric ethics, we need to ask not only what is problematic about them but also what makes them effective. Narrative structure may be part of the answer to both of these questions.

While it is often very helpful, a narrative structure is not sufficient, and perhaps not always necessary, for an effective environmental ethic. Further, not just any narrative will do. The content of the story is just as important to ethics as the narrative structure. What kinds of narratives might be both plausible and powerful for contemporary environmental ethics? Some writers have suggested that evolution can provide an overarching narrative to underpin a sustainable environmental ethic. This perspective frames human history as part of evolutionary history. As Colin Tudge writes, "Humans are not merely cultural beings, minds on legs, but are a biological species, as prone as any to the deep rhythms of the Earth itself. History and archaeology must become one; archaeology and paleontology must become one. We can understand ourselves and what is happening to us, and our own impact upon the rest of the world, only when we look at ourselves on the grand scale of time."[28] Both religious and secular writers have taken up this call to understand ourselves as a species and our place in the world in terms of evolution. Edward Wilson argues that science does not replace the human need for myth and story but in fact may help fill that need in a scientifically plausible and ecologically constructive way: "If the sacred narrative cannot be in the form of a religious cosmology, it will be taken from the material history of the universe and the human species. That trend is in no way debasing. The true evolutionary epic, retold as poetry, is as intrinsically ennobling as any religious epic."[29]

Some Christian thinkers echo Wilson's vision of evolution as a sacred narrative. Most influential, perhaps, is Thomas Berry's insistence that ethics requires a narrative and that the narrative most suited for our situation is evolution: "It's all a question of story. We are in trouble just now because we do not have a good story. We are in between stories. The old story, the account of how the world came to be and how we fit into it, is no longer effective. Yet we have not learned the new story."[30] Traditional Christian and Jewish narratives provided a meaningful framework in the West for a long period, Berry explains, but the biblical story is now "dysfunctional in its larger social dimensions." We require a different narrative that offers the meaning and guidance that religion previously supplied. For this "we must begin where everything begins in human affairs—with the basic story, our narrative of how things came to be, how they came to be as they are, and how the future can be given some satisfying direction. We need a story that will educate us, a story that will heal, guide, and discipline us."[31] This new story, he believes, is supplied by "the story of the universe as emergent evolutionary process over some fifteen billion years, a story that now provides our sense of where we are in the total context of universal development."[32] Similarly, Sallie McFague argues that evolution, especially the "common creation story," lies at the heart of the necessary "remythologizing of doctrines of God and human beings in light of the picture of reality from contemporary science" that environmentalism requires.[33]

Darwinian evolution generates a very powerful narrative. It has the potential to describe our origins, as well as the stages through which we have passed and the operating principles that brought us to where we are now. It also tells us that change is continuous and how change works. However, it does not, cannot, tell us where the changes will lead. Natural selection is not goal oriented, and viewing evolution as moving toward ever-higher goods (what Midgley calls the "escalator fallacy") seriously distorts scientific understandings of evolution.[34] In this sense, the evolutionary epic differs decisively from the narratives of Christianity, Marxism, and other teleological models, which describe not only where we came from and how history works but also where we will end up, at least if we act as we ought. The ending helps tie together the beginning and middle of the story and provides its ethical efficacy. A projected ending, a vision of where we can and ought to wind up, is one of the most powerful motivators of ethical practice, especially in the face of risks and uncertainties. This is evident, for example, in stewardship ethics, which conceptualize proper care of nature as part of the story of humanity's relationship with God, destined to end with redemption. As Jim Cheney argues, "To contextualize ethical deliberation is, in some sense, to provide a narrative or story, from which the solution to the ethical dilemma emerges as a fitting conclusion."[35] The absence of a clear picture of the future in the evolutionary epic weakens evolution's capacity to provide a motivational, as well as cognitive, basis for a lived ethic.

UTOPIA

For some thinkers, however, the nonteleological nature of evolution's epic makes it a better possibility for grounding a moral vision. Utopian narratives, such as those of Christianity and Marxism, can lead to dangerous consequences, as postmodernist critics in particular have emphasized. (The fact that stories require endings, and big stories require big endings, may be a primary reason that postmodernism rejects metanarratives so decisively.) Critics point to several problems with utopias. One problem is simply that they are implausible. At the beginning of the twenty-first century, how can any sensible person believe in the realization of an ideal human society? Quite plainly, we cannot get there from here. However, this critique is not really the most important one for ethics, since utopian narratives often influence even those who know they are fantastical.

Two other ethical and political problems of utopian thinking are especially relevant here. First, misguided efforts to force a certain goal, or a deluded conviction that a particular society will realize utopia, can lead to intolerance and even genocide. In religious terms, this reflects the arrogance of thinking that a given project has a divine mandate, that one is doing God's will. A second danger is the mirror image of this hubris, and it rests on the same foundations. This is the risk of falling into resignation and what Sharon Welch calls cultured despair, of thinking that since everything we might realize will fall short of perfection, then we should not try for anything. We are not responsible for trying to effect change, in this view, since anything short of unilateral achievement of the total goal is worthless. In religious perspective, this sometimes takes an otherworldly form, such as the Christian idea that we are only passing through, as the spiritual says, bound for the better home that awaits us by and by. This perspective can make present ills seem trivial, for, as Augustine contended, the greatest evil and the greatest good that people can experience in this life both pale in comparison to those that await us in the next.[36]

In response to these fears, a number of thinkers contend that ethics now must be anti-utopian. Welch writes, for example, that "it is possible to create and resist without the illusion of progress. It is possible to live fully and well without hopes for ultimate victory and certain vindication."[37] Elsewhere she describes her goal as an alternative to "utopian dreams of unending progress, absolute justice, and beneficent power and creativity."[38] I agree with Welch that the dangers of utopianism are real. However, there are also dangers involved in giving them up. Anti-utopian cynicism, for example, does not always avoid the arrogance of some forms of utopianism. Instead of the illusion that one's project is God's, there can emerge the conviction that one's own deconstructions constitute the only truth, and that all those who hope for real change are immature, sentimental, deluded. This infinite critique can be just as impotent and paralyzing, or just as likely to breed arrogance, as the disappointment of utopian dreams.

In rejecting utopias, contemporary critics relinquish not only the power to motivate repressive movements but also the capacity to inspire progressive ones. Images of a desirable future generate much of the compelling power of many religious and political movements. Utopian hopes can encourage people to transform their present lives so that they more closely resemble the better lives they imagine. Without such a vision of where change might lead, critique alone rarely motivates sustained effort to improve present conditions. Even when utopian visions lead to a sense of not belonging, of just passing through, that very alienation can sometimes provide a powerful political or ethical motive, if a desirable alternative is also presented. For example, images of the river Jordan and the promised land in African American Christianity have inspired generations of creative and persistent activism. Utopian dreams also provide compelling standards by which to evaluate concrete movements and projects. None may match the ideal, but some come closer than others. Put in other terms, religion's "already, not yet" carries more ethical and political force than postmodernism's "always already."

Perhaps we need a utopianism that is as chastened as our constructionism. While we need to take seriously the dangers of utopian narratives, we may not have to discard narratives and utopias entirely. Instead, we might look for contextual, partial understandings of narratives to replace the metanarratives of the Enlightenment and mainstream Christianity. Drawing on the insights of constructionist and feminist critiques, among others, we can begin to reconceptualize narratives and utopias in accordance with not just the intellectual but also the political demands of our time. In relation to environmental ethics, this means critically examining both our own stories and the alternative narratives of humanity's relations to nature, in order to explore the strengths as well as the flaws of both. This effort is evident in some streams of leftist thought and practice in Latin America, where progressive parties and social movements are revising notions of both what is possible and what is necessary, without giving up hope of a qualitatively better future—"without fear of being happy," as the Workers' Party of Brazil puts it. Recent works on progressive movements in Latin America hint at the possibilities: *Utopia Unarmed,* one is called; *The Limits of Utopia,* another.[39] Is it possible to have an unarmed, limited utopia? Is this a contradiction in terms? How might a chastened utopianism mobilize people? And what might this utopianism mean for human relationships with nature?

Rethinking utopianism requires, first, the postmodernist insistence that utopias are by definition unrealizable and, therefore, that no present or historical human community does or can fully realize our ideals. This recognition must be challenged, however, by a future vision that provides a horizon capable of motivating action for change. This horizon may be ever receding, but it is also ever present. Sallie McFague calls this modified utopia an "atopia": "an imagined world both prophetic and alluring from which we can judge what is wrong with the paradigm that has created the present crisis." An atopian vision not only provides grounds for critique but also, as McFague writes, points to "the breaking in of new possibilities, of hope for a new creation."[40] However, it poses dangers as well, especially that of imagining that we have found a God's-eye perspective, which time and again has generated domination. Despite the risks, without utopian or atopian hopes ethical and political action often lacks meaning and almost always lacks the enthusiasm necessary for long-term commitment. Visions of how things ought to be provide a goal toward which transformative action can aim, without needing guarantees of reaching the goal. Paul Tillich describes this in terms of anticipation: "The thing ultimately referred to in all genuine anticipation remains transcendent; it transcends any concrete fulfilment of human destiny; it transcends the otherworldly utopias of religious fantasy as well as the this-worldly utopias of secular speculation." Still, Tillich continues, "this transcendence does not mean that distorted reality should be left unchanged; rather it looks forward to a continuous revolutionary shattering and transforming of the existing situation."[41] This suggests that we allow the image of horizon to replace that of kingdom, that we celebrate small victories rather than insist on final triumph, and that we read ethical narratives not as maps reflecting present reality but as signposts to a different reality.

STORIED RESIDENCE

The question remains, however, which narratives might point us in the right direction. We need new stories, but where will we find them? And what is going to make us believe them? Many people no longer find the old stories of traditional religion compelling; some consider them downright dangerous. Even if the stories do retain appeal, we cannot return to what Sallie McFague terms "the naivete of organic belonging that permeated the lives of our foremothers and fathers."[42] Rather, as Rebecca Raglon and Marian Scholtmeijer write, "we must make the difficult effort to appreciate the new stories that we have, and to begin to value them as legitimate sources of knowledge."[43] Which new stories? Some environmental ethicists and activists, as noted above, find inspiration in the evolutionary epic. Others look to non-Western, especially Asian and Native American, cultures as sources of knowledge and models for less destructive relationships to nonhuman nature. Val Plumwood outlines what Westerners might learn from indigenous narratives in particular: "Those of us from the master culture who lack imagination can gain new ideas from a study, undertaken in humility and sympathy, of the sustaining stories of the cultures we have cast as outside reason. If we are to survive into a liveable future, we must take into our own hands the power to create, restore and explore different stories, with new main characters, better plots, and at least the possibility of some happy endings."[44]

The problem, again, is that we cannot find or invent narratives, however wise and beautiful they may be, and then just decide to live by them. To be powerful, narratives must emerge from a context, a whole worldview and lifeway. I discussed these issues in chapter 5, in relation to non-Native borrowing of indigenous traditions. In addition to the colonial undercurrents of such an approach, there is the simple fact that few narratives, Native American or other, either make sense or inspire dedicated followers outside the culture in which the stories originated or in which they have had time to become naturalized, as Christianity has done, for example, in much of Latin America and among African Americans in the United States. We then have to ask what is required for alternative narratives to become naturalized in contemporary Western cultures.

This restates the driving question of bioregionalism: what might it take to resettle or reinhabit the lands where we live, to become native to "our little places?"[45] And how do we decide who counts as a native? Gary Nabhan elaborates this problem in the contemporary context: "Do Mennonites, Lapps, Basques, and Bedouins qualify as 'traditional peoples,' 'ecosystem peoples,' or 'indigenes' as much as 'Native Americans' do?"[46] Nabhan suggests that origins and length of residence are not the only criteria that matter. Rather, being native means caring for a place in the fullest sense: knowing it, minimizing negative impacts to it, and preserving its full range of native species and ecological relations. In this light, as Nabhan indicates, some groups that are not original inhabitants or Native may qualify as native. He points, for example, to Mennonite farmers, who have spent generations getting to know, caring for, and making a living in the Midwestern United States while maintaining the health and diversity of the local ecosystems. It is neither accidental nor irrelevant that Mennonite culture and agriculture are deeply tied to a particular, highly theocentric version of the Christian narrative, encompassing a strong sense of stewardship, awareness of human fallibility, and commitment to mutual aid and pacifism. Mennonite agriculture and environmental ethics, in other words, gain legitimation and force from an overarching religious framework that situates humans in relation to God, nature, and other persons. European Mennonites brought this narrative and its associated ethic, along with agricultural technology and methods and forms of community life, to their new home in the United States. The narrative and the people have since become deeply embedded in the Midwestern landscape. Studies of such naturalized (neonative?) communities, their setbacks as well as their successes, can help us understand in more detail both what makes people live by a given moral system and, in meta-ethical terms, what can make moral systems livable.

Mennonite communities clearly benefited from their shared religious narrative and theological commitment. As Mennonites in the United States adapted to new ecological, cultural, and political conditions, they could modify their religious narrative without losing its original coherence and power. Bioregionalism points to more heterogeneous efforts to become native to a place from scratch, so to speak, or at least without a prior, overarching religious framework in and through which to understand our residence. Bioregionalism is a project of "reinhabitation," which has developed, as Doug Aberley explains, "in response to the challenge of reconnecting socially-just human cultures in a sustainable manner to the region-scale ecosystems in which they are irrevocably embedded."[47] For bioregionalism, the place itself, rather than faith in God or religious history, has to generate both the narratives and the ethical commitments. Place—the land, the relationships and histories embodied in it, the diverse lives it sustains—must provide meaning and motivation, or in Callicott's terms, fill the void left without a shared theology.

Holmes Rolston theorizes the connections among attachment to place, narrative, and ethics in his conception of "storied residence." Rolston writes, "An environmental ethic does not want to abstract out universals, if such there be, from all this drama of life, formulating some set of duties applicable across the whole. . . . The logic of the home, the ecology, is finally narrative. . . . If a holistic ethic is really to incorporate the whole story, it must systematically embed itself in historical eventfulness. Else it will not really be objective. It will not be appropriate, well adapted, for the way humans actually fit into their niches."[48] For Rolston and other bioregionalists, being at home in our niches helps us invent and adapt to the narratives that celebrate and sustain those places. These narratives reinforce our feeling of being native to particular bioregions, and in turn this feeling encourages us to take care of the places we love.

Rolston's felicitous concept of storied residence might help expand our understanding of ethics generally. Charles Kammer has suggested that ethics involve an integrally related set of factors, which together constitute a sort of ethical landscape. The five elements of Kammer's "moralscape" are worldview, loyalties, norms and values, experiential and empirical elements, and mode of decision making.[49] Kammer's model significantly broadens the traditional analytic emphasis on values, norms, and forms of decision making. I expand it further by adding conceptions of humanness, either as an aspect of worldview or as a separate category. We might also add narrative, as a structural dimension that ties the different elements of the moralscape together in meaningful ways.

Environmental ethics points to the further necessity of including nature or the land as an element of the moralscape, perhaps even as its underlying ground. Making this explicit in our conceptualization of ethics means bringing our dependence upon nonhuman nature out of the obscurity to which it is generally relegated by mainstream ethics.

This obscurity exemplifies what Val Plumwood calls the backgrounding of nature, in which people deny their dependence and treat nature "as a limitless provider without needs of its own."[50] Environmental ethics both foregrounds human dependence upon natural processes and points to the possibility of seeing nature in terms of nonhuman needs. No understanding of humanness or of human morality, in this view, can be complete without taking into account the ecological dimensions of human life. Along these lines, a fuller conception of ethics might also rescue from philosophical obscurity our physical bodies—the earth we carry—and the myriad ways they connect us to other humans, other species, and natural processes.

The image of a moral landscape underlines the fact that no single element determines ethical decisions. Instead, ethics weaves together different factors, including worldview, loyalties, norms, values, in different ways (i.e., in modes of decision making) and in different settings, understood in ecological terms as bioregions, and also shaped by human history and culture. Contrary to established deontological, utilitarian, and theological models, this approach insists that no single step or concept can determine an essence of morality, to which all other factors are accidental. Our understandings of ourselves and our world, our values and goals, our relationships, our histories, our physical embodiment, and our ecological embeddedment are neither trivial nor corrupting. Rather, together they constitute ethics. None of these elements by itself can properly be described as ethics, and there is no morality apart from the relations among them. In other words, these relationships are not external to something separate called morality. Ethics is the sum of these relationships; or better, "the sum of . . . relationships plus the uniqueness, the individuality, that emerges from just this particular blend of natural and social interactions."[51] These dimensions come together— not always but often and in especially powerful ways—in narratives. The moral landscape, like physical landscapes, is storied. We live both in and through the tales we hear, tell, and retell.

IDEAS AND PRACTICE

The image of a moralscape points to some of the different factors that shape ethical decisions and action. It underlines the ways that ethics are lived and concrete, encompassing histories and relationships as well as abstract principles. This model points us back to the question about how ideas about human nature shape action. What, again, are the relations between theory and practice in ethics? This is a complex, multifaceted question that will always escape final resolution. Nonetheless, we can answer it at least in part by exploring meta-ethical issues, such as the structural framework suggested by narrative and the different elements brought together in a moralscape. More concretely, we can explore some of the practical implications of particular elements of an ethical landscape, such as the chastened anthropology I have described.

One aspect of this anthropology is the characteristic of being terrestrial—being native to the planet as well as to the particular piece of it that we occupy. Sallie McFague emphasizes the practical implications of the image of earth as home for Christianity: "If we evolved here, if the earth is our home, then it follows that we will want to take care of it."[52] This claim echoes the central argument of bioregionalism. Is it justified? Can attachment to place lead people to take better care of it? In other words, is there really a link between ideas and practice in this particular case? Gary Nabhan suggests that there is, and for evidence he points to the correlation between species extinctions and mobility of human populations in given bioregions. This indicates, he argues, that there really is a correlation between being culturally rooted in a place and taking care of it. Other environmental writers have argued that immigrant groups, such as the English in North America or the Spanish and Portuguese in South America, are much more likely to cause serious environmental damage than native, or at least naturalized, populations.[53] Other cases show, however, that length of residence in itself is not sufficient to inspire care. Further, the reality of contemporary society means that we need to think hard about whether or not long residence in a given place is necessary, because it might not be possible. We are not merely a society but a world of immigrants, where traditional forms of attachment to place are increasingly difficult. This reality does not make the vision of bioregionalism impossible, but it does call for careful consideration of what being native might mean in a globalized world.[54]

In addition to the notion of being terrestrial or native, I have suggested, a chastened anthropology encompasses a relational understanding of human selfhood. This model contrasts with the vision of personal autonomy and separateness that is reinforced by multiple institutions of modern Western life, including the market economy, educational systems, and the family. The value of self-sufficiency is ingrained literally from the first day of life in our culture. For example, in much of Asia, Latin America, and Africa, children sleep with their mothers for the first few years of life (and often with siblings after that). However, at least in the middle classes in the United States most newborn babies sleep in their own beds, usually in their own rooms. According to the immensely popular guide to raising babies *What to Expect the First Year,* this practice is necessary to instill a sense of autonomy in the infant. Babies who sleep with their parents, the book suggests, will have problems "adjusting" later. "Co-sleeping, parents and children sharing a bed at night, does work well—but chiefly in other societies. In a society like ours, which stresses the development of independence and the importance of privacy, co-sleeping is associated with a wide range of problems."[55] Clearly, babies' sleeping habits do not a culture make, but they are a symptom of how profoundly contemporary Western cultures value individual autonomy, even to the extent of imagining that it should and can be attained by the most dependent of humans, a newborn baby.

Not only sleeping habits but other elements of child rearing both shape and are shaped by dominant understandings of personhood. Many psychologists and other theorists argue that early childhood experiences are crucial to notions of individual identity. Building on this claim, Nancy Chodorow suggests that collective child rearing, probably the norm for most of human evolution, generates very different understandings of self than does the nuclear family with mother as primary (often solitary) caregiver. Chodorow contends that although children grow up differently without exclusive mothering, these differences may not be undesirable. "Studies of more collective child rearing situations (the kibbutzim, China, Cuba) suggest that children develop more sense of solidarity and commitment to the group, less individualism and competitiveness, [and] are less liable to form intense, exclusive adult relationships, than children reared in Western nuclear families." Exclusive parenting, Chodorow argues, harms both mother and child. Both benefit from "situations where love and relationship are not a scarce resource controlled and manipulated by one person only."[56]

Patricia Hill Collins describes an alternative to exclusive parenting in her analysis of mothering practices in African American communities, which, she writes, recognize that "vesting one person with full responsibility for mothering a child may not be wise or possible."[57] "Othermothers," defined as women who share responsibilities and attachment to children who are not biologically their own, traditionally have been central to the institution of black motherhood, Collins writes. In this model, young women are groomed to become othermothers, and children may be disciplined by any of their othermothers. Evidence of this extended understanding of motherhood can be seen in the use of family language to refer to other community members, which anthropologists might term "fictive kinship," but which reflect nonfictional relationships that profoundly shape both the children and adults involved. Collins argues that "by seeing the larger community as responsible for children and by giving othermothers and other nonparents 'rights' in child-rearing, African-Americans challenge prevailing property relations."[58] They also challenge prevailing notions of what it means to be a mother, to be a member of a community, and to be a person. Collins suggests that exclusive mother-child relationships may limit understandings of one's responsibility to others and, ultimately, the potential for activism.

Collins's discussion of different conceptions of mothering complements the feminist insistence that the quality and not just the fact of relationship matters. In interpersonal relationships, the simple fact of relationship does not preclude exploitation, domination, or injustice. More broadly, in ethical and political terms, narrow definitions of acceptable relationality and caring—who or what you can care for and how—may be no better than extreme individualism. These definitions also shape the kind of community that emerges from the multiple relations among individuals. Collins argues that community othermothers "demonstrate a clear rejection of separateness and individual interest as the basis of either community organization or individual self-actualization. Instead, the connectedness with others and common interest expressed by community othermothers models a very different value system."[59] It also reflects a very different understanding of personhood, as related and answerable to a range of persons, not just to those to whom one is biologically related or to whom one has chosen to relate.

This points to the ways that new understandings of self and of interpersonal relationships undergird alternative definition and experiences of community. In the West, or at least in the United States, Sharon Welch explains, community has generally rested on similarities among members (thus "the Polish American community" or "the gay community"). In response to the challenges of increasing cultural diversity, Welch proposes a model of community based not on similarity but on contiguity.[60] Community need not be limited to those who are similar, she suggests: we can have important relationships and common ground with people who are very different from us. These connections, however, do not come easily. They require conversation, as theories of communicative ethics suggest, but "conversation alone is not enough. Emancipatory conversations are the fruit of work together, the result of alterations in relationships between groups. In work we create as much as we affirm the rational principle of shared humanity."[61] In order to create community with people from different backgrounds, in order even to hold meaningful conversations with them, we need to work together.

Further, we need not merely to accept their differences. Welch criticizes "models of tolerance and respect in which respect means not only not judging or trying to change others, but also, that there are no grounds then, for others to seriously challenge, and perhaps even change us."[62] We need more than pluralism, Welch insists, because "we can see foundational flaws in systems of ethics only from the outside, from the perspective of another system of defining and implementing that which is valued."[63] "Enlarging our moral vision" requires "a process of learning to see the world through multiple lenses."[64]

Although Welch is speaking, at least explicitly, only of interhuman communities, her model can be expanded to what Midgley calls "mixed communities" of humans and nonhuman animals. Creating and respecting cross-species relationships, like building diverse human communities, require both deliberate effort and a willingness to let the perspectives of the other become a lens for viewing our own worlds. While it is difficult to see the world through the perspective of other species, it need not be impossible. We can know nonhuman nature, to a significant though not full extent, because our senses serve as windows between our bodies and the outside world, and our bodies are not walls but semipermeable membranes. As Adrienne Rich writes, "We are neither 'inner' nor 'outer' constructed; our skin is alive with signals."[65] The challenge of living with diverse people and diverse species calls us to attend to these signals, to engage the coresidents of our neighborhood, our bioregion, and our planet in conversations and shared work, to be open to the possibility of transformation. If we make room for nonhuman others and get to know them, we might be able to let the worlds they construct and inhabit transform our own worlds.

LIVED ETHICS

Understandings of community based on contiguity as well as similarity, interaction as well as conversation, suggest that our ideas about community, including ideal communities, take shape only in concrete, partial, and ever-changing ways. Once we take seriously the varied interests and perspectives of contiguous others, human or not, we cannot simply apply our idea of community or any other ethical concept to nature or to human society. Rather, we alter our ideas in response to the thoughts of others and to our experiences together. This helps to give nuance to, or at least to complicate, the ways we think about efforts to identify and implement alternative ethical narratives in the larger context of becoming native to a place. In this process, we can and must draw on the narratives and ideals of other cultures. For practical and political reasons, however, we can neither adopt their ideas wholesale nor impose our visions on others. We can construct a livable and lived ethic only in and through a process of listening to others and working with them.

Many, even most, lived ethics in human history have been religious. Recognizing this, as I discussed in chapter 1, a number of environmental philosophers have recently turned their attention to religion. They hope to understand what can make environmental ethics, any ethics, practicable and compelling. On one level, most ethics are compelling for the prosaic reason that they have been ingrained since childhood. People do change their minds and their moral outlooks, however, or there would be no revolutions, no religious reformations, not even any individual conversions. Given that many of us grow up with belief systems that do not incline us to live gently on the earth, the urgent task for environmental ethics is to uncover what might make people change their ways of understanding and living on the earth, in its many particular ecosystems.

While they are not sufficient, meta-ethical inquiries can help us in this task. Exploring the ways that moral frameworks are shaped by understandings of self and of relationships, by narrative structure, and by other elements of the moralscape helps us understand what constitutes an ethic and what makes it compelling. The presence of these different elements, though, or even the understanding that they are present, does not necessarily mean that desired behavioral consequences will follow. In other words, just because we get one thing right does not guarantee that everything else we hope for will follow. This is a common misapprehension of many ethicists: they imagine, probably more wistfully than naively, that if we just get the philosophy (metaphysics, epistemology, theology) right, then we will get it right every other way.

Other thinkers have countered this idealism with reminders that the link between ideas and practice is neither straightforward nor allpowerful. Reinhold Niebuhr insists that achieving greater social justice requires not just spiritual enlightenment or moral education but also political force. While morality is valuable and necessary, by itself it is not sufficient to change societies, institutions, or laws. Those changes require political force, embodied in laws, armies, courts, economies, and even peer pressure. Niebuhr's critics point out that he may have underestimated the power of individual changes and that his brand of realism may encourage resignation, even despair. This is tied to the critique of utopianism noted earlier, the danger that impossible changes may seem to be the only worthwhile ones. This perspective makes social improvement seem so difficult that no one can be required to try for it (since, as Kant insists, "ought" must presume "can"). This cultured despair, in Welch's term, recognizes the scope of our problems and the limitations of our efforts to resolve them. This awareness, however, leads to "a failure of nerve" rather than to a realistic commitment to struggle in the face of limitations.[66]

We need alternatives both to the idealistic hope for a straight line from ideas to practice and to the cynical notion that no such line exists. The search for this balance, Zygmunt Bauman suggests, takes a peculiar form in our time: "The postmodern perspective offers more wisdom; the postmodern setting makes acting on that wisdom more difficult. . . . What the postmodern mind is aware of is that there are problems in human and social life with no good solutions, twisted trajectories that cannot be straightened up."[67] We will not achieve a quick fix, or indeed any total fix or utopian society. We must, therefore, accept the genuine biological, political, and personal limits we face in our efforts to change our societies. This humility, however, needs the counterbalancing force of imagination, the atopian hope that reaches toward the not yet. To transcend and transform experience, as Adrienne Rich puts it, we need to envision alternatives to the very lives we are living.

This hope becomes more necessary as we pay more attention to the condition of the nonhuman worlds around us. Ecological catastrophe is real, and much that has already been lost is irretrievable. It is easier and much less painful to avoid thinking about these losses. Aldo Leopold expresses this pain when he writes, "One of the penalties of an ecological education is that one lives alone in a world of wounds."[68] Our world is full of wounds, human and nonhuman. The point, however, is precisely that we are not alone in it. We are not alone because we are connected to the wounded. That is why we care about the wounds or even notice them in the first place. We are not alone, further, in loving the wounded bodies of our planet. Many people love and have loved them, in myriad embodied, storied ways. Expressing those ways, bringing them to bear on our own lives, defending what we love against further wounding, may well be the meaning of ethics.

Notes

CHAPTER ONE: INTRODUCTION

1. Raymond Williams, "Ideas of Nature," in *Problems in Materialism and Culture* (London: Verso, 1980), 70–71.

2. Esbjornson, "On Rethinking Resistance," 288.

3. A closely related approach is that of moral psychology, "the study of the person . . . with an eye towards its good." Horst, "Our Animal Bodies," 35. Both moral psychology and ethical anthropology have their "beginnings in the recognition that facts about what kinds of beings we are have implications, both for what vision we conceive of the human good, and for what methods we should adopt to pursue it," as Horst writes (ibid.). Moral psychology is distinguished, however, by its explicitly therapeutic methods and goals. Another related field is "virtue ethics," which contends that ethics depends on certain qualities of character rather than adherence to rules or pursuit of goals. Virtue ethicists, however, have not made explicit the ways that *all* ethical systems, including rule- and goal-oriented ones, rely on anthropological assumptions.

4. I am grateful to Les Thiele for drawing my attending to the ontological dimensions of these issues, which he also addresses in "Nature and Freedom," 171–90.

5. Benton, *Natural Relations*, 103.

6. This echoes Gustavo Gutiérrez's assertion that liberation theology represents not a new theme, but a new *method* for theology. Gutiérrez, *A Theology of Liberation*, 15.

7. Antonio Gramsci, "Observations on Folklore: Giovanni Crocioni," in *Gramsci: Selections from Cultural Writings,* ed. D. Forgacs and G. Nowell-Smith; trans. W. Boelhower (Cambridge: Harvard University Press, 1985), 189. See also Mary Midgley's claim that everyone has to do philosophy, i.e., to work out their own system of concepts, well or badly, whether they notice it or not. Midgley, *Beast and Man,* xxxv.

8. Tweed, "Introduction: Narrating U.S. Religious History," 12.

9. Oelschlaeger, *Caring for Creation*, 6.

10. Ibid., 11.

11. See the two influential works by Robert Bellah, Richard Madsen, William Sullivan, Ann Swidler, and Steven Tipton, *Habits of the Heart* and *The Good Society*.

12. Oelschlaeger, *Caring for Creation*, 29.

13. Ibid., 99, 186; see also 230.

14. Ibid., 119–20, 123, 222.

15. Ibid., 9, 112, 189–90. Oelschlaeger, like most environmental ethicists, at least in the United States, also shies away from explicit critiques of the free market economy and related social and political arrangements. Some environmental activists and theorists from the United Kingdom, Latin America, and elsewhere have pointed to the close links between capitalism and current forms of environmental degradation. Few environmental or social ethicists, however, have explored these links or their ties to dominant Western philosophical (and often religious) assumptions about human nature. See Benton, *Natural Relations*, for a more openly leftist perspective on some of these issues.

16. Paul Santmire's *The Travail of Nature* does highlight the fact that salvation and eschatology are at the center of different Christian attitudes toward nature.

17. Oelschlaeger, *Caring for Creation*, 176–77. See also Deloria, *God Is Red*.

18. Other works that look at the potential of non-Western religions include Roger Gottlieb, ed., *This Sacred Earth: Religion, Nature, Environment* (London: Routledge, 1996); Taylor, ed., *Ecological Resistance Movements*; Suzuki and Knudtson, *The Wisdom of the Elders*; and various studies of Asian religions and ecology, including J. Baird Callicott and Roger Ames, eds., *Nature in Asian Traditions of Thought: Essays in Environmental Philosophy* (Albany: State University of New York Press, 1989); Alan Hunt Badiner, ed., *Dharma Gaia* (Berkeley: Parallax Press, 1990); Mary Evelyn Tucker and Duncan Ryuken Williams, eds., *Buddhism and Ecology* (Cambridge: Harvard University Press, 1997); De Silva, *Environmental Philosophy and Ethics in Buddhism*; and L. Nelson, ed., *Purifying the Earthly Body of God*. Zimmerman, *Contesting Earth's Future*; and Garé, *Postmodernism and the Environmental Crisis*, both explore the role of postmodern science in environmental ethics.

19. Callicott, *Earth's Insights*, 198.

20. Callicott, "The Metaphysical Implications of Ecology," 60.

21. Callicott, *Earth's Insights*, 10.

22. Leopold, *A Sand County Almanac*, 239. Callicott discusses his interpretation of Leopold's ethic in *In Defense of the Land Ethic*.

23. Callicott, *Earth's Insights*, 82.

24. Ibid., 111, 121; John G. Neihardt, *Black Elk Speaks: Being the Life Story of a Holy Man of the Oglala Sioux* (Lincoln: University of Nebraska Press, 1961).

25. Ibid., 158.

26. Ibid., 186, 189. Callicott acknowledges that his endorsement of a single,

global ethic and of the universality of contemporary science is open to criticism (ironically, given his faith in postmodern science) from postmodernists, among others.

27. Ibid., 205–206.

28. Cheney, "Eco-Feminism and Deep Ecology," 144.

29. Johnson, *Moral Imagination*, 163. See also D. Carr, *Time, Narrative, and History;* and Holstein and Gubrium, *The Self We Live By*, for arguments about the narrative structure of human experience.

30. Johnson, *Moral Imagination*, 152.

31. MacIntyre, *After Virtue*, 191, 203, 205; the reference to "storytelling animals" is on 201.

32. Ibid., 216.

33. McCutcheon, "A Default of Critical Intelligence?" 459. McCutcheon sees only one dimension of this universalizing process—its oppressive potential. He fails, I believe, to recognize the liberatory possibilities of seeing one's local and particular experiences in larger spiritual, even universal terms.

34. See Peterson, "Religious Narratives and Political Protest," 27–44, and *Martyrdom and the Politics of Religion.*

35. Callicott, *Earth's Insights,* 223. See also Akula, "Grassroots Environmental Resistance in India," 127–45.

36. Such stories are common in many Native American cultures. Another powerful example, recounted by Gary Snyder, is the Athapaskan story of "the woman who married a bear," which "teach[es] humans the precise manners in regard to bears." Snyder, *The Practice of the Wild,* 169. See also Cheney, "Postmodern Environmental Ethics."

37. Flores, "Place," 44.

38. See Oelschlaeger, *Caring for Creation,* especially chap. 4; Callicott, *Earth's Insights,* 212–18.

39. See Peterson, *Martyrdom and the Politics of Religion;* and Roger Lancaster, *Thanks to God and the Revolution: Popular Religion and Class Consciousness in the New Nicaragua* (New York: Columbia University Press, 1988).

40. Macy, *Mutual Causality,* 209.

41. See, for example, de Waal, *Good-Natured.*

42. Rolston, *Environmental Ethics,* 349.

CHAPTER 2: NOT OF THE WORLD

1. Niebuhr, *The Nature and Destiny of Man,* 99.

2. Radner and Radner, *Animal Consciousness,* 8, quoting Charles Darwin, *The Descent of Man and Selection in Relation to Sex,* 2nd ed. (New York: A. L. Burt, 1874), 89.

3. Augustine, *City of God,* Vol. 1, bk. 11.

4. Revised Standard Version. In a second and less influential creation account, Genesis 2:18–19, other animals are made as "helpers" for the first man, who should not be alone. According to this text, Baird Callicott suggests, "man is neither essentially different from other animals nor separated from them by a metaphysical gulf." Callicott, *Earth's Insights,* 17.

5. Kaufman, "The Concept of Nature," 352.

6. Santmire, *The Travail of Nature*, 13.

7. The Roman Catholic Church attacked the Cathari brutally during the Inquisition and, in response to their opposition to reproduction, hardened its prohibition on birth control and abortion, which previously had not been a central or consistent teaching of the church.

8. This perspective is echoed in others of Paul's letters, including 1 Cor. 5: 10 and 7:29–35; Phil. 2:15; and Col. 2:20, and in the Gospel of John, especially 17:14–15.

9. Laitin, "Religion, Political Culture," 589.

10. Ibid., 571.

11. Augustine, *City of God*, 1:12.

12. Augustine, *De Genesi ad Litteram* 6.19.30, quoted in Santmire, *The Travail of Nature*, 65–66.

13. Augustine, *City of God*, 2:252.

14. Martin Luther, "On the Freedom of a Christian," in *Martin Luther: Selections from His Writings*, ed. John Dillenberger (New York: Anchor Books, 1961), 53

15. Northcott, *The Environment and Christian Ethics*, 220.

16. Niebuhr, *The Nature and Destiny of Man*, 26.

17. Ibid., 55.

18. Niebuhr, *Moral Man and Immoral Society*.

19. Santmire, *The Travail of Nature*, 81–82.

20. Aquinas, *Introduction*, 234, 616, 618.

21. Ibid., 263.

22. Ibid., 918.

23. Second Vatican Council, *Gaudium et Spes*, no. 24, p. 174.

24. Ibid., no. 12, p. 167.

25. John Paul II, *Redemptor Hominis*, no. 14, p. 332.

26. Northcott, *The Environment and Christian Ethics*, 229.

27. Callicott, *Earth's Insights*, 79.

28. Northcott, *The Environment and Christian Ethics*, 220.

29. René Descartes, "Discourse on Method," in *The Philosophical Writings of Descartes*, trans. J. Cottingham et al. (Cambridge: Cambridge University Press, 1969), 22–24.

30. Marx, *Economic and Philosophic Manuscripts of 1844*, 76. Some environmental philosophers have also pointed to helpful aspects of Marxist thought; see, Benton, *Natural Relations*.

31. Durkheim, *The Elementary Forms of the Religious Life*, 469, 487, 83.

32. Warren, "The Power and Promise of Ecological Feminism," 128–29.

33. Birke, *Feminism, Animals, and Science*, 98.

34. Aristotle, *The Politics*. See esp. 57, 68–69.

35. Johnson, *The Body in the Mind*, x. Zuleyma Tang Halpin argues that this concept of objectivity is central to scientific training. See Halpin, "Scientific Objectivity and the Concept of 'the Other,'" 285–94.

36. Johnson, *The Body in the Mind*, x.

37. Ibid., xxvi.

38. Ibid., xiv.

39. Richard Schmitt notes an alternative perspective on embodiment: having distinct bodies can be read as justifying claims to separateness. Schmitt argues against this interpretation of embodiment, although he does not highlight the ways that bodies might connect us to rather than separate us from others. See *Beyond Separateness.*

40. Ibid., 57.

41. L. White, "The Historical Roots," 1205.

42. Ibid., 1205.

43. Ibid., 1206.

44. Northcott, *The Environment and Christian Ethics.*

45. Santmire, *The Travail of Nature,* 212.

46. Ibid., 93.

47. Christians have also debated whether or not the body is involved in salvation, and some, including Luther, have insisted that the resurrection does in fact include the body (albeit a transformed, "spiritualized" body). Regardless of this debate, what is most importantly redeemed and reborn to eternal life— and what gives the body any value it may have—is the soul, the divine spark that longs to meet its maker.

48. Ibid., 116. See also Roger D. Sorrell, *St. Francis of Assisi and Nature.* Lynn White Jr. also praises Francis, proposing him as the "patron saint" for ecologists ("The Historical Roots," 1207).

49. Jackson, *Becoming Native to This Place.*

50. Snyder, *The Practice of the Wild,* 40.

51. Ibid., 39.

52. Weber, *The Protestant Ethic and the Spirit of Capitalism.*

CHAPTER 3: THE SOCIAL CONSTRUCTION
OF NATURE AND HUMAN NATURE

1. Berger and Luckmann, *The Social Construction of Reality,* 18.

2. Ibid., 183. In *The Structure of Scientific Revolutions,* Thomas Kuhn argues that scientific knowledge is also socially constructed. Scientific paradigms, writes Kuhn, not only emerge from scientific data but help determine what data scientists make use of and even what they can perceive in the first place: "What a man sees depends both upon what he looks at and also upon what his previous visual-conceptual experience has taught him to see." As a result, "when paradigms change, the world changes with them." Kuhn, *The Structure of Scientific Revolutions,* 113, 111.

3. Clifford Geertz, "The Growth of Culture and the Evolution of Mind," in *The Interpretation of Cultures* (New York: Basic Books, 1973), 83.

4. Geertz, "The Impact of the Concept of Culture on the Concept of Man," in *The Interpretation of Cultures* (New York: Basic Books, 1973), 53.

5. Ibid., 35.

6. Berger and Luckmann, *The Social Construction of Reality,* 89.

7. Butler, "Contingent Questions," 46.

8. Scott, "Deconstructing Equality-versus-Difference," 33.

9. Butler, "Contingent Questions," 47.

10. Wilson, *Sociobiology: The New Synthesis, Sociobiology: The Abridged Edition,* and *On Human Nature;* quote is from the last (17).

11. Ibid., 119.

12. This dominant interpretation probably does not do full justice to the sophisticated and often politically aware work of Wilson and some other leading sociobiologists, although undoubtedly a number of "cruder" writers fulfill all the constructionist stereotypes and more. I discuss sociobiological views of human nature in more detail in chapter 7.

13. See Tang-Martinez, "The Curious Courtship of Sociobiology and Feminism," 116–50.

14. Gould, *The Mismeasure of Man.* Many critics point to recent controversies surrounding *The Bell Curve* as evidence that scientific racism is still alive and influential. See Richard J. Herrnstein and Charles Murray, *The Bell Curve: Intelligence and Class Structure in American Life* (New York: Free Press, 1994).

15. Midgley, *Beast and Man.*

16. Watson, "What Is Behaviorism?" 61.

17. Derrida, "The End of the Book and the Beginning of Writing," 337–38.

18. Baudrillard, *Symbolic Exchange and Death,* 438. Italics in original.

19. Deleuze and Guattari, *Anti-Oedipus,* 404. Italics in original.

20. Ibid., 412.

21. Soper, *What Is Nature?* 129.

22. Berger and Luckmann, *The Social Construction of Reality,* 183.

23. Harvey, *Justice, Nature, and the Geography of Difference,* 166.

24. Soper, *What Is Nature?* 130.

25. Midgley, *Beast and Man,* 56.

26. Spretnak, "Radical Nonduality in Ecofeminist Philosophy," 433.

27. Williams, "Ideas of Nature," 67. Soper makes a similar point in *What Is Nature?* 2.

28. Descola, "Constructing Natures," 88.

29. Ingold, "Hunting and Gathering," 117.

30. Howell, "Nature in Culture or Culture in Nature?" 128.

31. Mick Smith highlights this contribution of social constructivism in "To Speak of Trees," 359–76. Smith contends, in particular, that social constructivism can provide an important critical element to the theories of Deep Ecologists. His arguments complement mine here and in a modified version of this chapter, which appeared as "Environmental Ethics and the Social Construction of Nature."

32. A recent article in the *Hartford Courant* makes this point, describing a wetland along the Susquetonscut Brook that "is not completely natural but was altered by Colonial farmers centuries ago." The article goes on to point to the environmental dangers of distinguishing sharply between "natural" and "unnatural": the finding about the wetland's origin "raises questions about whether and how a man-made wetland should be protected by Connecticut policy." Grant, "Altered States," F1.

33. Moran, "Nurturing the Forest," 531–55.

34. Soper, *What Is Nature?* 152.

35. McKibben, *The End of Nature*, 49.

36. Harrison, "Toward a Philosophy of Nature," 426.

37. Proctor, "Whose Nature?" 273.

38. Ibid., 288.

39. Cronon, "The Trouble with Wilderness; or, Getting Back to the Wrong Nature," 69.

40. Budiansky, *The Covenant of the Wild*, 116–17, 139, and 140–41.

41. Coates, *Nature*, 95. Along slightly different lines, Shepard Krech argues against the stereotype of the "ecological Indian": "For the sake of a simple narrative, critics who excoriate the larger society as they absolve Indians of all blame sacrifice evidence that in recent years, Indian people have had a mixed relationship to the environment. They victimize Indians when they strip them of all agency in their lives except when their actions fit the image of the Ecological Indian." Krech, *The Ecological Indian*, 216. Gary Paul Nabhan offers a thoughtful and incisive critique of some of these efforts to demythologize Native American conservation practices in *Cultures of Habitat*, 152–65.

42. Budiansky, *Nature's Keepers*. The most bizarre attack on environmentalists is probably Coates's claim that "the eco-socialist dystopia is a police state run by a green Hitler that mobilizes a vast network of informers to stamp out ecological incorrectness" (*Nature*, 172).

43. Cronon, "The Trouble with Wilderness; or, Getting Back to the Wrong Nature," 80.

44. White, "Are You an Environmentalist," 172.

45. Ibid., 184.

46. Budiansky, *The Covenant of the Wild*, 12. Budiansky ignores the obvious fact that hunting is necessary "daily work" for very few people in contemporary Western societies.

47. McKibben, *The End of Nature*, 48.

48. White, "Are You an Environmentalist," 183.

49. Cronon, "The Trouble with Wilderness; or, Getting Back to the Wrong Nature," 82.

50. Slater, "Amazonia as Edenic Narrative," 130.

51. Midgley, *Animals and Why They Matter*, 31.

52. See Ehrenreich and McIntosh, "The New Creationism: Biology under Attack," 12.

53. Gary Snyder is more blunt about the links between advocates of the social construction of nature and more traditional anticonservationists. Despite attempts to appear radical, he writes, social constructionists offer "the same old occidental view of Nature as a realm of resources that has been handed over to humanity for its own use." He goes on to conclude that postmodernist approaches to nature represent "simply the high end of the 'wise use' movement." Snyder, "Is Nature Real?" 32.

54. Rival, "Blowpipes and Spears," 148–49, 150.

55. Howell, "Nature in Culture," 131.

56. Keith Tester, *Animals and Society*, 46.

57. Soper, *What Is Nature?* 151.

58. Rolston, "Nature for Real," 38.

59. Evernden, *The Social Creation of Nature*, 89; Rolston, "Nature for Real," 42.

60. Rolston, "Nature for Real," 55.

61. Ibid., Rolston, "Nature for Real," 40, 53–54, 62.

62. In a response to some of his critics, Cronon presents a different interpretation in *Environmental History*: "I have *not* argued that we should abandon the wild as a way of naming the sacred in nature; I have merely argued that we should not celebrate wilderness in such a way that we prevent ourselves from recognizing and taking responsibility for the sacred in our everyday lives and landscapes. If we wish to preserve wild nature, then we must permit ourselves to imagine a way of living in nature that can use and protect it at the same time." Cronon, "The Trouble with Wilderness: A Response," 55. In this response, Cronon portrays his critique of wilderness advocacy as a result of his commitment to environmental justice (e.g., the need for attention to urban habitats and human health). While this is a plausible argument, it is not a central theme in "The Trouble with Wilderness; or, Getting Back to the Wrong Nature." While the concern for environmental justice emphasized in his *Environmental History* piece may reflect his ongoing reflections on this issue, it does not appear as the main thrust of his work in *Uncommon Ground*.

63. Haraway, *Simians, Cyborgs, and Women*, 184.

64. In Marshall Sahlins's words, "The creation of meaning is the distinguishing and constituting quality of all men—the 'human essence' of an older discourse." *Culture and Practical Reason*, 102, quoted in Tim Ingold, introduction to *What Is an Animal?* ed. Tim Ingold (London: Routledge, 1988), 11.

65. Snyder's phrase comes from this sentence: "For all the talk of 'the other' in everybody's theory these days, when confronted with a genuine Other, the nonhuman realm, the response of the come-lately anti-Nature intellectuals is to circle the wagons and declare that Nature is really part of culture" ("Is Nature Real?" 32).

66. Benton, *Natural Relations*, 17. See Birke, *Feminism, Animals and Science*, 146.

67. Benton, *Natural Relations*, 17.

68. Rolston, "Nature for Real," 61. Italics in original.

69. Birke, *Feminism, Animals, and Science*, 147. Birke's point calls to mind David Harvey's broader critique of postmodernism: "Radicals within the cultural mass became charmed by fields like semiotics, as if the really interesting thing about the homeless were the variety of coded messages of protest that cardboard boxes could convey." In Harvey's view, postmodernists "became so caught up in the world of images for their own sake that they failed to examine to what purpose the building of images might be put." Harvey, "Flexibility," 69.

70. Reed, "The Affordances of the Animate Environment," 111–12.

71. Donna Haraway, "Situated Knowledges: The Science Question in Feminism and the Privilege of Partial Perspective," in *Simians, Cyborgs, and Women: The Reinvention of Nature* (New York: Routledge, 1991), 198.

72. Hayles, "Searching for Common Ground," 58.

73. Ingold, "Hunting and Gathering," 120–21.

74. Ibid., 121. Italics in original.

75. Adrienne Rich, "Woman and Bird," in *What Is Found There: Notebooks on Poetry and Politics* (New York: Quality Paperback Book Club, 1994), 7.

76. Cronon, "Introduction: In Search of Nature," 52. Unfortunately, Cronon makes statements elsewhere that demonstrate that this constructionist insight need not lead to ethically or politically constructive positions. For ethics, it is not the simple acknowledgment of otherness but the step *after* that recognition that matters.

77. Rich, "Woman and Bird," 8.

CHAPTER 4: THE RELATIONAL SELF

1. Gaard, "Ecofeminism and Native American Cultures," 296.

2. Larson, "Conceptual Resources," 273.

3. Ibid.

4. Sponberg, "Green Buddhism," 372.

5. Lovin and Reynolds, "In the Beginning," 3, 4.

6. McCutcheon, "A Default of Critical Intelligence?" 454.

7. Harding, "The Curious Coincidence of Feminine and African Moralities," 308. Harding takes the notion of "language of challenge" from Maurice Bloch and Jean Bloch, "Women and the Dialectics of Nature in Eighteenth Century French Thought," in *Nature, Culture and Gender,* ed. Carol Mac-Cormack and Marilyn Strathern (Cambridge: Cambridge University Press, 1980), 25–42.

8. Lovin and Reynolds, "In the Beginning," 31.

9. A number of the essays in McGinnis, *Bioregionalism,* explore the global dimensions of environmental problems.

10. Callicott and Ames, "Introduction: The Asian Traditions," 3.

11. Larson, "Conceptual Resources," 277.

12. Lovin and Reynolds, "In the Beginning," 30.

13. Ibid., 31.

14. Rahula, *What the Buddha Taught,* 66.

15. Ibid., 26.

16. Cook, "The Jewel Net," 225.

17. Ibid., 215.

18. Ibid., 214. Italics in original.

19. Macy, *Mutual Causality,* 8.

20. Ibid., 18.

21. Ibid., 108.

22. Inada, "Environmental Problematics," 243.

23. Rahula, *What the Buddha Taught,* 66.

24. Macy, *Mutual Causality,* 184.

25. Rahula, *What the Buddha Taught,* 1.

26. Rita Gross, "Buddhist Resources," 296.

27. Ibid., 296

28. Ibid., 296–97. Italics in original.

29. Gary Snyder, "Nets of Beads, Webs of Cells," in *A Place in Space: Ethics, Aesthetics, and Watersheds, New and Selected Prose* (Washington, D.C.: Counterpoint, 1995), 71.

30. Gross, "Towards a Buddhist Environmental Ethic," 339.

31. Gross, "Buddhist Resources," 296.

32. Ibid., 294.

33. Macy, "Greening," 57.

34. Ibid., 61. Italics in original.

35. John Seed, Joanna Macy, Pat Fleming, and Arne Naess, *Thinking Like a Mountain,* 36.

36. Quoted in Macy, "Greening," 62. Naess appears to assume that the self is permanent and eternal, which Buddhism, of course, denies.

37. Gross, "Towards a Buddhist Environmental Ethic," 338.

38. Swearer, "The Hermeneutics of Buddhist Ecology," 26–27.

39. Codiga, "Zen Practice and a Sense of Place," 108.

40. Sponberg, "Green Buddhism," 370–71. Italics in original.

41. Ibid., 373.

42. Eckel, "Is There a Buddhist Philosophy of Nature?" 344.

43. Thich Nhat Hanh, quoted in Allan Hunt Badiner, ed., *Dharma Gaia: A Harvest of Essays in Buddhism and Ecology* (Berkeley: Parallax Press, 1990), 215.

44. Snyder, "Nets of Beads," 70.

45. Thich Nhat Hanh, quoted in ibid., 70–72.

46. Welch, *A Feminist Ethic of Risk,* 3.

47. Ibid., 76.

48. Ames, "Putting the *Te,*" 132.

49. Tu Wei-Ming, "The Continuity of Being," 68.

50. Ames, "Putting the *Te,*" 121.

51. Tu Wei-Ming, "The Continuity of Being," 73.

52. Ames, "Putting the *Te,*" 119–20.

53. Tu Wei-Ming, "The Continuity of Being," 76

54. Ibid., 76; Schipper, *The Taoist Body,* 43.

55. Callicott, *Earth's Insights,* 79, 80.

56. Ibid., 84.

57. Ibid., 82.

58. Tuan, "Discrepancies."

59. Kellert, "Concepts of Nature East and West," 115–17.

60. Tuan, "Discrepancies," 92.

61. Coates, *Nature,* 95.

62. Ileto, *Pasyon and Revolution,* 10.

63. Ibid., 18.

64. See C. Martin, *Keepers of the Game.*

65. Weber, *The Protestant Ethic and the Spirit of Capitalism.*

66. J. Baird Callicott, "Traditional American Indian and Western European Attitudes toward Nature: An Overview," in *In Defense of the Land Ethic* (Albany: State University of New York Press, 1989), 192.

67. Ibid., 192.

CHAPTER 5: PERSON AND NATURE
IN NATIVE AMERICAN WORLDVIEWS

1. Albanese, *Nature Religion in America,* 19.
2. Taylor, "Earthen Spirituality," 200.
3. Tinker, *Missionary Conquest,* 122.
4. Hultkrantz, *The Religions of the American Indians,* 19.
5. Taylor, "Earthen Spirituality," 204. While he attacks widespread exploitation of indigenous cultures, Vine Deloria also suggests that Western cultures can learn ecologically sounder practices from Native Americans. See Deloria, *God Is Red,* 2.
6. In his study of the Muskogee of what is now the Southeastern United States, Joel Martin traces a similar pattern, in which Western disease and consumer goods reached "untouched" Native American groups through trade with other Indians long before actual contact with whites. See *Sacred Revolt.*
7. Nelson, *Make Prayers,* 8.
8. Ibid.
9. Ibid., 14.
10. Ibid., 16, 79, 159.
11. Ibid., 20.
12. Ibid., 76, 131.
13. Ibid., 108, 220–21.
14. Nelson, *The Island Within,* xiii.
15. Nelson, *Make Prayers,* 223.
16. Ibid., 242.
17. Ibid., 246.
18. Schwarz, *Molded in the Image,* xi.
19. Hedlund, "More of Survival Than an Art," 49.
20. Luckert, "Toward a Historical Perspective on Navajo Religion," 210.
21. Fransted, "The Secular Uses of Traditional Religion," 209.
22. Anne Lane Hedlund points to weaving as an important aspect of this Navajo cultural endurance; see "More of Survival Than an Art," 47–48.
23. Schwarz, *Molded in the Image,* 16–17. Gladys Reichard, an influential early ethnographer of the Navajo, puts it in Western terms: "The body of Navaho mythology is to Navaho chanters what the Bible is to our theologians." Reichard, *Navaho Religion,* xlvii.
24. Walters, "The Navajo Concept of Art," 29.
25. Quoted in Kelley and Francis, *Navajo Sacred Places,* 29.
26. The importance of the mother-child relationship in Navajo culture does not necessarily stem from or indicate the existence of a Mother Earth deity. In fact, Sam Gill argues that for Native American cultures generally, most references to Mother Earth were initially metaphorical, not theological. They formed part of a larger indigenous effort to communicate with European colonizers and express ties to the land. Anglos often misinterpreted these efforts and assumed that Mother Earth was a widespread indigenous deity. Beginning in the mid-1900s, according to Gill, many Native Americans began using these

misinterpretations to construct a pan-Indian tradition, with Mother Earth as a central theme, as part of a political rejection of Euro-American culture. See Gill, *Mother Earth,* 66, cited in Kelley and Francis, *Navajo Sacred Places,* 99–100. In addition to the image of the mother, another basic type of positive relationship in Navajo culture is based on exchange and is voluntary and contractual. The model for this relationship is that between husbands and wives. See Witherspoon, *Navajo Kinship,* 57.

27. Witherspoon, *Navajo Kinship,* 125.

28. Witherspoon, *Language and Art,* 84.

29. Ibid., 126.

30. Schwarz, *Molded in the Image,* 240.

31. Gill, *Sacred Words,* 30.

32. Ibid., 82.

33. Witherspoon, *Language and Art,* 86; see also 92.

34. Ibid., 92.

35. Thomas, "Shil Yool T'ool," 36. Thomas defines *dah'iistl'o* as "the process of integrating the warp and the weft in the art of weaving on a set-up loom" (34).

36. Harry Walters explains that "art in Navajo society is considered alive. It is like a person. It has feelings. It has power—healing power." Walters, "The Navajo Concept of Art," 29. Wesley Thomas reinforces this theme, arguing that Navajo weaving does not simply produce a product for sale or display but rather envisions "an entity with a life of its own." (Thomas, "Shil Yool T'ool," 33). See also Reichard, *Navaho Religion,* 452, on mountains as persons.

37. Schwarz, *Molded in the Image,* 9.

38. Witherspoon, *Language and Art,* 34. See also Gill, *Sacred Words,* 53. Wesley Thomas explains that even theories need to have a life force: "An entity of any form has to have be'iina. It is imbued with be'iina through the process of creation. Theories are considered to 'have no life of their own' and, therefore, cannot make any valuable contribution to the lives lived by traditional Navajo people. To be beneficial, thinking must be brought to life. It is given life through overlap with empirical concepts that make thoughts absolute and real. They become tangible. Entities of all forms and shapes need be'iina. Thoughts and plans become real when coupled with speech, song, prayer, or action" (Thomas, "Shil Yool T'ool," 36).

39. Kelley and Francis, *Navajo Sacred Places,* 20.

40. Schwarz, "Unraveling," 45.

41. Ibid., 43.

42. Ibid., 44.

43. Kelley and Francis, *Navajo Sacred Places,* 2.

44. Ibid., 188.

45. Schwarz, "Unraveling," 51. Reichard also emphasizes the sense of dependency: "Every plant is a symbol of vegetation without which neither man nor animals could exist. Flowers, therefore, are treated ceremonially." *Navaho Religion,* 144. The Navajo elder Jessy Biakeddy makes this point dramatically: "The Dine people have lived on the Big Mountain longer than any other people

in the world. If we are removed, a terrible thing will happen." Quoted in Francis and Kelley, *Navajo Sacred Places*, 195.

46. Witherspoon, *Language and Art*, 88–89.

47. Schwarz, *Molded in the Image*, 240.

48. Witherspoon, *Language and Art*, 82. Sam Gill adds, "Death must not be inflicted except for creative purposes. When it is, as may occur in times of war, ill consequences may result which are ascribed to the ghost of the dead. Enemyway [ceremony] expels this ghost, but it may only do so by an act of creation. Until some creative act results from that death, the ghost can never be allayed" (Gill, *Sacred Words*, 116).

49. Witherspoon, *Language and Art*, 82.

50. Begay, "Shi' Sha' Hane'" 24.

51. James F. Downs, *Animal Husbandry in Navajo Society and Culture* (Berkeley and Los Angeles: University of California Press, 1964), 92–93, quoted in Gary Witherspoon, *Language and Art in the Navajo Universe* (Ann Arbor: University of Michigan Press, 1977), 83.

52. Catherine Robbins, "A Zoo in Peril Stirs a Debate," 34.

53. As noted above, the Koyukon also oppose keeping wild animals because they suffer in captivity. As one man told Nelson, "We have respect for the animals. We don't keep them in cages or torture them, because we know the background of animals from the Distant Time. We know that the animal has a spirit—it used to be human—and we know all the things it did. It's not just an animal; it's lots more than that." Nelson, *Make Prayers*, 108, 24.

54. Another recent controversy highlights the complexity of these dilemmas. In 1997, the International Whaling Commission gave the Makah Indians of the Olympic Peninsula in Washington State permission to revive the hunt for gray whales. Some environmentalists, animal rights advocates, and even Makah elders opposed the hunt, arguing, among other things, that the hunt was not necessary and that no Makah people even knew how to conduct the hunt or butcher a whale, since the last hunt had been in 1926. Others, including some environmentalists, accepted the tribal leadership's arguments that the Makah needed to hunt whales both for subsistence and to help young tribe members learn traditional cultural values and knowledge. See Krech, *The Ecological Indian*, 223.

55. Reichard, *Navaho Religion*, 142. More generally, Kelley and Francis point out, traditional stories rarely mention things the Navajo received from contact with U.S., Spanish, and Mexican colonists, including domestic livestock. (One exception is a story about the origin of horses, which is not included in all versions of the creation cycle.) Rituals have helped maintain stories close to their preconquest forms, Kelley and Francis argue, as has the stability in basic conditions of Navajo life. Most important, stories and the practices that preserve them have survived because extended families have continued to support themselves from their traditional land base. Kelley and Francis, *Navajo Sacred Places*, 210–11.

56. Nabhan, *Cultures of Habitat*, 2.

57. Ibid., 159.

58. Jackson, *Becoming Native to This Place.*
59. Nabhan, *Cultures of Habitat,* 4. Virginia Nazarea makes a related argument about traditional agricultural methods and the preservation of both cultural and biological diversity in *Cultural Memory and Biodiversity.*
60. Nabhan, *Cultures of Habitat,* 223.
61. Taylor, "Bioregionalism," 53. Taylor notes the influence of the poet Gary Snyder, whose Pulitzer-Prize-winning collection of poetry, *Turtle Island* (New York: New Directions, 1974), served as a foundational document for bioregionalists. The writer and agrarian advocate Wendell Berry is another early "father" of the movement. See particularly his book *The Unsettling of America.*
62. Jackson, *Becoming Native to This Place,* 2–3. Recent bioregional theory emphasizes the complexity of interrelationships among local and global factors, with some authors stressing a "cosmopolitan bioregionalism" rather than a simple localism. See the essays in McGinnis, *Bioregionalism,* especially Mitchell Thomashow, "Toward a Cosmopolitan Bioregionalism," and Ronnie Lipschutz, "Bioregionalism, Civil Society and Global Environmental Governance."
63. Nabhan, *Cultures of Habitat,* 159.
64. Krech, *The Ecological Indian,* 211.
65. Nabhan, *Cultures of Habitat,* 4.
66. Ibid., 164.
67. Ibid., 2–3; see Jackson, *Becoming Native to This place.*
68. R. Nelson, *The Island Within,* xiii.
69. Ibid., 267.
70. Ibid., 267–68. Marti Kheel criticizes Nelson for focusing on, even romanticizing, hunting as the primary aspect of Koyukon culture that non-natives can and should "borrow." See Kheel, "License to Kill," 85–125.
71. R. Nelson, *The Island Within,* 45.
72. Ibid., xii.
73. Albanese, *Nature Religion in America,* 19
74. Ibid., 20.
75. Brown, *Animals of the Soul,* 13.
76. Hallowell, "Ojibwa Ontology, Behavior, and World View," 158.
77. Tanner, *Bringing Home Animals,* 136–38.
78. Allen, "The Sacred Hoop," 16 and 8.
79. Deloria, *God Is Red,* 274; see also p. 89. Calvin Martin also concludes that most Native American cultures (at least prior to European contact) saw nonhuman animals as "people" who had social lives, kinship norms, relationships, and even vices akin to human ones. Martin, *Keepers of the Game,* 33–34.
80. Bron Taylor quotes a similar generalization by Dennis Martinez, an O'odham-Chicano activist from Oregon: "Everything is alive and has a spirit[;] . . . it's universal, that's true, all tribal peoples [have this experience]." Taylor, "Earthen Spirituality or Cultural Genocide," 192.
81. Hallowell, "Ojibwa Ontology, Behavior, and World View," 152. Emphasis in original.
82. Albanese, *Nature Religion in America,* 20.
83. Brown, *Animals of the Soul,* xiii.

84. Allen, "The Sacred Hoop," 7.
85. Gill, *Sacred Words*, xxiii.
86. Rival, "Blowpipes and Spears," esp. 149–50.
87. Descola and Palsson, introduction, 14.
88. Schwarz, *Molded in the Image*, 113.
89. Deloria, *God Is Red*, 195.
90. Albanese, *Nature Religion in America*, 21.
91. Kelley and Francis, *Navajo Sacred Places*, 41.
92. Ibid., 39, 40.
93. Schwarz, "Unravelling," 47.
94. Ibid., 50.
95. Basso, *Western Apache*, 102–3.
96. Ibid., 129.
97. Francis and Kelley, *Navajo Sacred Places*, 198.
98. Berry, *The Dream of the Earth*, 124.
99. Plumwood, *Feminism and the Mastery of Nature*, 103.

CHAPTER 6: RELATIONSHIPS, STORIES, AND FEMINIST ETHICS

1. Welch, *Sweet Dreams in America*, 64. See also Michel Foucault, *The Archaeology of Knowledge and the Discourse on Language* (New York: Harper and Row, 1972), esp. 215–37.
2. Thomas Kuhn notes, in relation to scientific debates, some parallels to this sort of political conflict. Scientists, like members of other groups, make arguments based on the premises and values of the guiding paradigms of their own community. These arguments cannot, Kuhn contends, be made logically compelling to outsiders. Rather, "each group uses its own paradigm to argue in that paradigm's defense," and in the end "there is no standard higher than the assent of the relevant community" in the choice of scientific theories as in political revolutions. Kuhn, *The Structure of Scientific Revolutions*, 94.
3. Rich, *Of Woman Born*.
4. Chodorow, *The Reproduction of Mothering*, 206.
5. Ibid., 169. See also p. 93: "Because of their mothering by women, girls come to experience themselves as less separate than boys, as having more permeable ego boundaries. Girls come to define themselves more in relation to others."
6. Ibid., 177.
7. Dinnerstein, *The Mermaid and the Minotaur*, 20.
8. Gilligan, *In a Different Voice*, 33.
9. Ibid, 59.
10. Gilligan, "Moral Orientation and Moral Development," 23.
11. Ibid.
12. Gilligan, *In a Different Voice*, 35.
13. Ibid., 105.
14. Held, "Feminism and Moral Theory," 112.
15. Ruddick, "Maternal Thinking," 349, 350.

16. Ruddick, "Remarks," 242.

17. Ruddick, "Maternal Thinking," 354–55.

18. Welch, *A Feminist Ethic of Risk*, 110.

19. Ruddick, "Maternal Thinking," 359.

20. Ibid.

21. Ruddick, "Remarks," 254.

22. Ruddick, "Maternal Thinking," 361.

23. Noddings, *Caring*, 4, 5. Italics in original.

24. Ibid., 24.

25. Ibid., 5, 45.

26. Ibid., 83, 104.

27. Ibid., 86.

28. Ibid.

29. Benhabib, "The Generalized Other," 163.

30. Ibid., 164.

31. Baier, "The Need for More Than Justice," 55.

32. Benhabib, "The Generalized Other," 165. Emphasis in original. See John Rawls, *A Theory of Justice* (Cambridge: Harvard University Press, 1971).

33. Benhabib, "The Generalized Other," 164.

34. Ruddick, "Injustice in Families," 209.

35. Baier, "The Need for More Than Justice," 56.

36. Haraway, "Situated Knowledge," 188. Italics in original.

37. Ibid., 189.

38. Bird, "The Social Construction of Nature," 255, 256.

39. Haraway, "Situated Knowledge," 196. The philosopher of science Joseph Rouse contends that the conviction that a more accurate picture of the world is possible, despite the inevitable partiality and relativity of all visions, distinguishes many feminist theorists, particularly in science studies, from some other constructionists. See Rouse, "Feminism and the Social Construction of Scientific Knowledge," 195–215.

40. Rich, *Of Woman Born*, 22, 21.

41. Adrienne Rich, "Notes towards a Politics of Location," in *Blood, Bread, and Poetry: Selected Prose, 1979–1985* (New York: W. W. Norton, 1986), 213.

42. Rich, *Of Woman Born*, 290.

43. Walker, "Moral Understandings," 142.

44. Benhabib, "The Generalized Other," 156

45. Clifford Geertz, "Religion as a Cultural System," in *The Interpretation of Cultures* (New York: Basic Book, 1973), 93–95.

46. Sommers, "Filial Morality," 79.

47. Gilligan, *In a Different Voice*, 30.

48. Schmitt, *Beyond Separateness*, 44–45.

49. Adrienne Rich, "Conditions for Work: The Common Ground of Women," in *On Lies, Secrets, and Silence: Selected Prose, 1966–1978* (New York: W. W. Norton, 1979), 205.

50. Schmitt, *Beyond Separateness*, 50.

51. Kheel, "From Heroic to Holistic Ethics," 261. Italics in original.

52. Tronto, "Women and Caring," 109.

53. Warren, "The Power and Promise," 127.

54. Ibid., 129.

55. Plumwood, "Androcentrism and Anthropocentrism," 337–38.

56. Warren, "The Power and Promise," 145.

57. Merchant, *The Death of Nature*, 195.

58. Lahar, "Ecofeminist Theory and Grassroots Politics," 5. See Shiva, *Staying Alive*.

59. McFague, "An Earthly Theological Agenda," 85.

60. Li, "A Cross-Cultural Critique of Ecofeminism," 276.

61. A. Carr, *Transforming Grace*, 74.

62. Plumwood, "Nature, Self, and Gender," 7.

63. Cheney, "Eco Feminism and Deep Ecology," 141.

64. Warren and Cheney, "Ecological Feminism," 184.

65. Ibid. Italics in original.

66. Ibid., 191.

67. Warren, "The Power and Promise," 134–35.

68. Raglon and Scholtmeijer, "Shifting Ground," 22.

69. See Cheney, "Postmodern Environmental Ethics," 117–4.

70. Roach, "Loving Your Mother," 62.

71. Ibid., 52.

72. Chodorow, *The Reproduction of Mothering*, 14.

73. Tang-Martinez, "The Curious Courtship of Sociobiology and Feminism," 117.

74. Child rearing, central to typically female experience, also challenges the plausibility of hard constructionism. Caregivers who closely observe children's development point out both how "hardwired" are certain general behaviors (notably, the ceaseless struggles to walk and talk) and how distinctive are the individual personalities even of newborns who have not been in the world long enough to be shaped by culture. It is hard to imagine how a hard constructionist approach could survive any extended period of caring for babies and toddlers. The dedication of Mary Midgley's *Beast and Man* makes this point: "To my sons, with many thanks for making it so clear to me that the human infant is not blank paper."

75. Adams, "The Traffic in Animals," 204.

76. Ibid., 202.

77. Lahar, "Roots," 91.

78. Adams, "The Traffic in Animals," 206.

CHAPTER 7: EVOLUTION, ECOLOGY, AND ETHICS

1. Gould, *The Mismeasure of Man*. In relation to Gould's discussion of efforts to measure the brain capacity of different races, it is worth noting Darwin's assertion in 1871 that "no one supposes that the intellect of any two animals or of any two men can be accurately gauged by the cubic contents of their skulls." Darwin, *The Descent of Man*, 145.

2. William Sumner, *The Challenge of Facts* (1887), 67, quoted in Midgley, *Evolution as a Religion*, 118.

3. Midgley quotes *Hitler's Table-Talk:* "If we did not respect the law of nature, imposing our will by the right of the stronger, a day would come when the wild animals would again devour us. . . . By means of the struggle the elites are continually renewed. The law of selection justifies this incessant struggle by allowing the survival of the fittest." H. Trevor-Roper, ed., *Hitler's Table-Talk* (London: Weidenfeld and Nicolson, 1963), quoted in Midgley, *Evolution as a Religion,* 119.

4. Wilson, *On Human Nature,* 79. Evolution is this change in the frequency of genes in a population. It is important to note that evolution can result from different agents, including drift, mutation, and migration, as well as natural and artificial selection. Thus natural selection alone is not evolution. Rather, selection is a phenotypic event (concerned with characteristics of individuals) that can lead to evolution, a genetic event. See Thornhill, "The Study of Adaptation," 120.

5. Darwin, *The Origin of Species,* 131.

6. Ibid., 443.

7. Weiner, *The Beak of the Finch,* 141–42.

8. Ibid., 143.

9. Darwin, *The Origin of Species,* 133. Recent research suggests that evolution sometimes operates much more rapidly, although the actual alteration of species usually does indeed require the "long lapses of ages" that Darwin described. For an accessible and informed discussion of this and of evolution generally, see Weiner, *The Beak of the Finch.*

10. Weiner, *The Beak of the Finch,* 39.

11. Tudge, *The Time before History,* 89.

12. Bonner and May, introduction, xix. Mendel's paper on the laws of heredity was published in 1866, five years before *The Descent of Man.* Darwin may have overlooked Mendel's work, Bonner and May suggest, because it was written in a mathematical jargon that he did not understand.

13. See Bowler, *Evolution,* 307.

14. Darwin, *The Origin of Species,* 454–55.

15. Ibid., 160–61.

16. Some pre-evolutionary theories grouped humans with monkeys and apes. In 1735, Linnaeus placed humans with other primates in the genus *Homo,* in a family he called Anthropomorpha. Other eighteenth-century scientists, however, separated humans from all other animals, including monkeys and apes. Linnaeus shared with Darwin a belief that the line between humans and apes was not clear-cut, although, unlike Darwin, Linnaeus believed that species were fixed and unchanging. See Kuper, *The Chosen Primate,* 19–20.

17. Bonner and May, introduction, xxii.

18. Foley, *Humans before Humanity,* 67, 69.

19. See Bowler, *Evolution,* 323–24. Darwin also speculated, correctly, that humans originated in Africa; see *The Descent of Man,* 19.

20. Kuper, *The Chosen Primate,* 32, quoting Grafton Elliot Smith, quoted in Phillip Tobias, "Piltdown, an Appraisal of the Case against Sir Arthur Keith," *Current Anthropology* 33 (1992): 281.

21. Kuper, *The Chosen Primate*, 49.

22. Gould, *Ever since Darwin*, 62.

23. Kuper, *The Chosen Primate*, 90.

24. Wright, *The Moral Animal*, 28.

25. Kuper, *The Chosen Primate*, 131.

26. Wilson, *On Human Nature*, 32.

27. Trivers, "Parental Investment and Sexual Selection," 795–842.

28. R. Dawkins, *The Selfish Gene*, 3. This clause is often cited as evidence that Dawkins is an unreconstructed Social Darwinist, content to let our "selfish" genes drive our behavior. However, if we read the quotation in context, this critique appears less justified: "If you wish . . . to build a society in which individuals cooperate generously and unselfishly towards a common good, you can expect little help from biological nature. Let us try to *teach* generosity and altruism, because we are born selfish. Let us understand what our own selfish genes are up to, because we may then at least have the chance to upset their designs, something that no other species has ever aspired to do" (italics in original). It is true, as Midgley notes (in *Beast and Man,* xviii), that Dawkins emphasizes competition and ignores the fundamental role of cooperation in the evolution of many animals, including humans. In other words, his idea that we must struggle to overcome innate egoism neglects the fact that cooperation and care are equally innate. As incomplete as Dawkins's picture of human nature may be, though, he clearly does not advocate unrestrained selfishness. It is also incorrect to assume (as Midgley does not) that Dawkins is alone in this view; his understanding of the essential egoism of human nature is very close to that of liberal political theory, which assumes, as Alison Jaggar writes, that "people tend naturally toward egoism, even though they are sometimes able to refrain from self-interested behavior." *Feminist Politics and Human Nature,* 31.

29. Wilson, *Sociobiology: The Abridged Edition,* 3.

30. Kin selection, like parental investment, is a complex idea elaborated by a number of researchers. The central figure in the development of kin selection is William Hamilton. See his "The Genetical Evolution of Social Behaviour," 1–52. It is interesting to note Darwin's prescience regarding this question, which he saw posed in starkest terms by the behavior of social insects such as ants and bees, who often give their lives in defense of the group. Hamilton also studied social insects in working out his ideas about kin selection and inclusive fitness.

31. Wright, *The Moral Animal,* 173.

32. Ibid., 158. Italics in original.

33. Reciprocal altruism, another key concept in sociobiology, also resulted from the work of various researchers, although it is most associated with George Williams, especially his influential book *Adaptation and Natural Selection.* Robert Trivers expanded Williams's ideas in "The Evolution of Reciprocal Altruism," 35–46.

34. Non-kin altruism is well documented in a range of species, including chimpanzees, dolphins, and vampire bats, among others. See, for example, M. Dawkins, *Through Our Eyes Only?* 57–61.

35. Cheney and Seyfarth, *How Monkeys See the World,* 102–3.

36. See Irenaus Eibl-Eibesfeldt, *Love and Hate,* trans. Geoffrey Strachan (London: Methuen, 1971; New York: Holt, Rinehart and Winston, 1972).

37. Midgley, *Beast and Man,* 136. Italics in original.

38. R. Dawkins, *The Selfish Gene,* 281. Dawkins uses the example of "brotherly altruism" in birds, which could emerge from changes in the genes shaping parental nurturing. Birds already have a complicated nervous apparatus, which is required to care for and feed offspring and which has been built up by many generations of step-by-step evolution. A gene for feeding younger brothers and sisters could work by accelerating the age at which these behaviors mature (e.g., by "activating" the "rule of thumb" which tells birds to feed squawking, gaping nest mates earlier). Thus a small variation, in this case in timing, could lead to apparently "new" behaviors, such as sibling care, in Dawkins's example.

39. Koenig and Mumme, "Levels of Analysis and the Functional Significance of Helping Behavior," 160. Koenig and Mumme are summarizing an argument made by J. L. Brown and E. R. Brown, in "Reciprocal Aid-Giving in a Communal Bird," *Zeitschrift fur Tierpsychologie* 53 (1980): 313–24.

40. Wright, *The Moral Animal,* 176. The "spigots" are often not turned off even when tendencies that emerged in the course of evolution, such as the desire for sweets and fatty meats, may harm individuals' well-being in contemporary settings. Sociobiologists describe a host of other features, including the link in humans between visual stimulation and sexual activity, which have far surpassed their original, adaptive confines. Especially in complex animals, many behaviors generated through natural selection are not highly compartmentalized. As Michelle Johnson-Weider puts it, evolution has no line-item veto.

41. I do not mean that creationist worldviews are irrelevant in general, but here I am interested in what is implied for ethics and anthropology when we take evolution seriously as the story of human origins.

42. Edward O. Wilson, "Altruism and Aggression," in *In Search of Nature* (Washington, D.C.: Island Press, 1996), 93.

43. Kuper, *The Chosen Primate,* 100.

44. Midgley, *Beast and Man,* xxxix.

45. Paul Davies, *The Mind of God* (New York: Simon and Schuster, 1992), 232, quoted in Dennett, *Darwin's Dangerous Idea,* 66.

46. Dennett, *Darwin's Dangerous Idea,* 66. Italics in original.

47. John Dewey, *The Influence of Darwin on Philosophy* (New York: Holt, 1910; Bloomington: Indiana University Press, 1965), 15, quoted in Dennett, *Darwin's Dangerous Idea,* 66.

48. Damasio, *Descartes' Error,* 126.

49. Wilson, *On Human Nature,* 73.

50. Ibid., 77. Wilson's emphasis on the constraints, rather than the possibilities, created by biology also opens his approach to charges of imbalance.

51. Gould, *Ever Since Darwin,* 253.

52. Dennett, *Darwin's Dangerous Idea,* 228.

53. Ibid., 487. Italics in original.

54. Ibid.

55. Wilson, *Consilience,* 223, 128. Adam Kuper, similarly, suggests that genes may "code potentialities rather than program fixed sequences of action." *The Chosen Primate,* 147.

56. Wilson, *Consilience,* 266.

57. M. Dawkins, *Through Our Eyes Only?* 22.

58. Ristau, "Aspects of the Cognitive Ethology of an Injury-Feigning Bird," 86.

59. De Waal, *Good-Natured,* 180.

60. Ibid., 181.

61. M. Dawkins, *Through Our Eyes Only?* 62.

62. Donald Griffin has pioneered this approach. See Griffin, *Animal Thinking,* and *Animal Minds.*

63. Allen and Bekoff, "Intentionality, Social Play, and Definition," 233. Italics in original.

64. Midgley, *Beast and Man,* 47. Italics in original.

65. Jamieson and Bekoff, "On Aims and Methods of Cognitive Ethology," 68. See also Griffin, *Animal Thinking,* esp. chap. 8.

66. Midgley, *Beast and Man,* 25.

67. Other distorted (or just plain inaccurate) versions of evolutionary theory pose different types of ethical problems, such as the "escalator fallacy," as Mary Midgley calls it, which envisions endless inevitable progress in human affairs or the cosmos as a whole. Some Christian evolutionists, notably Teilhard de Chardin, have adopted this approach. See Midgley, *Evolution as a Religion.*

68. Darwin, *The Origin of Species,* 263.

69. Midgley, *Beast and Man,* 163–64.

70. Ibid., 164.

71. R. Dawkins, *River Out of Eden,* 131–32.

72. Darwin describes the wasp in *The Origin of Species,* 263.

73. Midgley, *Beast and Man,* xv. See also *The Ethical Primate.*

74. Midgley, *Beast and Man,* xvi.

75. Gould, *Ever Since Darwin,* 50.

76. Midgley, *Beast and Man,* xxxiv. Italics in original.

77. Some biologists suggest that this very mode of thinking in terms of binary opposites might be an evolved human trait. See Wilson, *Consilience,* 153.

78. Stringer and McKie, *African Exodus,* 113.

79. Wilson, *On Human Nature,* 46.

80. Ibid., 48.

81. Worster, *Nature's Economy,* 114.

82. Darwin, *The Origin of Species,* 127.

83. Callenbach, *Ecology,* 80.

84. Worster, *Nature's Economy,* 298.

85. Ibid., 161.

86. Ibid., 335.

87. Walter Taylor, "Significance of the Biotic Community in Ecological Studies," *Quarterly Review of Biology* 10 (September 1935): 296, quoted in Worster, *Nature's Economy,* 320.

88. See Frederic Clements, *The Development and Structure of Vegetation* (Lincoln Neb.: 1904); and Lovelock, *Gaia*.

89. Callenbach, *Ecology*. The other two "laws" are "There's no such thing as a free lunch" and "Nature bats last." Callenbach did not originate all of the laws; the third and fourth laws may have first been devised by Paul Ehrlich and Barry Commoner, respectively.

90. Worster, *Nature's Economy*, 407.

91. Ibid., 411.

92. Interdependence is also a central theme in popular or political versions of ecology, which sometimes but not always accord with scientific approaches. The two streams come together in the contemporary emphasis on biodiversity, especially the need to prevent or at least slow the rate of species extinctions. This message also accords with the assertions of many Darwinists, who contend that diversity is the primary product of evolution and that if there is any ethical or political message at all to come out of natural selection, it is that diversity is a good that humans should strive to preserve or at least not damage.

93. Callenbach, *Ecology*.

94. Morovitz, "Biology of a Cosmological Science," 48.

95. Ibid., 47.

96. Callicott, "The Metaphysical Implications," 60. Italics in original.

97. Callicott, *Earth's Insights*, 206.

98. Naess, *Ecology, Community, and Lifestyle*, 55.

99. Callicott, "The Metaphysical Implications," 60.

100. Naess, *Ecology, Community, and Lifestyle*, 56. Italics in original.

101. Ibid.

102. Robert O'Neill, D. L. De Angelis, J. B. Waide, and T. F. H. Allen, *A Hierarchical Concept of Ecosystems* (Princeton, N.J.: Princeton University Press, 1986), 7, quoted in Warren and Cheney, "Ecological Feminism and Ecosystem Ecology," 182. Warren and Cheney often refer to hierarchy theory simply as ecosystem ecology, in the title and throughout the article. This suggests that perhaps hierarchy theory, or at least the broad themes that Warren and Cheney highlight, is less distinctive from ecological science as a whole than they imply.

103. Warren and Cheney, "Ecological Feminism and Ecosystem Ecology," 183, 186–87.

104. Leopold, "The Land Ethic," 251.

105. Rolston, *Environmental Ethics*, 58. Italics in original.

106. J. Baird Callicott, "Animal Liberation: A Triangular Affair," in *In Defense of the Land Ethic: Essays in Environmental Philosophy* (Albany: State University of New York, 1989), 33.

107. Rolston, *Environmental Ethics*, 58. Italics in original.

108. Ibid., 59.

109. Callicott, *Earth's Insights*, 207.

110. Ibid., 205.

111. Rolston, *Environmental Ethics*, 59.

112. Callicott, "Animal Liberation," 33.

113. See, for example, Zimmerman, "Ecofascism, 244–48. Zimmerman uses Callicott's early work, such as "Animal Liberation: A Triangular Affair," cited

in the previous paragraph, as an example of "ecofascism." Zimmerman acknowledges, however, that Callicott's more recent writings "emphasize the moral standing of human individuals" (248). Callicott gives an account of his "chastened" response to critics of the "repugnant misanthropic indications" of the "extreme monism" of some of his early work, in "Moral Monism in Environmental Ethics Defended," 58. Despite these revisions, Callicott continues to defend a holistic ethic, as is evident in *Earth's Insights* (84, 205) and elsewhere.

CHAPTER 8: IN AND OF THE WORLD

1. For a more detailed discussion of some of these issues, see Peterson, "In and of the World?"

2. Geertz, "The Impact of the Concept of Culture," 35, 43, 49.

3. Ibid., 44.

4. Geertz, "The Growth of Culture and the Evolution of Mind," 68, 79.

5. Geertz, "The Impact of the Concept of Culture," 49.

6. Ibid., 46–48. His "step-by-step" model contrasts, Geertz notes, with the notion that anatomically modern humans slowly discovered culture. Geertz claims to base his argument on a "finely graduated time scale in terms of which to discriminate the stages of evolutionary change" ("The Growth of Culture and the Evolution of Mind," 65). Geertz's time scale, however, does not accord with current evidence. As noted in the previous chapter, the most recent analyses suggest that most of what we term "culture," and especially symbolic culture, emerged well after *Homo sapiens* evolved as a distinct species with the same essential physical structures as contemporary humans.

7. Geertz, "The Impact of the Concept of Culture," 50.

8. Wilson, *Consilience*, 126–27, 166.

9. Ibid., 157.

10. Ibid., 166, 217–18.

11. Ibid.

12. Ibid.

13. Geertz, "The Impact of the Concept of Culture," 52.

14. Esbjornson, "On Rethinking Resistance," 288.

15. Hefner, *The Human Factor,* 148.

16. Wilson, *Consilience,* 166.

17. Geertz, "The Impact of the Concept of Culture," 45.

18. Ibid., 49–50.

19. Wilson, *Consilience,* 150.

20. See M. Dawkins, *Through Our Eyes Only?* 38–53, for fascinating discussions of cultural learning and transmission among species such as sparrows and rats.

21. Geertz, "The Growth of Culture and the Evolution of Mind," 57.

22. Geertz, "The Impact of the Concept of Culture," 44.

23. Ayala, "Human Nature," 32, 40–41, 43–44. While this analogy and Ayala's argument generally are very helpful for thinking about the relationship between cultural and biological evolution in shaping distinctive human traits, two factors weaken his case. First, he adopts too narrow a definition of ethical

behavior by restricting it to *judgments* between good and evil. Thus he leaves out a huge range of actions that philosophers and others understand as ethical behaviors. Partly because his definition is so limited, Ayala rejects the possibility that some aspects of ethical behavior might be related to reproductive fitness. For example, he discards all the discussions of kin and non-kin altruism and other possible links between fitness and certain ethical behaviors. Second, Ayala repeats the common attacks on sociobiology (that it is narrowly determinist and justifies racism, sexism, etc.), but fails either to cite examples of these errors in the sociobiological literature or to acknowledge the explicit rejection of such errors by writers such as Edward Wilson and Richard Dawkins. More generally, Ayala claims that he is challenging sociobiologists when he asserts that a capacity for ethics is biologically grounded but specific ethical norms are not. While Wilson, among others, believes that some very widespread behaviors, such as incest taboos, have specific genetic groundings, in general he and most other sociobiologists agree with Ayala. For example, Robert Wright, an advocate of evolutionary psychology, contends that "adherence to any moral rule has an innate basis. It is only the specific contents of moral codes that are not inborn." Wright, *The Moral Animal*, 184.

24. Hefner, *The Human Factor*, 20, 28.

25. Ibid., 29, 151, quoting Richard Dawkins, *The Selfish Gene* (London: Granada, 1978), vii. Note: This is not the edition of *The Selfish Gene* that I quote elsewhere.

26. Hefner, *The Human Factor*, 29, 43.

27. Ibid., 36.

28. Ibid., 27, 32, 39.

29. Ibid., 236–37.

30. "On Being Terrestrial" is the title of chapter 15 of Midgley, *The Ethical Primate*.

31. R. Nelson, *The Island Within*, xii.

32. McFague, *The Body of God*, 102.

33. T. Berry, *The Dream of the Earth*, 205.

34. Hefner, *The Human Factor*, 5.

35. Ruether, *Gaia and God*, 86.

36. T. Berry, *The Dream of the Earth*, 164, 166–68.

37. Jung, *We Are Home*, 31.

38. Ibid., 69. Emphasis in original.

39. Ibid., 5.

40. McFague, *The Body of God*, 31. Italics in original.

41. Midgley, *Beast and Man*, 195. Italics in original.

42. Emily Martin, *The Woman in the Body* (Boston: Beacon Press, 1987); Boston Women's Health Collective, *The New Our Bodies, Ourselves: A Book by and for Women* (New York: Simon and Schuster, 1992).

43. Rich, *Of Woman Born*, 22.

44. Adrienne Rich, "Motherhood: The Contemporary Emergency and the Quantum Leap," in *On Lies, Secrets, and Silence: Selected Prose, 1966–1978* (New York: W. W. Norton, 1979), 272.

45. Rich, *Of Woman Born*, 290.

46. Rich, "Notes Toward a Politics of Location," 213.

47. Ibid., 215.

48. McFague, *The Body of God*, viii, 16. It is worth noting that no one ever confuses the body of a chimp or tree with a mere outside cover. Nonhumans are "reduced" to their bodies, nothing more, like women are often "reduced." The problem, as McFague recognizes, despite her confusing parenthetical clause, lies in seeing bodiliness as a "reduction" in the first place.

49. Ibid., 19.

50. Ibid., 99.

51. Ibid., xi, 176.

52. Ibid., 25, 54. Italics in original.

53. Damasio, *Descartes' Error*, xvi. See also Midgley, *Heart and Mind*.

54. Damasio, *Descartes' Error*, 118.

55. And minds have not evolved alone, Paul Shepard adds: "The human mind is the result of a long series of interactions with other animals. The mind is inseparable from the brain, which evolved among our primate ancestors as part of an ecological heritage." Shepard, *The Others*, 15.

56. Dennett, *Kinds of Minds*, 98, 97.

57. Harding, "The Curious Coincidence of Feminine and African Moralities," 298.

58. Rouse, "Feminism and the Social Construction of Scientific Knowledge," 207–8, quoting Haraway, *Primate Visions*, 331.

59. Haraway, "Situated Knowledges," 191. The idea of taking the standpoint of the subjugated is also central to liberation theologians; see, for example, the Peruvian theologian Gustavo Gutiérrez's essay "Theology from the Underside of History," in *The Power of the Poor in History* (Maryknoll, N.Y.: Orbis Books, 1983), 169–221.

60. Haraway, "Situated Knowledges," 190.

61. Ibid., 201.

62. Ibid., 119.

63. Ibid., 134.

64. Copeland, *Economic Justice*, 97–98.

65. Callicott, "The Metaphysical Implications of Ecology," 61–62, citing Kenneth Goodpaster, "From Egoism to Environmentalism," in *Ethics and Problems of the 21st Century*, ed. K. Goodpaster and K. Sayre (Notre Dame: University of Notre Dame Press, 1979), 21–35.

66. Macy, "Greening," 61. Italics in original.

67. Seed et al., *Thinking Like a Mountain*, 36. It is important to keep in mind that theorizing in Deep Ecology does not necessarily reflect the thinking of radical ecological activists "on the ground." Their ideologies and commitments, as Bron Taylor points out, are often more plural and less abstract than philosophical arguments.

68. Plumwood, "Nature, Self, and Gender," 13.

69. Ibid., 14.

70. Ibid., 15.

71. For a thoughtful critique of Macy's notion of the "greening of the self" along these lines, see Sponberg, "Green Buddhism."

72. Hayles, "Searching for Common Ground," 58.
73. Cheney and Seyfarth, *How Monkeys See the World*; Nagel, "What Is It Like to Be a Bat?" 435–50.
74. Snyder, "Nets of Beads, Webs of Cells," 72.
75. Sponberg, "Green Buddhism," 370.
76. Welch, *A Feminist Ethic of Risk*, 111.

CHAPTER 9: DIFFERENT NATURES

1. Gould, *Ever Since Darwin*, 259. Unfortunately, Gould emphasizes his point about human difference by quoting Simone de Beauvoir's claim that we are "the being whose essence lies in having no essence."
2. This is exemplified by an experience I had at an academic conference. I gave what I thought was a carefully worded argument to the effect that continuity as well as distinctiveness characterizes human relations with nonhuman animals. The first response began thus: "These differences you want to erase . . ."
3. Hefner, *The Human Factor*, 27.
4. Ibid., 32.
5. Nasr, "Islam and the Environmental Crisis," 83–108.
6. McFague, *The Body of God*, 197; see also 108. Italics in original.
7. Ibid., 109. Italics in original.
8. Jung, *We Are Home*, 86.
9. McFague, *The Body of God*, 60. Italics in original.
10. Rolston, "Wildlife and Wildlands," 140.
11. Second Vatican Council, *Gaudium et Spes*, no. 69, pp. 203, 204.
12. Ibid., no. 71, pp. 204–5.
13. Jung, *We Are Home*, 21. Italics in original. More concisely, Jung quotes a note he has posted in his bathroom: "You are not absolutely, irrevocably, personally responsible for everything. That's my job. Love, God" (19).
14. Kehm, "The New Story," 89.
15. Santmire, "Healing the Protestant Mind," 60.
16. Ibid., 75.
17. Ibid., 77. Santmire's proposed model of cooperation has some similarities to Carolyn Merchant's vision of an ecofeminist "partnership ethics." See Merchant, "Partnership Ethics and Cultural Discourse," 212–23.
18. Midgley, *The Ethical Primate*, 180.
19. Callicott, *Earth's Insights*, 21, 22.
20. Ibid., 23.
21. Lovin and Reynolds, "In the Beginning," 3, 4.
22. Ruddick, "Remarks on the Sexual Politics of Reason," 244.
23. Benhabib, "The Generalized Other," 155.
24. Jane Goodall suggests this when she writes that she watched chimpanzee mothers as a model for her own efforts at parenting. See *In the Shadow of Man*, 237.
25. Midgley, *Beast and Man*, 359.
26. R. Williams, "Ideas of Nature," 85.

27. Warren, "The Power and Promise," 134–35.

28. Tudge, *The Time before History,* 17.

29. Wilson, *Consilience,* 265. See also Wilson, *On Human Nature,* 192: "The evolutionary epic is mythology in the sense that the laws it adduces here and now are believed but can never be definitely proved to form a cause-and-effect continuum from physics to the social sciences." For an insightful and informed discussion of the strengths and weaknesses of the evolutionary epic as a source for environmental ethics, see Thiele, "Evolutionary Narratives and Ecological Ethics," 6–38.

30. T. Berry, *The Dream of the Earth,* 123.

31. Ibid., 124.

32. Ibid., 111.

33. McFague, *The Body of God,* 81. For an excellent discussion of this issue, see Thiele, "Evolutionary Narratives and Ecological Ethics."

34. Midgley, *Evolution as a Religion.* Most instances of the escalator fallacy seek to justify human domination over the rest of nature because we have, presumably, achieved a higher stage of development than all other creatures. One influential, though eccentric, version of the escalator fallacy is Pierre Teilhard de Chardin's vision of evolution as a process of increasing "hominisation," leading to higher consciousness and eventually encompassing the rest of creation into humanity. Teilhard de Chardin, *The Phenomenon of Man.* Even some ecocentric thinkers interpret evolutionary theory in teleological terms. Thomas Berry, strongly influenced by Teilhard's reading of evolution, writes that "each stage of development was the consequence of a single process at work, a process that came to a new phase of its development in the human mode of consciousness." T. Berry, *The Great Work,* 29.

35. Cheney, "Eco-Feminism and Deep Ecology," 144.

36. Augustine, *City of God,* vol. 1, esp. bks. 19 and 21.

37. Welch, *Sweet Dreams in America,* xix.

38. Ibid., 61.

39. Jorge Castañeda, *Utopia Unarmed: The Latin American Left after the Cold War* (New York: Alfred A. Knopf, 1993); Manuel Vásquez, "The Limits of Utopia" (Ph.D. diss., Temple University, Philadelphia, 1994), published in revised form as *The Brazilian Popular Church and the Crisis of Modernity* (Cambridge: Cambridge University Press, 1998). See also Ken Silverstein and Emir Sader, *Without Fear of Being Happy: Lula, the Workers' Party, and Brazil* (London: Verso, 1991). In *Spaces of Hope,* David Harvey also argues the importance of a revised and revitalized utopianism for progressive political movements.

40. McFague, *The Body of God,* 198.

41. Tillich, *The Protestant Era,* 172. This quotation reflects Tillich's "eschatological reservation," which Sharon Welch summarizes as "the reminder that all of our good works are partial[;] . . . they cannot be directly identified as the work of God nor identified as the kingdom of God." Welch argues that this stance can so widen the gap between the human and the divine that all human projects are seen only in terms of their failure to be divine, and the real differences between human projects are not appreciated. Welch, *A Feminist Ethic of*

Risk, 106, 107. While Welch's concerns are important, she underestimates the ways Tillich, at least, valued and supported concrete political projects.

42. McFague, *The Body of God,* 34, 35.

43. Raglon and Scholtmeijer, "Shifting Ground," 38.

44. Plumwood, *Feminism and the Mastery of Nature,* 196.

45. Jackson, *Becoming Native to This Place,* 2.

46. Nabhan, *Cultures of Habitat,* 3. The term "ecosystem people" comes from Ray Dasmann, *Wildlife Biology* (New York: Wiley, 1964).

47. Aberley, "Interpreting Bioregionalism," 13.

48. Holmes Rolston III, "The Human Standing in Nature: Storied Fitness in the Moral Observer" (presented to the "Values and Moral Standing Conference," Bowling Green State University, Bowling Green, Ohio, April 1986), quoted in Cheney, "Eco Feminism and Deep Ecology," 124–25. See also Rolston, *Environmental Ethics,* 341–54.

49. Kammer, *Ethics and Liberation,* 16–31. Kammer's "moralscape" is a modified version of Ralph Potter's model, described in *War and Moral Discourse* (Richmond, Va.: John Knox Press, 1973).

50. Plumwood, *Feminism and the Mastery of Nature,* 21. In *Beyond Separateness,* Richard Schmitt discusses a parallel phenomenon in relations among persons, especially between women and men, with his idea of being "covertly" in relation. In both models, dependence upon the other (nature, women) is presumed and denied.

51. Callicott, *Earth's Insights,* 80.

52. McFague, *The Body of God,* 56, 57.

53. See Nabhan, *Cultures of Habitat,* 1–4. On immigrants and on native connections to place more generally, see David Suzuki, "A Personal Foreword," in *The Wisdom of the Elders: Sacred Native Stories of Nature,* by David Suzuki and Peter Knudtson (New York: Bantam, 1992), xxvii–xliv. On the loss of "native" ethics in the United States, see W. Berry, *The Unsettling of America.*

54. Reflections on globalization—its possibilities, its dangers, and the impossibility of ignoring it—are, in fact, becoming central to bioregional and other environmentalist writings; see McGinnis, *Bioregionalism;* and also Jerry Mander and Edward Goldsmith, eds., *The Case against the Global Economy, and for a Turn toward the Local* (San Francisco: Sierra Club Books, 1996).

55. Eisenberg, Murkoff, and Hathaway, *What to Expect the First Year,* 186. Recent research showing that babies who sleep with their mothers have a reduced risk of sudden infant death syndrome ("crib death") may be starting to weaken prejudices against "co-sleeping" in the United States, where perhaps only the fear of a dead baby can overcome the fear of a dependent one.

56. Chodorow, *The Reproduction of Mothering,* 217.

57. Collins, "Black Women and Motherhood," 120. Sarah Blaffer Hrdy suggests that many other cultures and groups have their own sorts of "othermothers, which she terms "allomothers," people who regularly care for children in their mother's absence. Hrdy, *Mother Nature.*

58. Collins, "Black Women and Motherhood," 124.

59. Ibid., 132.

60. Welch, *Sweet Dreams in America,* 70.

61. Welch, *A Feminist Ethic of Risk,* 135.
62. Welch, *Sweet Dreams in America,* xv.
63. Ibid., 64.
64. Ibid., 63.
65. Rich, *Of Woman Born,* 291.
66. Welch, *Feminist Ethic of Risk,* 14.
67. Bauman, *Postmodern Ethics,* 245.
68. Aldo Leopold, "The Round River," in *A Sand County Almanac; with Essays on Conservation from Round River* (New York: Oxford University Press, 1949; San Francisco: Sierra Club, Ballantine, 1970), 197.

Selected Bibliography

Aberley, Doug. "Interpreting Bioregionalism: A Story from Many Voices." In *Bioregionalism,* ed. Michael Vincent McGinnis. New York: Routledge, 1999.

Adams, Carol J. "The Traffic in Animals." In *Ecofeminism: Women, Animals, Nature,* ed. Greta Gaard. Philadelphia: Temple University Press, 1993.

Akula, Vikram. "Grassroots Environmental Resistance in India." In *Ecological Resistance Movements: The Global Emergence of Radical and Popular Environmentalism,* ed. Bron Taylor. Albany: State University of New York Press, 1995.

Albanese, Catherine. *Nature Religion in America: From the Algonkian Indians to the New Age.* Chicago: University of Chicago Press, 1990.

Allen, Colin, and Marc Bekoff. "Intentionality, Social Play, and Definition." In *Readings in Animal Cognition,* ed. Marc Bekoff and Dale Jamieson. Cambridge: Massachusetts Institute of Technology Press, 1996.

Allen, Paula Gunn. "The Sacred Hoop: A Contemporary Perspective." In *Studies in American Indian Literature: Critical Essays and Course Designs,* ed. Paula Gunn Allen. New York: Modern Language Association of America, 1983.

———. *The Sacred Hoop: Rediscovering the Feminine in American Indian Traditions.* Boston: Beacon Press, 1986.

Ames, Roger. "Putting the *Te* back in Taoism." In *Nature in Asian Traditions of Thought: Essays in Environmental Philosophy,* ed. J. Baird Callicott and Roger Ames. Albany: State University of New York Press, 1989.

Aristotle. *The Politics.* Translated by T. A. Sinclair. Middlesex and New York: Penguin Books, 1951.

Augustine. *City of God. Vol. 1.* London: J. M. Dent and Sons, 1945.

———. *City of God. Vol. 2.* London: J. M. Dent and Sons, 1945.

Ayala, Francisco. "Human Nature: One Evolutionist's View." In *Whatever*

Happened to the Soul? Scientific and Theological Portraits of Human Nature, ed. Warren Brown, Nancey Murphy, and H. Newton Malony. Minneapolis: Fortress Press, 1998.

Baier, Annette. "The Need for More Than Justice." In *Justice and Care: Essential Readings in Feminist Ethics,* ed. Virginia Held. Boulder, Colo.: Westview Press, 1995.

Basso, Keith. *Western Apache Language and Culture: Essays in Linguistic Anthropology.* Tucson: University of Arizona Press, 1990.

Baudrillard, Jean. *Symbolic Exchange and Death.* London: Sage, 1993. Reprinted in *From Modernism to Postmodernism: An Anthology,* ed. Lawrence Cahoone. Cambridge, Mass.: Blackwell, 1996.

Bauman, Zygmunt. *Postmodern Ethics.* Oxford: Basil Blackwell, 1993.

Begay, D. Y. "Shi' Sha' Hane' (My Story)." In *Woven by the Grandmothers: Nineteenth-Century Navajo Textiles from the National Museum of the American Indian,* ed. Eulalie H. Bonar. Washington: Smithsonian Institution Press, 1996.

Bellah, Robert, Richard Madsen, William Sullivan, Ann Swidler, and Steve Tipton. *Habits of the Heart: Individualism and Commitment in American Life.* Berkeley and Los Angeles: University of California Press, 1985.

———. *The Good Society.* New York: Knopf, 1991.

Benhabib, Seyla. "The Generalized Other and the Concrete Other: The Kohlberg-Gilligan Controversy and Moral Theory." In *Women and Moral Theory,* ed. Eve Feder Kittay and Diana T. Meyers. New York: Rowman and Littlefield, 1987.

Benton, Ted. *Natural Relations: Ecology, Animal Rights, and Social Justice.* London: Verso, 1993.

Berger, Peter, and Thomas Luckmann. *The Social Construction of Reality: A Treatise in the Sociology of Knowledge.* New York: Doubleday, Anchor Books, 1966.

Berry, Thomas. *The Dream of the Earth.* San Francisco: Sierra Club Books, 1990.

———. *The Great Work: Our Way into the Future.* New York: Bell Tower, 1999.

Berry, Wendell. *The Unsettling of America: Culture and Agriculture.* San Francisco: Sierra Club Books, 1977.

Bird, Elizabeth Ann. "The Social Construction of Nature: Theoretical Approaches." *Environmental Review* 11, no. 4 (winter 1987): 255–64.

Birke, Lynda. *Feminism, Animals, and Science: The Naming of the Shrew.* Buckingham, England: Open University Press, 1994.

Bonar, Eulalie H., ed. *Woven by the Grandmothers: Nineteenth-Century Navajo Textiles from the National Museum of the American Indian.* Washington: Smithsonian Institution Press, 1996.

Bonner, John Tyler, and Robert M. May. Introduction to *The Descent of Man, and Selection in Relation to Sex,* by Charles Darwin. Princeton: Princeton University Press, 1981.

Bowler, Peter. *Evolution: The History of an Idea.* Rev. ed. Berkeley and Los Angeles: University of California Press, 1989.

Brown, Joseph Eppes. *Animals of the Soul: Sacred Animals of the Oglala Sioux.* Rev. ed. Rockport, Mass.: Element, 1997.

Budiansky, Stephen. *The Covenant of the Wild: How Animals Chose Domestication.* New York: William Morrow and Co., 1992.

————. *Nature's Keepers: The New Science of Nature Management.* New York: Free Press, 1995.

Butler, Judith. "Contingent Questions: Feminism and the Question of Postmodernism." In *Feminist Contentions: A Philosophical Exchange,* ed. Seyla Benhabib, Judith Butler, Drucilla Cornell, and Nancy Fraser. New York and London: Routledge, 1995.

Callenbach, Ernest. *Ecology: A Pocket Guide.* Berkeley and Los Angeles: University of California Press, 1998.

Callicott, J. Baird. *In Defense of the Land Ethic: Essays in Environmental Philosophy.* Albany: State University of New York Press, 1989.

————. "The Metaphysical Implications of Ecology." In *Nature in Asian Traditions of Thought: Essays in Environmental Philosophy,* ed. J. Baird Callicott and Roger Ames. Albany: State University of New York Press, 1989.

————. *Earth's Insights: A Multicultural Survey of Ecological Ethics from the Mediterranean Basin to the Australian Outback.* Berkeley and Los Angeles: University of California Press, 1994.

————. "Moral Monism in Environmental Ethics Defended." *Journal of Philosophical Research* 29 (1994): 51–60.

Callicott, J. Baird, and Roger Ames. "Introduction: The Asian Traditions as a Conceptual Resource for Environmental Philosophy." In *Nature in Asian Traditions of Thought: Essays in Environmental Philosophy,* ed. J. Baird Callicott and Roger Ames. Albany: State University of New York Press, 1989.

Carr, Anne. *Transforming Grace: Christian Tradition and Women's Experience.* San Francisco: HarperCollins, 1988.

Carr, David. *Time, Narrative, and History.* Bloomington: Indiana University Press, 1986.

Cheney, Dorothy, and Robert Seyfarth. *How Monkeys See the World: Inside the Mind of Another Species.* Chicago: University of Chicago Press, 1990.

Cheney, Jim. "Eco Feminism and Deep Ecology." *Environmental Ethics* 9, no. 2 (spring 1987): 115–145.

————. "Postmodern Environmental Ethics: Ethics as Bioregional Narrative." *Environmental Ethics* 11 (summer 1989): 117–34.

Chodorow, Nancy. *The Reproduction of Mothering: Psychoanalysis and the Sociology of Gender.* Berkeley and Los Angeles: University of California Press, 1978.

Coates, Peter. *Nature: Western Attitudes since Ancient Times.* Berkeley and Los Angeles: University of California Press, 1998.

Codiga, Doug. "Zen Practice and a Sense of Place." In *Dharma Gaia: A Harvest of Essays in Buddhism and Ecology,* ed. Allan Hunt Badiner. Berkeley: Parallax Press, 1990.

Collins, Patricia Hill. "Black Women and Motherhood." In *Justice and Care: Essential Readings in Feminist Ethics,* ed. Virginia Held. Boulder, Colo.: Westview Press, 1995.

Cook, Francis. "The Jewel Net of Indra." In *Nature in Asian Traditions of Thought: Essays in Environmental Philosophy,* ed. J. Baird Callicott and Roger Ames. Albany: State University of New York Press, 1989.

Copeland, Warren. *Economic Justice: The Social Ethics of U.S. Economic Policy.* Nashville: Abingdon Press, 1988.

Cronon, William. "Introduction: In Search of Nature." In *Uncommon Ground: Rethinking the Human Place in Nature,* ed. William Cronon. New York: W. W. Norton, 1996.

———. "The Trouble with Wilderness; or, Getting Back to the Wrong Nature." In *Uncommon Ground: Rethinking the Human Place in Nature,* ed. William Cronon. New York: W. W. Norton, 1996.

———. "The Trouble with Wilderness: A Response." *Environmental History* 1, no. 1 (January 1996): 47–55.

Damasio, Antonio. *Descartes' Error: Emotion, Reason, and the Human Brain.* New York: Avon, 1994.

Darwin, Charles. *The Origin of Species by Means of Natural Selection; or, The Preservation of Favoured Races in the Struggle for Life.* London: John Murray, 1859; London: Penguin Books, 1968.

———. *The Descent of Man, and Selection in Relation to Sex.* London: John Murray, 1871; Princeton: Princeton University Press, 1981.

Dawkins, Marian Stamp. *Through Our Eyes Only? The Search for Animal Consciousness.* Oxford: Oxford University Press, 1998.

Dawkins, Richard. *The Selfish Gene.* New Oxford: Oxford University Press, 1989.

———. *River out of Eden: A Darwinian View of Life.* New York: Basic Books, 1995.

De Silva, Padmasiri. *Environmental Philosophy and Ethics in Buddhism.* London: Macmillan, 1998.

Deleuze, Gilles, and Felix Guattari. *Anti-Oedipus: Capitalism and Schizophrenia.* New York: Viking Penguin 1977. Reprinted in *From Modernism to Postmodernism: An Anthology,* ed. Lawrence Cahoone. Cambridge: Blackwell, 1996.

Deloria, Vine, Jr. *God Is Red.* New York: Dell, 1973.

Dennett, Daniel. *Darwin's Dangerous Idea: Evolution and the Meanings of Life.* New York: Simon and Schuster, 1995.

———. *Kinds of Minds: Towards an Understanding of Consciousness.* New York: Basic Books, 1996.

Derrida, Jacques. "The End of the Book and the Beginning of Writing." In *Of Grammatology.* Baltimore: Johns Hopkins University Press, 1974. Reprinted in *From Modernism to Postmodernism: An Anthology,* ed. Lawrence Cahoone. Cambridge: Blackwell, 1996.

Descartes, René. *The Philosophical Writings of Descartes.* Translated by J. Cottingham et al. Cambridge: Cambridge University Press, 1969.

Descola, Philippe. "Constructing Natures: Symbolic Ecology and Social Practice." In *Nature and Society: Anthropological Perspectives,* ed. Philippe Descola and Gisli Palsson. London: Routledge, 1996.

Descola, Philippe, and Gisli Palsson. Introduction to *Nature and Society: Anthropological Perspectives,* ed. Philippe Descola and Gisli Palsson. London: Routledge, 1996.

Dinnerstein, Dorothy. *The Mermaid and the Minotaur: Sexual Arrangements and Human Malaise.* New York: Harper and Row, 1976.

Durkheim, Emile. *The Elementary Forms of the Religious Life.* New York: Free Press, 1965.

Eckel, Malcolm David. "Is There a Buddhist Philosophy of Nature?" In *Buddhism and Ecology: The Interconnection of Dharma and Deeds,* ed. Mary Evelyn Tucker and Duncan Ryuken Williams. Cambridge: Harvard University Press, 1997.

Ehrenreich, Barbara, and Janet McIntosh. "The New Creationism: Biology under Attack." *The Nation* (June 9, 1997): 11–16.

Eisenberg, Arlene, Heidi Murkoff, and Sandee Hathaway. *What to Expect the First Year.* New York: Workman Publishing, 1989.

Esbjornson, Carl D. "On Rethinking Resistance." *Environmental Ethics* 15, no. 3 (fall 1993): 287–88.

Evernden, Neil. *The Social Creation of Nature.* Baltimore: Johns Hopkins University Press, 1992.

Fischer, Frank, and Maarten A. Hajer, eds. *Living with Nature: Environmental Politics as Cultural Discourse.* Oxford: Oxford University Press, 1999.

Flores, Dan. "Place: Thinking about Bioregional History." In *Bioregionalism,* ed. Michael Vincent McGinnis. London: Routledge, 1999.

Foley, Robert. *Humans before Humanity.* Oxford: Blackwell, 1995.

Fransted, Dennis. "The Secular Uses of Traditional Religion and Knowledge in Modern Navajo Society." In *Navajo Religion and Culture: Selected Views: Papers in Honor of Leland C. Wyman,* ed. David M. Brugge and Charlotte Frisbie. Museum of New Mexico, Papers in Anthropology, no. 17. Santa Fe: Museum of New Mexico Press, 1982.

Gaard, Greta. "Ecofeminism and Native American Cultures: Pushing the Limits of Cultural Imperialism?" In *Ecofeminism: Women, Animals, Nature,* ed. Greta Gaard. Philadelphia: Temple University Press, 1993.

Garé, Arran. *Postmodernism and the Environmental Crisis.* London: Routledge, 1995.

———. "MacIntyre, Narratives, and Environmental Ethics." *Environmental Ethics* 20, no. 1 (spring 1998): 3–22.

Geertz, Clifford. *The Interpretation of Cultures.* New York: Basic Books, 1973.

Gill, Sam. *Sacred Words: A Study of Navajo Religion and Prayer.* Westport, Conn.: Greenwood Press, 1981.

———. *Mother Earth.* Chicago: University of Chicago Press, 1987.

Gilligan, Carol. *In a Different Voice: Psychological Theory and Women's Development.* Cambridge: Harvard University Press, 1982.

———. "Moral Orientation and Moral Development." In *Women and Moral Theory,* ed. Eve Feder Kittay and Diana T. Meyers. New York: Rowman and Littlefield, 1987.

Goodall, Jane. *In the Shadow of Man.* Boston: Houghton Mifflin, 1971.
Gould, Stephen Jay. *Ever since Darwin: Reflections in Natural History.* New York: W. W. Norton, 1977.
———. *The Mismeasure of Man.* New York: W. W. Norton, 1981.
Gramsci, Antonio. *Gramsci: Selections from Cultural Writings,* ed. D. Forgacs and G. Nowell-Smith; trans. W. Boelhower. Cambridge: Harvard University Press, 1985.
Grant, Steve. "Altered States." *Hartford Courant,* November 3, 1998, p. F1.
Griffin, Donald. *Animal Thinking.* Cambridge: Harvard University Press, 1984.
———. *Animal Minds.* Chicago: University of Chicago Press, 1992.
Gross, Rita M. "Buddhist Resources for Issues of Population, Consumption, and the Environment." In *Buddhism and Ecology: The Interconnection of Dharma and Deeds,* ed. Mary Evelyn Tucker and Duncan Ryuken Williams. Cambridge: Harvard University Press, 1997.
———. "Towards a Buddhist Environmental Ethic." *Journal of the American Academy of Religion* 65, no. 2 (summer 1997): 333–54.
Gutiérrez, Gustavo. *A Theology of Liberation.* Maryknoll, N.Y.: Orbis Books, 1973.
———. *The Power of the Poor in History.* Maryknoll, N.Y.: Orbis Books, 1983.
Hallowell, A. Irving. "Ojibwa Ontology, Behavior, and World View." In *Teachings from the American Earth: Indian Religion and Philosophy,* ed. Dennis Tedlock and Barbara Tedlock. New York: Liveright, 1975.
Halpin, Zuleyma Tang. "Scientific Objectivity and the Concept of 'the Other.'" *Women's Studies International Forum* 12, no. 3 (1989): 285–94.
Hamilton, William. "The Genetical Evolution of Social Behaviour," pts. 1 and 2, *Journal of Theoretical Biology* 7 (1964): 1–52. Pt.1 reprinted in *Foundations of Animal Behavior: Classic Papers with Commentaries,* ed. Lynne D. Houck and Lee C. Drickamer. Chicago: University of Chicago Press, 1996.
Haraway, Donna. *Primate Visions: Gender, Race, and Nature in the World of Modern Science.* New York and London: Routledge, 1989.
———. *Simians, Cyborgs, and Women: The Reinvention of Nature.* New York: Routledge, 1991.
Harding, Sandra. "The Curious Coincidence of Feminine and African Moralities: Challenges for Feminist Theory." In *Women and Moral Theory,* ed. Eve Feder Kittay and Diana T. Meyers. New York: Rowman and Littlefield, 1987.
Harrison, Robert P. "Toward a Philosophy of Nature." In *Uncommon Ground: Rethinking the Human Place in Nature,* ed. William Cronon. New York: W. W. Norton, 1996.
Harvey, David. "Flexibility: Threat or Opportunity?" *Socialist Review* 21, no. 1 (January-March 1991): 65–77.
———. *Justice, Nature, and the Geography of Difference.* Oxford: Blackwell, 1996.
———. *Spaces of Hope.* Berkeley and Los Angeles: University of California Press, 2000.
Hayles, N. Katherine. "Searching for Common Ground." In *Reinventing Na-*

ture? Responses to Postmodern Deconstruction, ed. Michael Soulé and Gary Lease. Washington, D.C.: Island Press, 1995.

Hedlund, Ann Lane. "'More of Survival Than an Art': Comparing Late Nineteenth- and Late Twentieth-Century Lifeways and Weaving." In *Woven by the Grandmothers: Nineteenth-Century Navajo Textiles from the National Museum of the American Indian,* ed. Eulalie H. Bonar. Washington: Smithsonian Institution Press, 1996.

Hefner, Philip. *The Human Factor: Evolution, Culture, and Religion.* Minneapolis: Fortress Press, 1993.

Held, Virginia. "Feminism and Moral Theory." In *Women and Moral Theory,* eds. Eve Feder Kittay and Diana T. Meyers. New York: Rowman and Littlefield, 1987.

Holstein, James, and Jaber Gubrium. *The Self We Live By: Narrative Identity in a Postmodern World.* Oxford: Oxford University Press, 2000.

Horst, Steven. "Our Animal Bodies." In *Midwest Studies in Philosophy XXII: The Philosophy of Emotion,* eds. Peter A. French and Howard K. Wettstein. Notre Dame, Ind.: University of Notre Dame Press, 1998.

Howell, Signe. "Nature in Culture or Culture in Nature? Chewong Ideas of 'Humans' and Other Species." In *Nature and Society: Anthropological Perspectives,* ed. Philippe Descola and Gisli Palsson. London: Routledge, 1996.

Hrdy, Sarah Blaffer. *Mother Nature: A History of Mothers, Infants, and Natural Selection.* New York: Pantheon, 1999.

Hultkrantz, Ake. *The Religions of the American Indians.* Trans. Monica Setterwall. Berkeley and Los Angeles: University of California Press, 1979.

Ileto, Reynaldo Clemeña. *Pasyon and Revolution: Popular Movements in the Philippines, 1840–1910.* Manila: Ateneo de Manila University Press, 1979.

Inada, Kenneth. "Environmental Problematics." In *Nature in Asian Traditions of Thought: Essays in Environmental Philosophy,* ed. J. Baird Callicott and Roger Ames. Albany: State University of New York Press, 1989.

Ingold, Tim. "Hunting and Gathering as Ways of Perceiving the Environment." In *Redefining Nature: Ecology, Culture, and Domestication,* ed. Roy Ellen and Katsuyoshi Fukui. Oxford and Washington: Berg, 1996.

———, ed. *What Is an Animal?* London: Routledge, 1988.

Jackson, Wes. *Becoming Native to This Place.* Lexington: University Press of Kentucky, 1994.

Jaggar, Alison. *Feminist Politics and Human Nature.* Savage, Md.: Rowman and Littlefield, 1988.

Jamieson, Dale, and Marc Bekoff. "On Aims and Methods of Cognitive Ethology." In *Readings in Animal Cognition,* ed. Marc Bekoff and Dale Jamieson. Cambridge: Massachusetts Institute of Technology Press, 1996.

John Paul II. *Redemptor Hominis.* In *Proclaiming Justice and Peace: Papal Documents from* Rerum Novarum *through* Centesimus Annus, ed. Michael Walsh and Brian Davies. Mystic, Conn.: Twenty-third Publications, 1991.

Johnson, Mark. *The Body in the Mind: The Bodily Basis of Meaning, Imagination, and Reason.* Chicago: University of Chicago Press, 1987.

———. *Moral Imagination: Implications of Cognitive Science for Ethics.* Chicago: University of Chicago Press, 1993.

Jung, L. Shannon. *We Are Home: A Spirituality of the Environment*. New York: Paulist Press, 1993.

Kammer, Charles, III. *Ethics and Liberation: An Introduction*. Maryknoll, N.Y.: Orbis Books, 1988.

Kaufman, Gordon. "The Concept of Nature: A Problem for Theology." *Harvard Theological Review* 65 (1972): 337–66.

Kehm, George H. "The New Story: Redemption as Fulfillment of Creation." In *After Nature's Revolt: Eco-Justice and Theology*, ed. Dieter T. Hessel. Minneapolis: Fortress Press, 1992.

Kellert, Stephen R. "Concepts of Nature East and West." In *Reinventing Nature? Responses to Postmodern Deconstruction*, ed. Michael Soulé and Gary Lease. Washington, D.C.: Island Press, 1995.

Kellert, Stephen R., and Edward O. Wilson, eds. *The Biophilia Hypothesis*. Washington, D.C.: Island Press, 1993.

Kelley, Klara Bonsack, and Harris Francis. *Navajo Sacred Places*. Bloomington: Indiana University Press, 1994.

Kheel, Marti. "The Liberation of Nature: A Circular Affair." *Environmental Ethics* 7 (summer 1985): 135–49.

———. "From Heroic to Holistic Ethics: The Ecofeminist Challenge." In *Ecofeminism: Women, Animals, Nature*, ed. Greta Gaard. Philadelphia: Temple University Press, 1993.

———. "License to Kill: An Ecofeminist Critique of Hunters' Discourse." In *Animals and Women: Feminist Theoretical Explorations*, ed. Carol J. Adams and Josephine Donovan. Durham, N.C.: Duke University Press, 1995.

Koenig, Walter D., and Ronald L. Mumme. "Levels of Analysis and the Functional Significance of Helping Behavior." In *Readings in Animal Cognition*, ed. Marc Bekoff and Dale Jamieson. Cambridge: Massachusetts Institute of Technology Press, 1996.

Krech, Shepard, III. *The Ecological Indian: Myth and History*. New York: W. W. Norton, 1999.

Kuhn, Thomas. *The Structure of Scientific Revolutions*. International Encyclopedia of Unified Science. Vol. 2, no. 2. 2d ed., enlarged. Chicago: University of Chicago Press, 1970.

Kuper, Adam. *The Chosen Primate: Human Nature and Cultural Diversity*. Cambridge: Harvard University Press, 1994.

Lahar, Stephanie. "Roots: Rejoining Natural and Social History." In *Ecofeminism: Women, Animals, Nature*, ed. Greta Gaard. Philadelphia: Temple University Press, 1993.

———. "Ecofeminist Theory and Grassroots Politics." In *Ecofeminism: Women, Culture, Nature*, ed. Karen Warren. Bloomington: Indiana University Press, 1997.

Laitin, David. "Religion, Political Culture, and the Weberian Tradition." *World Politics* 30, no. 4 (July 1978): 563–92.

Larson, Gerald James. "'Conceptual Resources' in South Asia for 'Environmental Ethics.'" In *Nature in Asian Traditions of Thought: Essays in Environmental Philosophy*, ed. J. Baird Callicott and Roger Ames. Albany: State University of New York Press, 1989.

Leopold, Aldo. *A Sand County Almanac; with Essays on Conservation from Round River.* New York: Oxford University Press, 1949; San Francisco: Sierra Club, Ballantine, 1970.

Li, Huey-li. "A Cross-Cultural Critique of Ecofeminism." In *Ecofeminism: Women, Animals, Nature,* ed. Greta Gaard. Philadelphia: Temple University Press, 1993.

Lipschutz, Ronnie. "Bioregionalism, Civil Society and Global Environmental Governance." In *Bioregionalism,* ed. Michael Vincent McGinnis. New York: Routledge, 1999.

Lovelock, James. *Gaia: A New Look at Life on Earth.* Oxford: Oxford University Press, 1979.

Lovin, Robin, and Frank Reynolds. "In the Beginning." In *Cosmogony and Ethical Order,* ed. Robin Lovin and Frank Reynolds. Chicago: University of Chicago Press, 1985.

Luckert, Karl. "Toward a Historical Perspective on Navajo Religion." In *Navajo Religion and Culture: Selected Views: Papers in Honor of Leland C. Wyman,* ed. David M. Brugge and Charlotte Frisbie. Museum of New Mexico, Papers in Anthropology, no. 17. Santa Fe: Museum of New Mexico Press, 1982.

Luther, Martin. *Martin Luther: Selections from His Writings.* Ed. by John Dillenberger. New York: Anchor Books, 1971.

MacIntyre, Alasdair. *After Virtue: A Study in Moral Theory.* Notre Dame, Ind.: University of Notre Dame Press, 1981.

Macy, Joanna. "The Greening of the Self." In *Dharma Gaia: A Harvest of Essays in Buddhism and Ecology,* ed. Allan Hunt Badiner. Berkeley: Parallax Press, 1990.

———. *Mutual Causality in Buddhism and General Systems Theory: The Dharma of Natural Systems.* Albany: State University of New York Press, 1991.

Martin, Calvin. *Keepers of the Game: Indian-Animal Relationships and the Fur Trade.* Berkeley and Los Angeles: University of California Press, 1978.

Martin, Joel. *Sacred Revolt: The Muskogee Struggle for a New World.* Boston: Beacon Press, 1991.

Marx, Karl. *Economic and Philosophical Manuscripts of 1844.* In *The Marx-Engels Reader,* ed. Robert Tucker. New York: W. W. Norton, 1978.

McCutcheon, Russell. "A Default of Critical Intelligence? The Scholar of Religion as Public Intellectual." *Journal of the American Academy of Religion* 65, no. 2 (summer 1997): 443–68.

McFague, Sallie. *The Body of God: An Ecological Theology.* Minneapolis: Fortress Press, 1993.

———. "An Earthly Theological Agenda." In *Ecofeminism and the Sacred,* ed. Carol J. Adams. New York: Continuum, 1993.

McGinnis, Michael Vincent, ed. *Bioregionalism.* New York: Routledge, 1999.

McKibben, Bill. *The End of Nature.* New York: Random House, 1989.

Merchant, Carolyn. *The Death of Nature: Women, Ecology, and the Scientific Revolution.* San Francisco: HarperCollins, 1983.

———. "Partnership Ethics and Cultural Discourse: Women and the Earth

Summit." In *Living with Nature: Environmental Politics as Cultural Discourse,* ed. Frank Fischer and Maarten A. Hajer. Oxford: Oxford University Press, 1999.

Midgley, Mary. *Heart and Mind: The Varieties of Moral Experience.* New York: St. Martin's, 1981.

———. *Animals and Why They Matter.* Athens: University of Georgia Press, 1983.

———. *Evolution as a Religion: Strange Hopes and Stranger Fears.* London: Methuen, 1985.

———. *The Ethical Primate: Humans, Freedom, and Morality.* New York: Routledge, 1994.

———. *Beast and Man: The Roots of Human Nature.* Rev. ed. London: Routledge, 1995.

Moran, Emilio. "Nurturing the Forest: Strategies of Native Amazonians." In *Redefining Nature: Ecology, Culture, and Domestication,* ed. Roy Ellen and Katsuyoshi Fukui. Oxford: Berg, 1996.

Morovitz, Harold. "Biology of a Cosmological Science." In *Nature in Asian Traditions of Thought: Essays in Environmental Philosophy,* ed. J. Baird Callicott and Roger Ames. Albany: State University of New York Press, 1989.

Nabhan, Gary Paul. *Cultures of Habitat: On Nature, Culture, and Story.* Washington, D.C.: Counterpoint, 1997.

Naess, Arne. *Ecology, Community, and Lifestyle.* Trans. and ed. David Rothenberg. Cambridge: Cambridge University Press, 1989.

Nagel, Thomas. "What Is It Like to Be a Bat?" *Philosophical Review* 83 (1974): 435–50.

Nasr, Seyyed Hossein. "Islam and the Environmental Crisis." In *Spirit and Nature: Why the Environment Is a Religious Issue,* ed. Steven Rockefeller and John Elder. Boston: Beacon Press, 1992.

Nazarea, Virginia D. *Cultural Memory and Biodiversity.* Tucson: University of Arizona Press, 1998.

Nelson, Lance, ed. *Purifying the Earthly Body of God: Religion and Ecology in Hindu India.* Albany: State University of New York Press, 1998.

Nelson, Richard. *Make Prayers to the Raven: A Koyukon View of the Northern Forest.* Chicago: University of Chicago Press, 1983.

———. *The Island Within.* New York: Vintage, 1989.

Niebuhr, Reinhold. *Moral Man and Immoral Society.* New York: Charles Scribner's Sons, 1932.

———. *The Nature and Destiny of Man: A Christian Interpretation.* Vol. 1: *Human Nature.* New York: Charles Scribner's Sons, 1964.

Noddings, Nel. *Caring: A Feminine Approach to Ethics and Moral Education.* Berkeley and Los Angeles: University of California Press, 1984.

Northcott, Michael. *The Environment and Christian Ethics.* Cambridge: Cambridge University Press, 1996.

Oelschlaeger, Max. *Caring for Creation: An Ecumenical Approach to the Environmental Crisis.* New Haven: Yale University Press, 1994.

Peterson, Anna L. "Religious Narratives and Political Protest." *Journal of the American Academy of Religion* 64, no. 1 (spring 1996): 27–44.

———. *Martyrdom and the Politics of Religion: Progressive Catholicism in El Salvador's Civil War*. Albany: State University of New York Press, 1997.

———. "Environmental Ethics and the Social Construction of Nature." *Environmental Ethics* 21, no. 4 (winter 1999): 339–57.

———. "In and of the World? Christian Theological Anthropology and Environmental Ethics." *Journal of Agricultural and Environmental Ethics* 12, no. 3 (2000): 237–61.

Plumwood, Val. "Nature, Self, and Gender: Feminism, Environmental Philosophy, and the Critique of Rationalism." *Hypatia* vol. 6, no. 1 (spring 1991): 3–27.

———. *Feminism and the Mastery of Nature*. London: Routledge, 1993.

———. "Androcentrism and Anthropocentrism: Parallels and Politics." In *Ecofeminism: Women, Culture, Nature*, ed. Karen Waren. Bloomington: Indiana University Press, 1997.

Proctor, James D. "Whose Nature? The Contested Moral Terrain of Ancient Forests." In *Uncommon Ground: Rethinking the Human Place in Nature*, ed. William Cronon. New York: W. W. Norton, 1996.

Radner, Daisie, and Michael Radner. *Animal Consciousness*. Buffalo: Prometheus Books, 1989.

Raglon, Rebecca, and Marian Scholtmeijer. "Shifting Ground: Metanarratives, Epistemology, and the Stories of Nature." *Environmental Ethics* 18, no. 2 (spring 1996): 19–38.

Rahula, Walpola. *What the Buddha Taught*. Rev. ed. New York: Grove Press, 1974.

Reed, Edward S. "The Affordances of the Animate Environment: Social Science from the Ecological Point of View." In *What Is an Animal?* ed. Tim Ingold. London: Routledge, 1988.

Reichard, Gladys. *Navaho Religion: A Study of Symbolism*. 2d edition. New York: Bollingen Series XVIII, Pantheon Books, 1963.

Rich, Adrienne. *Of Woman Born: Motherhood as Experience and Institution*. New York: W. W. Norton, 1976.

———. *On Lies, Secrets, and Silence: Selected Prose, 1966–1978*. New York: W. W. Norton, 1979.

———. *Blood, Bread, and Poetry: Selected Prose, 1979–1985*. New York: W. W. Norton, 1986.

———. *What Is Found There: Notebooks on Poetry and Politics*. New York: Quality Paperback Book Club, 1994.

Ristau, Carolyn A. "Aspects of the Cognitive Ethology of an Injury-Feigning Bird, the Piping Plover." In *Readings in Animal Cognition*, ed. Marc Bekoff and Dale Jamieson. Cambridge: Massachusetts Institute of Technology Press, 1996.

Rival, Laura. "Blowpipes and Spears: The Social Significance of Huaorani Technological Choices." In *Nature and Society: Anthropological Perspectives*, ed. Philippe Descola and Gisli Palsson. London: Routledge, 1996.

Roach, Catherine. "Loving Your Mother: On the Woman-Nature Relationship." In *Ecological Feminist Philosophies,* ed. Karen Warren. Bloomington: Indiana University Press, 1996.

Robbins, Catherine. "A Zoo in Peril Stirs a Debate about Navajo Traditions." *New York Times,* March 28, 1999, sec. 1, p. 34.

Rolston, Holmes, III. *Environmental Ethics: Duties to and Values in the Natural World.* Philadelphia: Temple University Press, 1988.

———. "Wildlife and Wildlands: A Christian Perspective." In *After Nature's Revolt: Eco-Justice and Theology,* ed. Dieter Hessel. Minneapolis: Fortress Press, 1992.

———. "Nature for Real: Is Nature a Social Construct?" In *The Philosophy of the Environment,* ed. Timothy Chappell. Edinburgh: Edinburgh University Press, 1997.

Rouse, Joseph. "Feminism and the Social Construction of Scientific Knowledge." In *Feminism, Science, and the Philosophy of Science,* ed. Lynn Hankinson Nelson and Jack Nelson. Dordrecht, Netherlands: Kluwer Academic Publishers, 1996.

Ruddick, Sara. "Maternal Thinking." *Feminist Studies* 6, no. 2 (summer 1980): 342–67.

———. "Remarks on the Sexual Politics of Reason." In *Women and Moral Theory,* ed. Eve Feder Kittay and Diana T. Meyers. New York: Rowman and Littlefield, 1987.

———. "Injustice in Families: Assault and Domination." In *Justice and Care: Essential Readings in Feminist Ethics,* ed. Virginia Held. Boulder, Colo.: Westview Press, 1995.

Ruether, Rosemary Radford. *Gaia and God: An Ecofeminist Theology of Earth Healing.* San Francisco: HarperCollins, 1992.

Sahlins, Marshall. *Culture and Practical Reason.* Chicago: University of Chicago Press, 1976.

Santmire, Paul. *The Travail of Nature: The Ambiguous Promise of Christian Theology.* Philadelphia: Fortress Press, 1985.

———. "Healing the Protestant Mind: Beyond the Theology of Human Dominion." In *After Nature's Revolt: Eco-Justice and Theology,* ed. Dieter Hessel. Minneapolis: Fortress Press, 1992.

Schipper, Kristofer. *The Taoist Body.* Trans. Karen C. Duval; foreword by Norman Girardot. Berkeley and Los Angeles: University of California Press, 1993.

Schmitt, Richard. *Beyond Separateness: The Social Nature of Human Beings—Their Autonomy, Knowledge, and Power.* Boulder, Colo: Westview Press, 1995.

Schwarz, Maureen Trudelle. *Molded in the Image of Changing Woman: Navajo Views on the Human Body and Personhood.* Tucson: University of Arizona Press, 1997.

———. "Unraveling the Anchoring Chord: Navajo Relocation, 1974–1996." *American Anthropologist* 99, no. 1 (1997): 43–55.

Scott, Joan. "Deconstructing Equality-versus-Difference: Or, the Uses of Poststructuralist Theory of Feminism." *Feminist Studies* 14, no. 1 (spring 1988): 33–50.

Second Vatican Council. *Gaudium et Spes*. In *Proclaiming Justice and Peace: Papal Documents from Rerum Novarum through Centesimus Annus*, ed. Michael Walsh and Brian Davies. Mystic, Conn.: Twenty-third Publications, 1991.

Seed, John, Joanna Macy, Pat Fleming, and Arne Naess. *Thinking Like a Mountain: Towards a Council of All Beings*. Philadelphia: New Society Publishers, 1988.

Shepard, Paul. *The Others: How Animals Made Us Human*. Washington, D.C.: Island Press, 1996.

Shiva, Vandana. *Staying Alive: Women, Ecology, and Development*. London: Zed Books, 1988.

Slater, Candace. "Amazonia as Edenic Narrative." In *Uncommon Ground: Rethinking the Human Place in Nature*, ed. William Cronon. New York: W. W. Norton, 1996.

Smith, Mick. "To Speak of Trees: Social Constructivism, Environmental Values, and the Future of Deep Ecology." *Environmental Ethics* 21, no. 4 (winter 1999): 359–76.

Snyder, Gary. *The Practice of the Wild*. San Francisco: North Point, 1990.

———. *A Place in Space: Ethics, Aesthetics, and Watersheds: New and Selected Prose*. Washington: Counterpoint, 1995.

———. "Is Nature Real?" *Resurgence*, no. 190 (September–October 1998): 32–33.

Sommers, Christina Hoff. "Filial Morality." In *Women and Moral Theory*, ed. Eve Feder Kittay and Diana T. Meyers. New York: Rowman and Littlefield, 1987.

Soper, Kate. *What Is Nature?* Oxford: Basil Blackwell, 1995.

Sorrell, Roger D. *St. Francis of Assisi and Nature: Tradition and Innovation in Western Christian Attitudes toward the Environment*. New York: Oxford University Press, 1988.

Sponberg, Alan. "Green Buddhism and the Hierarchy of Compassion." In *Buddhism and Ecology: The Interconnection of Dharma and Deeds*, ed. Mary Evelyn Tucker and Duncan Ryuken Williams. Cambridge: Harvard University Press, 1997.

Spretnak, Charlene. "Radical Nonduality in Ecofeminist Philosophy." In *Ecofeminism: Women, Culture, Nature*, ed. Karen Warren. Bloomington: Indiana University Press, 1997.

Stringer, Chris, and Robin McKie. *African Exodus*. London: Jonathan Cape, 1996.

Suzuki, David, and Peter Knudtson. *The Wisdom of the Elders: Sacred Native Stories of Nature*. New York: Bantam, 1992.

Swearer, Donald. "The Hermeneutics of Buddhist Ecology in Contemporary Thailand." In *Buddhism and Ecology: The Interconnection of Dharma and Deeds*, ed. Mary Evelyn Tucker and Duncan Ryuken Williams. Cambridge: Harvard University Press, 1997.

Tang-Martinez, Zuleyma. "The Curious Courtship of Sociobiology and Feminism." In *Feminism and Evolutionary Biology: Boundaries, Intersections, and Frontiers,* ed. Patricia Adair Gowaty. New York: Chapman and Hall, 1997.

Tanner, Adrian. *Bringing Home Animals: Religious Ideology and Mode of Production of the Mistassini Cree Hunters.* New York: St. Martin's Press, 1979.

Taylor, Bron. "Earthen Spirituality or Cultural Genocide? Radical Environmentalism's Appropriation of Native American Spirituality." *Religion* 27 (1997): 183–215.

———. "Bioregionalism: An Ethics of Loyalty to Place." *Landscape Journal* 19, no. 1 (spring 2000): 53–81.

———. "Deep Ecology and Its Social Philosophy: A Critique." In *Beneath the Surface: Critical Essays on Deep Ecology,* ed. Eric Katz, Andrew Light, and David Rothenberg. Boston: Massachusetts Institute of Technology Press, 2000.

———. ed. *Ecological Resistance Movements: The Global Emergence of Radical and Popular Environmentalism.* Albany: State University of New York Press, 1995.

Teilhard de Chardin, Pierre. *The Phenomenon of Man.* New York: Harper and Row, 1959.

Tester, Keith. *Animals and Society: The Humanity of Animal Rights.* London: Routledge, 1991.

Thiele, Leslie Paul. "Nature and Freedom: A Heideggerian Critique of Biocentric and Sociocentric Environmentalism." *Environmental Ethics* 17 (summer 1995): 171–90.

———. "Evolutionary Narratives and Ecological Ethics." *Political Theory* 27, no. 1 (1999): 6–38.

Thomas Aquinas. *Introduction to St. Thomas Aquinas: The* Summa Theologica, *the* Summa Contra Gentiles. Ed. Anton C. Pegis. New York: Modern Library, 1948.

Thomas, Wesley. "Shil Yool T'ool: Personification of Navajo Weaving." In *Woven by the Grandmothers: Nineteenth-Century Navajo Textiles from the National Museum of the American Indian,* ed. Eulalie H. Bonar. Washington: Smithsonian Institution Press, 1996.

Thomashow, Mitchell. "Toward a Cosmopolitan Bioregionalism." In *Bioregionalism,* ed. Michael Vincent McGinnis. New York: Routledge, 1999.

Thornhill, Randy. "The Study of Adaptation." In *Readings in Animal Cognition,* ed. Marc Bekoff and Dale Jamieson. Cambridge: Massachusetts Institute of Technology Press, 1996.

Tillich, Paul. *The Protestant Era.* Chicago: University of Chicago Press, 1957.

Tinker, George E. *Missionary Conquest: The Gospel and Native American Cultural Genocide.* Minneapolis: Fortress Press, 1993.

Trivers, Robert L. "The Evolution of Reciprocal Altruism." *Quarterly Review of Biology* 46 (1971): 35–46.

———. "Parental Investment and Sexual Selection." In *Sexual Selection and the Descent of Man, 1871–1971,* ed. B. Campbell. Chicago: Aldine, 1972. Reprinted in *Foundations of Animal Behavior: Classic Papers with Commentaries,* ed. Lynne D. Houck and Lee C. Drickamer. Chicago: University of Chicago Press, 1996.

Tronto, Joan. "Women and Caring: What Can Feminists Learn about Morality from Caring?" In *Justice and Care: Essential Readings in Feminist Ethics,* ed. Virginia Held. Boulder, Colo.: Westview Press, 1995.

Tuan, Yi-Fu. "Discrepancies between Environmental Attitudes and Behavior." In *Ecology and Religion in History,* ed. David Spring and Anita Spring. New York: Harper and Row, 1974.

Tudge, Colin. *The Time before History: 5 Million Years of Human Impact.* New York: Scribner, 1996.

Tweed, Thomas. "Introduction: Narrating U.S. Religious History." In *Retelling U.S. Religious History,* ed. Thomas Tweed. Berkeley and Los Angeles: University of California Press, 1997.

Waal, Francis de. *Good-Natured: The Origins of Right and Wrong in Humans and Other Animals.* Cambridge: Harvard University Press, 1996.

Walker, Margaret Urban. "Moral Understandings: Alternative 'Epistemology' for a Feminist Ethics." In *Justice and Care: Essential Readings in Feminist Ethics,* ed. Virginia Held. Boulder, Colo.: Westview Press, 1995.

Walters, Harry. "The Navajo Concept of Art." In *Navajo Religion and Culture: Selected Views: Papers in Honor of Leland C. Wyman,* ed. David M. Brugge and Charlotte J. Frisbie. Museum of New Mexico, Papers in Anthropology, no. 17. Santa Fe: Museum of New Mexico Press, 1982.

Warren, Karen. "The Power and Promise of Ecological Feminism." *Environmental Ethics* 12, no. 2 (spring 1990): 125–46.

Warren, Karen, and Jim Cheney. "Ecological Feminism and Ecosystem Ecology." *Hypatia* 6, no. 1 (spring 1991): 179–97.

Watson, J. B. "What Is Behaviorism?" In *Behaviorism.* New York: W. W. Norton, 1924. Reprinted in *Foundations of Animal Behavior: Classic Papers with Commentaries,* ed. Lynne D. Houck and Lee C. Drickamer. Chicago: University of Chicago Press, 1996.

Weber, Max. *The Protestant Ethic and the Spirit of Capitalism.* New York: Charles Scribner's Sons, 1958.

Wei-Ming, Tu. "The Continuity of Being." In *Nature in Asian Traditions of Thought: Essays in Environmental Philosophy,* ed. J. Baird Callicott and Roger Ames. Albany: State University of New York Press, 1989.

Weiner, Jonathan. *The Beak of the Finch: A Story of Evolution in Our Time.* New York: Knopf, 1994.

Welch, Sharon. *A Feminist Ethic of Risk.* Minneapolis: Fortress Press, 1990.

———. *Sweet Dreams in America: Making Ethics and Spirituality Work.* New York: Routledge, 1999.

White, Lynn, Jr. "The Historical Roots of Our Ecologic Crisis." *Science* 155 (1967): 1203–7.

White, Richard. "Are You an Environmentalist, or Do You Work for a Living? Work and Nature." In *Uncommon Ground: Rethinking the Human Place in Nature,* ed. William Cronon. New York: W. W. Norton, 1996.

Williams, George. *Adaptation and Natural Selection: A Critique of Some Current Evolutionary Thought*. Princeton, N.J.: Princeton University Press, 1966.

Williams, Raymond. *Problems in Materialism and Culture*. London: Verso, 1980.

Wilson, Edward O. *Sociobiology: The New Synthesis*. Cambridge: Harvard University Press, 1975.

———. *On Human Nature*. Cambridge: Harvard University Press, 1978.

———. *Sociobiology: The Abridged Edition*. Cambridge: Harvard University Press, 1980.

———. *In Search of Nature*. Washington D.C.: Island Press, 1996.

———. *Consilience: The Unity of Knowledge*. New York: Alfred A. Knopf, 1998.

Witherspoon, Gary. *Navajo Kinship and Marriage*. Chicago: University of Chicago Press, 1975.

———. *Language and Art in the Navajo Universe*. Ann Arbor: University of Michigan Press, 1977.

Worster, Donald. *Nature's Economy: A History of Ecological Ideas*. 2d ed. Cambridge: Cambridge University Press, 1994.

Wright, Robert. *The Moral Animal: Why We Are the Way We Are: The New Science of Evolutionary Psychology*. New York: Vintage Books, 1994.

Zimmerman, Michael. *Contesting Earth's Future: Radical Ecology and Postmodernity*. Berkeley and Los Angeles: University of California Press, 1994.

———. "Ecofascism: A Threat to American Environmentalism?" In *The Ecological Community: Environmental Challenges for Philosophy, Politics, and Morality*, ed. Roger Gottlieb. New York: Routledge, 1997.

Index

CPSIA information can be obtained at www.ICGtesting.com
Printed in the USA
BVOW010703180112

280798BV00001B/72/A